A Statesman and a Seeker

A Statesman and a Seeker

The Extraordinary Life and Legacy of Dr Karan Singh

An Authorized Biography by

Harbans Singh

SPEAKING TIGER

SPEAKING TIGER BOOKS
125A, Ground Floor, Shahpur Jat, near Asiad Village,
New Delhi 110049

First published by Speaking Tiger Books in 2026

All photographs courtesy the Amar Mahal Museum and Library,
unless otherwise specified.

ISBN: 978-93-6336-968-9

10 9 8 7 6 5 4 3 2 1

Typeset in Adobe Garamond Pro by
SÜRYA, New Delhi

Printed at Chaman Enterprises, New Delhi

Contents

1

An Heir is Born

THE WINTER OF 1930-31 in Srinagar was colder than usual. Until spring began in the early days of March, those who could go away to more pleasant climes, usually left the city. The Dogra rulers of Jammu and Kashmir always did, moving every year to their winter capital, Jammu. That year, the reigning Maharaja had left Srinagar early, taking his family and close staff not across the Pir Panjal range that separates the Kashmir Valley from the Jammu plains, but several thousand miles away, to the French Mediterranean coast. His wife was into her seventh month of pregnancy and he wanted to take no chances. Too much depended on the yet unborn child—the fate of the State, and of the Maharaja and his dynasty. He had waited for this moment for almost two decades, and he would spare no expense to ensure a safe delivery. He wanted a son, as did his wife, it was the reason the Maharaja had married her. The Maharani was much given to prayer and ritual, the Maharaja was not, but it is said that he had asked for special prayers in the temples of his State through those anxious months. In the end, the prayers were answered.

So it was that the last heir to the Dogra throne of Jammu

and Kashmir—Yuvraj Karan Singh—was born a continent away, in the fabled, glamorous resort town of Cannes.

Much of the history of the Dogras in general, and Jammu in particular, is steeped in myths, legends and oral narratives, and therefore subject to debate. It is often claimed that the word Dogra has its roots in the Sanskrit word *Dwi-garta*, referring to the twin lakes of Mansar and Surinsar, located just east of Jammu city. With time, the Sanskrit word became *Durgara*, and from this was derived the word *Duggar*, or *Dogra*, to describe the inhabitants of the region. The Durgara region was not confined just to the vicinity of Jammu, as its other half was to the east of the Ravi River. *Dwi-garta*, therefore, came to be not just the lands around the twin lakes of Mansar and Surinsar but, in the broader context, the lands between the rivers Chenab and Ravi and Ravi and Beas. Some experts claim that the eastern borders of *Dwi-garta* extend up to the Sutlej River, as dialects of the Dogri language are spoken in much of the hill region between the Beas and Sutlej.

In these two connected regions, two distinct families, or lines, of Dogra Rajputs, both equally illustrious and claiming near divine origins, came to rule. The family inhabiting the region between the Ravi and the Sutlej calls itself *Chandravanshi*, of the Moon-born lunar dynasty. The most famous Chandravanshi is Susarma Chandra, who is believed to have married the daughter of Duryodhana, the main antagonist of the epic *Mahabharata*, and participated in the *Mahabharata* war as one of the commanders of Duryodhana's Kaurava army. The second family of the Dogras claims descent from one Agnigiri, who is believed to have migrated from Ayodhya to the area between the Ravi and the Chenab, which is the Jammu region. Agnigiri belonged to the *Suryavanshi* or Sun-born dynasty, the dynasty of Lord Rama, the hero of the other great Indian epic, the *Ramayana*. There are other narratives of Dogra origin, too, but the dominant one remains that they trace their history to the *Mahabharata* and the *Ramayana*. The Dogra dynasty into which Karan Singh was born, belongs to the Suryavanshi family.

In history as we know it, reference to the region appears only with the Muslim invasions. The first reference is to the Katoch Dogras of Kangra, who had their capital in Jalandhar and were forced to withdraw to the hills of Kangra when Muhammed Ghori invaded the area at the close of the 12th century. But the first detailed reference is found in accounts of Timur's army sweeping through the region on its way back after destroying the capital of the Delhi Sultanate in January 1398. During the march, Timur captured Kangra and looted it, and punished Jammu severely, by sacking it and carrying out a general massacre, for its Dogra ruler's audacity of supporting the Sultanate and attacking the Timurid army.

However, during periods of stability for the Delhi Sultanate, Jammu and the Dogras prospered, as Jammu became the bulwark of the Sultanate against the recalcitrant Khokhars, a martial tribe of the Northwest. References to this fact first appear in accounts from the reign of Mubarak Shah, the most powerful ruler of the Sayyid dynasty (1421-34). Jammu's rulers, Raja Hamir Dev and Bhiram Dev, assisted him against the Khokhars. This alliance continued during Lodhi rule, when Bhiram Dev was instrumental in quashing the Khokhars during the reign of Sultan Sikandar Lodhi. During the Mughal era, Jammu rulers like Ghoggar Dev, Sangram Dev, Hari Dev and Ghansar Dev were Mughal allies. Sangram Dev was a *mansabdar* at the Mughal court and aided Jahangir in many of his campaigns against Gujarat, Deccan and even Kangra. Later, Hari Dev and his son Gaje Singh were Aurangzeb's *mansabdars* and participated in his Deccan campaigns.

The Sultanate rulers, and later the Mughals, were able to reign for so long and carry out their campaigns in the south and east of the Indian Subcontinent mainly because they were secure that their empire was well defended from the invaders from the Northwest because of the loyalty and martial traits of their allies, the Dogras. But this changed when the Mughals lost their vigour and vitality after the death of Aurangzeb and gradually yielded space not just to new invaders from the Northwest—chiefly Nader Shah and Ahmed Shah Abdali—but also to emerging regional powers like the Marathas, as well as Britain's East India Company. It was only by the close of the 18th century that it became clear which forces would determine the course of history in the different regions of North India.

Interestingly, the puritanical rule of Aurangzeb, followed by the successive invasions of Ahmad Shah Abdali, triggered the transformation of the Dogra states of the Punjab hills. With the ban on music and arts during Aurangzeb's rule, painters and artists who lived on the patronage of the Mughals migrated to the hills, giving birth to the world-famous Pahari painting schools of Basholi, Jasrota and Mankot in the Jammu region, and Kangra, Guler and Chamba across the Ravi. After Aurangzeb, the Mughal empire went into decline, and Abdali's invasions led to the disruption of trade, making the caravan routes unsafe. Consequently, the caravans followed the hill route between Delhi and the Northwest, which brought prosperity to the small principalities of the Punjab hills through toll collection. In time, this gave rise to the Sikh *misls*—sovereign confederacies—and the subsequent rise of Maharaja Ranjit Singh, chief of one of the *misls*, and the fading of the Dogras. Soon, the whole of the Dogra region was brought under Ranjit Singh's rule.

The first half of the nineteenth century was bad for most Indian rulers. The century had begun with the Marathas being decisively beaten and reduced to a few vassal and fragmented states in Central India; in the second decade, the Gurkhas had not only been pushed out of the Kumaon Hills but also forced to enter into a peace treaty on British terms; the Jats, who had briefly threatened to displace the remnants of the Mughals in Agra and Delhi, had been reduced to a minor force around Bharatpur. Only the Sikhs in the north had succeeded in carving out an empire for themselves—one of the largest that India has seen—that extended from Sutlej in the east to Attock in the north-west and had forced the British to enter into a treaty of friendship to become their equal in 1809. However, even before the first half of the century had closed, the Sikh Empire built by Maharaja Ranjit Singh, with the fabled city of Lahore as its capital, had imploded and gone out of existence. Only the Jammu Dogras, who were part of the Sikh Empire, survived this carnage.

The Dogras of Jammu survived this upheaval because they were led by Raja Gulab Singh, who was able, shrewd and a great general and statesman. Descended from the family of Maharaja Ranjit Dev, whose immediate family had fallen on bad days following the turmoil of the 18th century, he had sought employment in the service of Maharaja Ranjit Singh and had rapidly risen through the ranks because of his soldierly qualities and loyalty. He made his mark during the first—and failed—Kashmir campaign of Maharaja Ranjit Singh. Before the Kashmir campaign, Maharaja Ranjit Singh had undertaken to secure his rear by conquering the Muslim rulers of Akhnur, Rajouri and Bhimbar. All these states to the west of the river Chenab owed loyalty to Kabul, and hence, when the Sikh armies were crossing the Pir Panjal, they had chosen to betray the Sikhs, forcing the armies to beat a hasty retreat. It was during this retreat that the organizational skills of Gulab Singh were noticed, and after playing significant roles in the conquests of Garh Dhamala, Multan and Attock, his stock had skyrocketed in the Sikh Durbar in Lahore. But the Kashmir retreat had made very clear to Maharaja Ranjit Singh that unless the smaller hill states of the Dogras and others on the western side of the Ravi were under the control of the Lahore Durbar, his dream of conquering Kashmir could not be realized. He also understood that it was not easy for outsiders to rule over the Dogras, as they were warriors of independent disposition. A shrewd judge of men, the Maharaja chose Gulab Singh as his representative in the hills to bring the unruly people under some kind of order, as he had seen that neither his Sikh Governors nor his son, Prince Kharak Singh, had succeeded in establishing Sikh authority in the region.

Gulab Singh established the authority of the Sikh Empire by bringing the Hindu states on the eastern side of the Chenab—Jammu, Jasrota, Mankot, Lakhanpur, Bhadu and Billawar-Basholi, etc.—under his control. This he did by negotiating peace deals, by marriage alliance, and, where necessary, by military strength. On the western side of the Chenab were the Muslim states of Akhnur, Bhimbar and Poonch, and all of them were not only conquered by Gulab Singh but their rulers punished according to the degree of their defiance. Maharaja Ranjit Singh had by then concluded that, since Gulab Singh had time and again proven his loyalty and ability to organize and establish the authority of the Sikh Empire, it was best to hand over control of the Dogra states to him. Thus, in 1822, Maharaja Ranjit Singh made Gulab Singh the hereditary Raja of Jammu. Being an efficient administrator and a statesman, Gulab Singh gave a system of governance that convinced the people of the hill states that all of them had an equal stake in the stability and well-being of the new rule in Jammu. Thus, for the first time in the history of the Dogras, they had one identity, having accepted the larger identity of Jammu, instead of the smaller identities of fragmented states. With this, a genuine Dogra state had come into existence, and it would soon become far larger than anyone had imagined. This happened through chance, some genuine military genius, and some clever and pragmatic political manoeuvring.

With the passage of time, Raja Gulab Singh and his two brothers, Dhyan Singh and Suchet Singh, became the most powerful nobles in the kingdom of Maharaja Ranjit Singh. This, however, lasted only as long as Ranjit Singh was alive, because none of his successors possessed the abilities keep the kingdom in good health. What followed his death is a story of betrayals, treachery, incompetence and conspiracy leading to the disintegration of the mighty Sikh Empire. How Jammu survived the carnage of the 19th century is a miracle of sorts. Badly scarred by the intrigues and conspiracies of the Lahore Durbar after Maharaja Ranjit Singh's death, Gulab Singh managed to survive and come out alive from Lahore after losing his two brothers, two sons and a nephew. Although he did not sever his links with the Lahore Durbar, he concluded that with a succession of incompetent and corrupt princes occupying the throne and their advisors egging them on to reverse Maharaja Ranjit Singh's policy of a peaceful partnership of equals with the British, there was little hope for the Sikh empire. Therefore, he decided to wash his hands of the affairs of Lahore. Since the Treaty of 1809, the boundary between the British and the Sikhs had been a settled issue. The British were to confine themselves to the eastern bank of the Sutlej. But this treaty that had served so well for so long came under stress due to the bloated egos of the lot who succeeded Maharaja Ranjit Singh, bringing the two sides face-to-face in hostile posturing. Finally, when war did break out between the Sikhs and the British in 1846—the First Anglo-Sikh War—Gulab

Singh, although his territories were part of the Sikh Empire, chose to remain neutral. When defeat of the Sikhs looked imminent, the Lahore Durbar turned to Gulab Singh to broker peace with the British, who were favourably disposed towards him, so that something of the old empire could be salvaged. But as luck would have it, the war indemnity reparations that had been imposed by the British could not be paid by the Lahore Durbar in full, and to make up for the shortfall, they offered to cede parts of their empire to the British—specifically the territories that were controlled by Gulab Singh, which comprised Jammu and the conquests he had made in Ladakh and Baltistan. The British, with Governor-General Lord Henry Hardinge in charge, then made Gulab Singh an offer, that they would recognize him as the sovereign ruler of his territories, independent of the Sikh Empire, if he paid the remaining indemnity on behalf of the Lahore Durbar. Which Gulab Singh did. Later, he was offered Kashmir, which was also part of the Sikh Empire, for a sum of 75 lakh Nanakshahi rupees, which he gladly accepted.

And so it was that the Dogra State of Jammu and Kashmir came into existence—as a sovereign State under British suzerainty, with Gulab Singh as the first Maharaja. In was an artificially put together State, comprising disparate regions—Jammu, Ladakh, the Kashmir Valley, Baltistan, and later Gilgit—that had little in common but were brought together by Sikh and Dogra conquests and sale deeds between Gulab Singh and the British.

Thus, the Jammu Dogras under Maharaja Gulab Singh had not only survived the great turmoil and churning in the Subcontinent during the 19th century, but also prospered and created a unique position for themselves, where they became rulers of India's largest princely state by area, and allies of the most important imperial power.

The euphoria, however, was short-lived as the forces that were antagonistic to the Dogras were neither mute nor weak. When the Sikh Empire was liquidated by the British, the Empire of Queen Victoria was at its zenith. The British hold on India had been consolidated, and vital concessions had been extracted from the Chinese Empire following the First Opium War. Drunk on ever-increasing power, many in London believed that Governor General Lord Hardinge had erred in not divesting Gulab Singh of his lands and power back in 1846 when there was a genuine opportunity to do so. This was also the lobby that advocated a Forward Policy to secure the northern frontiers of their Indian Empire against expansionist Czarist Russia. In the 19th and early 20th centuries, the British and the Russians were locked in a rivalry for the control of Central Asia, which made Afghanistan, the Northwest Frontier and Tibet of great importance to the British and they pursued a policy of taking control of kingdoms and principalities along the northern frontiers either by invasion, annexation or treaties to create buffer states. It was as part of this policy that Lord Hardinge had signed the treaty with Gulab Singh, and given him Kashmir as well, in order to create a bulwark against the Russians in the north. However, a powerful section of the British establishment had always believed this had been a mistake—these areas should have been made a part of their Indian Empire, rather than being put in the care of an ambitious Raja who was within hailing distance of the Russians across the Pamirs.

Hence, many efforts were made to take direct or indirect control of the newly created Jammu and Kashmir State. This Forward Policy lobby did not make much headway during the reigns of Gulab Singh and his successor Ranbir Singh, but finally succeeded in 1885 in getting a British representative appointed in the State, thus gaining a foothold there. Not long after, a new group of officials became so brash and bold as to hatch a conspiracy to dethrone the third Dogra Ruler, Maharaja Pratap Singh, and bring the State under the direct administration of the British Viceroy.

In fact, the British had sensed an opportunity during the last years of Pratap Singh's father, Maharaja Ranbir Singh, who, when his health was failing, had written to them that after his death, his younger son Raja Amar Singh should be recognized as his successor owing to his sterling qualities as an administrator. The British had declined to entertain the request and stuck to anointing his eldest son, Pratap Singh, as the ruler. But this had placed Pratap Singh at a disadvantage, as the British put the condition that in return for their recognizing him as the Maharaja, he should first accept the permanent stationing of a Political Agent, something that Maharaja Gulab Singh and Maharaja Ranbir Singh had refused since it was violative of the Treaty of Amritsar, 1846. But a cornered Pratap Singh had no choice but to accept the appointment of a Political Agent. Ultimately, he was recognized by the British and crowned as Maharaja in 1885, but more was in store. The era of British interference in the affairs of the State had begun.

Not too long after, the British accused Maharaja Pratap Singh of misgovernance and disloyal dealings with Russia against the British, and divested him of his powers, even though he had taken steps to appoint a Settlement Commissioner to root out the maladministration of land that had impoverished the farmers of Kashmir for centuries, through the rule of the Afghans, the Sikhs and also the Dogras. Pratap Singh was accused of conspiring with the British enemies to act against the Queen. However, a timely exposure by the Calcutta (now Kolkata) newspaper *Amrit Bazar Patrika* of the conspiracy to dethrone him caused such an uproar in the British Parliament that the conspirators had to abandon their plans. After that, some of his powers were restored, but his full powers were restored only in 1905. This brush with danger made the Dogra ruler wiser and more pragmatic, and hence, comprehensive reforms were carried out to give the State as progressive and modern an administration as there was anywhere in the subcontinent. During his reign, not only were educational institutions, including colleges, opened, but the State was also linked to Punjab by rail, and to Gilgit and Ladakh by road. He also had to deal with the aftermath of the famine of 1877-79, which had decimated the population of Srinagar.

After the initial setback, Maharaja Pratap Singh had learnt that while the British left the Indian Princes to their own devices, his State was different. It would remain their particular target and the slightest excuse would be used against him. He would need to take special care of his State, especially of its governance and infrastructure. What followed was a remarkable period of development and progress, marred by the unfortunate fact of the Maharaja not having an heir. The next in line of succession was his nephew, Prince Hari Singh, son of his younger brother Raja Amar Singh, whom Ranbir Singh had actually wanted as his successor. Since it was known quite early that Hari Singh would be the next ruler, no effort had been spared to impart a modern and Western education to the young prince so that he could fit in the world of the imperial rulers with ease. In this, the British worked closely with Pratap Singh, keen to groom the future Maharaja as an ally, a man whose sensibilities would align with theirs and whom, they thought, they could control. Hari Singh was eight years old when he was made a 'page of honour' to Lord Curzon, Viceroy of India, at the spectacular Delhi Durbar of 1903 organized to celebrate King Edward VII's accession as Emperor of India. Six years later, when his father died, the British appointed Major H.K. Barr as his guardian. In 1915 Maharaja Pratap Singh appointed him Commander-in-Chief of the State Forces, and in 1918 he was made a Knight Commander of the Order of the British Empire (KBE).

Hari Singh's progress to the throne, however, was far from smooth. His aunt—Maharaja Pratap Singh's chief queen—Maharani Chadkan, was hostile to him and vigorously tried to convince her husband to adopt a prince from the family of Maharaja Gulab Singh's brother, Raja Dhyan Singh, who ruled Poonch. She also tried to get one of her nephews adopted so that Yuvraj Hari Singh could be deprived of the throne. The suspicion and hostility between Chadkan and Hari Singh only grew in later years.

Politically, however, Yuvraj Hari Singh was having a smooth ride as he had established a rapport with the Prince of Wales and had generally made a good impression in England during his first visit. Although there was a scandal, which, fortunately for him, did not have a serious impact in the end. Hari Singh was 26 when he sailed to Europe, his first visit abroad. Reaching Paris from Marseille, he spent some days in the French capital, like a lot of Indian royalty, before arriving in England. The Yuvraj had already acquired a reputation for his flamboyance and extravagance, and for his love of horses and hunting. He spent well over a million pounds buying race horses in Dublin and cars in London, and hosted hunting parties. All of this was reported in the press, and it is generally believed this was what resulted in him being drawn into an intimate encounter with a woman in a Paris hotel. The consequent attempt at blackmail was widely reported, his identity barely concealed. It was a very strange incident, and Hari Singh and his supporters believed it to be some sort of conspiracy, although it was never clear who might have been behind it.

This episode apart, the Yuvraj's study tour was a success. He interacted with senior functionaries, engineers and scholars, keen to understand the British system of governance, education, manufacturing and transport infrastructure. After his return to Jammu and Kashmir, he continued preparing himself for his future role as ruler of the State. He worked closely with his uncle and the British to introduce several reforms, especially in education and judicial and revenue laws. In February 1926, five months after the death of his uncle, Hari Singh was formally crowned as Maharaja.

However, even as Hari Singh consolidated his reign and modernized his kingdom, there was anxiety about the future of the Dogra dynasty. Hari Singh's three marriages had produced no children. His first marriage, when he was eighteen, to a princess of Dharampur had resulted in pregnancy, but she had died with the child in her womb. Yuvraj at that time, Hari Singh was not reconciled to the death and suspected that some evil palace intrigue had caused it. At that time, he used to live with the extended royal family in Mandi Mubarak, the complex of palaces in Jammu which had for decades been notorious for rivalries and there were frequent rumours of 'black magic' and poisoning. Maharani Chadkan, in fact, had taken his wife under her care during her pregnancy and barred the Yuvraj from meeting her. The young bride had died shortly after. Hari Singh could never really shake off that tragedy, and this episode, together with the scandal during his first visit to England in 1919, appears to have made it difficult for him to fully trust anyone, and this was to affect his personal and political relationships for life.

Hari Singh married twice after that. His second marriage ended with the death of the wife, and the third failed. Both were childless. As the Maharaja himself was an only child, the fear grew that after him, in the absence of a 'natural' male heir, the British might invoke the infamous Doctrine of Lapse and annex the state. It is said that as Hari Singh's three royal marriages had not given the dynasty an heir, astrologers suggested that he marry a 'commoner', and so one of his ministers, General Janak Singh Katoch, was assigned the task of finding a suitable match from among Rajputs of relatively modest means who had no connection with royalty. Janak Singh looked for a suitable girl among his own people in Kangra in the Punjab Hills (now a district in Himachal Pradesh), and finally selected Tara Devi from a small village called Vijaypur, not far from the river Beas. The Maharaja did not see his bride till she was brought to Srinagar for the wedding.

Happily for the anxious Dogras of Jammu, this fourth marriage resulted in conception. The 35-year-old Maharaja now took matters into his own hands and made sure that the new Maharani would be away from the reach of the extended royal family, especially the zenana, which many believed—as the Maharaja did, too, after the mysterious death of his first wife—was rife with jealousy, malice and murderous intrigue. Fortuitously, the period coincided with the First Round Table Conference that was to be held in London between November 1930 and January 1931, and where Hari Singh was to speak on behalf of the Indian princes. Therefore, his pregnant wife also accompanied him, so that she could be taken away from any possibility of harm. But London, cold, foggy and damp, with sunshine a rarity and rain a constant companion, was not a pleasant place to live in, especially for someone from the tropics. Besides, it was too public and bustling a place. The Maharaja decided to shift his wife to sunny Southern France.

Cote d'azur—the French Riviera—on the Mediterranean coast of France, has for long been the favoured holiday destination of the rich and famous of the world. In the late nineteenth and early twentieth centuries, the ruling families of India's princely states were among the more generous patrons of the elegant luxury hotels built here, especially in the resort town of Cannes. It was here that Maharaja Hari Singh brought his 21-year-old pregnant wife at the start of 1931 and checked into Hotel Martinez, a newly built Art Deco hotel facing the Bay of Cannes. The Maharaja had booked the entire third floor of the hotel, where Maharani Tara Devi would stay, attended by a retinue of maid servants, many of whom had travelled with her from India and a few who had been hired in France. The Maharaja himself would be out most of the day, playing polo, and also much of the night, drinking champagne with other royals from the British Empire and Europe. He was absent during the actual childbirth as well, which was unusually long and difficult, with last-minute complications. But he had arranged for a famous obstetrician, Sir Henry Simson, to assist his personal physician, Dr J.H. Hugo, and they ensured a safe delivery. The heir to one of the most prized thrones of India finally emerged into the world on 9th March 1931, a healthy nine-pound baby.

Back in Jammu and Kashmir, the announcement of the birth of the heir was made in Srinagar by General Janak Singh Katoch. The news was greeted with great joy and enthusiasm by all the people of the State, irrespective of region, religion, caste or creed. By an official proclamation, the slaughter of animals, fishing, or shooting was banned for three days—from 10th March to 12th March—which were also declared as public holidays. Offerings were made in temples, mosques and gurudwaras, and sweets were distributed among school children across the state. Later, on 17th March, General Janak Singh was to make an interesting observation in a note:

> The 9th of March was the first bright day when the weather in Kashmir cleared after a long spell of bad winter. It was on this day that the newspapers containing the happy news of the Gandhi-Irwin agreement reached Srinagar. The people of Kashmir thought these happenings were a good omen and believed that the future destiny of the Prince was bright.

When, at the end of April, the entourage from Cannes finally arrived in Bombay (now Mumbai), on a P&O Steamship, *Kaiser-i-Hind*, many officials and courtiers from the State, along with many other princes, had assembled at the Gateway of India to welcome the Maharaja, his wife and the newborn. Among the princes who had gathered at the Gateway in welcome was the celebrated Maharaja of Bikaner, Ganga Singhji of Bikaner, and Nawab Taley Khan of Palanpur, a close friend of Hari Singh's. The birth of an heir was an occasion to be celebrated by all the princes since it meant that one more Indian State would be beyond the reach of the British. Also present to welcome the young prince was the 'Nightingale of India', Sarojini Naidu.

After a brief stay in Bombay, the royal party finally arrived in Jammu by train, where a sea of humanity welcomed them. The short journey from the railway station on the banks of the Tawi to the palace was a triumphal march. While the Maharaja and Maharani drove in a horse carriage, the infant prince was driven in a car along with his English nurse, Miss Doris Trunchell. Another huge welcome was repeated in Srinagar, and there was a mood of immense relief and optimism among the Maharaja's supporters.

The people, however, were unaware of the behind-the-scenes correspondence regarding the newborn's birth certificate and citizenship that had been going on between officials on behalf of the Maharaja and the British authorities even before the birth of the heir. There appears to have been some apprehension on the part of the Maharaja and his ministers—and perhaps a hope among some officials of the Empire—that if, by virtue of his birth in France, the child were to be regarded as a French citizen, then there would be no 'British-recognized natural male heir' to Hari Singh, and in time the state would fall into the lap of the British. However, a certain G. Patrick from the London office allayed all fears and informed one of the Maharaja's Ministers,

Pyare Kishen Wattal, in January 1931 that if neither parent had been born in France, 'the child does not forthwith become the citizen of France. But a child born in France of foreign parents, if domiciled in France when he attains his majority at 21, will then become a French citizen...' But he also added that in that case, within a year of attaining majority, i.e., before turning 22 years of age, the person could renounce his citizenship. The fear of the newborn being barred from ever ascending the throne of Jammu and Kashmir had thus been laid to rest. But troublemakers created confusion about the registration of the child's birth. While there was an opinion that the registration could be done at the Pro Consulate of Great Britain, some officials in London opined that it could only be done in the Registration Office of Cannes, where the birth had taken place. The French authorities, though, wanted the name of the newborn for registration, and it was hard work for the Maharaja's team to explain to them that among the Hindus a name could be assigned only after certain religious ceremonies had been carried out, and in this case, only after the parents had returned home with the child.

Even then, there were last-minute hurdles as the birth certificate signed by Sir Henry Simson and Dr. J.H. Hugo was misplaced. So once again Sir Simson certified that he 'attended Her Highness, the Maharanee of Kashmir, at her confinement at the Hotel Martinez, Cannes, France, on Monday March 9th, 1931, when Her Highness was safely delivered of a living healthy male child.' Accordingly, the Registration Office of Cannes also recorded the birth and issued a birth certificate.

Finally, on the 11th of May, amidst traditional and religious ceremonies, the baby was formally given a name, and Mr. Wakefield, one of the Maharaja's ministers, officially announced that the prince was to be called 'Shree Yuvraj Karan Singhji Bahadur.'

Dr Karan Singh sometimes wonders why he was given that first name. Who would have thought of it, for it is an unusual name, rarely favoured by Hindu families, especially royalty. Karna, or Karan, is a prominent character of the epic Mahabharata—born of the Sun and a teenaged woman who would grow up to marry the king of the Kuru Kingdom and birth the mighty Pandavas, the most illustrious of whom—Arjuna—later kills Karna with Lord Krishna's help in the battle of Kurukshetra. Karna is a great and noble warrior, famed for his generosity, loyalty and charity, but also a tragic figure—abandoned at birth, a loner who never truly belonged anywhere, wronged by fate and tricked by divinity, though he refused to be broken by either. Perhaps the name was chosen for the Yuvraj in the belief that it would ward off misfortune, just as a black dot on a baby's forehead is believed to protect it from the 'evil eye'.

Like his namesake, the Yuvraj would survive and surmount the challenges that life threw at him. But unlike Karna, who was defeated, Karan Singh would not be vanquished; he would write his own destiny and achieve a quiet and sure triumph.

2

Early Years

GENERAL JANAK SINGH'S OPTIMISM expressed at the news of the birth was shared by the courtiers and the people at large in the Jammu region, but there was trouble in the Kashmir Valley. Even before the birth of the heir, as the plants and greenery were struggling to break free of the cold earth and freezing air, the Valley was lashed by the vagaries of the weather, and the administration was hard-pressed to meet the challenge caused by incessant rains and consequent flooding. The officials, though, succeeded in limiting the damage, but before they could congratulate themselves for doing a competent job, the Valley was rocked by communal discord, the like of which had never been witnessed before. The suddenness of the violence against the Kashmiri Pandits had been so disturbing that Maharaja Hari Singh cancelled his scheduled visit to London to attend the Second Round Table Conference. The Maharaja was convinced that with the birth of the heir-apparent, the British had lost another chance of grabbing the State and had hence engineered the rioting and communal violence.

Even as euphoria had spread through Jammu after the birth of Maharaja Hari Singh's heir, the State administration seems to have been completely unaware of the dark clouds that hovered over the Dogra dynasty in Srinagar. Two parallel and complementary forces were about to be unleashed. The young and educated Kashmiri Muslims had become vocal about their identity and rights, questioning the prevalent poverty and squalor in the Valley, which was overwhelmingly Muslim, and the moral authority of the Dogras to rule over them. Their university education, in Lahore and Aligarh, had created an awakening that bred Kashmiri—and eventually Islamic—nationalism, though initially the movement was influenced by communist ideology. While the propagandist element in the movement these young Kashmiris started, and the means they adopted, can be questioned, it is true that Kashmiri Muslims, despite being the majority in the State, had very limited representation in the administration and in the senior ranks of the army. Credible observers like Sir Albion Banerjee, who served as Prime Minister of Kashmir from 1927 to 1929, had also recorded that there was very little contact between the administration of the Dogra State and the vast majority of Kashmiri Muslims, who 'were absolutely illiterate, labouring under poverty and very low economic conditions', and that the administrative machinery required 'overhauling from top to bottom' as it had 'little or no sympathy with the people's wants and grievances'. This was the situation when Hari Singh ascended the throne. The Kashmir Valley was ready to explode, should someone decide to light the fuse.

Simultaneously, the Dogra establishment had also failed to take notice of the fact that in the Subcontinent's politics and literature, a revolution had begun to take place. The progressive, often radical ideology of communism had become popular among the educated youth. Also, following the Russian Revolution of 1917, the flexing of communist muscles in Central Asia had again raised the phantom of what the British called the 'Great Game'. The possibility of the Soviet Union marching towards the

Subcontinent worried the British, and hence, they wanted control over the frontier region as a kind of buffer between Central Asia and their Indian Empire. In pursuit of this goal, the British Indian Government had been trying to persuade the Maharaja to lease them the Gilgit Agency that lay close to the northern frontier of Afghanistan. The intelligence agencies and administration of the State failed to appreciate the gravity of these changes and had no strategy to meet the challenge, depending solely upon the goodwill of the British rulers and the hope that they would be more trusting of Hari Singh than they had been of his uncle, Pratap Singh. The incompetence of the State's intelligence agencies had also resulted in a dangerous ignorance about the level of disaffection among large sections of Kashmiri Muslims. Subsequent events showed that even before the festivities over the birth of an heir to the Maharaja had subsided, the fuse of trouble had already been lit in Kashmir.

For almost a century, the state's rulers had been wary of outsiders entering the valley and sowing seeds of discord among the people, especially given the British regret at their inability to take direct control of the State in 1846. The Dogra rulers had known for long that they would remain susceptible to conspiracies to remove them. Yet, that summer of 1931, the administration failed in its duty. The antecedents of outsiders were supposed to be closely scrutinized before they were allowed to enter, and they were monitored after they did. However, the British and the Europeans were exempt from this scrutiny. That summer, a European tourist arrived in Srinagar with a person of Indian origin who was said to be his cook. This man, Abdul Qadir, turned out to be more than a cook. How he established his contacts among the local people in Srinagar in a short time and assumed enough influence to deliver fiery speeches after the Friday prayers remains a mystery to this day. He aroused the religious passions of the Kashmiris by accusing the Hindu Dogras of Reasi of demolishing a mosque and of preventing the Imam of a mosque in Jammu from saying his customary *khutba* after the Friday prayers. He also claimed that torn pages of the Holy Koran had been found strewn in a public facility. The Muslims of Kashmir fell for this propaganda against the State government and soon this snowballed into an agitation that culminated on 21st June, 1931, when the said Abdul Qadir delivered a dangerously inflammatory and communal speech after the Friday prayers in the precincts of the Khanqah of Shah Hamdan. He repeated his accusations and rumours and so inflamed passions that, perhaps for the first time in Kashmir's history, communal rioting, targeting Pandits and Hindu shopkeepers, took place not only in Srinagar but many other places in the Valley as well. The arrest of Abdul Qadir that followed worsened the situation to such a degree that the trial of the rioters could not be held in the normal courts and had to be shifted to the Srinagar prison. Even this measure turned out to be inadequate, as thousands of Kashmiris marched towards the prison in an attempt to free the prisoners. In response, the administration ordered a firing that killed 22 Kashmiris.

It had become clear that the smug administration had completely failed: it did not know the credentials of either the European tourist or his so-called cook, and worse, it failed in gathering intelligence about the political discontent that had been simmering among the people. It was only in hindsight that the administration started asking questions, but by then Abdul Qadir had already lit a terrible fire, started the countdown for the exit of the Dogra dynasty, and vanished as mysteriously as he had appeared. Later, it was suggested that he was a Rawalpindi-based spy in the service of the British with the task of creating conditions that would weaken Maharaja Hari Singh and thus force him to concede their demands.

This may indeed have been the case. Although the British had groomed Hari Singh and then helped instal him as the Maharaja, they found that he could be unpredictable, refusing to always toe the line. At the First Round Table Conference of 1930-31, for instance, he had shocked them by virtually endorsing the idea of an independent India. In his speech as the Chairman of the Chamber of Princes, he had said: 'While Indian Princes valued the British connection, they had full sympathy for the aspirations of their motherland for an equal and honourable place in the comity of nations.' Therefore, it is not surprising that he was branded as an 'unreliable ally' by the British, and they would have wanted to create trouble in his State in order to control him.

Both before and after his ascension, Hari Singh had also tried to address some of the failures of his predecessors by initiating reforms that were fairly progressive for his times. He introduced the State Subject law that prioritized land ownership by locals, brought in measures to regulate money-lending and tackle corruption, outlawed child marriage, threw open the doors of temples to Harijans (as the Dalits were then known), banned the practice of untouchability, built hundreds of schools and set up scholarships for poor children of all communities.

Unfortunately, these and other reforms were not effectively implemented on the ground and the Maharaja, overly fond of leisure and the good life, was too hands-off a ruler to notice or to push his administration to deliver results. The 1931 agitation, therefore, was in many ways inevitable, and it was the precursor to more serious challenges in the coming years.

Thus, in a twist of fate, the joy and optimism that the birth of an heir had brought came to be inextricably linked to the trials and tribulations that Jammu and Kashmir went through in subsequent decades. Yuvraj Karan Singhji Bahadur was to be called upon to play an important role in shaping the destiny of the Kashmiri people, whose leader Sheikh Mohammad Abdullah's political birth had also coincided with the birth of the Yuvraj.

The early childhood of the young prince was spent in Jammu's Amar Mahal—a mini-castle and, now, a museum and a library—that was commissioned by his grandfather, and designed by a French architect. No other place in Jammu gives such a panoramic and glorious view of the Tawi River and the Bahu fort across it. There he lived in the care of his mother, who doted on him. He remembers looking up at the sky above the palace and feeling awed and dazed by the vast blue expanse. And to this day he remembers seeing his image in a large mirror and becoming aware of himself as a person, an individual separate from his mother—to whom he ran back in some confusion.

The physical proximity of mother and child and the resultant joy were not to last long, and life was to change forever. When he was about four years old, the prince was separated from his mother and taken to another part of the palace and into an independent establishment. This arrangement was strictly followed in both Srinagar and Jammu, and he was allowed to be with his mother for only an hour every day and with his father thrice a week for an even shorter duration. These rules were set by the Maharaja, and the trauma of the harsh separation would haunt both mother and son for many years, and affect their relationship with the Maharaja—stern father to one and remote, seemingly loveless husband to the other.

Hari Singh and Tara Devi were very different people, and most of the time, neither appears to have made any serious attempt to understand or reach out to the other. As Karan Singh has observed often, this did not make for a very happy family environment. There was 'always tension, it affected everything' and it 'flowed from a deep incompatibility' between his parents. The only purpose of this apparent mismatch, it appears, was to get an heir for the dynasty. Otherwise, they had almost nothing in common. She was a village girl, and he the ruler of India's largest princely state and one of the richest. She had grown up in a large family and he, an only child, had been brought up for the most part under the strict, impassive supervision of British guardians. She was a gregarious person who loved children and people. She was of simple tastes and traditional values, where puja was a daily habit, *bhajans,* folk, and other songs came naturally and spontaneously. Her ambitions, too, were those of many young brides of her time: to be loved and wanted, to become a mother, take care of the needs of her child and family and be appreciated for it. She had not sought to be the Maharani but was catapulted into the role by destiny. On the other hand, the Maharaja was born into royalty and had been identified as the future king very early in life, heir to the burden but also the immense privileges of a famed dynasty. He was a man of reserved habits who preferred a select band of friends—with whom he could be jovial and frank—and largely appeared to be aloof from his surroundings. His presence was formidable and could be intimidating for many, thereby making conversation difficult. He could also be paradoxical—an agnostic, he could yet be ritualistic and easily influenced by astrologers and soothsayers. By most accounts, he was a psychologically complex and difficult person with trust and commitment issues. The only person who remained his favourite for a long time in the court was Brigadier Faqir Singh. Outside the court, only Victor Rosenthal, a jeweller and aesthete of Russian descent, was to be his long-lasting friend. Otherwise, many occupied and lost that position as fast as they had gotten it. He could also be stubborn.

And so could Tara Devi. Even after becoming the Maharani of the biggest princely state in the country, she did little to change her attitude towards life except learning the ways of courtly life and also the manners of a royal hostess, though she retained her warmth and sensitivity in all the glitz. Her rural, conventional background did not inhibit her. In the early years of her marriage, she would don a *shikari's* dress when she had to be part of royal hunting trips and enjoyed every bit of it. Like most of the Rajput women of her time, she also enjoyed a smoke, trading the hukkah for expensive cigarettes. Karan Singh recalls a delightful episode from the 1940s, when the Maharaja and she were at a private lunch hosted by Jawaharlal Nehru who had just become Prime Minister. The table had barely been cleared after the last course when she turned to the host and said in Hindustani, 'Mr Nehru, don't you offer cigarettes to your guests?' A flustered Nehru quickly produced a silver cigarette case.

But outside of these public gatherings, she remained distant from her husband, retreating into her rituals of puja and preferring the company of her relatives from Kangra, a good number of whom, including her brother, Thakur Nachint Chand, who had a strong influence on her, had become almost permanent residents of the palaces in Jammu and Srinagar. And she continued to yearn for her young child. To her, the Maharaja's decision to take him away from her was cruelty, and she never really forgave him for it. She would not make allowances for the Maharaja's anxieties. To him, the future ruler of a large and complex state needed to be trained in discipline and shielded from too much emotion, especially a mother's irrational love. The Maharaja was also prejudiced by his own experience, and considered the women's quarter, the zenana, as a den of disorienting passion and vicious envy and intrigue. Like the Dogra rulers before him, perhaps he too was acutely aware that had Maharaja Ranjit Singh taken as much care of the education and upbringing of his sons as he took of his horses, the Sikh Empire would not have met the fate that it ultimately did—a spectacular collapse that gave Raja Gulab Singh the opportunity to build an empire for himself and his family.

The mother and son both had to be deprived of the need they had of each other. Every day, much before the appointed hour, Tara Devi eagerly awaited the arrival of the child who had become her reason to exist, and when he arrived, she showered him with love and affection and took him first to her puja room, where she put flowers and coins in his small hands to offer the pictures of gods and goddesses installed there. Then they would play games with her maidservants and many of her nieces and nephews who lived there. They were the only children in the palace, since there were none from the Yuvraj's father's side. Sometimes, they would all gather in the large veranda of Amar Mahal to admire and absorb the magnificent view of the Shivalik range with the triple-peaked Trikuta mountain, the abode of Vaishno Devi, dominating the skyline, and below it, the river Tawi snaking down to the plains. Everything appeared so calm and peaceful that it suspended all thoughts that might torment the soul. That was also the time for the Maharani to light the earthen diyas and carry them to the sacred tulsi plant in one of the flower pots, singing a devotional Dogri prayer. Karan Singh remembers those brief moments as near magical, when a piece of divinity appeared to have descended upon them all. His mother had a sweet yet powerful voice and played the dholki, the traditional double-headed drum, with great skill and an infectious joy. He traces his love of Dogri devotional and folk music to those late afternoons and evenings spent with his mother.

But the appointed hour in the company of his mother passed too quickly, and the parting was always painful. The Maharani broke down each time, her tears making the child's own misery even keener. For a long time, young Karan would softly cry himself to sleep every night, haunted by his mother's distress and tear-stained face. It was only natural for the child to both fear and resent his father for causing so much unhappiness. Looking back to that time, Karan Singh says, 'You could say there was some trauma. It was painful seeing my mother suffer like that—delighted when she saw me and crying helplessly when I had to go. It is likely this had some long-lasting effect, but back then, after some time one fell into the routine. Children can be very resilient. But maybe something stays…something subconscious.'

About a year later, the Yuvraj's one-hour daily meetings with his mother were reduced to thrice a week, and the father now met him only once a week. While the boy looked forward to the hour with his mother for its uninhibited love, the meetings with his father were marked by both fear and awe. It was difficult to say anything unless spoken to. Hari Singh had a formidable reputation and his moods could be unpredictable. He could be affectionate, but in a distant and very formal way. He carried a photograph of his son in his gold cigarette case, but demonstration of love was not a part of his personality. He appears to have been deeply suspicious of intimacy, and his son would later see this as a kind of defence mechanism. An only child and identified as the presumptive successor to his uncle Maharaja Pratap Singh, who did not have any son of his own, Hari Singh had grown up in an atmosphere of insecurity, because of the competing ambitions and consequent intrigue that afflict all royal families. The palace, during his childhood, was a den of conspiracies and cunning planning—he was a marked child, and his guardians had made him live behind a curtain of caution and suspicion. The habit of controlling his emotions and being on his guard at all times would have been something he developed very early in life. He had grown up to become intimidating and aloof not only as monarch, but also as husband and father, with whom it was very difficult to open up, let alone speak from the heart. One occasion that

Karan Singh remembers clearly to this day—because the likes of it were so rare—was when his tonsils were removed. He was four. A room in one of the smaller palaces had been converted into an operation theatre for a prominent surgeon, Colonel Harper Nelson, who had come up from Lahore. Sometime after the operation, the Maharaja came to visit the Yuvraj and sat on his bed, showing him a jigsaw puzzle he had brought with him.

When Yuvraj Karan Singh was five, the Maharaja decided to give him a separate establishment, consisting of fourteen employees and a series of British guardians to oversee every aspect of his life. While this was the practice in most princely states, Hari Singh was more particular than most, being an Anglophile. He impressed upon his son's guardians and teachers that he was to be taught to speak English like the British aristocracy. He also made it a point to speak to the Yuvraj only in English himself, although he was fluent in Dogri, the language in which he conversed with his wife and several of his courtiers.

At about this time, two young boys, both a little older than the Yuvraj, came to live there and be his constant companions. Both belonged to the Rajput community of Jammu. One was Digvijay Singh, nicknamed 'Digby', and the other Digpal Singh, known as 'Bilti', the former the son of Rao Bahadur Kartar Singh, a senior and important administrator of the Maharaja, and the latter, son of Major Faqir Singh, later to become Brigadier, who remained a favorite courtier of the Maharaja for a long time. It speaks volumes about the kind of upbringing the Maharaja wanted for his son and heir that he instructed the two boys to slap the Yuvraj twice, in case he ever hit them! The occasion to test this instruction never arose since both companions were bigger and stronger, and Karan himself was gentle and peaceable, despite the nickname he'd been given—'Tiger'. When he was still an infant, the young prince had once crawled on all fours into a room where his father was sitting with his close friend, Maharaja Ummaid Singh of Jodhpur, and the guest gave him the name 'Tiger'. This is what the father called him after that day, and the name stuck. Many of his friends and even Jawaharlal Nehru addressed him by that name even as an adult.

The three boys, Tiger, Digby and Bilti, lived happily together for several years under a succession of British guardians, first Colonel Wyndham and Mrs. Wyndham, to be followed by the Ritchies. Mr. Ritchie had been a Master in Aitchison College, Lahore. They lived in the enchanting cottage located on Shankaracharya Hill, then known as Taley Manzil, which Taley Muhammad Khan of Palanpur had built. From that cottage, they had a commanding view of the Zabarwan mountain range that dominated the skyline, and a stunning panoramic view of the Dal Lake and the city of Srinagar. In Jammu, the three boys lived in the small Karan Niwas, which was originally a staff house attached to the larger palaces on the estate. It was a happy period, as they had a full complement of servants who doubled up as their play mates, especially to form football and cricket teams. The Maharaja's Goan butlers, too, came down to their part of the estate to play badminton with the three boys. This was part of the regimen that the Maharaja had drawn for the three of them, a fixed academic, dietary, and recreational schedule from which no deviation could take place. As for the food, the instruction was that no Indian food or sweets were to be served, which meant that the boys had to be content with English food, which the British guardian and his wife relished, but not the boys. For them, the best meal of the day was at tea-time, when they feasted on buttered scones and sponge fingers, delicious shortbread made by Huntley and Palmers, and sandwiches served on silver dishes.

For their studies, an Indian tutor, Amar Nath Khosla, would come to teach English, Mathematics, and other subjects. Every month in his neat handwriting, he meticulously prepared a report of the three of them, including an appraisal of their progress in games and general behaviour, and submitted it to the guardian, who, after perusal, put it before the Maharaja. This was the time when Britain was plunging into the Second World War, but much of India was peacefully protesting to free itself from British imperial rule. Even in their sequestered and somewhat unreal world, the boys would get news, from papers and many of the staff around them, of the massive movement for independence led by Mahatma Gandhi. It was a heady time, and like most young people, they were immediately on the side of revolution. But even at that young age they instinctively recognized that though what Gandhi was saying or doing might cause their hearts to flutter in excitement, the 'establishment' under which they lived would not appreciate their excitement. One day the very sedate-looking Masterji—as they called Amar Nath Khosla—surreptitiously brought a black marble tablet that had the figure of a frail, dhoti-clad man, who he told them was Mahatma Gandhi, a man who had become famous across the world. This was the leader of the freedom movement that they had heard about, he told them, but advised them not to speak about this to their English guardian. The boys obeyed, but the idea of India standing up to the British appeared very attractive to them, and they were delighted by the image conjured up by a wisecrack that they heard—the whole of India urinating simultaneously to wash away the British into the seas! When the War finally broke out, the three boys were privately rooting for the Germans, so that the battered English would be forced to leave India. In their establishment, only one servant, Raghunath Singh, was certain that the English reverses in the War were temporary and that soon they would rally their forces and return to the scene to regain the lost territories and launch a counter-offensive into the German heartland. His dogged insistence and belief in the invincibility of the British was infuriating to the boys.

In due course, the Ritchies were replaced by Captain and Mrs. Wreford. They were the favourites of the boys. Captain Wreford had lost an arm in the First World War, but that had not diminished him and he'd had an impressive career, retiring as the Census Commissioner of the State. But what impressed the boys most was that he was still a good shot, using his stump of an arm to good effect in shooting parties and hunts. With him as guide, the boys developed a great interest in badminton, tennis, hockey, and football as well as in general outdoor life. They were also introduced to cricket and became such fans of the two legends of world cricket, Don Bradman and Wally Hammond, that they wrote letters to them in Australia and England. But the Yuvraj could not sustain his interest in that slow and time-consuming game for long. The high point of the boys' life under the Wreford couple was that while in Srinagar, they went shopping in Gulmarg, the favourite summer resort of British high society, with glittering shops that stocked expensive and fashionable foreign products. During the winter, when in Jammu, the destination for a fortnightly outing was Sialkot, an hour's drive away. There, they had tea at Ghulam Qadir's department store and bought comics from a nearby bookshop. They also subscribed to three comics from England—the Yuvraj got *Tiger Tim*, Digby *Donald Duck,* and Bilti *Puck.* For a short while, they also had Ram Chandra Kak, who was later to become the Prime Minister of Maharaja Hari Singh, and his English wife, Margaret, as their guardians.

One sport that the Yuvraj could not take to with any great enthusiasm was polo, although the game and racing remained a significant part of his childhood and early youth because the Maharaja was an excellent horse rider and six-handicap polo player, and wanted his son to be a great player. So when the Yuvraj was just three, he was made to ride every day, beginning with a box-saddle and a tiny horse, and moving gradually to larger ones. The experience wasn't a happy one; he fell several times, and on one occasion when the horse bolted under him in the Jammu polo ground, the Yuvraj hung in the stirrup, terrified and screaming till the animal finally stopped after it had exhausted itself. Fortunately, there was no major damage done, at least not immediately. This misadventure apart, the business of horses and polo was fun. The finest polo players arrived in Srinagar to play matches, and famous teams like the one from Jaipur, which, with a combined handicap of 35 out of a possible 40, was a favourite with the spectators. Such occasions were also an opportunity for the young prince to see his older female relatives—his grandmother and grand aunts—who would be sitting in the Zenana pavilion, dressed in white.

In 1941, the Maharaja had purchased a block of flats on Nepean Sea Road in Bombay, as he used to spend four months every winter in the city because horse racing was his greatest passion, and there was no better place in India for racing than Bombay. Regardless of what was unfolding in his State, the Maharaja's annual routine never changed—six months of the summer in Srinagar and in the winter, two months in Jammu and four in Bombay. It is not surprising that many believed that he neglected governance for sport and leisure. His wife believed he wasn't really aware of what went on outside the palace. 'Your father doesn't meet the people,' she would say to her son. 'He surrounds himself with his fawning courtiers and favourites, and never gets to know what is going on outside.' As for herself, although she enjoyed the glitz and the riches, because of her humble background she was particular about helping her poorer relatives and the destitute in Jammu, on whom she spent a large sum of money. She would impress upon her son that this was a duty. 'If you help the rich', she would say, 'they will only take your money and turn against you when you stop giving. If you help the poor, they will pray for you and bless you.'

In Bombay, the Maharaja occupied the top floor—the sixth—of the block of flats on Nepean Sea Road, and the ground floor, with the lawns, was reserved for the Yuvraj. The Maharani, when she accompanied them, had a separate floor. Digby and Bilti would travel with the Yuvraj to Bombay and they would all spend a few months there. By then, the practice of having British guardians had been phased out, and one Colonel Kailash Narayan Haksar had been appointed. An honest and blunt man, he had an aura around him that, young Karan Singh thought, made even the Maharaja a little cautious in dealing with him. He was hugely satisfied that there was someone who could make his formidable father uncomfortable! Haksar had become the boys' guardian because the Maharaja had wanted him to be his political adviser but the British did not approve of the appointment. Determined to have him, the Maharaja had found this roundabout way to keep him close. Although, in the end, Haksar did not stay long—almost no one could have the trust of the Maharaja for any length of time, and this resulted in some of the most brilliant men in the country coming to the state as his ministers and prime ministers, only to be replaced after a couple of years or less. The only exception was Gopalaswamy Iyengar, who was Prime Minister for close to six years, from 1934 to 1939. Colonel Haksar took his job as guardian very seriously and, therefore, even when acting as the political adviser of his employer, if he noticed that, contrary to good advice, the Maharaja was making questionable decisions, he would tell the young Yuvraj, 'Tiger, look very carefully so that when you grow up, you will know what *not* to do.' The most exciting development of that phase was that the Colonel's eldest daughter coaxed the Yuvraj into writing an eight-page book, a collection of handwritten poems and mini-essays. Thus, he became an author at a very young age.

In 1940, Tiger, Digby and Bilti attended the Cathedral High School, their first school, in Bombay. It predominantly catered to English, Parsee, and Anglo-Indian boys, and the three boys were known in class as Singh I, II, and III. The education and life in that school did not leave any significant mark, but a beginning in formal schooling had been made. None of the princes at that time were aware of the dark clouds that had been gathering on the horizon, and, therefore, their lives continued as before. Maharaja Hari Singh's world of racing and parties was populated by a select band of friends, among whom Victor Rosenthal was the most prominent. A French jeweller, of Russian origin, he had moved out of Russia as the communists took control of it and had been a friend of the Maharaja for many decades and remained so till the end. During the summers, he was a regular guest in Kashmir and introduced the young Yuvraj to the world of Maupassant and O. Henry, and brought him boxes of Swiss chocolates. Also among the regular friends was the Stileman couple, Freddie and Beryl. Beryl was not only beautiful and vivacious but also the only person who could tease and laughingly admonish the Maharaja and get away with it. There were Indian friends as well, like Ahmedbhoy, with a racing background, and his wife Rukhsana. Ahmedbhoy was also an amateur singer whose *thumris* had earned him a fantastic reputation. With him as adviser, the Maharaja organized some of the best music parties in Bombay right up to his final years, where legendary singers like Kesarbai Kerkar, Siddheshwari Bai, Begum Akhtar, and Meneka Shirodkar came to perform. Among his father's Bombay friends Karan Singh remembers best were the Modys, Homi and Jerbai, from whom the Maharaja later bought a large bungalow, 19 Nepean Road.

He recalls being delighted by Lady Mody's wit and flamboyant eccentricity even as a young boy. He remembers her saying, 'I'm so unpunctual that even in my lifetime I'm known as the Late Mrs Mody!'.

In Srinagar, the Maharaja's close friends—besides Victor Rosenthal, who was not a permanent resident—were Sardar Abdur Rehman Khan Effendi and Nawab Khusroo Jung, whom the Yuvraj called Effendi Uncle and Nawab Uncle. Effendi was an Afghan prince who had settled in Srinagar. Interestingly, his story was similar to Hari Singh's. Born into the Afghan royal family, he was orphaned young and then the British had taken responsibility of his education and groomed him, with the intention of installing him as King of Afghanistan, a country they had coveted for a long time. But the prince had refused to ascend the throne and become a puppet, and had recommended his cousin Nadir Shah instead. He then settled in Srinagar, welcomed by the Maharaja. He lived on Gupkar Road just outside the royal palace gates. Nawab Khusroo Jung was a nobleman from Hyderabad, whose services had been loaned to Maharaja Hari Singh by the Nizam of Hyderabad. He was a prominent member of the Maharaja's court and his Military Secretary, well-known for his administrative skill and elegance, and for his amorous nature—even as a young boy Karan Singh had heard of his reputation as a great ladies' man. There were other Muslims in the Maharaja's court, but most of them from outside the Valley. The Kashmiri Muslims that the Yuvraj met were usually gardeners and the shooting and fishing guards.

One Kashmiri Muslim the Maharaja did know well was Ghulam Ahmed, a reputed jeweller and carpet manufacturer and his art adviser. One morning, the Maharaja asked Ghulam Ahmed to take the Yuvraj round Srinagar, and that drive opened his eyes to the realities of life for the first time. He realized with great shock that parallel to the world of ease and luxurious comfort that he inhabited, was another world of squalor and poverty. He saw rows of dilapidated buildings standing on the banks of the Jhelum, as if about to collapse into the river. The few people he saw were at a distance, looking tired and ragged. 'These are your people,' his guide said to him dramatically. The sight and those words left the young prince disturbed for many days. Until that day he had seen only palaces and villas and the elegant shops in upmarket Srinagar where he went to buy some books (he was given ten rupees for this whenever he went), or to get the pictures he took with his Brownie camera developed. He was just about eleven, but in a sense it was a loss of innocence, and he was keenly aware of it. Did his father, the Maharaja, want him to be introduced to the realities of life, or was it that he did not care? Did he accept the misery of the people as part of their destiny and wanted his son to accept this as well? Was he introducing the Yuvraj to the challenges that would lie ahead when he became the ruler? But that couldn't be, because he had not said anything before he asked Ghulam Ahmed to show him around the city. And he said nothing at all afterwards, either.

Karan Singh believes that brief drive into parts of the city he did not even know existed made him aware subconsciously that the world he lived in was feudal.

On their return to Srinagar from Bombay in 1940, Yuvraj and his two companions had been admitted to the Presentation Convent School in Raj Bagh. It was a clean and efficient school run by a group of Irish nuns led by Mother Peter. It was also periodically visited by the head of the Mission, Father Shanks. The Yuvraj almost always stood first in class ('alas, I suspect, not entirely on merit,' he writes in his autobiography!), and he made his first appearance in a play, as Robin Hood.

The Yuvraj's daily travel to the school was very unusual, but he did not realize this at the time. It was only later that he saw this as a forewarning of things to come. To reach Raj Bagh, ordinarily one had to travel over the Amira Kadal, the first of the famous seven bridges over the Jhelum. But the three boys were taken in a car to a designated spot on the bank of the river and then taken by boat across it. In the meantime, the car drove over the Amira Kadal, picked them up on the other bank of the river, and then drove on to their school. This was again according to the instructions of the Maharaja. He did not want to take any risk regarding the safety of his son. During the past decade, the Kashmiris had risen against the authority of the Dogra Rule, and Sheikh Abdullah and his All Jammu and Kashmir Muslim Conference—which he co-founded in 1932 and later renamed National Conference—had been getting belligerent, unafraid of openly challenging the Maharaja's authority and demanding an end to Dogra rule.

This would lead to events that would change Jammu and Kashmir forever, but those events but were still a little distance away.

3

The Years of Anxiety

AT TALEY MANZIL, IN the company of Digby and Bilti, Tiger had gradually settled down. The school, the teachers, and the activities there had just begun to appear attractive, making the separation from his mother less painful, when his father took what seemed to him another abrupt and arbitrary decision—to send him away to a boarding school. Many schools had been set up over the previous century specifically to educate the princes from all over the Subcontinent, among the most prominent being Mayo College of Ajmer, where Hari Singh himself had studied. Still, in a move that surprised everyone, he chose Doon School, Dehradun for his son. Established in 1935, it was a public school, with no special privileges for the wards of Maharajas or Nawabs. It was a school where the boarder had to make his own bed, clean his shoes, and tidy up everything in the room. For the first time, eleven-year-old Tiger had to live a life without retainers and had to perform all his daily chores himself.

Doon School also had a peculiar rule where all the students had to travel in a third-class compartment of a train. This rule was strictly adhered to when they were allowed to go home during the vacations. Some parents found it odd, but it helped in keeping the students grounded and aware of the realities of life in the country. It was, of course, still an institution for the privileged, but not entirely cut off from the rest of India. Unlike in Srinagar, it wouldn't be possible here to be permanently shielded from even the sight of the harsh living realities of common people. Because of the reticent nature of the Maharaja, the reasons why he chose this school for the Yuvraj are not clear, but it is likely that he could sense the era of royal privilege and exclusivity might not last long and wanted to prepare his heir for the change. There is also the fact that Doon school had been set up to build future 'leaders of India' within the British Empire—its first headmaster was an Etonian—and from the point of view of some Indian princes like Maharaja Hari Singh, an education here would prepare their heirs for a more stable and egalitarian relationship with the British.

Not surprisingly, Tiger found it difficult to adjust to the harsh life of an ordinary person, and a life so far away from the comfort of his mother and the company of his childhood friends. He was miserable and lonely at first. The food was tasteless and he began to lose weight and felt tired through the day. The loneliness was made worse by the fact that his father had forbidden anyone from visiting him at school. There were times when he wondered if his father was not subjecting him to cruelty yet again. Some nights he would be in tears, but knew that none of the other boys, let alone the masters, should ever see him crying.

In September 1942, when Tiger joined Doon School, A.E. Foot, a forbidding personality, was the Head Master. The school had four Houses: Kashmir, Hyderabad, Jaipur, and the Tata, and students were a part of one or the other House. Tiger was, appropriately, given the Kashmir House. Like all other students, he too was subjected to ragging, though it was a mild one. But more than the general ragging, he realized to his misery that the boys had found out that he was mortally afraid of black beetles, and when he approached his bed for sleep, he would invariably find a beetle on it. More than the ragging and the bad food, what troubled Tiger the most was that since he had been well tutored at home and was naturally inclined to learn, he had been put two classes ahead of the boys of his age. The consequence was that he was the youngest in class, but the most senior in academic record, and had a hard time being accepted by his classmates. Therefore, at a very young age, he had to earn the art of adjusting even in asymmetric conditions. Gradually, as he settled down, he found a congenial atmosphere that encouraged his interests, and he soon came to be accepted by the other boys, though a distance remained and it prevented him from making any real friends.

In public schools, a great deal of emphasis is placed on physical fitness and excellence in multiple sports. Tiger, though endowed with a good physique, was a little underconfident due to his early experiences of frequent dislocation and the sheltered and privileged life he had lived. However hard he tried, he could not overcome either his timidity or his inhibitions. This deprived him of the joy of fully enjoying the outdoor life in the hills around the school. But, as if to compensate for this, he had developed a passion for chess as he found duelling over the board a fascinating challenge. His father had donated a trophy for the Inter House chess championship of the school, and Tiger made his father and his Kashmir House proud by winning it. He also captained the school chess team for two consecutive years. Pitting the mind against the opponent was, however, one thing, but physically competing with them was quite another. He found that he could not coordinate his body in the school gym. Though he pushed himself, he could not perform the front roll; his body froze. No amount of encouragement or mocking would make his body relax and perform an exercise that everybody else seemed to do with great ease. Swimming appeared to be a bigger challenge, as those who were good at it watched him, probably enjoying his discomfort and also waiting for a chance to push his head under the water and delight in his panic and terror. But he knew there was no escape from this routine, so when he was in Bombay for the holidays, he learned to swim at the Willingdon Club, where the atmosphere was more congenial.

Gradually, Tiger began to feel confident and explored the school, where he found the library a place where he was most at home. It became his comfort zone, and his place of wonder and discovery. He devoured the hilarious Jeeves stories of Wodehouse and the dark tragedies of Hardy. He explored the French and Russian masters—Maupassant, Dumas and Hugo; Chekhov, Dostoevsky and Gorki. And it was here that he came upon the books that he believes shaped his outlook on life and India: Jawaharlal Nehru's *An Autobiography* and *The Discovery of India*. In the latter, he encountered India as an ancient and grand civilization, rich in history and human experience, a fascinating tapestry and mosaic, so vast and varied—an inheritance that made the young boy feel grand and noble himself. *An Autobiography* astonished him for the writer's passionate commitment to his people and his absolute certainty about his life's purpose, and for the candour with which he made his own conflicts and shortcomings so public. The young prince realized that the kingdom that would one day be his and the dynasty that he was told—and had instinctively believed—was his main identity, were but a tiny part of a history that had been flowing like a great river, uninterrupted for ages, and that his own life was so small, but could, perhaps, become larger, and in some way significant. The experience of reading those books shifted something in the young mind, and the true effects would unfold over the years to follow. More significantly, Nehru, who had been only a name till now, became a kind of hero. The Yuvraj went back to these books several times over the next few years, also reading other writings by Nehru and thinkers like him, and began to develop ideals that would be at variance with his feudal family background.

At school, he was also deeply impressed by his teacher V. Siddarthachari, who helped him come close to the new horizons that had emerged in learning and scholarship and encouraged him to explore them for himself. Siddarthachari later resigned from his teaching profession and qualified for the Foreign Service, where he spent the rest of his years. But before he left, he gave Tiger the gift of reading and reciting poetry with correct enunciation and emphasis, which remained with his student all his life. Other teachers who left a deep mark on the young mind were Gurdial Singh, who taught Geography, and Nandu Dayal, who was a great mountaineer. School had begun to look interesting and attractive, a new home, away from the tension of the palaces in Srinagar and Jammu. It appeared that the nightmares had finally left him.

During one of the summer vacations of that period, the Maharaja officially gave the Yuvraj his first public assignment, and he inaugurated a handicrafts exhibition in Srinagar and made a public speech. He had made that speech with a fluttering heart, but apparently, he had done an impressive job—Col. Haksar, who escorted him to Dachigam, where his father was, gave an impressive report of the event and the Maharaja demonstrated the rare emotion of pride in his son. It was an unexpectedly happy holiday and the vacations that followed were also largely pleasant. By a strange coincidence relations between his parents also remained surprisingly cordial during his vacations. His separate establishment had been wound up and Digby and Bilti had been sent back to their homes, so he spent his holidays with his parents. There were quite a few outdoor lunch and dinner parties. With a whole retinue of liveried servants assisting them, both the Maharaja and Maharani would cook for long hours while their friends gossiped over whisky and wine.

In December 1945, Tiger appeared for the Senior Cambridge Examination and passed with a first division. Elated, he telegraphically informed his parents. As this news spread in the State, the loyal subjects of his father responded with a flood of telegrams of congratulations. The school found itself in confusion as its office was unable to handle the large number. The same year, he felt a disconcerting pain in his hip but paid no further attention to it as it remained just a niggle. By then, he had begun to enjoy his studies, as he had discovered that he possessed the gift of quick learning and sharp memory. He found that he was able to understand and remember whatever he had read or heard better than many of the older boys. The Doon School offered facilities for students to appear for the Intermediate Science or Intermediate Arts from the Uttar Pradesh Education Board. Normally, all the bright students opted for the science stream, but Tiger decided to study Arts and his father approved, agreeing that subjects like economics, civics and history would be more useful to him as the future ruler. This choice proved to be a boon, as he not only passed but also topped the examination. His confidence had grown tremendously and for the first time he began to feel he might be up to the responsibility that he knew everyone expected him to shoulder one day. This was new. In the past, he had always been uncertain and feared that he might let everyone down, his father most of all. There was no strong yet approachable figure he could turn to for guidance and reassurance, without fear of being judged as a weakling. There is a poignant passage about this state of mind that he would write some four decades later in his autobiography: 'I did not have [anyone] upon whom I could rely during those formative years, someone who might have filled the inner vacuum of uneasy insecurity that afflicted me. I remember once how a casual remark by Pandit Ramchandra Kak (appointed my guardian after Colonel Haksar) to the effect that he had great hopes and faith in my future as Yuvaraj gave me tremendous sustenance for months.'

He did not doubt himself now; it was an entirely new feeling and it was both liberating and empowering. Life appeared attractive, and he was in a very happy frame of mind, when 1946 arrived and his world began to change in ways few had imagined.

The Second World War had ended, but it had devastated the British economy and it was generally accepted that the Sun was about to set on the British Empire. India was anxiously awaiting its independence, but the Muslim League, led by Mohammad Ali Jinnah, who had declared that Muslims and Hindus were separate nations, was demanding a separate Muslim state. During the early months of 1946, the communal question began to dominate everyday life, culminating in Jinnah's Direct Action—a call for a nationwide agitation to press the League's demand for a separate Muslim homeland. Communal riots erupted in Calcutta and Noakhali, and reports began to come in of killings in other parts of the north, including Rawalpindi and other districts of Punjab bordering Jammu and Kashmir. In Kashmir, Sheikh Abdullah—the undisputed and tallest leader of his people—and his National Conference, supported by many communist sympathizers from Punjab, had intensified the agitation against Dogra rule and there was the danger of both political chaos and communal discord.

The Maharaja, however, succumbed to the temptation of the racing season in Bombay during the winter of 1946-47 and left his state in the hands of his ministers. Strangely, his luck seemed to have run out on him at the track as his best horses lost. The Maharaja's letters from Bombay to Tiger were full of details about the racing results, with occasional reference to his wife and how he missed her and Tiger's company. He was also worried by the speculation that when the Congress Party assumed power after Independence, it might ban horse racing. One of his letters reflected how the royal elite viewed the approaching future. He wrote: 'The general feeling is that life is not going to be worth living in a Congress Province. They will stop smoking, drinking, racing, and wearing decent clothes and so on till everybody is limited to two meals (one course each) a day and restricted to wearing only a "langoti".' But his worries were far deeper than the jocular tone of the letter indicated. The thought of an independent India unsettled him, as it did all other rulers of the princely states. What would their future be in a free India? After the British left, would they lose their kingdoms?

There were other warning signs, too, that raised concerns about the future. In a letter dated 13 January 1947, the Maharaja wrote about the communal rioting that had taken place in the Bombay Central and Byculla regions after a Maratha had been stabbed to death. During the funeral, clashes had broken out and left almost 300 dead or injured. A similar incident following the Royal Indian Navy mutiny had claimed over 200 lives. According to the Maharaja, the Muslims had struck first, and the Hindus retaliated. Consequently, the Pathans had stopped going out unless in a group of 20 or 30, he wrote, and the Muslim horse trainers had started coming to the stables in European caps instead of their traditional red tasseled caps.

As the incidents of communal violence began to spread across much of the country, the Maharaja felt concerned about the safety of his heir, particularly since, while returning home for the school vacations, he was to travel in a third-class compartment.

One mad or determined man was enough to destroy not only the future of a dynasty but also of the State. And so he decided to pull his son out of Doon School. This was the second time that the Maharaja had withdrawn the Yuvraj from a school that he had just begun to like. Typically, he did not inform, leave alone consult, the Yuvraj, who in any case had grown used to his father's peremptory decisions.

By now, Tiger had taken to studies as a serious scholar, and he was determined to continue his studies. He opted to appear for the final year of the Intermediate Examination as a private candidate of the Allahabad University, and also attend English, civics, history, and economics classes at Sri Pratap College, Srinagar. Though he was accompanied to the college by his aide-de-camp, he participated in all the activities there like any other student. Despite the disruptions in his studies that year, he performed satisfactorily by passing in the second division. He had also won a prize during the annual declamation contest, which, to his embarrassment, was given away by his mother as the chief guest.

Meanwhile, the demand for the creation of Pakistan had snowballed into widespread communal rioting in the areas of Punjab that were on the north-western borders of Jammu and Kashmir. To prepare for the uncharted road ahead, the Maharaja began searching for advisors who would help him navigate the rough waters. Surprisingly, he also involved the Maharani in the affairs of the State, notably by sending her to Lahore to talk to Mehr Chand Mahajan. A reputed judge in the Lahore High Court with Congress connections, Mahajan was, like the Maharani, from Kangra, so the Maharaja sent his wife to discuss with him the possibility of taking up the position of Prime Minister of the State. Maharani Tara Devi was accompanied by the Yuvraj and sent word to Mahajan to meet them at Faletti's, the hotel where they were staying. When they met, she suggested that he give up his judgeship to become Prime Minister of Jammu and Kashmir. However, Mahajan explained that he could not resign from his judgeship without the permission of His Majesty the Emperor, and therefore he was unable to take up the offer. At this point young Yuvraj impetuously asked Mahajan if he considered the State of Jammu and Kashmir too insignificant for his consideration! This trip to Lahore was the first serious assignment that the Yuvraj was part of, and he had surprised even himself by his reaction. Perhaps it was this that worked, or the Maharani's tact and patience, for the meeting ended with Mahajan assuring them that once he had been elevated to the High Court, he would consider the matter if he were asked again. And some months later, he did become the Prime Minister.

On returning to the State, Tiger realized that the niggling pain in the hip that had been troubling him for some time was becoming difficult to bear, but he still did not inform anyone and pretended to walk normally in the presence of others. The daytime passed somehow, but at night a sudden, searing pain would make him shudder whenever his leg fell outward in sleep, and he began to dread falling asleep. As before, he decided not to talk about the pain—it was probably something to do with the traumatic falls he'd had during his early horse-riding days and he did not want to bring up the subject. But he was to pay a lifelong price for this neglect. Finally, it was his father who noticed a constant limp in his walk and called up the Palace physician, Dr. S.K. Shangloo, who began treating him with some oil massage for a few weeks. Since this did not work, his father decided to fly him to Bombay for specialist consultation. A series of tests and X-rays were carried out by Dr. Khanolkar, founder of the Tata Cancer Institute, as he suspected cancer. Finally, after ruling out cancer, he sent them back with the medical advice that if the pain continued, the hip should be put in a plaster and the joint temporarily immobilized.

It was a depressing period for Tiger. The excruciating pain had not been satisfactorily diagnosed, and it refused to go away. He would wander around, limping, spending time in the Amar Mahal with his mother or in Karan Niwas, where a certain Swami Sant Dev was staying. This Swamiji, a kind of godman who claimed to have special powers, had mysteriously reappeared on the scene some time ago after being banished by the Maharaja from the state many years ago. His acceptance in the court only showed that even though an agnostic, the Maharaja had already begun to feel the pressure of circumstances. He was floundering in the face of emerging forces that he could not reconcile himself to and, hence, was seeking some divine intervention, even the occult powers of a man he had distrusted earlier. The Maharani's elder brother, Thakur Nachint Cand, whose influence at the court was growing, became the intermediary between the Maharaja and the Swami. Tiger, influenced by his mother's piety, also wondered if Swamiji could intervene on his behalf with the gods, and gravitated towards him.

During these months, Sheikh Abdullah launched the 'Quit Kashmir' movement against the Maharaja, demanding that he abdicate and end Dogra rule over Kashmir. The Maharaja and his Prime Minister, Ram Chandra Kak, responded by putting him and other leaders of the National Conference behind bars, eliciting strong protests from Nehru, arguably the tallest national leader of the time, a Kashmiri by descent, and a personal friend of Sheikh Abdullah's. Apart from Nehru, Shiekh Abdullah also had the support of a large section of the Indian National Congress, which saw his campaign as a people's movement. Nehru announced that he would visit the State to show his solidarity with Sheikh Abdullah and his party, the National Conference. There was a counter announcement from the Maharaja's administration, banning Nehru's entry, and when he decided to defy the ban and enter Kashmir from Panjab, taking the Kohala bridge over the Jhelum, he was stopped by gun-wielding soldiers of the State Forces. Not one to back down, Nehru dared them to do their worst and kept walking across the bridge. Fortunately, the Gorkha commander of the troops defused the tension by ordering the troops to retreat and politely explained to Nehru that he had orders to arrest him and asked for the leader's cooperation. Nehru agreed, and was detained at a State Rest House. The Yuvraj was with his father when Ram Chandra Kak walked in and informed the Maharaja in a hushed but proud voice: '*Hum ne Nehru ko pakad liya* (We have arrested Nehru)', adding that he had been detained in a rest house. Tiger was stunned by the news. Here was the presumptive Prime Minister of India coming to the State, and instead of welcoming him and holding talks, the State had arrested him. The young man was convinced his father had made a blunder. Later, as events spiralled out of control and Tiger himself was involved in attempts to pull the State out of a crisis, he would identify this moment as the first clear sign of the Maharaja miscalculating his strength and thus making repeated and serious errors of judgment. He would also discover that the feudal mindset that had begun to dominate the court—and was sycophantically predicting that once the British left India, the Dogra flag would fly even in Lahore—had got the better of him.

The Maharaja was turning away from reality. Would the British leave? The Maharaja hoped not, as that would plunge not only all the princely states into uncertainty but set his own State on a course that had never been charted before. In that moment of uncertainty, he became indecisive. As the summer of 1947 arrived, the Maharaja appeared reluctant to undertake the annual move to Srinagar till the Maharani began to complain about the rising heat in Jammu. It was finally towards the end of May that the family moved to Srinagar, by which time Lord Mountbatten, who had replaced Lord Wavell as Viceroy and then Governor General of India, had announced his visit to the State. Mountbatten was president of the Executive Council of the Interim Government—with Nehru as Vice President (and de facto Prime Minister) and Sardar Patel as Home Minister—which was formed to oversee British India's transition from a colony to a free country, and he wanted to personally impress upon Maharaja Hari Singh to accede to either India or Pakistan before 15 August, the date when the British proposed to hand over power. Lord and Lady Mountbatten came and went. The Viceroy could not engage the Maharaja in meaningful discussion, though he explained clearly the dangers that lay ahead if the Maharaja failed to make a timely decision. Every princely state had to choose between India and Pakistan, independence was not an option for any of them. The Viceroy went to the extent of saying that if the Maharaja decided to accede to Pakistan, that would be acceptable to the Dominion Government of India, and that he had 'firm assurance on this from Sardar Patel himself'. But the Maharaja vacillated. All available evidence suggests that he preferred independence—as did others, like the Nizam of Hyderabad. But even if he did have to choose, what choice could he make? There were multiple religions practiced in his State, and it was difficult to take any decision in the vitiated atmosphere that prevailed at the time, with rioting at the borders and growing distrust between the Kashmiri Muslims and the Dogras. His Prime Minister, Ram Chandra Kak, had also been advising him to accede neither to India nor to Pakistan and remain independent. In the end, the Maharaja ducked, avoiding a final meeting with Mountbatten by sending word that he was unwell. The Viceroy gave up and left.

Karan Singh sees his father's response to the unstoppable

changes that came with India's Independence and Partition as tragic—that a man so intelligent, and in many ways progressive 'should have in those last years so grievously misjudged the political situation in the country'. This was, after all, the same man who, when he ascended the throne at just thirty years of age, had inspired great confidence in his people and political observers by declaring that justice would be his religion and promising a modern and efficient administration. He had shown clarity of mind and foresight by accepting the recommendations of the Glancy Commission—constituted after the 1931 agitation—and setting up the Praja Sabha, a legislative body under the Maharaja's control, but with some seats reserved for Muslims, Hindus and Sikhs. This eventually led, in 1944, to an experiment in dyarchy, or dual governance, when the Sabha was given the right to nominate a panel of six legislators, out of which the Maharaja would pick two for inclusion in his Council of Ministers, thus introducing a small element of democracy in his government.

But in 1947, the Maharaja was a changed, diminished man. The changes unfolding in the Subcontinent seemed too large and dramatic for him. He failed to read the signs—or even to accept the inevitable. He could not rise above the limited vision and insecurities of a dynastic monarch. He ended up believing the sycophants in his court and entertained hopes of becoming the undisputed ruler of an independent State.

Tiger's condition worsened through these months, with the pain in his leg making it difficult for him for walk even a short distance. Ultimately, Colonel Mirajkar, an eminent surgeon from Lahore, was called. In June 1947, a plaster cast was put to immobilize the hip joint and this reduced Tiger to a virtual invalid. The cast began at his waist and went all the way down to the right ankle. There was no way he could move and had to seek help even to relieve himself. During the day, he could at least be put in a wheelchair to be brought to the company of his parents, but the nights were long, lonely, and depressing. Confined to his bed or the wheelchair, he read in the papers about the enormous, even cataclysmic changes that the Indian Subcontinent was on the verge of.

Independence, it was clear, would come only with the dismemberment of the Subcontinent. And as Partition approached, Northern and Eastern India descended into chaos and violence. In Punjab, especially, the situation was catastrophic. Minorities in the different regions of the Province, whether Hindu, Muslim or Sikh, were subjected to loot, arson, rape, abductions and killings. Since Jammu and Kashmir had a border with Punjab, a stream of refugees poured in as the State was considered safe because of its communal harmony. But with every passing week the fear grew that the State may not for long remain peaceful, as many of the refugees would be itching to avenge their losses, and the local people of different faiths may also be communalized. It was in this scenario that Mahatma Gandhi arrived in Kashmir, where he also met Maharaja Hari Singh and Maharani Tara Devi. The meeting took place under the big Chinar tree of the Gulab Palace (now the Lalit Palace Hotel). Tiger also insisted on being present during the meeting. It was a lengthy conversation in which much of the talking was done by the Mahatma while the Maharaja listened. All that Tiger could make of the conversation was that Mahatma Gandhi urged that whatever the Maharaja might decide to do, he should ensure that the will of the people of the State was taken into account.

As 15 August neared, the communal forces consolidated themselves, and with the uncertainty over the Radcliffe Award—detailing which areas would go to Pakistan and which would remain with India—adding to the prevalent confusion and hostilities, it became clear that Jammu and Kashmir too might not remain immune to the virus of communalism. The British were determined to get out of India, and all that Mountbatten wanted to ensure was that they had no role to play in the consequences of Partition. In this way, 15 August came and passed, but not without leaving a trail of terrible death and destruction. The Maharaja had still not decided on the question of accession. All that he did was to offer a Standstill Agreement to both India and Pakistan. While Pakistan accepted it, India wanted time to study the Standstill Agreement. It is possible that India's hesitation was read by Pakistan as its lack of interest in Jammu and Kashmir State, and it slowly started to put pressure on the Maharaja by throttling the supply of essential goods. Since all entry points to the State were from the part of Punjab that had become Pakistan, the State soon felt suffocated. Mehr Chand Mahajan, who was by this time Prime Minister of the State, wrote to Jawaharlal Nehru, now Prime Minister of newly independent India, asking for help. India was overwhelmed with Partition violence and a massive refugee crisis within its own borders—immensely bigger than what Jammu and Kashmir State was contending with. In his reply to Mahajan, Nehru wrote:

> You will appreciate that there are some difficulties at present in establishing proper communications between India and Kashmir. We hope that these difficulties will be overcome soon by our joint efforts. In regard to sending necessary commodities to Kashmir, we should like to know what exactly you require. You are aware that the situation in India in regard to commodities is also a serious one and many important articles are rationed because of short supply. It is not easy for us to spare them. Nevertheless, we shall try our utmost to send you anything that you particularly need. I understand that salt and kerosene oil are specially needed by your people. Could you kindly let me have some idea of what you require urgently?

> Regarding other forms of assistance, you have our good-will but you will appreciate that these will depend on circumstances.

With India not offering much help to the State, Pakistan was further emboldened and in October, it launched an attack on the State in the guise of a tribal invasion. Around 20th October, intelligence reports began coming in of killings, rape and looting in the frontier areas of Poonch and Mirpur, and also parts of Sialkot district. The Maharaja would sometimes hand the reports to his son and ask him to explain them in Dogri to the Maharani. Tiger remembers his embarrassment in translating the word 'rape'. On 22 October, the Maharaja called for Brigadier Rajinder Singh, then Chief of Army Staff of the Jammu and Kashmir State Forces, and directed him to take a force and halt the advance of the attackers, fighting 'to the last man, last bullet'. Tiger was in the room when his father gave the orders in Dogri, and recalls the Brigadier saluting the Maharaja and Maharani and smiling at him before marching out with determined step.

Despite news of the invasion, the Maharaja thought it fit to hold the annual Dusshera Durbar, a grand, celebratory affair, in Srinagar on October 25. Perhaps he thought this would give the appearance of normalcy to the residents of the city. And, perhaps, he was confident that his State Forces would repel the invasion. It was in the middle of the Durbar that he discovered he was wrong. The Durbar was disrupted when the city plunged into darkness; it was feared that the State's only power House, at Mohra, had been captured by the invaders—which meant that they had reached Baramulla, 'the Gateway of Kashmir'. Tiger was alone in his room in the palace, as his parents and most of the senior officials were at the Durbar, and he sat in his wheelchair in the pitch darkness. He could hear jackals howling, unusually loud and eerie that night, while the staff lit lamps and torches. It was later discovered that the State Forces had not been able to repel the invaders. Neither the Maharaja's intelligence agencies, nor even the senior officers of the State Forces had realized how drastically things had changed.

The State Forces, raised a century earlier by Maharaja Gulab Singh during the founding of the State, comprised both Hindu and Muslim troops and had an enviable military record. Historically, the main recruiting areas for the Muslim contingents of the Forces had been the Poonch and Mirpur districts of Jammu Province. These areas had seen periodic unrest, with organized rebellions against Dogra rule. At Partition, a good number of the Muslim officers and soldiers from these regions had opted for Pakistan and joined its army, and in the prevalent atmosphere of hate and sectarian killings on both sides, many of those who remained had been affected by the communal virus. As a result, not only were the Forces depleted in numbers and overstretched, but about a third had turned against the State and their compatriots of other faiths, and were waiting to defect. The result was tragic. When Brigadier Rajinder Singh reached the Uri-Domel border, he found that not only was he hopelessly outnumbered, but several of his own men had also turned hostile. Showing extraordinary bravery, the Brigadier and those still loyal to him succeeded in holding the advancing hordes back for three vital days before they could reach Baramulla, the 'gateway of Kashmir'. The Brigadier himself died fighting, almost alone in the end, with just a revolver as his weapon.

Karan Singh recalls seeing his parents return from the Durbar ashen-faced that night of October 25th. There was a flurry of activity through the night and much of the following morning, and by the close of the 26th, the Maharaja had signed the instrument of Accession to India, giving it control of the State's defence, foreign affairs and communications only.

This limited accession was stated very clearly in the Instrument that the Maharaja signed, in which he wrote: 'Nothing in this Instrument shall be deemed to commit in any way to acceptance of any future constitution of India or to fetter my discretion to enter into agreement with the Government of India under any such future constitution.' He also stated that 'Nothing in this Instrument affects the continuance of my Sovereignty in and over this State...or the validity of any law at present in force in this State.' And Mountbatten, in his letter accepting the accession as Governor General, committed India to a course of action that was to have serious consequences later. He wrote: '...it is my Government's wish that as soon as law and order have been restored in Jammu and Kashmir and her soil cleared of the invader the question of the State's accession should be settled by a reference to the people.'

On the 27th morning, the Indian Army began arriving in Srinagar by air, even as the invaders were closing in on the city. It took the Indian Army several months to clear the Kashmir Valley of the invaders and push back the Pakistan Army—which had soon come out into the open as the aggressor—and gain control of two-thirds of the original State of Jammu and Kashmir. A third was still occupied by Pakistani forces when the United Nations-brokered ceasefire agreement was signed in August 1948, with the suggestion, arising from Mountbatten's commitment as Governor General of India, that a plebiscite be held at a later date to determine which of the two countries the people of the State wanted to join.

That plebiscite question would become a particularly intractable problem, making the Kashmir issue extremely messy. Jawaharlal would come in for a great deal of criticism for agreeing to a plebiscite. Karan Singh's opinion on the matter, which he detailed in his autobiography, remains to this day one of the most mature commentaries on the subject, and deserves to be quoted in full:

> While accepting the Instrument of Accession signed by my father, Lord Mountbatten as Governor-General of India had said in his reply:

In the special circumstances mentioned by Your Highness, my Government have decided to accept the accession of Kashmir State to the dominion of India. Consistently with their policy that, in the case of any State where the issue of accession has been the subject of dispute, the question of accession should be decided in accordance with the wishes of the people of the State, it is my Government's wish that as soon as law and order have been restored in Kashmir and its soil cleared of the invaders, the question of the State's accession should be settled by a reference to the people.

This 'offer' became the main source of trouble and difficulty later, and Jawaharlal Nehru came in for a good deal of criticism for having unnecessarily internationalized the Kashmir dispute. Indeed, my father's earlier reluctance to accede to either dominion, and Jawaharlal's later offer of a plebiscite, are both matters upon which future historians will doubtless lavish generous criticism. And yet the trouble with historians is that they are seldom 'there', and therefore find it difficult to appreciate the intangible parallelogram of forces and factors at play at any given point in time and space. I have already had something to say about my father's dilemma. Jawaharlal also must have found himself in a difficult predicament. On the one hand was his deep attachment to Kashmir, the land of his forebears, and the compulsions of newly resurgent Indian nationalism. On the other was his genuine idealism, his total commitment to democracy, and his personal affection for Sheikh Abdullah. No doubt Sardar Patel would have handled the situation differently as, in fact, he did in Hyderabad and Junagadh. And yet when a nation has the fortune of a genuine visionary as its leader, it sometimes has to pay the price of idealism itself.

Plebiscite being the watchword at that time, this became the trump card in the hands of Sheikh Abdullah. As the man who was supposed to win the plebiscite for India, he could virtually demand his pound of flesh. And this he did repeatedly;

> not only by assuming power, but also by pursuing my father relentlessly[.]

In the chaotic conditions prevalent at the time the tribal invasion began, V.P. Menon, who was Secretary in the Ministry of States and working under Sardar Patel to integrate the princely states into India, happened to be in Srinagar to assess the conditions in the State, and he advised the Maharaja to leave the city and move to Jammu, lest he fall into the hands of the invaders who were on the outskirts of the summer capital. By now, Mehr Chand Mahajan was Prime Minister, appointed on the advice of Sardar Patel after, inexplicably, Ram Chand Kak was dismissed and put in jail, suspected of treason. It was now decided that Mahajan would take charge, working closely with representatives of the Indian government. Thus, at short notice, the Maharaja and his family, along with several officers, left Srinagar in a hurry well before day break on 28th October. Tiger was still in his plaster cast, and a station wagon that the Maharaja used for his hunting expeditions had to be modified to accommodate his wheelchair. The Maharaja drove himself, with Victor Rosenthal by his side, and the Maharani was in the convoy of cars behind them with several other ladies. Karan Singh writes of that exodus as a nightmarish experience:

> It was bitterly cold as the convoy pulled out of the palace... The raiders were pouring in from across the border, pillaging, looting and raping as they came, and there were rumours that the road to Jammu had been cut and that we were likely to be ambushed on the way. There was no armed escort except for the palace guards, and as we left we had only our faith in God to sustain us. The journey was interminable, with numerous stops *en route.* I fell into an uneasy sleep, half hoping that I would awake to the comfort and security of my room and that the whole sequence was only a bad dream. But each time I awoke

> the night was colder and darker, and suddenly my hip started throbbing with pain.

The royal family of the Dogra dynasty finally arrived at its base in Jammu one last time. Everybody there seemed to be waiting for something to happen. The senior officers of the Indian army came and went, holding confabulations with the Maharaja and occasionally taking a drink or two before leaving. For Tiger, there was little to do except to remain glued to the radio to follow the news from the front, praying and wondering if he would ever be able to walk again. Even for the Maharaja, there was little to do as the State Forces had been put under the operational command of the Indian army, and decisions as to where they were to be deployed or in what role were being taken by the Brigade Commanders of Srinagar and Jammu. But the Maharani, who had kept her composure through the crisis, got busy immediately, organizing relief for the refugees, mainly Hindus from across the new border, who were still pouring into Jammu. She plunged into the relief work wholeheartedly, and this meant that Tiger had even less company, and he could do little except to get through the days somehow, practically bedridden. As week followed week, he would lie awake at night, afraid that he would be an invalid for life. During the day, he did his best to remain cheerful, surprising everyone, because he had learned early that expressing any anguish would be of little use. The only bright spot for him during this period was his first meeting with his ideal, Jawaharlal Nehru, now Prime Minister of India. Almost eighty years later, Karan Singh broke into a smile talking to this biographer about that encounter:

> It was almost fleeting, but I have never forgotten it…The first time Nehru came to see my father in Jammu—I think it was November'47—he was very busy and I missed seeing him. I

> was very disappointed when I found out and I complained to my father, so the second time he came my father brought him into my room. I forgot I was on a wheelchair and desperately unhappy, though I wouldn't show it. Here I was, face to face with the man who had become something of an idol for me. I remember thinking how remarkably agile he was, and there was his trademark smile, unforgettable for anyone who received it—pensive yet so intimate and human, as if you were a friend of many years...My father introduced me and said, 'Tiger is your great admirer.' That's when he smiled. He asked how I was, and apologized for not having seen me the last time. I was too overwhelmed to say anything. He was my hero, I didn't want to sound unintelligent...I asked him to autograph my copy of his autobiography. I still have that with me.

As the year was drawing to a close, Sardar Patel also arrived at the Jammu palace. On seeing the Yuvraj in a heavy plaster cast, he enquired about it, and on being told what had happened, he advised the Maharaja to send the Yuvraj to America for treatment at the earliest. The Maharani was aghast at the suggestion, unable to bear the thought of separation, but Sardar Patel told her bluntly that in his opinion, if a timely decision was not taken, her son would remain in a wheelchair for the rest of his life. He also assured the Maharaja that adequate foreign exchange would be released by the Government of India for the treatment.

Without wasting any time, the Maharaja asked Victor Rosenthal to make inquiries about a suitable hospital in New York and also arrange for admission. Brigadier N.S. Rawat, a Gurkha officer of the State Forces, and Captain Ranjit Singh, an aide of the Maharaja, were given the responsibility of taking care of Tiger during the period of his treatment. Within a few weeks, all arrangements had been made, and the three were ready to fly to New York. A DC-3 had been chartered to fly them to

Bombay. Before leaving, Tiger asked his mother to distribute all his clothes among the refugee children. On the advice of an astrologer, he left the palace a day earlier and spent the night in the Satwari Cantonment. That day, Tiger saw cracks in the iron mask of his father who was visibly moved by emotion, while his mother bade a tearful farewell. They saw him off together, but the distance between them had grown in the past few months and the old tension of a less-than-happy home had returned. Tiger saw his father retreat into a hard shell, helplessly watching his State slip out of his control, and occasionally raging against the irrelevance being forced upon him. In contrast was his mother, full of purpose, immersed in her work for the refugees that kept her away from the palace most of the time. Tiger knew he would miss them, but a part of him was also relieved that he was leaving the tension of home and the turmoil of the State far behind. Besides, there was new hope—he might walk again.

It took the plane a whole day to reach Bombay, where the three boarded a TWA Skymaster flight. Tiger was lifted into the cabin and placed on two seats with several cushions in between to make it a kind of bed. As he was being lifted into the cabin, two emotions assailed him: sorrow at leaving the country, and excitement at the prospect of discovering a new world. The plane took off in the evening and after one stop in the Gulf, it halted for its second stop in Cairo and then flew to Rome. From Rome, the plane reached Paris at night, the city looking like an illuminated, magical carpet as they touched down. The flight then took off for Shannon in Ireland, and from there started the interminable flight across the Atlantic towards Gander in Newfoundland. Throughout the flight, whenever despair built up, threatening to displace the hope he had felt at the start of the epic journey, Tiger clung to the picture of the Goddess Durga riding a lion that his mother had given him, and recited the Devi mantra she had taught him. Strangely, this comforted him more deeply than it had ever done before. Finally, the plane landed late in the evening of 31 December 1947 in New York. The city had received its heaviest snowfall in over half a century, and a piercing cold wind blew in when the door was opened. One of his companions went down to the runway where Rosenthal's representative, a Mrs. Toole, was waiting for him. It was a long time before the formalities were completed and a stretcher was brought into the cabin to carry him down and into an ambulance that had driven up to the plane. His arrival on American soil was recorded by a press photographer.

It was a nearly two-hour drive to the hospital through the falling snow. Ironically, this was the first time the Yuvraj saw snow. He had never spent a winter in Kashmir. Through the ambulance window, he saw New York's massive buildings rising through the swirling snow into a strangely lit night sky. When the Prince and his party finally arrived at the Hospital for Special Surgery on East 42nd Street, he was taken up in a large, deep elevator to the fifth floor and wheeled into Room 509, where he would stay far longer than he had anticipated. When he had been lifted onto his bed and tucked in, the paramedics left—eager, Tiger assumed, to join friends or family to ring in the new year. Ranjit's room was right next to his, 508, and he said he would go see it and return shortly. Before he left, Tiger asked him to put the picture of Durga and a photograph of his parents on the high table next to his bed.

Then Ranjit left, shutting the door gently, and Tiger was alone. After some time, he heard a clock strike the midnight hour somewhere in the distance, and he thought he heard muffled whistles and cheering. He lay still, strangely empty of all feeling. Perhaps the enormity of the change had finally hit him, and left him numb.

4
New York and Recovery

AMERICA WAS A DIFFERENT world. There was an openness of manner and a frank, good-natured curiosity that were welcome after the frigidity and sycophancy of the feudal world of Jammu. Tiger's arrival in the USA had been noticed and had been announced by the *Daily Mirror* with his photograph, and the nurses and the staff of the hospital would often come in to have a look at him. He was an object of curiosity since Princes of the East were thought of almost as delightful freaks. Americans were also surprised to hear him not only speaking English but good English that was probably better than theirs. Of course, they found his English accent and phrases a little odd, but being a quick learner, he soon learnt the difference between English and the American expressions. Biscuits were 'Crackers' here and pastries were 'cookies'!

A day after he arrived at the hospital, Tiger was visited by Dr. Philip Wilson, a renowned orthopedic surgeon in America, and after months, he felt optimistic. The doctor had brought a positive energy with him. The first thing that he did after asking a few questions was to ask for the plaster to be removed, and then, after x-rays, ordered a series of blood tests. He replaced the plaster cast with an eight-pound traction on Tiger's foot so that the joint remained in its position. His hip joint and ankle were both stiff after being in the cast for six months and could not be moved. As a remedy, every day he was taken to a heated swimming pool for a specialized treatment of muscular atrophy. Just getting into the water after six months was in itself a relief, and unfettered by the cast, he could move around in the water with ease. Gradually, he also started putting on weight on his legs and was soon allowed to stand in his room with the support of crutches. Meanwhile, the Maharaja wrote letters every few weeks. In one, dated 8th January 1948, he wrote: 'Your Mummy hopes they [Rawat and Ranjit Singh] are looking after you properly and not gadding about.' Three months later, he wrote, 'I got one [letter] only from Rawat and none from that scoundrel Ranjit. I think your party is bone idle, lazy.' Tiger knew better than to ask why his mother had not been allowed to accompany him.

Soon, a radio was brought into Tiger's room. Unlike at home, there was a plethora of radio stations that broadcast programmes for eighteen hours straight, from six in the morning to midnight. The variety of music, plays, talks, news, and sports commentaries was initially bewildering, but soon he was able to identify the stations of his choice that played mainly pop music. Shortly afterwards, a television was installed in his room. That was an even greater delight than the radio, and a revelation. Almost none of the nurses and hospital attendants had ever seen a TV set—just about one per cent of American households had one in 1948 and they would come to Tiger's room to watch a broadcast whenever they could. There was also a weekly screening of a film on the third floor for those patients who could be wheeled in, and a solarium on the sixth floor—a large, glass-paneled room with potted plants and trees. It was a great experience to enjoy the warmth of the sun there at a time when bone-chilling winds were blowing outside. Apart from the hospital staff, who went out of their way to be pleasant, there were visitors—mostly Victor Rosenthal's friends, some of whom were Indian. They would drop in every couple of days, bearing flowers and cookies and crackers, and stay for hours with him, chatting and playing card games.

When he was alone, Tiger devoured the American newspapers, intrigued by the supplements that ran into a hundred pages and covered almost every field of interest. That being the early period of the United Nations, it had its temporary headquarters in Lake Success, a village in New York, and Kashmir being the earliest issue that came before it, it was extensively reported by the newspapers. Tiger noted with some dismay that the Pakistani chief delegate, Sir Zafarullah Khan, appeared to be getting the better of Sir Gopalaswami Ayyangar, who had been the Prime Minister of Jammu and Kashmir from 1937 to 1943, and was now leading the Indian delegation at the UN. A prominent member of the Indian delegation was Sheikh Abdullah, and he came to see Tiger in the hospital. Tiger had heard so much about him since his childhood that he felt excited at the prospect of his visit. So the two men whose political lives were to become so closely intertwined met for the first time not in their home state but half a world away. Tiger found the Shiekh to be an impressive person, not just for his sheer physical presence—over six feet tall, with a robust build—but for his obvious charisma and gracious manner. Later, Shiekh Abdullah would surprise the younger man with his extreme insensitivity towards Maharaja Hari Singh and the Dogras in general, but their own relationship, though edgy, would remain cordial.

By the end of January, Dr. Wilson had decided that a full surgery was not immediately necessary, and he would try some manipulation and replastering of the hip joint. This would involve several painful procedures and the use of anaesthesia. Tiger understood enough about anaesthesia to be gripped by the anxiety that he might regain consciousness even before a procedure was completed and implored the doctor to make sure that nothing of that kind happened. He had to go under anaesthesia several times, and fearing that he might lose his memory and mental clarity, after each session, he would try to recall the definition of 'optimum population' that he had read while preparing for his Economics paper, and recite a tongue-twister: 'Peter Piper picked a peck of pickled pepper./ A peck of pickled pepper Peter Piper picked./ If Peter Piper picked a peck of pickled pepper,/ where's the peck of pickled pepper Peter Piper picked?' To his intense relief, he found that his memory and mind were sound. But there were moments of pessimism too, for he still could not move on his own, and remained dependent upon others, requiring sponge baths and bedpans. Some days were dark and it was a miracle that he didn't come undone.

Time marched on and the icy New York winter gave way to a warm and sticky summer. With a will and determination that he now wonders where he found in himself, Tiger kept his spirits up, humming the hit pop songs he heard on the radio. He also decided to take formal chess lessons. He was good at chess, but decided that he wanted to be better. So, Boris Siff, a player from the Empire City Chess Club in Bronx, was engaged to come thrice a week and help Tiger improve his game. On the other days of the week, except Sunday, a certain Mr. J.E. Brown from Columbia University came to give him lessons in political science and economics. He had a Central European accent, and Tiger was convinced that Brown was his assumed name. Tiger found him fascinating—in capitalist America, he was a fierce leftist. He was highly critical of a system where the armaments industry had such a disproportionate influence on national policy that civil wars were constantly being engineered in South America so that arms manufacturers could reap huge profits. He also said there wasn't much difference between the Republicans and the Democrats, since both believed that capitalism was fundamental to American life. Tiger sometimes wondered what his father would think of the lessons he was learning.

The Maharaja's letters kept him informed of developments in his State. The tribal invasion was growing into a full-scale war, with the Indian Army fighting valiantly to wrest the regions of Jammu and Kashmir that had been occupied by Pakistan. Mehr Chand Mahajan, the Prime Minister appointed on the advice of Sardar Patel, had left the State, but not before the Maharaja had issued a Proclamation, on 5th March 1948, appointing Sheikh Abdullah as the Prime Minister of an interim government with the charge of holding elections in the State as soon as possible to elect members of a Constituent Assembly that would draft a constitution. It was obvious this decision was not the Maharaja's own. Tiger now understood that after the Instrument of Accession had been signed, everything had begun to change in a manner that left very little room for his father. The State Forces had already been put under the administrative control of the Indian army, and the Maharaja remained only its nominal commander-in-chief. Now the political and administrative powers, too, were shifting, with the Maharaja remaining the head only in name as all powers would be exercised by the new Prime Minister, his inveterate enemy, Sheikh Abdullah, who had made it known very clearly that the future of Kashmiris would be more secure in a country led by a secular and socialist leader like Nehru, and not Pakistan, a country founded on the belief that diverse communities could not live together.

In Delhi, hectic activities were taking place as India's Constituent Assembly had taken up the task of framing a constitution that reflected the aspirations of a new India. In one of his letters, Tiger's father wrote, 'I have no idea of how the new

Constitution for India is going to affect us beyond the fact that before very long the Rulers will disappear even in name.' Many years later, Tiger would wonder how his father, a man who had handled the British with unusual intelligence and guarded his State's independence and stability, could not see the consequences of trying to hold on to some vestige of power when all the forces of the day were uncompromisingly arrayed against him. But at that time in the hospital, he admired his father's pride and wisdom. In his replies, he would keep his father posted on the proceedings in the UN Security Council regarding Kashmir. Tiger also wrote to his mother in Hindi, and she, too, would reply in her hard-to-read handwriting—she was always more comfortable with the spoken word than the written.

In the American papers—the *New York Times* being his favourite—Tiger found little news about India. But they were an education as they opened up a whole new world for him, a world less stuffy and more exciting than the one he had grown up in. The presidential election was to be held in 1948, and Tiger found the process of primaries and conventions not only a novelty but also dramatic and exhilarating—with the energy and liveliness that he saw on the streets of New York from his hospital windows. In the papers, and on radio and TV, he followed the energetic campaigns of Hubert Humphery and Harold Stassen to wrest the presidential nomination from President Truman on behalf of the Democratic Party. He also watched the Republican convention where Thomas Dewey won the Republican nomination and created such euphoria that it felt as if his victory at the polls was assured. The tumultuous drama of the competing candidates, the enthusiasm and excitement of the cheerleaders, and the catchy tunes of the bands were electric and contagious. The theatre of American democracy was such a fascination that he often spoke about it to the doctors and nurses and Rosenthal's friends who came to see him. In March, his birthday was celebrated in the hospital, and a picture of him receiving a cake from Dr. Wilson, flanked by two of his nurses and a fellow patient of Chinese origin, was published on the front page of the *New York Times*. The accompanying report said: 'Sir Hari Singh has recently liberalized his formerly despotic government, and his son is said to have democratic ideas. The youth declined, however, to discuss any political matter.' Tiger also made his debut on the radio, giving an interview for a show called 'Junior Reporter', where teenagers discussed a topic of the day. He spoke of his hope that India would soon occupy its rightful place among the great nations of the world and that the young everywhere would create an atmosphere of mutual understanding and love.

———

It was July, and a full year since Tiger's hip had been immobilized by the plaster. It had not responded to Dr. Mirajkar's treatment, and it did not respond to Dr. Wilson's, either. Finally, on 6 July, Dr. Wilson entered his room and announced that he had decided to operate on him the next morning. The good doctor had, in fact, already decided on that course of action and had also obtained the Maharaja's consent, but had not told his patient, in order to spare him long days of worry and anxiety. The surgery turned out to be much more serious than anyone had anticipated, as it eventually required a semi-circular incision that was twelve inches long, and a permanent immobilization of the hip joint through a bone graft and insertion of a six-inch metal pin. The operation went on for several hours and it was late afternoon by the time that Tiger regained consciousness. To this day he has not forgotten the immediate aftermath of that operation—five days that remain the darkest of his life. In his autobiography he writes, 'If heaven or hell actually exist outside one's consciousness, I think I got a fair approximation of the latter during those terrible post-operation days.' The body revolted against the trauma of the surgery. The pain was beyond tolerance. The bed shook each time his body convulsed with the pain. He was given sixteen injections every day—eight of penicillin, eight painkillers—and five bottles of blood by transfusion. Ranjit Singh remained by his side all the time, besides three nurses who looked after him in eight-hour shifts.

The after-effect of the anaesthesia killed his appetite. In any case, he had no energy to eat and was put on a liquid diet for a week. His heart sank when, after a few days, he was casually informed about the pin that had been inserted in his hip. He was convinced he would never walk again, or if he did, it would never be like a normal human. In the consuming depression that came with this realization, he had to summon all his faith and courage to resist a mental breakdown. Dr. Wilson came to see him every day, to tell him the operation had been a remarkable success and that there was not the slightest doubt that in a few months Tiger would be one hundred percent fit and on his feet. He would explain the whole procedure of using the bone graft from the newly developed bone bank. Knowledge heals, he would say. He was one of those great surgeons who was also a master of patient psychology. His fatherly figure and confidence were reassuring. Later, the doctor also gave Tiger a replica of the special alloy pin that had been inserted in his hip, and that remained with him as a reminder not only of the darkest period of his life, but of the fact that he survived it; that miracles happen.

Tiger had not realized that nature had blessed him with a robust physique. His body responded to the post-operative medication very quickly. Barely a week after the operation, he had written his father a short letter, and a couple of day later, we wrote a seven-page epistle. By then, the wounds had begun to heal and the twenty-five stitches of the cut had been removed, the pain too began to subside gradually, and his appetite returned. All his newfound acquaintances in New York, and his carers and several fellow patients in the hospital, had been kind and affectionate, and his room was always full of flowers and cookies. It was then that he realized that since he had courageously borne the pain and concealed the distress that he had suffered, he had earned the reputation of a brave young man among the doctors and nurses. This news had also travelled to his father, who wrote, 'You have patiently gone through a very great deal of trouble bravely…I am really proud of you.' Coming from a reticent person like him, it was high praise, indeed! When the ordeal was long over, the memory of this letter would warm Tiger's heart, making up for the sadness of another memory—that neither parent had come to be with him even for a few days during that year in hospital.

Some weeks after the operation, Dr. Wilson decided to remove the heavy plaster and replace it with a lighter one. The day Dr. Wilson made him stand on his legs was to remain etched forever in Tiger's memory. The first day, the sensation of standing on his legs was a giddy experience, and he was afraid of falling over. But gradually, he was made to stand for longer periods each day. It was almost like learning to walk all over again. September 25 was a memorable day, as that was the first time he was allowed out of the hospital. Nine months after the ambulance brought him to the hospital, he took a short drive in an open car. Viewing New York for the first time in daylight was a thrilling experience. Inexplicably, he also suffered a kind of sensory distortion at the sight of the towering skyscrapers. Then he was filled with an intense sense of well-being and smiled at every face he saw.

When he was back in the hospital, the euphoria died down a little, but he remained optimistic. The doctor's talks with him had taught him that hope needed to be tempered by realism for it to be truly empowering. He also did not want his parents to nurse false hopes and, therefore, wrote to his father: 'The loosening and strengthening of the muscle of my right leg will be a long, slow process, but once I get rid of the plaster permanently, it will only be a matter of time. Of course, as you know, my right hip will always be stiff, but after some practice and adjustment in my way of walking and sitting, I do not think that should trouble me too much in life. It will, however, take some time to get used to it.'

Meanwhile, he continued to learn chess as his recovery continued. And he continued the political science sessions with Mr. Brown. His association with this extraordinary man was to set a pattern for the rest of his life. In a wonderful irony, the people whose company this heir to a feudal order has enjoyed the most all his life are those known for their liberal and socialist views. But much of his time in hospital was spent watching and listening to the great electoral drama that was unfolding. He followed Truman's and Dewey's progress, as they crisscrossed America making endless speeches. Most importantly, he recognized the importance of the vote in modern governance and saw the two top leaders work tirelessly to win the support of every class of people. But he also saw how the Blacks were still denied full voting rights and when he made this observation, Mr Brown was pleased that his young student had begun to recognize the importance of all people and their opinions and of civil rights. Tiger also read a great number of books on contemporary politics recommended by Mr. Brown, but to relax, he also read novels and poetry.

His father had continued to write to him regularly, but his tone had become more guarded, and he would say there was 'tension'. He had warned his son once that their letters were being subjected to censorship. But the real reason for tension was that although the Maharaja had given in to Nehru's demand and appointed Sheikh Abdullah first as the Head of the Emergency

Administration after Accession and then as the Prime Minister of Jammu and Kashmir to conduct a democratic election in the State, it had not dissipated the old antagonism between the two leaders and their relations remained strained. In one of his letters, the Maharaja wrote about how Sheikh Abdullah had been trying to take over the State Forces but that he, the Maharaja, had vehemently opposed the move, and had been invited by Sardar Patel to New Delhi to resolve the matter. In the end, the State Forces had been put under the administrative control of the Indian Army. It was evident that the days of the Dogra monarchy were all but over. The Maharaja was fighting a losing battle.

All this while, Tiger's mobility had been increasing and, in the company of Ranjit and with the support of the crutches, he had started walking out of the hospital to the corner store for ice cream, and a little further, to buy a couple of suits, ties, and a felt hat. Even more thrilling was walking to the building of the *Daily News* on 42nd Street, as it had set up a special room for the coverage of the presidential election. It was a fascinating place to be in as it contained many huge charts, news flashes, and maps which kept changing as the days passed. The final election result was something of a shocker for many people in America, as much of the sound and fury had been coming from the Dewey camp, and it was generally thought that he would win. But it was Truman who scored a stunning victory, and Tiger was all the happier as he had wagered a bet with one of the hospital doctors and he was now richer by ten dollars!

On the first of November, the plaster cast was finally removed, and Tiger was once again able to go into the pool. Miss Helen Clark, the silver-haired physiotherapist, began giving him an underwater massage, as a result of which his right leg and hip gained sufficient strength for Dr. Wilson to advise that shifting to a hotel or a private accommodation after some days would be good. It would be the start of his gradual return to regular life. The physiotherapist would attend to him there, and the doctor would visit to monitor his recovery. Finally, after nearly eleven months in the Hospital for Special Surgery, Tiger moved out to the Barclay Hotel, East 48th Street. It should have been a very happy day, and indeed, he was happy, but the hospital had become a home, and he had also developed special bonds with the doctors, nurses, other staff and some of the patients too. He had struggled with fate and his demons there and emerged whole, even happy. He left feeling emotional.

Barclay was a comfortable and spacious place, which was fortunate, given that the dollar remittances from India were comparatively limited. The most cherished luxury at that time for Tiger was a proper hot bath in a tub after nearly a year. When discharged from the hospital, he was still on crutches, but soon he was strong enough to discard them and walk with the support of two canes. His physiotherapy continued, and he went thrice a week to the hospital where Miss Clark would give him underwater muscle therapy, and the other three days she would come to the hotel and give him an hour-long massage. Gradually, he was also able to get into taxis, and this gave him a new freedom, and along with Rawat and Ranjit, he was able to move around the great metropolis, impressive in the daytime and absolutely magical after sunset—Times Square and Broadway lit up with thousands of neon signs. There were massive bill boards—the most eye-catching at that time being the one of the newly released film *Joan of Arc* starring Ingrid Bergman. The cutout of Ingrid Bergman was bigger than any building that Tiger had seen in India. He and his two companions watched *Joan of Arc,* and The *Three Musketeers* starring Gene Kelly, Lana Turner, June Allyson, and Angela Lansbury; and plays on Broadway, among them, *Mister Roberts,* with Henry Fonda, and Noel Coward's *Private Lives.*

They went up the Empire State Building, visited the Rockefeller Centre, shopped at Saks and Macy's, visited Radio City Music Hall, and even went to see a fast-paced and aggressive ice-hockey match at the famous Madison Square Garden. They also undertook an overnight journey to Buffalo, from where they went to the Canadian border to see Niagara Falls. Tiger experienced the best moments of his life during those days, away from the toxic environment of a feudal court, away from the uncertainty of a world trying to survive the onslaught of history, away from the undercurrent of tension between his parents, and away from the smell of disinfectants, medicines and the cold, bare walls of the hospital.

By then, the year 1948 was nearing its end. The contrast between the previous New Year and this one could not have been starker. Last year, he had been strapped to a stretcher and driven in an ambulance to an imposing, alien hospital and then wheeled into a silent, impersonal room. This year he was out, celebrating in sparkling, shining Times Square, in the company of half a million New Yorkers. The bitter cold of the winter deterred no one, and as the midnight hour struck, people went berserk, welcoming it with cheers and hugs and kisses. Luckily, the three of them found an Indian restaurant that served them steaming cups of saffron tea.

It was soon time to leave, but not before a visit to Washington, where Gurbachan Singh of the Indian Foreign Service arranged passes for Truman's Inaugural Parade on the 20th of January 1949. Then a brief return to New York to visit Roosevelt House at Hyde Park along with the late President's son Elliott Roosevelt and his wife Faye. Elliot's mother, the legendary Eleanor Roosevelt, was gracious enough to show them around. Later, she wrote in her newspaper column about 'The young Prince of Kashmir', who was going back home after a long recovery to complete his education and who hoped 'to serve in the United Nations and help to build a peaceful world'. The party of three left New York in early February, stopping in London and Paris for a few days to shop—the Maharaja had sent his son a long list. Tiger wanted to visit the city of his birth, Cannes, but his father refused permission, insisting they had been travelling too long already.

Shortly before Tiger's return, his father had written him a letter in which he had brought up the question of his marriage. When he was about twelve, in the feudal tradition prevalent at the time, the Maharaja had got him engaged to the princess of Ratlam, Chandra Kunwar, nicknamed Shanti. It had been a glittering affair in Gulab Mahal, with the prince dressed in brocade and jewels, and had been covered by the Indian and international press as an exotic, extravagant affair typical of Eastern royalty. Thereafter, Shanti and her younger brother had come to Srinagar with their English governess and spent some months there. Tiger and Shanti were too young to pursue any kind of relationship back then, but when he was in New York, they had reconnected and exchanged a few letters. Tiger's parents were now keen on an early marriage. But Tiger had other ideas. In December 1948, he had written to his father: 'I would have preferred to be married when I was about 21, firstly, because I think that one is much more emotionally mature and ready to enter into a married life at that age than at 18, and secondly, because it would give me time to finish my BA at least, uninterrupted.' The Maharaja had responded, saying: 'You know your Mummy belongs to an old school of thought, and to a degree, so do I. Situated as we are today, we have to look at many things, e.g., public opinion and especially other factors, so as to maintain our position and prestige in the State. Keeping these things in mind, we can ill afford to be ultra-modern. It is our duty to guide you in selecting your life partner, and needless to say, whatever we do, it will be entirely in your interest, and that of the dynasty. You have always been an affectionate and dutiful son, and we are proud of you...You realize how worried we have been for the last one year. Massacres, loot, rapes, abductions and uprooting of the minorities, uncertain and unsettled conditions, administrative difficulties coupled with your illness and being away from us have been too much of a strain for us.'

Realizing that early marriage was a distinct possibility, Tiger had relented, but reluctantly: 'I am sorry that I will not be able to see more of Shanti and get to know her a little better before we are married because I am sure that if two people know each other well there is more chance of successful marriage than if they are almost strangers.' But on the subject of education, he was more emphatic and had virtually delivered a sermon to his father on the importance of education. He wrote: 'I would like you to know that I am very keen to continue my studies up to B.A. and further, that I sincerely believe, and I am sure you do too, that in these rapidly changing times, a sound education (in my case subjects such as Economics and Law) is essential. It is not enough to be born in a high position. I believe that one should be, in these times, capable enough and well enough equipped educationally to make a mark for oneself regardless of any accident of birth in a high position.'

And so it was that Tiger completed the final lap of his journey home with mixed feelings. Not only was he worried about the issue of his proposed marriage, he was also aware that he had moved far away in a very fundamental sense from the world he had been born into. He was confident he would regain his health fully soon enough, but he was not looking forward to the atmosphere of political uncertainty and ideological conflict in his home state, nor to the tense environment at home. In his father's recent letters, he had sensed the unspoken—that his parents had drifted further apart. Perhaps in the absence of the only real link between them, neither saw any reason to inhabit the same space.

When the Pan-American flight finally landed in Bombay, it was with a sense of foreboding that he stepped out.

5

Uneasy Homecoming

WHEN TIGER FINALLY LANDED in Bombay after almost fourteen months, he was greeted at the bottom of the ladder by one of his father's friends, Fatehsinghji of Limbdi, a small state of Kathiawad, Gujarat. Fatehsinghji quietly asked Tiger to accompany him to a car where the Maharaja was waiting. Throughout the flight, Tiger had felt a mild unease about the circumstances back home, but that had not prepared him for this cloak-and-dagger welcome. Tiger never found out the reason. Probably the Maharaja had some information that an assassination attempt might be made.

When the car reached 19, Nepean Road, he was received by his mother, who too had come down to Bombay, and as he had expected, she hugged him to her bosom. The fatigue of the long flight and the anti-climactic welcome had dampened his spirits, but not those of his father, who wanted him to open his bags immediately and show him all the stuff that he had instructed Tiger to get. Dutifully, Tiger showed his father the shaving kits, cigarette lighters, and other mechanical and electrical gadgets that his father was fond of collecting. The crisis through which his State was going had not taken away any of the Maharaja's enthusiasm for the good things of life. True to his character, Tiger had also thoughtfully brought some perfumes and cosmetics for his mother that pleased her. But this family reunion could barely mask the tension in the air.

The next morning, he was gradually made aware of the grim political situation that had developed in the State. When the great political drama of the exit of the British from India had unfolded, the Maharaja had placed himself against all the major forces that were to play any role in its denouement. Antagonism between him and Sheikh Abdullah could be explained by the history of the State and the fact that the National Conference had long been agitating for the end of the Dogra dynasty. In fact, although he still regards Sheikh Abdullah as one of Kashmir's most remarkable leaders, Karan Singh does not shy away from expressing his frank opinion that the Shiekh had 'terrible anti-Dogra' feelings and could be vicious about Maharaja Hari Singh. But the Maharaja had also failed to cultivate one of the leading figures of the freedom movement in India, Jawaharlal Nehru. The ideological differences between a democrat and a Maharaja had developed into something personal. The credentials of the Maharaja as a reformer and a ruler who was not interested in exercising his absolute powers—many of which he had delegated to successive prime ministers—had failed to impress Nehru. Perhaps Nehru saw the Maharaja's delegation of powers to his ministers as evidence only of his unwillingness to be constrained by the task of administration, so that he could pursue his frivolous pastimes of horse-racing, hunting, polo and partying. The Maharaja, in turn, was loath to be seen as a weak man who could be pushed by ambitious, populist leaders to cede all executive powers. Although he did not himself enjoy unqualified and universal support in his feudal State, he was absolutely convinced that Sheikh Abdullah did not represent all the regions of the State either. Nehru was equally convinced that the Shiekh did represent the entire State and this had led him to trust the latter as a fellow democrat and also consider him a kindred spirit and a friend. The Maharaja also did not believe that Sheikh Abdullah was capable of ruling at all. On the other hand, Nehru had an instinctive dislike of the feudal order.

Nehru did grow disenchanted with his friend, but it took a long time. Reference of Kashmir to the UN Security Council and the proposal to hold a plebiscite had become a weapon in the hands of Sheikh Abdullah, who extracted all the support that he needed from Nehru by claiming that without his hands being strengthened, he could not win the proposed plebiscite in favour of India—he was, after all, the undisputed leader of the Kashmiri Muslims, who comprised over 70% of the State's population. By strengthening his hands, the Sheikh meant that all the executive and legislative powers that were vested in the Maharaja should be transferred to him to convince the people of Kashmir that the changes that had happened post 1947 were permanent and that Dogra rule had been brought to an end. The Maharaja, for his part, saw this as blackmail and remained convinced all his life of the destructive and negative mind of Abdullah, and therefore, among other reasons, felt that Nehru could do no good.

Tiger, who had admired Nehru since his Doon School days, and who had recently been exposed to the workings of the American democracy, found himself in a dilemma. On one side was his loyalty to his father; on the other was his ideal leader, who promised to rejuvenate India through the tools of democracy.

Tiger soon found himself caught in another dilemma of his father's making. It was the issue of his marriage to Shanti. This was finally resolved, but in a manner that was somewhat shabby. The Maharaja could be an impulsive man, and for reasons that never became clear—perhaps some lapse in protocol or a fall from grace—less than two months after he had written to Tiger urging him to an early marriage, he decided to break off the engagement with the Ratlam princess. Even before this was formally done, however, the project to find another suitable match for Tiger had begun. At this time India had launched a 'Police Action' in the princely state of Hyderabad as the Nizam had been defying logic and geography on the question of Accession and had wanted to either accede to Pakistan or declare independence. Finally, when Sardar Patel's patience ran out, the Indian army launched a police operation to merge the state with India in September 1948. In support of the Indian action, and to show solidarity with India, the Rana Prime Minister of Nepal, Maharaja Mohun Shumsher, had sent a contingent of his forces under the command of his elder son, General Sarada Shumsher. Tiger's parents met General Sarada and his wife and children at a wedding at the Nepalese Ambassador's residence. General Sarada's eldest daughter, Yasho Rajya Lakshmi, was barely twelve years old, and it is said that Sardar Patel noticed the young princess, and he mooted the idea of the Kashmir and Nepal royal families entering into a marriage alliance, as that would be valuable to India as well as Nepal. Apparently, Maharaja Hari Singh also liked the idea, and since he had already begun to cool towards Ratlam, this gave him the incentive to hasten the break-off. Unfortunately, it did not happen gracefully as he sent a messenger to call off the engagement and also demanded that the jewellery that had been given to Shanti at the engagement be returned. Outraged by the rebuff, Shanti's brother, who had replaced his father as the Maharaja, refused to return anything.

When Tiger was betrothed to Shanti, his opinion and consent had not been sought but, by 1949, times had changed, and perhaps his father remembered that Tiger had evolved and had formed his own opinions about marriage and so, just when they were moving to Jammu from Bombay, he decided that Tiger's opinion should be ascertained before committing him to an alliance. It was arranged that on their way back to Jammu, a brief halt would be made in Delhi so that the two families could meet in Faridkot House over lunch. They were welcomed by General Sarada, his wife, and the princess in Delhi, and Tiger noted that even at the young age of twelve, Yasho Rajya Lakshmi looked very beautiful. For the men, lunch was a quiet affair, and most of the talking was done by the mothers. After the meal, when Tiger and his parents got into the car, he said, 'Yes.' Thinking back over seven decades later, Karan Singh believes that monosyllabic assent rescued him from what might have become a life of emotional and psychic barenness, or at best a dull satisfaction. In that moment, he had found the one person who would become his anchor and his harbour.

Arrival in Jammu was a tumultuous affair. Tiger had only heard of the joy and euphoria that had gripped the State when he was born, but now, he could see for himself what the dynasty and its destiny meant to the people of Jammu. Ever since the plan for the British to leave India and partition it before going back had been announced, unforeseen developments had overwhelmed the State. In the process, the monarchy and the dynasty had been cut to size by Nehru's insistence that India could not send any military help unless the Instrument of Accession to India was signed and executive power was handed over to Sheikh Abdullah for a democratic transformation. This had affected the balance that the Dogra dynasty had created in the State, with the scales getting heavily tilted to favour the Kashmiris. The hip injury of the Yuvraj, his prolonged treatment at home, and then in far-off America, where he took almost a year to recover, had only worsened the apprehensions among the Dogras about their future. But finally, he was back, walking on his feet, and they saw this as a sign of good fortune returning to Jammu. When the chartered DC-3 touched down, the whole of Jammu turned out to welcome the Yuvraj and his parents. It took almost three hours for the royal party to cover the distance from the airport to the palace at the north end of the city. The only stop on the way was at the Raghunath Temple, where a thanksgiving prayer was offered and blessings for the heir sought by the grateful parents.

From the next day, the reality of what had happened to Jammu after the Pakistani invasion struck Tiger as he was taken around the many refugee camps where people narrated their horrendous experiences—witnessing massacre, rape, and worse in Muzaffarabad, Mirpur, Rajouri, Bhimber and many other towns and villages. These proud people had lost everything and had become dependent upon whatever doles were given. He heard and later witnessed how his mother had helped people rebuild their lives. It was she, and not Tiger's father, the king, whose shoulder the people sought. She moved from one camp to another to find out what the people needed, canvassed support for the relief work, and arranged for the delivery of goods according to the needs of each refugee camp. In this work that required the heart as much as the mind to make decisions, the Maharaja found himself out of place. He could not hug someone or speak words of consolation, he did not have the temperament for that. He could still make decisions and give orders, but he was no longer in a position to ensure they were implemented. All the powers, including those to provide relief to the needy, were vested with Sheikh Abdullah, who showed no inclination to provide relief to the refugees.

Politically, the powers of the Maharaja had been eroded ever since he signed the Instrument of Accession. Interestingly, the path to Sheikh Abdullah's induction in the State administration had been paved by the Maharani's brother, Thakur Nachint Chand. In September 1947, he had prevailed upon Abdullah, who was still in prison, to write a letter of allegiance to the Maharaja so that he could be released. It says something about the state of mind of the Maharaja during that unsettling time, that although he had never really trusted or liked Thakur Nachint Chand, yet at this crucial juncture, he had allowed him to play a role in State affairs. On a personal level, he had firmly adhered to the principle that when he married, he not only married the Maharani but also her family, and hence her two brothers, nephews, and nieces used to live in the Jammu palaces. And although the men were given high positions in his court, he had never allowed any of the Maharani's relatives to interfere in or influence the affairs of the State. But when faced with a challenge, the dimension of which was unknown to him, he was willing to take the support of anyone who could offer it.

Thakur Nachint Chand had convinced Sheikh Abdullah to write a letter in the manner befitting a loyal subject, in which he had assured the Maharaja of his loyalty and desire to work under the Maharaja to make the State a model for others to follow. This letter expressing allegiance and loyalty had made Sheikh Abdullah's release from prison possible, and soon afterward, when the crisis hit the State, it gave an excuse for Nehru to write to the Maharaja, urging him to repose full confidence in Sheikh Abdullah and hand over power so that he could enable a peaceful transition to Jammu and Kashmir becoming a part of the Indian Union. Nehru expressed full confidence in his friend and asserted that he was more likely to be correct on the big issues and had proved his credentials by maintaining communal harmony in Kashmir. Nehru also argued that even if trusting Sheikh Abdullah was a risk, it was worth taking, as he was, without doubt, the tallest and most popular leader in the State. This letter had worked, and Sheikh Abdullah had been appointed as the Emergency Administrator to deal with the challenges that had arisen with the tribal invasion from Pakistan—which, it is true, the Sheikh had condemned and which the National Conference cadre had valiantly resisted.

However, for Sheikh Abdullah, the challenges arising from the invasion were not the only issue. No sooner had he taken control of the reins of power than he was back to his old ways of hostility, launching a vilification campaign against the Maharaja at a time when all the forces in the State needed to be united. As far back as 1945, when the Second World War had just concluded and the Maharaja had returned after touring the War Front, he had been presented with a document by Sheikh Abdullah and his colleagues on behalf of the National Conference. It was titled 'Naya Kashmir', and envisaged a form of government where the monarch was a titular head. It also suggested radical reforms that were closer to communism and visualized the presence of Political Commissars in every organ of the government. It is hard to say if Nehru was aware of this or if he thought that even going to this extent was a risk worth taking. The problem, therefore, was that it was expected of the Maharaja that he should stand and watch as his inherited world, feudal but stable, was dismantled by the new forces.

But there had been other changes, too. The Indian Army was in complete operational command in the state, and though the Maharaja continued to be the commander-in-chief of the State Forces, decisions about their deployment and how they were to be used were being taken by the Indian Army. There was a time in early 1948 when the Maharaja had expressed his dissatisfaction with the conduct of the war by the Indian Army's commanders, and the reference of the Kashmir issue to the Security Council, but in 1949, he had come to terms with what had happened.

But what he could not countenance was the idea of the Security Council suggesting that a plebiscite be conducted to determine the will of the people regarding accession to India or Pakistan. He was frustrated by the idea that though he had signed the same Instrument of Accession that other princely states had signed, his Accession had been accepted by the Government of India on the condition that it would be subject to determining the will of the people. This, he thought, had made his accession meaningless. On the other hand, the concept of holding a plebiscite had become a potent weapon in the hands of Sheikh Abdullah, who found that with it he could browbeat and bully the leaders in Delhi to accede to all his demands. First and foremost, he wanted the Maharaja to be reduced to a mere figurehead, if not removed. To achieve his goal, he had launched a vicious propaganda campaign against him to convince leaders in Delhi and the media that the Maharaja was complicit in the massacres of Muslims in the State. This was a serious charge that had long-term consequences, as it meant that the safety of the Muslims in a Hindu-dominated India was also suspect.

However, Sheikh Abdullah found that Sardar Patel, the realist, had been backing the Maharaja and was in favour of retaining him in the constitutional setup till other matters had been settled. His intervention had thwarted Abdullah's ambition to take administrative control of the State Forces, an army largely made up of Dogras. Having failed in this, the Sheikh had launched an attack on the Forces too, accusing them of perpetrating Muslim massacres in the State. He had also prevailed upon the Government of India to disband a few battalions of the State Forces. This had hurt the Dogras specifically, as most of them depended on employment in the army, and now hundreds of families had no source of livelihood. The Maharaja could do little except wring his hands.

Two other issues rankled the Maharaja, and both were

personal. Sheikh Abdullah had begun to publicly accuse him of fleeing the summer capital on 26 October 1947 to ensure his personal safety and leaving the people of Kashmir at the mercy of the tribal invaders. This accusation had even been made in his speech to the United Nations and had then been publicized in the form of a pamphlet by his administration. He had also added that while fleeing, the Maharaja had carried away as much as he could from his Srinagar Palace. This had so outraged the Maharaja that he had written personally to his Prime Minister—for that is what Sheikh Abdullah was at the time—pointing out that it was the Indian government that had instructed him to leave Srinagar so that its army could come in and operate effectively. But Prime Minister Abdullah had not even cared to acknowledge the letter. The Maharaja had also approached Sardar Patel on this issue as it tarnished his image, and Patel's ministry did issue a clarification about it, but in the State, Sheikh Abdullah's vituperative attacks on the person of the Maharaja continued unabated. He was winning the battle of the propaganda, and it appeared that either Nehru was no longer in a position to control his friend or he, too, was complicit in the accusations.

There were other issues, too, that technically fell under the 'Reserved Subjects'. These subjects were to be the domain of the Maharaja but had been challenged by Sheikh Abdullah. Among them were the hospitality department and pensions of various members of the royal family, but the more serious subject that concerned the Maharaja's honour was the Dharmarth Trust. It was a religious endowment that had been created by Maharaja Gulab Singh and administered more than a hundred Hindu temples and shrines in different parts of the State. Funds from the personal incomes of the successive rulers of the dynasty had been added to it. Sheikh Abdullah now accused Maharaja Hari Singh of using the Dharmarth funds for political purposes in the vitiated communal environment. By then, the communal question had become a very sensitive subject for Nehru; therefore, these accusations were lapped up by Delhi. His access to State funds having been cut off, the Maharaja had used lakhs of rupees from the Dharmarth Trust funds to feed thousands of refugees who had been languishing in the camps. These differences snowballed into such a bitter controversy that Sardar Patel had to intervene, and a compromise was worked out. It was resolved that a reputed firm of Chartered Accountants be appointed to thoroughly audit the accounts of the Trust, so that no unauthorized expenditure was incurred.

Karan Singh believes that the accusations and counter accusations were symptomatic of the inherent regional differences of needs and opinions in any multi-religious and multi-cultural state. But they were also the result of the ideological conflict between the two strong personalities. The Maharaja had lived in a traditional, feudal world in whose permanence he had implicit faith, and acted accordingly. On the other hand, Sheikh Abdullah had created a world in which challenging the existing order and striving to change it by constant disruption was a legitimate goal. The Maharaja had hoped that the changes that had become necessary because of the departure of the British would be gradual and involve give-and-take; Sheikh Abdullah was impatient and was not ready to see the monarchy exist a minute longer.

During this confrontation between the two, Sheikh Abdullah enjoyed the complete support of Nehru, while the Maharaja had built some kind of understanding with Sardar Patel. The Sardar was among the towering leaders of the freedom movement, but now his health had begun to falter, and being wise and pragmatic, he had lent all his support to Nehru. All the talk about the differences between the two have always been vastly exaggerated, as more often than not, they worked as a team to achieve their goal, which was always a free, secular and modern India. The

Maharaja appears to have believed the rumours about differences between Patel and Nehru and so he erred in judging who among the Delhi leaders could forcefully appreciate his and the Dogras' point of view. There is no doubt that there were many occasions when Patel had been able to help in the tug-of-war between the Maharaja and Sheikh Abdullah, who had Nehru's full backing, but the Maharaja had failed to see that Patel and Nehru were always on the same page on the important issues and that they complemented each other. Still, for the Maharaja it was some consolation that there was a sympathetic ear in Delhi for him too.

The Yuvraj was caught between these powerful forces, his sympathy being with his father for emotional reasons. But he also knew that the march of democracy was inevitable and a modern, democratic world was the world he wanted to be a part of.

On 9 March 1949, the Yuvraj celebrated his eighteenth year. It was nothing like it used to be before 1947. There was no public celebration, public holiday, or the banning of animal slaughter, hunting, or fishing. It was a quiet affair with the family and their well-wishers. During the past year, he had matured not only physically but also intellectually. The American experience had made him wise beyond his years. The maturity and insight that he had gathered during the past year made him wistfully wonder what might have been the fate of his State if his father and Sheikh Abdullah had been able to forge a working relationship. He did not know Sheikh Abdullah at all, but he knew his father, and it was the Maharaja's inability to change with the changing times that troubled him.

By then, Sheikh Abdullah had made it clear that he was no longer prepared to have Maharaja Hari Singh as the Head of the State, least of all as a Maharaja. With the weapon of a plebiscite in his hands, he was dictating terms to Delhi, and Nehru found himself conceding all his demands. Finally, Abdullah made it very clear that unless the Maharaja was made to abdicate, he could not guarantee victory if a plebiscite was held in the State, for the majority, he said, did not trust the monarch. So the Sheikh and his cabinet, including two Hindu representatives, Sham Lal Saraf and Girdhari Lal Dogra, passed a resolution demanding the removal of the Maharaja from the State. With this ultimatum, Nehru and Patel realized that the matter could no longer be delayed and that a decisive moment in history had arrived. This was in February 1949, shortly before the Yuvraj's eighteenth birthday. About two months later, his father received an invitation from Sardar Patel to come to Delhi for consultations. He also suggested that the Maharani and the Yuvraj should accompany him. This was the time of the year when the royal family of Jammu and Kashmir would be making preparations for the annual move to the summer capital in Srinagar, where many of their friends and their families too made their way to escape the oppressive heat of the plains. But now, on a warm April day, a DC-3 was chartered for a journey to sweltering Delhi.

Before the flight, there was some tension and foreboding, but no one knew that once the Maharaja flew out of Jammu, only his ashes would return.

6

The End and a Beginning

THE DAY AFTER THEY arrived in New Delhi, Prime Minister Nehru invited the Maharaja, the Maharani, and the Yuvraj to lunch at Teen Murti House. It was a very formal lunch, and though the Prime Minister and the Maharaja engaged in cordial conversation, the undercurrent of tension between them was unmistakable. To their credit, the conversation was civil. The Maharani, at least, was her usual, carefree self and it was soon after this lunch that she left Nehru a little flustered and apologetic by asking why he didn't keep any cigarettes out for his guests. This was also the first time that Tiger met Indira Gandhi and had a closer and longer look at Nehru.

Soon thereafter, on 29 April, Sardar Patel invited the family for a meal. Also present were Maniben, Patel's daughter, and his Private Secretary, V. Shankar. After the dinner, the Maharaja and the Maharani were invited to another room by Sardar Patel, and the Yuvraj was left in the company of Maniben to make small talk. The more serious conversation bearing long-term consequences, not only for the royal family but the State as well, took place in the other room where Sardar Patel delivered a blow to the Maharaja and unsuspecting Maharani. The Sardar must have been aware of the injustice that he was about to inflict, and therefore, he spoke as gently as he could. He said that Sheikh Abdullah had been arguing that the Muslims of Kashmir believed that the Maharaja and the Maharani had been supporting Hindu communalists in Jammu, thereby causing unease among the Muslim population. Therefore, he was pressing for the abdication of the Maharaja so that he could win the Muslims of the State over to the side of India. Patel and the Government of India, on the other hand, believed that the same purpose could be achieved if the Maharaja and the Maharani abstained from the State for a few months. Their absence was required to serve the national interest, given the complications that had arisen out of the plebiscite proposal that was pursued in the United Nations. He added that since the Yuvraj had turned eighteen, the Maharaja could appoint him his Regent for the period of his absence so that the royal duties of the Maharaja could be carried on unhindered.

It was a stunning blow to the Maharaja, and, coming from the Sardar, it was very painful. The rumours of his abdication had been doing the rounds in the State, but he had not given much credence to them, and certainly, he did not expect that the ultimatum would be delivered to him by Sardar Patel himself. It had come suddenly and there was no space left for him to mask his shock. The Yuvraj was taken aback when he saw his father emerging from the room speechless and ashen-faced, and the Maharani barely able to hold back her tears. The Maharaja had placed all his trust in the hands of Patel, and he had asked him to make a sacrifice that no other ruler had been asked to make. It had been forgotten that without his signing the Instrument of Accession, India would not have had any case for the inclusion of the State in the Indian Union. Not even the Nizam of Hyderabad had been treated like this. The Nizam had been offered a very liberal deal after he had resisted the merger with India and had given crores of rupees to Pakistan, which were probably used to fight the Indian forces in 1948. But it was too late for recriminations and arguments now, the Maharaja knew there was nothing that he could do.

The Yuvraj noticed that Sardar Patel looked grim as he came to the door to see them off. He realized that something serious had happened in that room, but so heavy was the atmosphere that he dared not break the silence that his parents maintained during the ride back to their hotel. On reaching the hotel, the Maharaja immediately went into a huddle with his advisors, Bakshi Tek Chand and Mehr Chand Mahajan, and his staff officers. The Yuvraj followed his mother, who went straight to her room, flung herself on the bed, and burst into tears. After she had calmed down, she told him that she and the Maharaja were being forced to leave the State and that the Government of India wanted the Yuvraj to be appointed Regent. This proposal had been broken so suddenly that Yuvraj was also nonplussed, as this scenario had not been imagined by anyone, least of all by him, although he had often felt that in recent months his father had been courting some kind of danger. Sometimes, when he was in school, the Yuvraj had imagined that when it was time for him to take over as king—and back then he had believed this was as natural as day following night—he would be a modern ruler, loved by all the people, who would transform the kingdom into a modern State. But he had understood that as a daydream, he hadn't imagined there would come a day when his father would be around but not the Maharaja.

Shortly after that fateful meeting with Patel, Nehru invited the Yuvraj to the first of the several breakfasts they were to have together in the months to follow. When he walked up to the dining room of the Teen Murti House, he noticed that the table had been set for only two persons, and he learned that Indira Gandhi and her children had finished their breakfast. Nehru walked into the room with a friendly 'Hello, Tiger,' and the breakfast lasted almost an hour, during which he asked the young guest a few general questions. But after the perfunctory conversation, he launched into a monologue about how a new India was being created and emphasized that the feudal order was in the process of collapsing and that a young person like him should be able to readily adjust to the new situation. During his first one-to-one conversation with Tiger, Nehru did not shy away from discussing the Kashmir problem and expressing his view that Sheikh Abdullah's role was crucial in ensuring a harmonious situation in Kashmir and safeguarding India's interests. He added that the reason for the present deadlock was the Maharaja's unwillingness, or inability, to adjust to the new dispensation, and, therefore, Sheikh Abdullah and he had concluded that to break the impasse, Tiger should be appointed as the Regent. New India needed him. When Nehru spoke of building a new India, his eyes glowed and Tiger felt uplifted by the excitement and enthusiasm in his voice. The confusion and anxiety he had been feeling ever since he saw his parents' distress after the meeting with Sardar Patel fell away in that moment, and he was to wonder often in the years to come at the effect Nehru's sheer idealism had on him that morning.

All that Tiger had heard from his father and his advisors was about preserving the past, but it is the future that a young, eager mind wants to inhabit. And it was the future that Nehru was showing him, where India would make its place in a modern world. The greatest Indian leader of the time was personally inviting him to be part of a gigantic project, and Tiger understood instinctively that his loyalty to his father notwithstanding, the old world was dead, and his place was in the world that was about to be born. Tiger had a lot to think about after that breakfast, but of one thing he was certain: he was excited at the prospect of what Nehru had told him.

The tension since the ultimatum to the Maharaja continued to mount in the following days, with a constant stream of visitors coming to meet him. It has never been disclosed what advice he was getting from those people, and the Maharaja never spoke to his son about the matter, either. But Tiger could see that his father had gradually resigned himself to the shocking 'proposal'. Not even Mehr Chand Mahajan, who has written about his period as the Prime Minister and then the Dewan of the State, has disclosed anything about the regular confabulations that the Maharaja held with him, nor has he written about his subsequent association with the Maharaja till the Maharaja's death, by which time he had given up his Sanatani traditions and become associated with the Arya Samaj.

Not long after the Maharaja's meeting with Sardar Patel, the Sardar's health began to deteriorate rapidly. V. Shankar became increasingly important in the States Ministry. Patel also invited Tiger one evening for a long and friendly talk about the situation as it had evolved. Tiger did not fail to notice the difference between Nehru and Patel. While the former had the broader sweep of imagination and idealism, the latter was a practical solver of problems who confined himself to the narrower margins. While Nehru had said that the Maharaja was unable or unwilling to adjust to the new situation, Patel admitted that injustice had been done to him. But he also invoked the national interest to defend the decision. He did his best to inspire Tiger to be brave and confident and to be prepared to shoulder his new responsibility with courage. This pep talk enthused Tiger, coming as it did from the most pragmatic and dispassionate leader of India.

Soon thereafter, Sardar Patel left for Dehra Dun to regain

some of his failing health, and since the allied matters of the Maharaja and Maharani leaving the State had not been fully resolved, they, along with Tiger, followed him after some time. During these days, as his father grappled with the horror of the ultimatum of the Government of India, he also realized the inevitability of it and began preparing himself to appoint his son as the Regent. This was not appreciated by some of his loyalists, as they found the prospect of the son replacing the father under duress abhorrent. They failed to see that Tiger's refusal would have led to the dissolution of the monarchy and put the Dynasty in peril, and also pushed the State into turmoil. Had either the father or the son demurred, it would not have deterred stalwarts like Nehru and Patel from finding an alternative. They would not risk India losing Jammu and Kashmir.

The Maharaja had reconciled to the idea of leaving the State, even the possibility that he may not be allowed to return, but he was clear that under no circumstances, or pressure, would he abdicate. After a great deal of thought, on 6 May, he wrote a letter to Sardar Patel giving a detailed response to everything that had been said by Patel during that fateful night. Apart from the subjects of appointing Yuvraj as Regent and how he felt let down and deeply disappointed by the turn of events, he addressed other issues arising out of the proposed action. He argued that it was a matter of paramount necessity that the Maharani should stay with her son, as he was young and required paternal guidance and personal supervision of at least one of the parents. He also emphasized that the safety and protection of the Yuvraj should be the concern of the Government of India and that the State and Indian Military should guard his person. There were also reproaches. He pointed out that ever since he had signed the Instrument of Accession, he had followed every advice that had been given to him by the Prime Minister, Sardar Patel, or the

States Ministry, but he regretted that Sheikh Abdullah had time and again gone back on the undertaking that he had given by constantly shifting his goal posts. He, the Maharaja, had been repeatedly asked to adjust accordingly, and yet he was being asked to make one final sacrifice so that, in the name of national interest, the ego of Sheikh Abdullah could be assuaged. When Sardar Patel replied, he was straightforward enough to admit that the decision that was ultimately taken was not an easy one, but when all considerations were taken into account, that was the best, not only for the Maharaja and his dynasty but also for the country. He then went on to assure the Maharaja that Sheikh Abdullah had been told in no uncertain words that the Maharaja would not be made to abdicate, but also added that the future course of events would be decided by the Jammu and Kashmir constituent assembly that would be framing the constitution. Thus, it was made clear that ultimately the fate of the dynasty and the Maharaja would be decided by the duly elected representatives of the State.

Patel also wrote that Sheikh Abdullah had a soft corner for the Yuvraj, and that the Sheikh would also realize that protecting the Yuvraj and the royal properties was in his interest as well. He also assured the Maharaja that the safety and protection of the Yuvraj was indeed the responsibility of the Government of India and this would be taken care of. But the Sardar did not agree to the plea that a mother should not be deprived of the proximity to her only son, but added that the Yuvraj could occasionally visit her and the Maharaja. Some observers maintain that Sardar Patel's refusal to concede on the matter of the Maharani staying on in the State was due to accusations that she had been partisan in her relief work and stoked the fire of Hindu communalism in Jammu. Patel's reply also dealt with some outstanding matters that the Maharaja had raised, and conveyed that the Civil List, the annual privy purse, of the Maharaja had been fixed at fifteen lakh rupees, out of which the Maharaja would have to make an allotment to the Maharani and the Yuvraj. But he added that since the Yuvraj would be discharging the duty of Regent, his expenditure would be much more, for which the Maharaja would have to make an allowance. The crux of the correspondence was that the Maharaja would have to follow the road map that had been drawn by Nehru and Patel in consultation with Sheikh Abdullah.

The same day, a copy of Sardar Patel's letter was sent to Nehru. The covering note to that letter contained an interesting paragraph that spoke volumes about Nehru and Patel and how they were working in tandem to influence and inspire the young Yuvraj. It read: 'As regards the Yuvraj, we have had a very detailed talk with him and I have impressed upon him the significance and importance of the agreements reached and the consequences which flow therefrom. He is a sensible lad, and I think he appreciated the situation fairly well and realizes his responsibilities. He is, of course, still in his teens and would require some guidance. I am looking for a suitable advisor for him on whose advice he can lean. We shall have to be very careful in the choice of a suitable person.'

After the correspondence between the Maharaja and Sardar Patel, the family too shifted once more to Dehra Dun on the latter's suggestion. This must have been part of Patel's plan to influence the Yuvraj and prepare him for future responsibilities, as he invited him to stay with him in the Circuit House known as Doon Court, while his parents stayed in a hotel. There, the Yuvraj spent three weeks in the company of the stalwart, who was recovering from another bout of ill health and was being taken care of by his daughter Maniben. Patel usually had his meals in his room, where he would occasionally invite the Yuvraj and talk about Kashmir. During his conversations, he exuded the quiet confidence of a man for whom no problem was too difficult to solve. He never spoke much about the government's handling of Kashmir, but Tiger gathered that he distrusted Sheikh Abdullah and disapproved of Nehru's relationship with him.

Meanwhile, Tiger's parents had returned to Delhi, where they had more consultations with the Maharaja's advisors, and it was finally decided that the Yuvraj would be appointed the Regent on 20 June and fly directly to Srinagar to take up his new responsibilities. The Maharani too had reluctantly agreed to leave the State, but she said she found the heat of Bombay oppressive, and opted to go to Kasauli, betraying the first clear sign of the marriage being over in all but name. But before she left, she insisted that as a devout Hindu, the *yajna-o-paveet*—the sacred thread ceremony—of her son be held. This was done at Mehr Chand Mahajan's residence at 5, Hastings Road, New Delhi. The Pandits came down from Jammu, and two young Rajput servants of the Maharaja also went through the ceremony along with the Yuvraj. All three of them were clad in dhotis, but a piquant situation arose as the Yuvraj was not prepared to have his head tonsured—usually a must for this ceremony—since he did not want to look like a monk when he assumed the Regency of Jammu and Kashmir State. Finally, only a tuft of hair was cut off.

As the appointed day neared, the three members of the family, staying at Delhi's Imperial Hotel, struggled with the turmoil of emotions. The Maharaja was unhappy and made no effort to hide it. On one occasion, finding the Yuvraj excited at the prospect of becoming the Regent, he testily remarked that he should not get carried away because Sheikh Abdullah would not waste any time in throwing him out of the State. The Maharani objected to his manner, and even the Yuvraj was irritated, but he did not realize then that a new distance had emerged between his father and him and that it would one day become almost unbridgeable. In his heart, the Yuvraj also knew that even if he was going to

Srinagar as the Head of the State, it was at the sufferance of Sheikh Abdullah, and there would be many, both in Kashmir and in Jammu, waiting for a misstep. The Maharani added another dimension to the emotional instability of the situation. She tried hard to come to terms with the situation but kept breaking down now and then. With both parents caught up in their own emotions, Tiger had, as always, only himself to rely on, and the inspiring words of Nehru and the calm assurance of Patel. The night of June 19 was a long and sleepless one, and he woke up in the morning with mixed feelings.

On the morning of 20th June, the Maharaja, his staff, and servants left for the station to catch the early morning train for Bombay. Before leaving, the Maharaja had signed a proclamation. It was short and cryptic, and read:

> PROCLAMATION
>
> Whereas I have decided for reasons of health to leave the State for a temporary period and to entrust to the Yuvaraj Shri Karan Singhji Bahadur for that period all my powers and functions in regard to the Government of the State.
>
> Now, therefore, I direct and declare that all powers and functions, whether legislative, executive or judicial which are exercisable by me in relation to the State and its Government, including in particular my right and prerogative of making laws, of issuing Proclamations, Orders and of pardoning offenders, shall during the period of my absence from the State be exercisable by Yuvaraj Shri Karan Singhji Bahadur.
>
> HARI SINGH
> MAHARAJADHIRAJ

His departure was followed by the Maharani, with her brother and maidservants, leaving for Kasauli by road. Yuvraj Shree Karan Singhji Bahadur was left alone to ponder over what had happened and wondering if he was up to the challenge. Finally, he pulled himself together and walked out of the hotel, accompanied by his staff officer, Captain Mahel Singh. Together they drove to Safdarjung Airport, where a DC-3 was waiting to fly him to Srinagar along with Vishnu Sahay, Secretary for Kashmir Affairs, a senior ICS officer deputed by Prime Minister Nehru to accompany him. The Yuvraj could not shake off his father's remark. He had not liked it, but deep inside, he knew that the warning of further humiliation delivered by his father was a possibility that could not be ruled out. After all, Sheikh Abdullah, then, was the undisputed leader of the Kashmiris and was at the zenith of his popularity and wouldn't want any obstacle in his way. In addition, he was also calling all the shots in Delhi. The Maharaja's grim prophecy could not be summarily dismissed.

7

Tiger in the Den of a Lion

THE WEATHER IN SRINAGAR had forced the flight of the Regent to land in Jammu, and after a brief halt, when it again took off and crossed the Banihal Pass, the clouds broke. Down below was the valley of Kashmir, with the Jhelum snaking its way past several human habitations along its banks. At the Srinagar airport, Sheikh Abdullah and his entire cabinet, and senior officials, had gathered to welcome the Regent. There were nine cabinet ministers in all, and among them, the most important were Deputy Prime Minister Bakshi Ghulam Mohammad, and the Revenue minister, Mirza Mohammad Afzal Beg. While Bakshi was the main organizer of the National Conference and a moderate in respect to Kashmir's relationship with India, Beg was universally viewed as a shrewd politician and a hardliner—he had also been in the government that had been formed during the short-lived self-rule experiment under Maharaja Hari Singh before crises overwhelmed the State. Among the other ministers were Ghulam Mohammad Sadiq, who brought intellectual fervour to the National Conference; the Pandit Sham Lal Saraf and the Dogra Girdhari Lal; Colonel Pir Mohammad, a Jammu Muslim and an ex-State Forces officer;

and Sardar Budh Singh, representing the Sikh community. After welcoming the Regent, Sheikh Abdullah introduced his colleagues. It appeared that the Sheikh was determined to make a clean break with the past and give a fresh start to his relationship with the scion of the Dogra dynasty.

Karan Singh too approached his new life with a calm mind; at least he maintained an outward calm that belied the mixed feelings of apprehension and exhilaration at what lay ahead. He was happy to be returning to the place where he had spent many years of his childhood, and no sooner had he come out of the car, his spirits lifted at the sight of manicured lawns and the beds of blooming flowers, and when the cool breeze coming from the Dal Lake swept over his face, he forgot the suffocating heat of Delhi where the royal family had been forced by circumstances to stay in May and June. After almost two years, Karan Singh was back in the beautiful villa where he could put aside the tension and turmoil of the past two months. During those early days of the Regency, Vishnu Sahay, from the Indian Civil Service (ICS), who had accompanied him from Delhi, was a great help as, without fanfare, he put everything in its proper perspective. His presence for a fortnight greatly helped Karan Singh to settle down.

For the first time in his life, Karan Singh was living entirely independently, and he loved the experience. He was not unaware of the pressures he would face. While being primed for his role as a Regent, Prime Minister Nehru had specifically tasked him to work in harmony with Sheikh Abdullah, which his father, understandably, had been unable to do. There was no mistaking the towering presence of Sheikh Abdullah. He commanded the unconditional loyalty of the Kashmiris and was at the height of his popularity and power. This was a time when no sacrifice would have been too big if he had demanded it of his people. But he seemed to be making efforts to build a new relationship, free of past animosities. He visited the young Regent, twenty-five years his junior, and delivered long lectures on the political situation, but he took care not to mention his father. Though Karan Singh got the impression that Sheikh Abdullah had a genuine warmth towards him, he was always aware that he was on some kind of trial as his moves were being closely watched by the people of Kashmir and also of Jammu, where the Dogras were still in a state of shock at the forced departure of their Maharaja and disapproved of his son becoming the Regent. The challenge before Karan Singh was that he had to follow the instructions of Prime Minister Nehru to work in tandem with Sheikh Abdullah, but this he needed to do without appearing to be subservient to the Sheikh. Yet he could not be seen to be acting in a manner that was confrontational, as that would have offended Sheikh Abdullah and Jawaharlal Nehru and made things difficult both in Srinagar and in Delhi.

But those apprehensions did not prevent him from enjoying himself. The Kashmir issue was very much alive at this time and was being hotly debated in the United Nations. In Kashmir, this was reflected in the frequent visits and activities of the United Nations observers drawn from several European and South American countries who often came with their families. This meant that there were endless rounds of parties at various venues, including the residence of the Divisional Commander, General T.S. Thimayya (Timmy to his friends) and his wife. Karan Singh took to the General, who exuded an easy confidence, was witty, and fun to be with; importantly, he was a hero to his soldiers and also well-liked in the civil administration. Soon after they met, he accompanied the General to the forward areas along the Ceasefire Line. After crossing the 10,000-foot-high Nashtachum Pass, they reached Tangdhar and Tithwal. Though he had spent many years of his life in the Kashmir Valley, Karan Singh had only seen the mountains from afar and it was only now that he realized what it meant to be among the mighty Himalayas. It was an experience beyond the imagination of those who had never been there.

Being high-spirited, Timmy drove the jeep himself and, on the way, regaled his young companion with accounts of his encounters with the enemy in those forbidding heights not too long ago. This was also the first time that Karan Singh met the soldiers of the Indian Army up close and was impressed by their sense of duty and the ability to adapt to alien and harsh conditions. He also noticed that the population across the Pass was not Kashmiri-speaking but Punjabi-speaking and that there was cordiality between the civilian population and the army. On a personal level, he was pleased to note that he was, perhaps, the only member of the Dogra dynasty who had visited those places and felt proud of the fact that there did not seem to be any signs of ill-will towards the Dogras. Enthused by the trip, he accompanied Timmy to the Zojila Pass and across to see the terrain where the General had taken the tanks to rout the enemy, a Herculean feat comparable to Hannibal crossing the Alps on elephants. Across the Pass, they spent the night in Dras, said to be the coldest place in the world.

During those early days, the Regent also met Durga Prasad Dhar, popularly called 'DP'. He belonged to a distinguished family of Kashmiri Pandits and had associated himself with the National Conference at a very young age because of his left-leaning ideas. Though only a Deputy Minister in the cabinet, he was widely acknowledged as the brain behind Sheikh Abdullah's government. Karan Singh soon learned that DP was excellent as a liaison between the civilians and the army, the state government and the Government of India. He was also the youngest in the State cabinet, and this helped Karan Singh to strike a friendly chord with him. The friendship continued till DP's untimely death, in 1975, and during those difficult and anxious early years, it proved extremely valuable for Karan Singh.

The summer of 1949 made way for autumn. During this time, Nehru made two visits to Srinagar, and Karan Singh also went to Delhi twice, staying at Teen Murti House. He noticed that though Nehru always had a busy schedule, he found time to enquire about the comfort of his guests. It was during one of these visits that Karan Singh met the towering Pandit Govind Vallabh Pant with his walrus mustache, the Mephistophelian-looking Krishna Menon, and the good-humored Padmaja Naidu whose mother Sarojini had been among the welcoming dignitaries at the Gateway of India when the newborn heir to the throne of Jammu and Kashmir had landed on Indian soil in 1931.

But Regency did not mean that Karan Singh had to be always in the company of much older and important people. Whenever he was free from official tasks, he would visit his childhood haunts, particularly Dachigam and Thricker. He enjoyed shooting and fishing there and also hosted lunch and tea parties for visiting and local dignitaries. He had also inherited a spirit of religious devotion from his mother, and, therefore, he made it a point to visit as many temples and shrines as he could. He also invariably performed a small puja before he began his official day. His devotion was to soon land him in a rather unpleasant situation with Sheikh Abdullah, which was also an indication of the undercurrent of tensions in Kashmir.

The incident occurred about a month after he had arrived in Srinagar as Regent. The occasion was the annual festival at the shrine dedicated to Goddess Kheer Bhawani situated in the village of Tulmulla in Ganderbal district, not too far from Srinagar. This shrine has been at the core of the Kashmiri Pandits' faith, and they believe that the colour of the water of the pool at this shrine predicts approaching events—it is said, for instance, that months before the invasion of 1947, the water here had turned black. On that occasion in 1949, a delegation of Pandits, led by Pandit Parmanand, a very respected and able officer who had recently retired as Accountant General, approached the Regent to visit the shrine on the auspicious day. There was nothing unusual about the request, and Karan Singh accepted the invitation and announced his acceptance. It was obvious to him that, despite the secular claims of the National Conference and the support that Sheikh Abdullah had among the Pandits, there was an undercurrent of insecurity among them after the end of Dogra rule. He thought that his visit to the shrine on that auspicious day would be reassuring. But he was shocked to get a message from Sheikh Abdullah that it would be better if he did not visit the shrine on that particular day. The Prime Minister of the State had put the Regent in an embarrassing situation. After giving thought to the matter, Karan Singh decided that since he had committed himself to the visit, he could not let the Pandit community down. So, he went and received a tumultuous welcome from the thousands of Pandits who had gathered there. The elderly ladies embraced him and kissed his forehead, a gesture reserved only for close and dear ones. The puja was a long affair and lasted almost three hours. Periodically, the air was rent with the slogan '*Dogra Raj Zindabad* (Long live the raj of the Dogras)'. Later, Karan Singh was informed that the news of the welcome and the raising of that slogan had greatly disturbed Sheikh Abdullah, though to his credit, he never mentioned it to the Regent.

Amidst the formal duties of the Regent and the newfound independence to spend his spare time as he wished, Karan Singh made two life-altering decisions. The acquaintance that he made with Pandit Parmanand yielded the immediate result of Sanskrit lessons. The Pandit would come to Karan Mahal thrice a week and started by teaching simple Sanskrit verses. Karan Singh's ability to remember and recite long passages with ease, which he had discovered at Doon School, helped him to learn Sanskrit in a short time. He discovered that the key to this classical language was the musical and metrical quality of the verses, and anyone who could learn to operate this key had easy access to the majesty of the Vedas, the wisdom of the Upanishads, the teaching of the Bhagavad Gita, and the hymns of Adi Shankaracharya.

Even as he had started his Sanskrit lessons, he also decided that he wanted to reestablish his contacts with the academic world. So, he asked the Director of Education to suggest a scholar who could regularly discuss with him the current economic and political problems. Thus, he got in touch with Professor P.N. Chaku, an accomplished intellectual, and struck up a friendly and fruitful relationship. Chaku introduced him to the economic theories of Keynes that had transformed the world by taking America out of economic depression; and the ideas of Marx, in the context of the developing economies of the world, and of Harold Laski, who had also made a deep impact upon those who had wanted to strike a balance between communism and capitalism. In Chaku's company, Karan Singh also discovered the writers Bertrand Russel and Aldous Huxley, with whom he also exchanged some letters.

As Regent, Karan Singh had replaced his father as the Head of State, and, therefore, had some formal duties, and one of them was being Commander-in-Chief of the State Forces. Effectively, the State Forces were under the administrative and operational control of the Indian Army, but they had not yet been merged into the Indian Army because of the accession of the State being considered a dispute by the United Nations. Being the Commander-in-Chief was a very formal kind of title that entailed signing a few papers now and then, but still, it made the State and its Forces a distinct entity that carried prestige. But there was one more formal function that was closer to his heart. After the Partition and independence of India, the Panjab University, to which the colleges in the State were affiliated, had suffered disruption, making it necessary for the State to have its own University. Therefore, Maharaja Hari Singh had, by issuing a Proclamation in 1948, created the Jammu and Kashmir University. Being the Head of State, Karan Singh also became its Chancellor. On 24 September 1949, the first formal convocation of the University was to be held in Srinagar. This meant that at the age of eighteen years and six months, he was to preside over that proud occasion for the State. A little nervous, he drafted his speech and sent a copy of it to Nehru, who, after reading it, commented humorously that he must be the youngest Chancellor of any University in history! Karan Singh took the remark in his stride, made improvements to his speech and hoped for the best. Pandit Nehru came for the convocation, where everyone wore black gowns and pink turbans. Since Sheikh Abdullah was the Pro-Chancellor, he, Karan Singh, and Pandit Nehru walked together in a procession. After giving away the degrees and the prizes, Karan Singh read out his speech before Pandit Nehru delivered his. It had been a trial almost by fire, but once it was over and he received generous praise, his confidence was sky high—he had stood shoulder to shoulder with the two veterans of the art of public speaking. After this, there could be no looking back!

In the afternoon, Nehru and the dignitaries accompanying him were taken out in a procession of boats along the Jhelum. This was the second time that Karan Singh had participated in such a procession. Almost a decade ago, he had sat with his father in a barge covered with brocade and enjoyed being rowed by young Kashmiri boatmen wearing white and sporting yellow turbans. This time, the context had altogether changed, and he sat in the main barge with Pandit Nehru and Sheikh Abdullah. Gopalaswami Ayyangar, Sardar Baldev Singh, Rajkumari Amrit Kaur, V.N. Gadgil, all cabinet ministers in Delhi, and General Cariappa, Commander-in-Chief of the Indian Army, followed in smaller barges. It was a memorable ride as the banks of the Jhelum were overflowing with admiring crowds, and when the procession passed under the seven historical bridges of the river, they were so crowded by the people that it appeared that any moment they would collapse under their weight. While Karan Singh basked in the reflected glory of a great national leader, the Sheikh used the opportunity to demonstrate his and his party's political strength. The colorful procession and the cheering crowds demonstrated to anyone who cared to see that the visit had touched the emotions of the Kashmiris. It gave the lie to Pakistani propaganda about the people of the Valley groaning under the occupation of the Indian Army. Here they were, the men, women and children of Kashmir, pouring out their love and affection for Nehru, showing him that they shared his dream of a great future. Significantly, the event was well covered by the foreign press that had arrived in impressive numbers.

When the euphoria of the convocation and historic boat procession had subsided, it was time for the State Government to prepare for the annual Durbar move to Jammu. This annual exercise entailed a lot of expenditure but was politically useful as it gave equal importance to the two main regions of the State. Normally, the offices reopened in Jammu on the first Monday of November. Similarly, they opened on the first Monday of May in Srinagar. Karan Singh had decided that he would travel to

Jammu on 7 November. However, before that, he could not resist the temptation of some more fishing and shooting since both improve as the autumn moves towards winter. He was enjoying one of the best periods of his life, his health having improved to such a degree that despite the stiffness in his hip, he could once again play tennis. He intended to stay for a few weeks in Jammu and then travel to Bombay to meet his father, who had been in touch with the Ranas of Nepal, and his marriage had been fixed for 15 January 1950.

Because of this, one last Chakor shoot had been planned for 29 October at Khrew, a few miles out of Srinagar. Karan Singh sat in the front seat of the jeep with the driver, and Brigadier Rawat and his ADC, Captain Mahel Singh, sat behind, along with his black Labrador Dusky. The night had experienced rain, making the muddy edges of the tarred road slushy and slippery. The party had hardly travelled a few miles when near the Panderthan temple, a truck came from the opposite direction and moved onto the slushy verge of the road to give way to Karan Singh's vehicle, but no sooner had it done that, it skidded and to the horror of the hunt party, it came and hit their jeep. Instinctively, Karan Singh pressed his left foot forward to protect his right hip. The impact of the collision broke his left leg between the knee and ankle and he saw it twist, almost at a right angle. Adding to this horror was a sharp pain in his right hip. He had not even had a full year of normal life and here he was, trapped in a mangled vehicle. He was extricated with great difficulty, taken to the nearby military hospital for an X-ray, and put once again under anaesthesia for treatment. The nightmare had returned.

His leg was put in plaster, but even more unbearable was the fact that his right hip, too, was back in plaster. The next day, his Prime Minister, Sheikh Abdullah, visited him in the hospital and enquired about his condition with genuine concern. Meanwhile, as soon as his father was informed of the accident, he insisted that he be flown to Bombay instantly. Karan Singh wanted to wait till the pain had subsided. However, the Maharaja was insistent, and an Air Force DC-3 was chartered to take Karan Singh to Bombay. The news had also reached his mother, who, finding that the chartered flight was to stop in Delhi for refuelling, had come down there from Kasauli to see him. Looking at his condition, she was too shocked even to speak. In Bombay, his father met him at the airport and brought him to Nepean Road, where he arranged for two eminent orthopedics, Dr. Kini and Dr. Mulgaonkar, to examine him. They had the plaster removed and put him under anaesthesia before examining the leg. It was a mass of blisters, and had his father not been adamant about bringing him to Bombay, his leg might have had to be amputted. The hard reality of the situation was that his condition was far worse than it had been when he had been flown to America. His operated hip was back to square one as it had cracked under the impact of the accident, and now his left leg was in an equally bad condition, as both bones had broken.

For weeks thereafter, Karan Singh remained in plaster with the bones not healing. Yet, the bigger question was his marriage. Soon, Yasho Rajya Lakshmi's uncle, General Bijaya Shumsher, Nepal's Ambassador to India, also came to see him, and it was agreed that the January date for the marriage was no longer possible, but a new date could not be fixed as everything depended on the speed of recovery. The good doctors found that even the blisters on his left leg were taking an inordinately long time to heal. This began to worry them, and after some time they concluded that an operation had to be carried out to put a metal strip and six screws in his left leg to balance the metal pin in his right hip. When the operation was taking place, his mother did what was within her control—she locked herself in her puja room, praying for her son till the operation had been completed and her son had regained consciousness.

As he lay on his back for months, momentous changes took place in the country. On 26 January 1950, India adopted a new Constitution to become a sovereign nation after shedding the status of a Dominion and electing Dr. Rajendra Prasad as its first President. Bombay celebrated the occasion with an unprecedented procession lasting almost three hours. Silently, Karan Singh thanked his stars for belonging to a generation that had not wielded the power of the princely era. Though deeply attached to his State, yet at that moment he felt proud to be an Indian, and also regretted the fact that on the two most important dates in the history of modern India, he had not been in a state to participate in the joyous celebrations. First, on Independence Day and now on Republic Day, instead of being in the streets enjoying the pulsating moments, he had been lying on his back with nothing but the ceiling of the room to stare at.

Sheikh Abdullah and his Deputy Prime Minister Bakshi Ghulam Mohammad maintained contact with Karan Singh, with the former also writing to him from New York, where he had gone as a member of the Indian delegation to the Security Council to put forth the Indian and the Kashmiri case before it. Meanwhile, the doctors had assured the Maharaja that his son would be up on his feet after six weeks, and this had encouraged him to draw up plans for his marriage. He was determined that even the marriage of his son should not in any way disrupt his racing season, and the Pandit had been appropriately briefed. Thus, 5 March 1950 was the auspicious date that the Pandit came up with. At that time, his bride-to-be's grandfather was still the all-powerful Prime Minister of Nepal. He would lose that position the following year. The Ranas, like the Dogra dynasty, had come to power almost a hundred years ago, and it was a strange coincidence that both families lost their power at about the same time.

The marriage date having been fixed, Yasho Rajya Lakshmi's parents, General and Rani Sarada Shumsher, along with their five children, moved to Bombay—to Kutch Castle on Nepean Sea Road. Normally, the family of the groom would have travelled to Nepal to bring the bride home, but because of Karan Singh's condition, it had been decided to have the marriage solemnized in Bombay. On another auspicious day, a formal betrothal ceremony was held in the hall of Kashmir House. By then, Karan Singh had begun to get out of his bed and had started walking with the support of walking sticks. He was at the threshold of a new life. During his childhood and boyhood, he had been made to live a segregated life where girls had no place. His boarding school had been a boys' school, and hence he had no experience of interacting with girls. For all but nine months of the past three years, he had been immobilized, and hence his teenage years too had passed without any interaction with girls. And now he was about to tie the knot with a girl he had only seen once. A more immediate worry was whether his leg had become strong enough for him to go through the long marriage ceremonies without collapsing. It was then that he displayed some ingenuity: he would use the sword that Rajput grooms carry as his walking stick.

For the wedding, he wore a long brocade coat—an *achkan*—a turban with an emerald ornament, and a jewelled sword. He sat in a Packard belonging to the Thakore Sahib of Dhrol, one of the fattest men in the world, who had an unusually spacious car in which the groom with a stiff hip could travel in some comfort. The ceremonies were spread over two days, though the rituals were not as elaborate as they would have been in Jammu, and the entire wedding was of course not even a tenth as extravagant as it might have been had Tiger's father still been the Maharaja of old.

But after all the ceremonies were over and Karan Singh brought the bride home to Napean Sea Road, champagne flowed literally like water, for the Maharaja was still determined to celebrate his son's wedding in a manner that would be remembered for a long time. The next few days were a blur as there were parties hosted by the Maharaja, the Ranas of Nepal, and mutual friends. It was a happy time for the Maharaja after the gloom of the past three years, and often he would ask Karan Singh to sing during the parties, who, though out of practice, could still render the tunes and ragas with a fair degree of control. Meanwhile, the newly married couple too were trying to know each other better. The bride had been given a new name by her father-in-law, Asha. In a nice gesture, Asha gave her husband a Japanese transistor, a rarity then, for his birthday, which fell a few days after the marriage, on 9th March.

The marriage concluded, and with Karan Singh on his feet, it was time to return to the State of which he was the Regent. So, it was decided that the young couple would leave for Srinagar on 28 April. By then, Bombay too had begun to get warmer, so the Maharani also decided to leave for Kasauli. She departed three days before her son was to leave for Srinagar. When it was time for her to leave for the station, she came to the Maharaja and bowed low with her folded hands in a gesture of goodbye. That was the last time Karan Singh saw his parents together.

8
The Catalyst

Karan Singh—the Yuvraj—and Asha—the Yuvrani—flew first to Jammu, where, along with Bakshi Ghulam Mohammad and many officials, huge, enthusiastic and affectionate crowds welcomed them. The next day, Sheikh Abdullah arrived in Jammu and hosted a reception in honour of the newlyweds in Mubarak Mandi, the old palace. In a touching and graceful gesture, he presented a diamond *sarpech* for the Regent's turban on behalf of the State. The next few days were a blur of activity as there were ladies' receptions and a constant stream of visitors. The young husband was relieved to notice that his thirteen-year-old bride was not flustered or nervous. She did not know a word of Dogri and could speak only a smattering of Hindi, but she had managed to overcome the language barrier and was enjoying every bit of the attention and the hectic coming and going of visitors. After about a fortnight, the couple flew to Srinagar and settled into Karan Mahal.

It was new territory for Karan Singh. Emotionally, he had lived almost a solitary life. He had no siblings, and he had spent more time with guardians than with either of his parents.

The closest he had come to unregimented intimacy was in his childhood friendship with his playmates Digby and Bilti, who were like quasi siblings. But in that friendship, too, despite the Maharaja's instruction to his companions to strike him twice if he ever hit them, there was a distance because they were, after all, sons of officers in the service of the Maharaja. There was a hierarchy. Now, he had a constant companion with him at day and at night, who would see him at his best and his worst, in moments when he was happy and feeling confident but also when he was depressed and vulnerable. Strangely, that did not unsettle him—for, from their first moments together, Asha had felt like a familiar. It was as if they had grown up together. In an interview for this biography, Karan Singh attributed that instant connection and their ease with one another to the fact they were both so young, and also to Asha's 'naturally sunny' temperament. 'She came from a large family. Back in Nepal, she had grown up with many siblings and cousins, and besides her parents, there were several aunts and uncles. And suddenly here she was with this lone wolf! It's remarkable that she didn't get fed up,' he said, laughing. 'She adjusted very quickly and seamlessly to her new life…You know, in the days just before our marriage I used to think I was going to be responsible for another human being. I rather liked the idea of taking care of her, it made me feel very grown up and mature. But *she* turned out to be the more mature one. Pretty soon it was she who was looking out for me and taking care of me!'

They had been in Srinagar just about three months when the young Regent was reminded of the purpose that he had been charged with by Prime Minister Nehru, and the challenges that came with that responsibility. Ever since the rioting and unrest of 1931 that had left 22 Kashmiri Muslim protestors dead in police firing, 13th July has been commemorated as 'Martyrs Day' in the Valley. As 13 July 1950 approached, Sheikh Abdullah decided that as part of the commemoration that day, he would announce the abolition of the jagirdari system of land tenancy and landlordism. The State would put a ceiling on land-holdings and take over surplus land without paying compensation. The Sheikh was at the pinnacle of his popularity at this time, and now also had political power. He was, of course, a brilliant mind, brimming with confidence, and was also charming and affectionate when he wanted to be. But he had also begun to show authoritarian traits, and like all authoritarian leaders, he periodically needed to make grand gestures to reinforce his image of a revolutionary leader. On the face of it, the proposals to abolish the jagirdari system and impose a land ceiling were progressive, but needed fine-tuning as they would have destroyed the orchards of Kashmir and badly affected the agricultural economy of the Jammu region where the Dogras lived. The proposals could also have been seen as communal, as orchards in Kashmir were owned mostly by the Pandits and the large landowners in Jammu were Hindu Rajputs. This imbalance in land ownership in the State could not be denied, and yet, whatever the merits of the Sheikh's proposals, these communities would have justifiably felt that they were being specifically targeted.

Karan Singh realized the need for the land-ceiling proposals to be re-examined and fine-tuned and, therefore, referred the matter to Vishnu Sahay, who was Secretary of Kashmir Affairs in the Government of India. When Sheikh Abdullah learned of this, he was furious and he castigated the Regent in a memorandum by reminding him that he was only a Constitutional Head of the State and had no say in the executive or legislative subjects, and that according to the March 1948 Proclamation of the Maharaja, under which Sheikh Abdullah had been appointed Prime Minister, the Head of the State would act only on the advice of the Prime Minister. He also pointed out that the Regent had no business involving the Government of India in this case, as it had no jurisdiction in the said matter since the Accession to India—which the Maharaja himself had signed, had been limited only to Defence, Foreign Affairs, and Communications.

However, young and inexperienced as he might have been, Karan Singh refused to buckle and, after consultations with the Government of India, replied that not only was he aware of his constitutional limitation, he was also aware that the proposals were of far-reaching consequences as they affected a large segment of the population. Moreover, he pointed out that because of the far-reaching consequences, such an important decision needed to be taken by a forum that represented all the people of the State. In other words, he reminded Sheikh Abdullah that he was a *nominated* and not an *elected* Prime Minister, and that the Proclamation that had appointed him as the Prime Minister had also enjoined him to take steps to get a Constituent Assembly elected which could draft a Constitution for the State, so that a duly elected government could then take executive and legislative measures following the functions and duties mentioned in the Constitution. But by then, Sheikh Abdullah had gone too far in his idea about the autonomy of the State in the Indian Union, and he announced the land reforms in a long speech at Lal Chowk on 13 July 1950.

His defiance and the abrupt and imperious manner in which he had asserted his will jolted New Delhi. It was to be just the start of a series of more serious jolts. What made the Sheikh's move questionable was the haste. He knew well that the Government of India was already seized of the issue of landlordism, as all the states of the Union were plagued by it, and the Congress had been supporting the tenants and tillers everywhere in the country, but was still trying to find a democratic and fair system to deal with the problem. But the Sheikh had disregarded that and resorted to a populist and divisive proclamation instead of a fair and sustainable one.

This episode also added a new dimension to the Kashmir problem, which was still under consideration by the United Nations. This had been further complicated because of geo-political interests in the changed world order after World War II. The United States and the Soviet Union had emerged as competing 'superpowers'. In this scenario, the State of Jammu and Kashmir had assumed great significance, as geographically it was part of a pivotal region in the struggle for power and influence between the Soviet Union and the United States and its allies. The Americans had decided to renew what the British called the 'Great Game', and Sheikh Abdullah was becoming a much sought-after leader, as it was known that India would steer clear of global conflicts and rivalries and focus on its reconstruction as a nation. It soon became obvious that, like Maharaja Hari Singh, Sheikh Abdullah too had been tempted not only by the State's geographical contiguity with Pakistan, but also its geostrategic advantages in the new Great Game, and had begun to toy with the idea of independence.

The experience of this brief confrontation with Sheikh Abdullah necessitated a visit to the Indian capital for further consultations. So, Karan Singh and Asha flew to Delhi. Asha drove to Kasauli to meet her mother-in-law, while Karan Singh stayed for a few days in Teen Murti House. During this visit, he could not meet Sardar Patel because of his failing health, but he did visit Dr. Rajendra Prasad, the first President of India. Karan Singh briefed him about the situation and understood that Rajendra Prasad's approach to Kashmir was almost similar to that of Sardar Patel's and he was concerned about the Hindus of the State. He also had reservations about Sheikh Abdullah.

The differences over the Proclamation about the land reforms were finally settled with the intervention of the Government of India. Sheikh Abdullah agreed to make some amendments, notably, taking the orchards out of the purview of the proposed reforms. Despite his failing health, Patel had intervened to help resolve the matter

The issue of land reforms was the opening move in Sheikh Abdullah's game plan to achieve complete constitutional legitimacy and have the monarchy abolished. He had already succeeded in getting the Maharaja out of the State, and now that the need for a Constituent Assembly had already been raised in the context of land reforms, he pushed for it decisively. The Proclamation of 5th March 5 1948, which appointed Shiekh Abdullah as Prime Minister of the State's interim government, had also required him to ensure that a Constituent Assembly was elected and convened as soon as possible. However, the approval of the Regent was needed before the Assembly could be elected and convened.

The Government of India, too, was keen that the Constituent Assembly be elected soon. India had committed itself to holding a plebiscite over the question of the State's accession. Pakistan had not met the conditions for a plebiscite in the areas under its occupation, yet the uncertainty in Indian Kashmir had allowed it to give the impression internationally that the Muslim-majority State actually wanted to vote in favour of Pakistan, so India was finding excuses to avoid the plebiscite. Many countries of the world were inclined to accept Pakistan's narrative. Therefore, the Government of India thought that if a Constituent Assembly were convened and it ratified the State's accession to India, it would create a favourable opinion among the comity of nations. It was another matter that the Constituent Assembly would give Sheikh Abdullah a constitutional tool to strike a final and fatal blow to the Dogra dynasty.

Much of the year 1950 was devoted to consultations between the State Government and the Union Ministry for Kashmir Affairs. The problem, however, was that even though Maharaja Hari Singh had appointed his son as the Regent, legally he was still the ruler—and therefore the Head of State—since he had not abdicated. This made it incumbent upon the Government of India to consult him over the issue. Consequently, on 30 November 1950, Vishnu Sahay wrote to the Maharaja and also enclosed a copy of the proposed Proclamation. On 10 December 1950, the Maharaja replied to Sardar Patel, making several points.

The Maharaja expressed his total agreement with the object and spirit of the Proclamation, but argued that he was the authority in law to promulgate the constitution of a Constituent Assembly and not his Regent. He also wrote that the powers and functions of such a body should be clearly expressed and worded, and anything that was not included in it should be beyond its purview. He further added that the Constituent Assembly should report to the appointing authority, that is, him, and then he would seek the advice of the Parliament of India. He separately wrote to Karan Singh, informing him that he was taking up the matter with the Government of India and that he should not sign the Proclamation till the matter had been clarified. Soon thereafter, Sardar Patel passed away, leaving behind a vacuum. The only voice of caution on the Kashmir issue that carried weight was no longer there, leaving it to Nehru and others to navigate through the rough waters.

On 25 January 1951, Vishnu Sahay wrote to Karan Singh, enclosing a copy of the Proclamation for the Constituent Assembly, and suggested that whenever Sheikh Abdullah made a submission in that regard, he should sign it. The submission duly came on 27 January 1951. In it, Sheikh Abdullah argued that the State government 'has always been committed to the position that it is for the people of the State to draw up a Constitution for the State', and that the 'Ruler also supported this idea' and had tasked his government to constitute such an Assembly as soon as the conditions were normal. He also pointed out that the Government of India too was supportive of the idea, and that the Proclamation had been drafted after consultations with the Government of India. Shri Yuvraj was, therefore, requested to affix his signature to it and return it forthwith.

This put Karan Singh in a dilemma as on the one hand, the Governments of India and the State were urging him to sign the Proclamation, and on the other, his father, the Maharaja and legally the Ruler who had appointed him as his Regent, had explicitly barred him from signing any such Proclamation without his express approval. He, therefore, flew to Delhi and met Gopalaswami Ayyangar, who had taken over the States Ministry after the demise of Sardar Patel. After consultations, he wrote a note on the submission of Sheikh Abdullah, explaining to Ayyangar that he was not a free agent as he derived all his powers from the Maharaja, and since the matter had far-reaching consequences, it had been sent to him for his comments. The Maharaja's response had been sent to the Minister for States, but what transpired after that was not known to the Yuvraj, and, therefore, in the absence of any express direction from his father, he stood precluded from signing the document. This was on 30 January 1951.

Meanwhile, Ayyangar replied to the Maharaja, pointing out to him that when societies and countries are on the cusp of revolutionary changes, legalities and rights of individuals and dynasties are often swept away and this was inevitable. He reiterated the commitment of the Government of India to convening the Constituent Assembly of the State to draft a new

Constitution. But significantly, he also wrote that the 'Assembly will be held whether the formal Proclamation issues or not'. The blunt message persuaded the Maharaja to lift the ban on the Yuvraj, and the Proclamation was duly signed on 21 April 1951.

It was a futile and ill-advised resistance on the part of the Maharaja, and it was clear that his legal advisors had taken into account only the legalities of the matter and not the realities of political power. The Maharaja had also given Sheikh Abdullah an opportunity to paint him and his dynasty as anti-people, and repeat his accusation that the Maharaja and his wife had been complicit in the instigation of communal violence and the killing of Muslims during Partition. He launched a bitter and personal attack on the Maharaja and the Yuvraj during a public speech a few miles from Jammu on 9 April 1951. It was not the first time that he had attacked the Maharaja, but it was the first time that he had included the Yuvraj as a legitimate target. It was a rude shock for Karan Singh as he had come to believe that Sheikh Abdullah had a genuine concern and affection for him.

Deeply hurt by the unprovoked attack, Karan Singh wrote a letter of protest to his Prime Minister and sent a copy to Jawaharlal Nehru with a covering letter wherein he expressed his pain and shock at the vicious accusations. Sheikh Abdullah responded with a five-page letter and made it very clear that he expected the Regent to be a virtual captive of his government, to the extent that he could make no public appearance without the prior approval of the government. This attack reminded Karan Singh of what the Maharaja had predicted—that the Sheikh would waste no time to 'throw him out' of the State. Nehru was prompt in his reply to Karan Singh and regretted that Sheikh Abdullah had made a personal reference to the Regent and expressed satisfaction that he had chosen to immediately communicate with Sheikh Abdullah directly. But he also argued that the situation in Kashmir was a difficult one, and great powers were waiting for a chance to intervene in it. Karan Singh got the message that he had been asked to lie low at that moment, which he did.

Karan Singh was just twenty. Through these challenging times Nehru's genuine affection for him, regular correspondence and meetings with him in Delhi, gave him confidence and remained a source of inspiration. Also, fortunately for Karan Singh, while Nehru trusted his friends and ideological peers to a fault, he was not averse to hearing contrary views from others whom he also trusted. Thus, as Karan Singh and D.P. Dhar too had direct access to him, their narrative of the events in Kashmir somewhat neutralized the aggressive Muslim-Kashmiri views put forth by Sheikh Abdullah and his belligerent Revenue Minister Mirza Afzal Beg. However, he could be deaf to opinions about people and groups whose ideology he was strictly opposed to. Karan Singh and others were to realize this whenever the subject of the Jammu Praja Parishad, the State's main opposition political party came up. Founded in November 1947 by members of the Hindu-right Rashtriya Swayamsewak Sangh (RSS), the Praja Parishad also had links with the political wing of the RSS, the Bharatiya Jana Sangh, and with the Hindu Mahasabha. It was also seen primarily as the party of the Dogras. One of the main demands of the Praja Parishad was complete integration of Jammu and Kashmir with India and it did not support the idea of a separate Constitution for the State. Because of its links with the militant Hindu right, Nehru had a deep suspicion of the Praja Parishad. He was convinced that its actions only fanned communalism and gave fodder to the propaganda machine of Pakistan. Therefore, he had no time for the opinions of Praja Parishad leaders like Prem Nath Dogra. Karan Singh felt, then and later, that these opinions should at least be considered, but Nehru was adamant.

In June, shortly after the Proclamation regarding the Constituent Assembly had been made, Nehru came to Srinagar. Karan Singh learned later that in Nehru's meetings with Sheikh Abdullah, the issue of the latter's intemperate remarks targeting Karan Singh came up, and the Sheikh suggested that the Regent should have a secretary on his staff through whom communications should be made to avoid further misunderstanding.

While all these moves and counter moves were playing out, the Regent and his wife had not lost sight of what they wanted in their personal lives. Karan Singh enrolled for a BA course with the Jammu and Kashmir University, choosing English, Political Science and Economics as his subjects at Professor Chaku's suggestion, and appeared for the examination as a private candidate. The University, of which he was the Chancellor, offered to make arrangements so that he could write his papers at his residence, but he declined, and joined the other students at the Sri Pratap College centre. The only concession he asked for was a high table and a chair to help him sit comfortably because of his stiff hip.

Asha, meanwhile, began to study Hindi on her own, and Mrs Hanley, an Indian lady brought up by missionaries in Kashmir, was engaged to coach her in English. Asha was interested in painting, so Lilian Purbi, an Englishwoman married to a retired Kashmiri civil servant, was hired as her art teacher.

While pursuing his BA course, it struck Karan Singh that the dynasty's Gulab Mahal palace in Srinagar could be put to better use and what could be better than donating it to the newly created Jammu and Kashmir University. He mentioned it to Jawaharlal Nehru and Gopalaswami Ayyangar, who reacted favourably, saying the gesture would be greatly appreciated by the people of the State. When the Maharaja learned of the plan, he was furious and wrote an angry letter to his son. Taken aback, Karan Singh replied, explaining that the family didn't really need the palace, no one used it any longer, and by donating it to the university they would earn the goodwill of not just Kashmiris but people from all parts of the State who came to study there. All of the Maharaja's pent-up anger after repeated humiliation by Sheikh Abdullah and the Indian government was now directed at his son. When his friend 'Fatty', Fateh Singhji Limbidi, came to visit him in Bombay around this time, the Maharaja poured out his heart to him, and Fatty wrote to Karan Singh, urging him to be mindful of his father's feelings, for he had been slighted and wounded too often. Echoing the Maharaja, he said the new rulers of the State were trying to use the young heir to divest the Dogra dynasty of its property. Thwarted in his attempt, Karan Singh later donated 120 acres of extremely valuable orchard land near Hazratbal, which he had inherited from his grandfather, Raja Amar Singh, to the university. It was there that the present campus was built.

Amidst all this, the process for electing members of the Constituent Assembly had been completed, but it had put a question mark over the democratic credentials of Sheikh Abdullah. All his life, Sheikh Abdullah had accused the Maharaja of being an absolutist and an autocrat, but when it was his turn to rule, he displayed the same tendencies. The nomination papers of the candidates who stood against the National Conference were arbitrarily rejected by pliant officials of the interim government. In Jammu, the main—in fact, virtually the only—opposition party, the Praja Parishad, boycotted the electoral process when the nomination papers of 13 of its 28 candidates were rejected. In the valley too, the candidatures of the opposition were declared invalid, resulting in 72 out of 75 members getting elected unopposed, all of them being the nominees of the National

Conference. It was a farcical election that became a sore point for all time to come—denied any democratic representation, the Praja Parishad woud soon take to the streets in protest. But unaffected by questions about his integrity and credibility, Sheikh Abdullah went on to brush aside protocol and propriety. Karan Singh was the Regent and, therefore, effectively the Head of the State, so on the momentous occasion when the members of the Constituent Assembly were to meet to draft a new Constitution for the State, he should have been the person making the opening address. But Sheikh Abdullah decided to appropriate that honour. No one protested, not even Delhi.

In his address Abdullah outlined the issues that would be debated and decided by the Assembly, foremost among them being the framing of the Constitution for the future governance of the State, a 'reasoned conclusion regarding the accession', land reforms that had been passed by the government, and the vital issue of the future of the Royal Dynasty. Then he went on to give the historical background of the Dogra dynasty, and launched a scathing attack against Maharaja Hari Singh. He declared that the Maharaja had 'forfeited confidence of every section of the people', and that he was incapable of adjusting to the changed circumstances with his antiquated ideas. Then he spoke of the need to be impartial about individual deeds and said that he and his colleagues had found during their association with Yuvraj Karan Singh that he was intelligent, had a broad outlook, and wanted to serve his country. Finally, he added: 'There is no doubt that Yuvraj Karan Singh in his capacity as a citizen of the State, will prove a fitting symbol of the transition to a democratic system in which the ruler of yesterday becomes the first servant of the people, functioning under their authority, and on their behalf.'

It was obvious to most observers at the time that this appreciative reference to the Regent and the hint that he would be the new Head of State was made on the advice of Nehru and other officials of the Government of India. This would, if not appease the Dogras, at least help to avoid offending them by maintaining the constitutional authority of the Dogra family. But there was another reason why this endorsement of the Yuvraj, now the Regent, was important. Jammu and Kashmir's accession to India rested on the signing of the Instrument of Accession by the Yuvraj's father, the Maharaja. Yet, for the Indian Union, as of course for Sheikh Abdullah, it was now necessary to eliminate the Maharaja from the political scene and end the monarchy. This could lawfully be done only by the Constituent Assembly—whose existence had been made possible by a proclamation signed by the Regent. And the final, fatal blow to the Maharaja, which the Constituent Assembly would be used to deliver, would be difficult, if not impossible, to deliver if the Regent were alienated completely.

9

Cutting the Umbilical Cord

JAWAHARLAL NEHRU AND SHEIKH ABDULLAH had drawn up a plan to cast aside the Maharaja without disrupting the continuity of the Dogra dynasty—the Maharaja would be replaced as Head of State by his son. The Dogras, when they realized what was happening, were first shocked, but soon this turned into anger that was also to singe the Yuvraj. Sheikh Abdullah's reference to the Yuvraj, in his address to the Constituent Assembly, as 'an intelligent person who did not carry the burden of the past' and was keen to 'serve the State' had led them to conclude that the Yuvraj had agreed to become a 'puppet' Head of the State. Given the traditional rivalry, even hostility, between the Valley and Jammu, nothing could have been more infuriating for the Dogras than to have to play second fiddle to Kashmiris in general, and Sheikh Abdullah in particular. The idea that the Yuvraj—their hero's own son—would lead them to this situation was galling. The Dogras were already angry at his having accepted to become the Regent. They had not taken into account the negative consequences of his refusing the Regency, as they were driven by emotions that did not see reason and reality.

As for the Yuvraj, he was well aware that his father was still seething at the unceremonious manner in which he had been cancelled out from the State. He was also aware that even when his father had appointed him as his Regent, he had done so reluctantly and under duress. Now, the son was being used to completely cut the Maharaja off and still maintain a semblance of historical continuity. His detractors had found an alternative to abdication, which the Maharaja had pretty much indicated would happen over his dead body. The Yuvraj understood only too well that he was being offered the position of Head of State to give legitimacy to the unsavoury actions that had been planned. But deep down in his heart, he also had the urge to prove himself in the new environment, and do it on his own terms. He also understood that the currents of politics and history had made the changes inevitable and that with or without him, a Head of State would be elected. As it was, Sheikh Abdullah had already thought of the next move in case the Yuvraj refused to toe the suggested line. The name of Mahasha Nahar Singh, a Dalit leader of Jammu, was already doing the rounds as a possible Head of State.

Karan Singh weighed the pros and cons of accepting or rejecting the offer and saw that in case he declined the offer, he too would be exiled from the State since Sheikh Abdullah was not going to tolerate the presence of an uncooperative or hostile Dogra symbol around whom the people of Jammu could rally. Karan Singh also did not see any future for himself in Bombay; he could not see himself leading a life similar to his father's. His life had just begun, and he had started to enjoy the world of academics and the company of intelligent people who had become an integral part of his life. He also knew that a whole new world was opening up and there was the 'exciting adventure of building a new India,' as Nehru would often say. Surely, his declining the offer would not have helped anyone—not him, individually, nor the people of Jammu or even the Kashmiris, as the confrontation between the two regions would have intensified. In such an environment, Pakistan and the inimical West would have found an excuse to meddle in the affairs of the State and also force some solution upon India. He was also convinced that if he, the only member of the Dogra ruling family in the State, also left, Sheikh Abdullah would most probably proceed to take over not only the property and lands belonging to the family, but also the Dharmarth and other family trusts.

He had also gathered from his many conversations with Nehru that he was needed in the State to play a useful part in serving the national interest in that sensitive period. Thus, at this critical juncture of his life, he faced the dilemma of choosing between his father and Nehru. Becoming a Regent had not been his choice, as he had been appointed by his father, whose natural successor he was, but getting elected as the Head of State was to be a conscious choice taken under the influence of Nehru. Tremendous pressure was brought upon him by the staff members of his father and the various Dogra leaders, who told him that acceptance of the office would be a betrayal and he would go down in history as a traitor to the dynasty of Maharaja Gulab Singh. Some even warned him that if he defied his father, he might be disinherited and would lose patrimony worth hundreds of crores of rupees. Some even suggested that the offer of Headship was part of an elaborate plan of Sheikh Abdullah's. They said Abdullah had secured the Maharaja's exile, and then his exclusion from Headship of the State, and he would now not hesitate to deliver a similar blow to the Yuvraj as well in his bid to annihilate the Dogra dynasty. As it was, he had already spewed poison against the Yuvraj only recently in Jammu, and it was possible that he would create such a situation that the Yuvraj would be humiliated and would be forced to throw in the towel and leave. The Yuvraj was also reminded of the Sheikh's history of reneging on agreements with the Maharaja.

Since making a reasoned decision was difficult, Karan Singh's instinct was to gain some time and watch events closely as they unfolded, in order to gain some clarity, and also consider the contradictory advice he was being given. The Constitution of the State had not yet been framed, consultations between the State and the Government of India were going on regarding the constitutional arrangements, covering not only the Headship of the State but also subjects like citizenship, fundamental rights, the Supreme Court, financial integration, and the flag. On 26 July 1952, Karan Singh received a letter from his guide and mentor, Nehru, assuring the young Regent of his support, and advising him to cheerfully accept the changes that would be suggested, so that he would be seen to be in the forefront, rather than as someone stuck in the past who was being dragged against his will into a new, modern world. When the inevitable needed to be done, he wrote, it must be done gracefully so that the goodwill and respect of others could be earned.

The letter provided Karan Singh with the opportunity to express his concerns, based on his own understanding of the situation he was in, and advice from his own and his father's friends and well-wishers, including some Dogra leaders who had reached out to him. Karan Singh made it clear to Prime Minister Nehru that he wanted to serve the country in whatever way he could, and had no qualms about taking up any position. But in the circumstances, where the Constitution of the State was yet to emerge and no one knew what shape the Constituent Assembly would give it, he couldn't make up his mind. Moreover, a decision regarding the Headship could be taken only when the duties and functions of the Head of the State had been defined and he was clear about the responsibilities that he would have to carry. In addition, he also needed to know the conditions under which he would have to work.

Meanwhile, Sheikh Abdullah called upon the Yuvraj to reiterate the need to take an early decision as to whether he would or would not accept the post of Head of State—Sadr-e-Riyasat—elected for a five-year term by the Constituent Assembly, of which Sheikh Abdullah's National Conference had absolute control. The Yuvraj gave him the same arguments that he had put before Nehru, but he brushed them aside, saying that the drafting and adoption of the full Constitution might take many more years, and he was not prepared to wait till then to resolve this important matter. The Constitution would be adopted in phases, the issue of Head of State was part of the first phase and it was absolutely crucial. It was obvious that, not content with the removal of Maharaja Hari Singh from the scene, the Sheikh was now impatient for the freedom to act unilaterally in the State. Again, Karan Singh had no option but to turn to Nehru to protest against what he felt was Sheikh Abdullah's dictatorial attitude. Nehru agreed that hustling through a part of the Constitution was neither normal nor was it desirable, but he said the issue of adopting a part of the Constitution now and the rest in phases was something that the Indian Government had discussed and agreed with the Kashmir delegation when they were in Delhi. This was known as the Delhi Agreement, aimed to strike a balance between autonomy for the State and its integration with India, involving give and take on both sides. Nehru argued that since Delhi had already agreed to this mode of drafting and implementing the State's Constitution, going back on it and reopening the arguments would only complicate the matter.

During this period of uncertainty, Karan Singh expressed his desire to go abroad for studies but Nehru understood this as a sign of the pressure the young Regent was feeling—he wanted to take himself away, so that he could avoid taking a decision. Nehru urged him not to delay or decline the offer of being made Sadr-e-Riyasat, as that would not only be bad for the State but would also be of no advantage to him personally. He would be in a better position to educate himself by staying in his State, where he would have enough time for himself as Sadr-e-Riyasat. Moreover, Nehru argued, Western universities were not at their best in the aftermath of the World War and now the emerging Cold War between the Eastern and Western blocs. Besides, foreign countries were good for short visits only and he would learn much more by facing the problems of life at home. Nehru suggested that Karan Singh should accept becoming the Sadr-e-Riyasat, so that he may serve the people of his State in many ways that are not always obvious.

Still not able to dispel his doubts and misgivings, Karan Singh decided to go to Delhi to meet Nehru, who affectionately welcomed him in the drawing room of Teen Murti House. Busy as he was, he took time to explain to the young Regent why he and his colleagues were anxious that he accept the offer. It was also obvious to Karan Singh that the Kashmir team, consisting of Sheikh Abdullah, Mirza Afzal Beg, D.P. Dhar, and M.A. Shahmiri, Sheikh Abdullah's constitutional adviser, had taken a rigid stand, forcing Delhi to succumb to the pressure. But he also noticed that for the first time, there was a note of displeasure as Nehru spoke about Sheikh Abdullah. He also felt that Nehru wanted him to be on the scene if ever some difficulty arose in the State—another sign that he was beginning to feel a little uncertain about Sheikh Abdullah. When Karan Singh then spoke to Nehru about the matter of handling public opinion in Jammu, represented by the Praja Parishad, he softened his stand towards them and suggested that Karan Singh invite some of the

Jammu leaders to Srinagar so that he could personally explain the whole situation to them. Nehru appeared to have changed his mind about the Praja Parishad, whom he had always condemned as communalists and not worth engaging with in any manner. Perhaps he could also see that Karan Singh needed support at this time and while he had always found it in him—Nehru—he may also have sought and found it in the leaders of the Praja Parishad. Nehru may have realized that extreme opinions on either side would do neither the young Yuvraj and Regent, nor the state of Jammu and Kashmir any good.

Therefore, on his return to Srinagar, the Yuvraj began consulting Pandit Prem Nath Dogra, the President of the Praja Parishad, and other leaders from Jammu. After meetings held over three days, Prem Nath Dogra issued a statement wherein he reiterated his party's old demand for complete accession and merger with India. But he concluded the statement by adding that 'till the new Constitution for the State assumes a concrete shape, it would be premature to give any definitive answer on this single issue of accepting the office of the Head of the State by Shree Yuvaraj Bahadur'. Given their intransigence on the issue, this too was a significant concession. The Yuvraj had thus been able to buy a little more time. At about this time, in a separate development, he learned that his father had written a memorandum to the President of India, and press reports claimed that he had demanded a referendum in the State over the issue of retention or abolition of the dynasty.

With these twin developments in mind, Karan Singh wrote a letter to Nehru on 1 September 1952, reporting what had transpired during the parleys with the Praja Parishad leaders and urged that senior Indian leaders like Maulana Azad, Dr. K.N. Katju—the then Home Minister—and Gopalaswami Ayyangar, Minister for Kashmir Affairs, should also meet the Jammu leaders and listen to their point of view. But before concluding his letter, he could not resist the temptation of referring to the Maharaja's memorandum, even though he knew that Nehru would not be happy to read that. He brought up the issue of the referendum that his father was said to have demanded and suggested that to him, it appeared a good idea as it would democratically settle the question of whether the people of Jammu and Kashmir State wanted the dynasty to exist or not. Tongue firmly in cheek, he also added that there were indications that the outcome of such a referendum could not be considered a foregone conclusion—in other words, even the Valley's Muslims might spring a surprise and support the Maharaja!

Nehru replied the very next day and conceded that the Jammu leaders had many grievances that were justified, but then he went on to castigate the Praja Parishad for its intolerant mode of functioning. He also addressed the memorandum written by the Maharaja, and categorically said that there was no reference to the referendum in it, but added that it was an 'angry and tendentious document'. He again reiterated that the Yuvraj's father was unable to accept that the world was changing rapidly. After this, he expressed his surprise that the Yuvraj had brought up the subject of referendum without thinking the matter through. It was not possible to hold a referendum over that smaller issue in a smaller area—by which he meant the part of the original State that was presently with India—when the bigger question of plebiscite over a larger area—that is, Jammu and Kashmir as it was before the tribal invasion of 1947—had not been held, even though it was mandated by the United Nations. Moreover, he said, even if a referendum were held over a smaller question, Pakistan would then demand that the whole of the State as it existed in 1947 should be participating in this referendum, which was clearly not possible. He closed the argument by saying that, in the circumstances that existed, only Pakistan would profit from such an idea and no one else.

Despite these pressures, away from routine politics, Karan Singh had an exciting and dramatic experience when, in the company of Nehru, he took a flight to the newly constructed airfield at Chushul in Eastern Ladakh. This airfield, at a height of 14,270 feet above sea level, was reportedly the highest in the world. The flight was flown by Air Marshal Mehr Singh with Indira Gandhi and Sheikh Abdullah as the other passengers. During the flight, everyone had to wear oxygen masks because of the height. From above, the Himalayas appeared spectacular to Karan Singh, like 'some vast, frozen ocean stretching endlessly in all directions.' When the flight landed, sensory perceptions played tricks on their minds. The mountains near the runway appeared as if they were very close and, taken in by the illusory effect, Indira Gandhi began to walk towards them till she was informed that they were at least ten miles away. After staying there for about 90 minutes, the party departed, but the beauty of the landscape which had no vegetation and sparse habitation remained etched in Karan Singh's the mind. Himalaya, the abode of snow, the home of Lord Shiva, he felt, really belonged to another planet.

Ladakh has a special place in the consciousness of the Dogras. It was in these forbidding heights and debilitating climatic conditions that the Dogra forces under the legendary General Zorawar Singh, General Basti Ram and General Baj Singh had defeated the Namgyals, effectively ending that dynasty. With this conquest, 36,000 square miles of land, which comprised Ladakh, were added to the then Jammu kingdom of Raja Gulab Singh. There were quite a few occasions in the history of Ladakh when it had been conquered by invaders from the south or the west, like Lalitaditya of Kashmir and Mirza Haider Dughlat, the Chagtai-Mongol prince from Kashgar, but none of them had been able to hold on to it. Only the Dogras had achieved this historical feat and transformed the economic history of both Ladakh and Kashmir. Therefore, it was natural for Karan Singh to feel attracted to this forbidding yet fascinating land, more so because no member of the Dogra dynasty had ever set foot there, though they had been ruling it since 1834. As long its economic and strategic interests were secure, the Dogra dynasty had been content to rule Ladakh through the office of *Wazir Wazarat* and had not interfered with the Ladakhis' religious and cultural lives. In 1947, Pakistan had come close to occupying Ladakh. Neighbouring Tibet, which shared its culture and religion with Ladakh, had been appropriated by the Chinese after the communist takeover. This meant that both Pakistan and the Chinese were near Ladakh, and if they found the conditions conducive, they would not hesitate to make a bid to take it over.

The visit to Chushul ignited a desire in Karan Singh to visit Ladakh and understand its people and their culture—they were, after all, people of the State of which he was the Regent. So, in September 1952, the Yuvrani and he landed in Leh. Led by the Head Lama Kushak Bakula, the whole town and the population of neighboring villages had come out to greet them. It was a fairy world that greeted them under the clear and deep blue sky. They wore their traditional robes, and the women were adorned with their gorgeous turquoise headpieces. Asha, the Yuvrani, was so fascinated by those headpieces that when the opportunity arose, she grabbed them to admire them closely. The couple had taken with them several thousand yards of cloth so that every inhabitant could get enough for at least a coat.

They stayed in Leh for three days during which they visited all the leading monasteries, made appropriate offerings, and were deeply fascinated by the beauty of the statues of Buddha and Bodhisattvas, the most outstanding among them being the three-storey-high image of Buddha at Shey. Then they took a flight to Kargil, the second important town and region of Ladakh. It was mostly Shia and very close to the ceasefire line. It was here that Karan Singh noticed that though India derived its name from the river Indus, yet, after the Partition of India, Ladakh was the only place in India where the mighty river could be seen.

In his discussions with Kushak Bakula, the leader of Ladakh, and his colleagues, Karan Singh was surprised to discover a feeling of unease and insecurity because of Sheikh Abdullah's administration. It was much more intense in Ladakh than in Jammu. A microscopic minority, the Ladakhis needed constitutional protection for their distinct cultural identity, but with only two members in the State Assembly, their position was precarious and subordinate to that of the Kashmiris. If the State had moved away from a feudal system, there should now be fair representation of all regions and communities. They suggested that, given their problems and insecurities, there should be a Statutory Advisory Committee to which all legislation that vitally affected them should be mandatorily referred. They also demanded that a special administrator for Ladakh be sent from the Centre. On his return to Srinagar, Karan Singh wrote to Prime Minister Nehru about the visit, and enclosed a separate note with his impressions of the situation there and suggestions to improve the situation. He pointed out that Ladakh was strategically more important for India than the rest of the State, and that 'it would be a tragedy if, for lack of the State's accommodating spirit, the people of Ladakh remain unhappy and discontented, and thus easy prey to all sorts of exploitation, both communalist and communist'. Nehru replied promptly but expressed his inability to take up the construction of the Leh-Kulu Road—to open a new route connecting Ladakh to the rest of the country—as suggested by the Regent, because of the heavy expenditure involved. He also dismissed Kushak Bakula as someone who had no remedy for Ladakh's economic backwardness.

Back in Srinagar, Karan Sing was racked again by the dilemma over the offer of becoming the first elected Head of State of Jammu and Kashmir. The dilemma triggered an internal response, and he immersed himself in reading Edwin Arnold's *The Light of Asia*, a wonderful book on the life and teachings of the Buddha. He also went to Dachigam and shot a bear. Unfortunately, it did not die instantly, and lay on the ground for long, shrieking pitifully. Those cries haunted Karan Singh for a long time, and he resolved not to shoot or fish again, a promise that he kept all his life. But this incident also triggered another impulse, and he recorded in his diary that his long-term aim was to achieve spiritual enlightenment and to work for harmony and peace. Over the years, he says, he has realized that saving the world from falling into an abyss is not as simple a task as it appeared in those youthful years. Extreme positions come easily to people. His belief in accommodation, in the interest of social and political harmony, and in civility despite opposing beliefs has sometimes earned him the displeasure of the liberal and the illiberal alike.

As Karan Singh, still only twenty-one, grappled with the dilemma over the Sadr-e-Riyasat offer in a period that he has described as the most excruciating of several difficult moments in his life—he passed his B.A. examination. The convocation was addressed by the Vice President of India, Dr. Radhakrishnan, and created an amusing situation. As Chancellor of the University, Yuvraj presented the degrees to the graduates, but since he too had graduated that year, he could not have given that degree to himself. Hence, after presenting the degrees to others, he stepped down and, thus, had the honour of receiving his degree from Dr. Radhakrishnan. This was probably the only occasion when a Chancellor became a graduate of his own University. But this embarrassment aside, it was a proud moment for him—receiving his degree from a learned scholar like Dr. Radhakrishnan, who was also a spellbinding orator, peppering his speeches with quotations from the Sanskrit and other classics. This ability so impressed Karan Singh that he decided to work on a similar style for himself, and followed it all his life.

While pressure on the Regent mounted from both Shiekh Abdullah and his government and the Government of India, the Maharaja wrote letters to the State Ministry, protesting that promises made to him when he signed the Instrument of Accession and later, when he was forced to leave the State 'temporarily', were being broken time and again. The Government of India had persistently disregarded his rights 'thereby weakening my position and securing very unfair advantage to my persecutors.' He wrote: '[Am] I not entitled, may I ask you, to be told either that I am wrong or that the Government of India are committed to carry out a certain policy emanating from Sheikh Abdullah even though it may mean sacrificing myself, my dynasty and certain cherished principles of justice and equity? Have I lost the elementary right of a person who considers himself aggrieved and seeks justice?' But it was a lonely, futile battle he was fighting. No Indian leader of consequence stood by him. Rulers of all other princely states had also, willingly or otherwise, made their peace with the Indian Republic.

The time for his son, the Yuvraj and his Regent, to decide about accepting the Headship of the State had run out. The Indian government had made it clear to his father that times had changed, the assurances of the past were no longer valid. And in the State of Jammu and Kashmir, Sheikh Abdullah would wait no longer. If the Regent refused to accept the offer of being elected the Sadr-e-Riyasat, Sheikh Abdullah had a reserve nominee of his own for the post. He was in a win-win situation. If the Yuvraj accepted to become the Sadr-e-Riyasat, then a Dogra and the heir of the dynasty would have been reduced to becoming Sheikh Abdullah's puppet and a titular head, and if he refused, the Sheikh would have his candidate from a Scheduled Caste elevated to the high office, even if a ceremonial office. For the Yuvraj, there was the risk that if he accepted the office, Sheikh Abdullah would most likely contrive to create an opportunity to force him into leaving the State as well, and after that, nobody could say whether the properties, land, legacy of the dynasty of which he was the heir would be safe or not. On the other hand, if he refused, he might have to leave anyway. But the greater risk of his refusal would be letting down Nehru and India. Refusal would also mean that he would have effectively retired even before he had started, and he would be consigned to the ranks of anachronistic one-time royals who now squandered their lives in race courses and *shikargahs*.

But if he accepted the proposal, then cracks in his relationship with his father, which had emerged since the Maharaja had been forced to appoint him as the Regent, would not only widen but also, very likely, lead to a painful rupture. Acceptance would also mean that he would have to constantly fight for his space in the system, in order not to allow anyone to push him around and prevent him from playing a positive role in the lives of the people.

In reality, he had to choose between his father and Pandit Jawaharlal Nehru; by refusing, he would be joining his father in exile, and by accepting, he would join hands with Nehru in the 'exciting adventure of building India', in however small a manner.

On 30 October, Nehru wrote to Karan Singh, saying he hoped that he would agree to take the steps that were suggested to him by Delhi and consent to becoming the Head of State.

'That is the only course that is open to us now, and we should not hesitate to take it. Any other course or any attempt at postponement will only lead to difficulty and trouble.' He added that it was no longer possible to delay a decision on the issue of Sadr-e-Riyasat, and that by the middle of November, the election would take place. Still apprehensive about the future and an honest commitment on the part of Sheikh Abdullah, Karan Singh decided to visit Delhi once again. Nehru spoke in greater detail about the implications of his decision, and that at critical junctures in life, a person had to take a clear stand regardless of the pressures. He was frank that Delhi's relationship with Sheikh Abdullah had entered a difficult phase, and, therefore, it was important that Karan Singh be present in the State in case some problems arose. Even after this frank conversation, Nehru neither sought nor gave any assurance. But as he left Teen Murti House that day, Karan Singh had made up his mind.

He returned to Srinagar on 12 November 1952, and on 15 November, the Constituent Assembly met and elected him as the first Sadr-e-Riyasat for a term of five years. He was 21, well below the age that would have made him eligible for the high office. Therefore, the Assembly reduced the age of eligibility from 35 to 21 and cleared the path for his election. On his election, Prime Minister Nehru wrote him a formal letter of congratulations. But he also wrote that the office 'puts great responsibility upon you, for you have to not merely follow an established convention but rather help in making conventions for the future'.

The night of 16 November turned out to be a long one for Karan Singh, the former Yuvraj. He sat with his wife, unable to sleep. He realized she was the only real support he had. She sat up with him till the early hours of the morning, listening. She did not question his decision even for a moment, making it known by her presence that they were in this together. She was barely fifteen.

His decision had been momentous, as he had not only severed his relationship with his feudal background but had also put his relationship with his father in serious jeopardy. He was aware that his father would not forgive him, though on the surface he might maintain a cordial relationship. He also realised that he had taken a huge risk, as Sheikh Abdullah had repeatedly proved his visceral hatred for the dynasty, and now the scion of the dynasty would probably be at his mercy. He also knew that he would have to face the wrath of the Dogras, who, in any case, were already angry at the exile of the Maharaja and his acceptance of the Regency. The fact that he had chosen Nehru over his father would be an additional cause of anger for them. But he told himself that by cutting himself from the past, he had linked his destiny to the much larger cause of building and shaping the destiny of one-seventh of humanity.

On the morning of 17 November 1952, he drove to the old Rajgarh Palace on the Jhelum, where rulers before his father lived, and entered the Darbar Hall, which had a magnificent papier-mâché ceiling and had now been converted into the Constituent Assembly. Earlier, the courtiers would sit on the carpet and only the Maharaja on the throne, but for the Assembly, benches had been installed and only the Speaker sat on an elevated platform. At the entrance of the Hall he was received by Sheikh Abdullah, Bakshi Ghulam Mohammad, and the Speaker, G.M. Sadiq, and escorted into the Assembly to thunderous applause by the members. The event was symbolic of the transformation that had taken place, with the last representative of the old order becoming the first servant of the new. As he stood there, flanked by Sheikh Abdullah and his colleagues, Chief Justice Janki Nath Wazir administered the oath of office. After the oath, he read out a short speech in which he admitted that he was initially hesitant to shoulder the responsibility because he felt that there were better and more experienced men who qualified for the office. He then enumerated the challenges that the State had to face during the preceding years and lauded the courage, grit, and determination of the people while facing the invaders from Pakistan. He also paid tribute to the gallant resistance that had been put up by the heavily outnumbered State Forces with the timely assistance of the Indian Army. He concluded by drawing the Assembly's attention to the multi-religious nature of the State and emphasizing the need for greater unity in the future, and added that in 'building the equal partnership of all the people and all the regions of this State, a solemn duty devolves upon each one of us to do our bit, to make our contribution'.

There was no looking back now. A week after the oath-taking, the Government moved to Jammu for the winter.

10

Jammu Takes to the Streets

As EXPECTED, OUTRAGED DOGRAS of Jammu rallied under the banner of the Praja Parishad and threatened to welcome Sadr-e-Riyasat Karan Singh with black flags. On 24 November, when he flew in an Indian Airlines plane to Jammu, he was shocked by the hostile reception he received. It was in sharp contrast to the earlier receptions that had been accorded to him by the people of Jammu when he arrived in February 1949 from New York after his prolonged hospitalization, and in 1950 when he had brought his bride home. This time, there was a sea of humanity from the airport to the gates of the palace waving black flags and shouting themselves hoarse with angry slogans.

After the initial shock, Karan Singh composed himself to put up a brave face. He waved at the sea of black flags and found some strength when he noticed that a few acknowledged him by waving back. There was some hope! He rationalized to himself that the hostile welcome was not as much against him as it was a mark of the people's solidarity with his father, as legally now the Maharaja and the dynasty had been abolished.

An agitation against Sheikh Abdullah had already been

launched by the Praja Parishad on 13 November, a day before the Constituent Assembly had met to elect the Sadr-e-Riyasat, demanding the complete integration of the State with India. Its slogan summed up the aims of the agitation: '*Ek Vidhan, Ek Nishan, Ek Pradhan*'—'One constitution, one flag, one head of the State.' The agitation represented the popular sentiment of Jammu, and it gathered momentum during the next few months. Karan Singh was stunned by how widespread the agitation was, and worried by the intensity of the anger among the Dogras, which had manifested itself in the aggressive participation of women in the agitation, and also in violence. He informed Prime Minister Nehru that 'an overwhelming majority of the Jammu Province seems to be emphatically in sympathy with the agitation. Fundamentally responsible for this, I feel, [are] very deep-seated and genuine economic and psychological reasons, and I do not think it will be a correct appraisal to dismiss the whole affair as merely the creation of a reactionary clique.' He also added that on 1st December, 'the new State Flag was hoisted upon the Secretariat here [Jammu], but I am afraid my suggestion about hoisting the Indian Flag has not been accepted. I feel that would have been a graceful and becoming gesture, which might have had a very healthy psychological effect and would have forestalled much trouble.' Sheikh Abdullah, he said, had curtly turned down the suggestion, letting go an opportunity to mollify the Dogras. Karan Singh too refused to hoist the State Flag unless the National Flag was hoisted, giving an early indication that he would not be the rubber stamp that Sheikh Abdullah wanted him to be and that, on a matter of principle, he would not hesitate to take a stand.

Karan Singh's letter to Nehru was a long one, detailing the nature of the grievances of the majority in Jammu and his opinion of what the way forward could be. 'At the root of all this trouble,' he wrote, 'are certain deeply felt psychological and economic factors...The people feel that they have not only been treated with scant regard but that consistent and vindictive efforts have been made to ruin them economically over the last five years and to outrage their deepest and most cherished sentiments... They would not have minded the abolition of the [Dogra] State Flag if they had seen the State Government adopting the Indian National Flag, and they would not have minded the abolition of hereditary rule if a system of Rajpramukh—as in other Part B States—had been introduced. What has caused great resentment is that while their deeply cherished flag and the rule [of the Dogra dynasty] have gone, they have not been given what has been given to the rest of the Part B States, and that a new flag and a new kind of Head of the State has been foisted upon them.'

He added, 'Up till now, the movement has been basically peaceful, despite a few unpleasant incidents. But a situation of this kind is liable to take an ugly turn at any time, causing considerable loss of life and widespread suffering. For this reason, and also for the fact that the agitation is not only disrupting the smooth functioning of the administration but is also being fully exploited by Pakistan and is likely to have undesirable international repercussion, it is very essential that conditions be speedily created in which this agitation can be called off, or at least lose its appeal with the masses, and the people of Jammu be made to feel that their rights, culture and interests are safe and that they are not being treated in a discriminatory manner.'

Karan Singh went on to write that unless Sheikh Abdullah was made to agree to full integration, there were only three alternatives to the unpleasant situation, and he gave his opinion on each:

'A) Jammu and Ladakh separate from Kashmir. Under the present international complications, this will be a very undesirable and dangerous development, as it is likely to have the effect of pushing the Kashmir Valley into the hands of Pakistan…It is no doubt true that the people of Jammu are culturally and linguistically much more closely allied with the Dogra areas of Kangra and Himachal Pradesh, and are also geographically contiguous to them. But as I said, any realignment at this stage is likely to prove disastrous.

'B) The present status quo as regards the internal and external relations of the State be maintained. This also will not be satisfactory, as in the ultimate analysis the three units of the State can remain together only by common consent, and if the present unrest and discontent continues there is a strong possibility of the situation deteriorating considerably. It is clear that forcible repression can at best act as a palliative, and a very temporary one at that. At worst it can sow such seeds of hatred and resentment as will completely inhibit any solution or settlement for many years to come…Our attitude, therefore, while dealing adequately with violent elements, should be one which is conducive to arriving at an amicable and mutually satisfactory solution.

'C) A formula is evolved whereby while remaining with Kashmir as one unit, the people of Jammu and Ladakh are made to feel happy and contented. This, to my mind, is the only solution possible under the circumstances. For its attainment, however, it is very necessary that certain measures be swiftly adopted. I feel that if the measures suggested in this note are specially implemented, and full efforts are made to consolidate the goodwill and confidence they are bound to generate, the whole problem can be peacefully and satisfactorily settled within a short time.'

As remedial measures, Karan Singh suggested that the National Flag should fly along with the State Flag immediately over at least the Secretariats in Jammu and Srinagar. He pointed out that at the moment, there was not a single building in the State where the National Flag was flown. Another problem that needed immediate remedy was the universal complaint of corruption in the working of the government machinery. This had been very noticeable in the implementation of the Big Landed Estates Abolition Act. On paper, the beneficiaries were not supposed to pay anything for the allotment of land to them, but in practice, bribes had to be paid to the *patwaris, girdaurs,* and *tehsildars* who were instrumental in the implementation.

Karan Singh also called for speedy economic integration of the State with the rest of the country. He advocated the abolition of State Custom Duty so that trade and commerce opened up between the State and the rest of India, and pointed out that opening linkages with the rest of the world was necessary—even the traders of Kashmir had been demanding the opening of the Rawalpindi route so that their products could find profitable markets. He also expressed his dissatisfaction with the land reforms and wrote that the Big Landed Estates Abolition Act had proved highly unsatisfactory for the Jammu region because of the arbitrary ceiling of 182 Kanals. This had been done without taking into account the productivity and fertility of the land, rendering many land units in the Jammu region uneconomical. The hardest hit section was the small landowners, mostly Rajputs, who had no savings and no jobs as they lived entirely on the land. Similarly, the small *jagirdars* too had been affected. Such *jagirdars,* having been rendered landless, needed some support from the Government for their existence. But even those *jagirdars* who had large units of land, had been hit, as with the abolishing of the *jagirdari* system, they had forfeited their land.

Karan Singh also took up the issue of the alarming rate of unemployment in the Jammu region. This had been aggravated by the State Government, as it disbanded three Units of the

State Forces in 1951 in an act that the Dogras felt was vengeful. Karan Singh suggested that to ameliorate their lot, they be re-employed in the Militia, Home Guards, Police, etc., and, also, an unemployment commission be constituted to recommend the measures that ought to be taken for its solution. For the development of the region, he pointed out that since the biggest problem of the Kandi region was water scarcity, a dam on the river Tawi could revolutionize the lifestyle.

After sending this note, Karan Singh went to Delhi and then to Kangra to meet his mother, where, on the third day of his visit, he got the news that the agitation in Jammu had taken a violent turn and the police had resorted to firing, killing some agitators in Sunderbani. On returning to Jammu, he came to know that Sheikh Abdullah had written a long letter to Nehru on 23 December 1952, in which, after blaming 'communal organizations' and the Jammu land-lords and other upper classes, he had claimed that the 'real problem of Jammu does not relate to the completion of its association with India and Kashmir, nor to the propriety of this or that symbol', but the 'wretchedness, poverty and degeneration of the vast masses', which needed to be tackled by all. This he had written in response to Nehru's letter dated 13 December 1952. In the face of the apathy of Sheikh Abdullah and worry over the ugly turn the agitation had taken, Karan Singh had had to curtail his visit to be back in Jammu and he again wrote to Nehru, urging him to tackle the whole problem himself, as it appeared that there were forces outside the State that were fanning and manipulating the agitation, which was having an unhappy effect on Indian public opinion as well as opinion in the Kashmir Valley. He also suggested that since the 58th session of the Indian National Congress was to be held in Hyderabad from 15 to 18 January 1953, and Sheikh Abdullah was expected to attend it, the Prime Minister could use that opportunity to prevail upon the Sheikh to hold direct talks with the leaders of the national parties supporting the Jammu agitation.

The New Year began with some positive signs as Begum Abdullah, her two daughters, and three sons visited Karan Singh's home for tea. Later that day, when D.P. Dhar—Karan Singh's old friend who was Deputy Home Minister in the Sheikh Abdullah government—came over and they were discussing the situation in the State, they heard loud and angry slogans from a Praja Parishad procession, followed by gunshots. They both agreed that the situation was getting out of control and the only way of bringing the confrontation to an end was to honestly implement the Delhi Agreement in full at the earliest, and give provincial autonomy to Jammu and Ladakh. That night, Karan Singh noted in his diary, 'If Sheikh Abdullah is not prepared to take those steps, then the sooner we find out, the better. In that case, if he cannot be induced to take them, then the only alternative is a break for which we must mentally prepare ourselves. If a break has to come, we should not let it come upon us suddenly, with a terrific explosion which would fling Kashmir into Pakistan and ruin us all.' He added, that D.P. Dhar agreed with him that if the break came, then to make the best out of a bad situation, Hindu-majority areas of the State should be merged with India, forming a Dogra state together, preferably, with Himachal Pradesh and Kangra [which had not been made a part of Himachal yet]. Also, that Leh and Zanskar should be centrally administered, and Kashmir and Kargil could become one unit with a special relationship with India.

Even as he was struggling for some answers, Karan Singh saw, on the morning of 7th January 1953, that parts of a letter he had written to Prime Minister Nehru on the 4th had appeared in an Urdu paper, *Hind Samachar*, published from Jalandhar. He immediately wrote to Nehru about it, saying that the leak could not have come from his side as he had typed the letter himself and delivered it personally at the Prime Minister's house. He also assured Nehru that his files containing their letters were always under lock and key, hence the source of the leak could only be Delhi. Even before Karan Singh's letter could reach Delhi, Nehru too had written to him and expressed his hope that Sheikh Abdullah would come to Hyderabad to attend the Congress Session and that he would then talk to Abdullah and take some proper action. He also said that any defeatist attitude regarding the problem could not be a solution, therefore he disapproved of the proposal by the belligerent Praja Parishad and its supporters in India—mainly the RSS, Jana Sangh and the Hindu Mahasabha—regarding the breaking away of the Jammu province from the rest of the State. But more significantly, he drew Karan Singh's attention to a news item in *Veer Arjun*, a Hindi newspaper from Delhi, claiming that Karan Singh had written a letter to Nehru regarding the Jammu agitation and had made various suggestions. This, Nehru further wrote, meant that someone had got hold of the letter and the note, and cautioned him to be careful. The letter written by Karan Singh and the one written by Nehru on the same day had crossed each other, but what was a cause of concern was that someone in Delhi had wanted to embarrass both Nehru and Karan Singh and was working to sabotage any reasonable solution to the Jammu agitation.

Karan Singh could not shake off the feeling that there was some kind of conspiracy against him. He noticed that whenever Colonel Bhagwan Singh or Captain Dewan Singh, his father's old loyalists, met him, their superficial politeness could not mask their resentment towards him. Even the level-headed Brigadier Ghansara Singh seemed to have joined their club. All of them averred that they were not part of the Praja Parishad's agitation or leadership but, not surprisingly, declared their sympathies with it. Meanwhile, his understandably angry father had begun to get as much furniture, art and artefacts, rugs, and even silver utensils, which the Yuvrani often used for cooking, from the State to be sent to him in Bombay. Karan Singh discovered on return to Jammu from Srinagar that Ranbir Mahal had been stripped of all the furniture on his father's instructions. Even more painful was the fact that his last few letters to the Maharaja had remained unanswered.

Karan Singh and D.P. Dhar had agreed that a break-up of the State of Jammu and Kashmir could only be the last resort, but soon he discovered that the prevalent mood in the Sheikh Abdullah government was that if Jammu wanted to break away from Kashmir, then it would not stand in the way, but it would accept only the Hindu majority areas of Jammu breaking off. Karan Singh was shocked, as it meant that the State Government, instead of trying to solve the problem, had decided to just sit back and let the matter drift. This, he felt, was dangerous and wrote to Nehru again, suggesting that the Delhi Agreement be implemented in full, including working out a system of provincial autonomy, to which the National Conference had committed itself. Since forces outside the State were playing an active role in the Praja Parishad agitation, he also urged the Prime Minister to hold talks with the leaders of national parties to find a consensus, and also to hold talks with the Praja Parishad, despite his strong reservations about this party. Had the Parishad's leaders participated in the 1952 elections, some of them would have been elected and would have been members of the Constituent Assembly. Sheikh Abdullah and the Government of India could not have avoided a dialogue with them then, so they should not shy away from a dialogue now.

He followed up his letters and the detailed note with a visit to Delhi and held talks with the Prime Minister, the Home

Minister, and the President, Dr. Rajendra Prasad, and reiterated his assessment. He urged Delhi that the agitation should not be treated as a law-and-order problem alone and together with police intervention there should be concrete political, economic and administrative measures. As a consequence, Nehru wrote a letter to Sheikh Abdullah, but the latter was adamant that his government's hard response was justified and, once again, dismissed the agitation as the handiwork of a communal organization with the violent support of Jammu landlords. Nehru also responded to Karan Singh's letter and agreed that though police action may be necessary, it was a negative reaction to any situation. But he urged that such situations needed a cool and dispassionate approach. In other words, while not endorsing Sheikh Abdullah's action completely, he was not ruling out that the agitation was indeed the handiwork of reactionary and communal forces.

Meanwhile, meddling in the affairs of the State by mysterious agents continued—not only through leaks but also misinformation. On 11 January 1953, Karan Singh was constrained to write to Nehru about a news item in *The Tribune* that referred to a supposed interview by the Sadr-e-Riyasat in which he was said to have condemned the Praja Parishad for starting an agitation that was dangerous for both India and Kashmir. He was also reported to have heaped praise on the State Government, saying, 'The State has, however, under the plan of New Kashmir, made greater progress than India in several aspects, such as the abolition of landlordism without compensation.' This was the second time that his name and his office had been dragged into the controversy in the media. It was obvious there were forces desperate to damage him in Delhi as well as among his people in Jammu. To put a stop to such plans, he issued a Press Note to say, 'Yuvraj Karan Singh wishes to make it clear that no press interview has been given by him within the State or elsewhere in India...

As Head of the State, he does not wish to be dragged into any controversy in this manner. Of course, the welfare of the State and all its people are his primary concern, and his efforts, consistent with his constitutional position, are always directed towards that end.'

Shortly afterwards, when Karan Singh and Asha were celebrating Makar Sankranti with some visitors, news came in that a young Dogra boy who had been injured in police firing had died. The news greatly upset Karan Singh, but he was informed by the State's Deputy Prime Minister and Home Minister Bakshi Ghulam Mohammad, who came to visit him later in the day, that the news was false. Bakshi also gave details of a firing incident at Hira Nagar, in which, according to the Praja Parishad, 18 people, including two women, had been killed. Bakshi claimed it wasn't the police that had fired shots but the agitators. Shots had also been fired at him, he said, but the bullets providentially missed him. He went on to give more details and said that if anything, he had been guilty of using less force against the agitators, and that the police force was angry that the constraints put on them were causing them to suffer beatings and stone pelting at the hands of protesters. Bakshi was categorical that Pandit Prem Nath Dogra and Pandit Durga Chand were not responsible for the violence as much as the people 'sitting in rooms holding meetings, such as Ghansara Singh, Bhagwan Singh, Haveli Ram, Kartar Singh, Ganga Ram' and threatened to arrest them and put them behind bars, whatever the consequences. At this, Karan Singh impressed upon him the need to hold talks and reminded him sharply that the agitation had been going on for two months and the government had not taken any steps to reach out to the agitation leaders. Arbitrary arrests and use of force were not going to solve any problem. Bakshi agreed with him about the need for talks, but obviously, the problem was Sheikh Abdullah.

By 17 January, a new dimension was added to the problem when the Akali Dal, under the leadership of veteran freedom fighter Master Tara Singh of Punjab, announced it was joining hands with the Praja Parishad in the agitation. Master Tara Singh, for his own political purposes, had attended the joint meeting of the Jana Sangh, the Hindu Mahasabha and the Ram Rajya Parishad in Delhi on 10 January 1953, wherein they had resolved to work unitedly. The newly formed Jana Sangh was headed by Dr. Syama Prasad Mukherjee, who had been a Minister in Nehru's first cabinet after independence. Ram Rajya Parishad was led by the maverick Hindu revivalist Swami Karpatri Maharaj. Another important leader who had pitched in for the Praja Parishad was N.C. Chatterjee who was at that time President of the Hindu Mahasabha. When the Akali Dal decided to join hands with all of these groups and the Praja Parishad agitation, it was considered a matter of grave concern as there were fears of the agitation becoming far more aggressive. It was also feared that the Communists would take advantage of the growing bitterness in society. As feared, the police resorted to lathi charges, tear-gassing, and, on several occasions, firing, resulting in injuries and, in some cases, deaths. Gradually, the agitation had also spread to the rural areas. Because of these developments, Karan Singh suggested that some persons of high standing be sent to the State on behalf of Delhi to study the situation on the spot. He suggested the names of Dr. Radhakrishnan and Maulana Azad, as both were considered to be above partisan politics. He was confident that since the two of them commanded great respect among all sections of the people, their efforts might yield results and put an end to the unfortunate consequences of the agitation on all sides.

Prime Minister Nehru wrote to Karan Singh on 14 February 1953 and shared his views about the Jammu situation. He, too, had noticed that Praja Parishad was getting support from national parties based outside the State, which could lead to the agitation assuming an all-India character and becoming entirely communal. To prevent this, he had corresponded with the parties that had come together to support the Praja Parishad agitation, but found that their views on the subject were not only unhelpful but also irritating and belligerent. N.C. Chatterjee, for one, was not only constantly finding fault with Nehru, but in a letter declared that the differences between the Mahasabha and Nehru were so fundamental that a reasonable understanding was not possible. In other words, he had already closed the door on negotiations before they had even begun.

Meanwhile, Syama Prasad Mukherjee had warned that if the government did not explore the possibility of a peaceful settlement, the agitation would spread to other parts of the country. He asked for the leaders of the Praja Parishad who had been arrested by the State government to be released for the negotiations. Meanwhile, Chatterjee continued to apply pressure with threats and ultimatums, even as he demanded that a round-table conference involving the Praja Parishad representatives be held and the agitation could be suspended for that period. But by now Nehru had run out of patience with the aggressive communal speeches and the bullying. The bottom line was that outside communal support was threatening a confrontation on a much larger scale and Nehru, understandably, could not buckle under their pressure. As for Sheikh Abdullah, negotiations with Jammu representatives were out of the question, he was not prepared to give an inch. To Karan Singh, he seemed blinded by his antipathy to the Dogras. It was not surprising that he still did not appreciate the seriousness of the economic havoc that his land reforms had caused in Jammu, becoming a major reason for the intensity of the agitation.

Much of Karan Singh's focus was on how the agitation could be brought to an end and how the Dogras could be assuaged. So, he frankly wrote to Nehru on 23 February 1953 that he was impressed by the statements of Dr. Mukherjee and other senior leaders in the Parliament. Dr Mukherjee had offered to withdraw—not just suspend—the agitation if the arrested Praja Parishad workers were released and invited to a round table conference on the subject. But he lamented the fact that Sheikh Abdullah was adamant about the 'absolute impossibility' of his meeting with the Praja Parishad leaders. He pointed out to Nehru—as Karan Sangh had done in his letter—that, after all, if the Praja Parishad leaders had not 'foolishly boycotted' the elections, and had been elected to the Assembly, then whether Sheikh Abdullah liked it or not, he would have been discussing the matter on the floor of the Assembly with them. He added that 'in a matter in which the whole future of the country is involved, I feel that we should rise above our predilections to serve the interests of the country'. He said that if Sheikh Abdullah were to invite the political leaders, not in a gesture of surrender, but to explain the whole situation, then the chances of a settlement were good.

Karan Singh was aware that mere meetings would not solve problems; therefore, he drafted a road map to be followed. To begin with, he suggested that since there were misgivings in Jammu about the direction that the Constitution-making was taking, a period for finalising it should be announced. But it should also be ensured that it was drafted in the context of the Delhi Agreement. In his opinion, a three-month period should suffice for this exercise, but it could be extended. Simultaneously, a committee consisting of people mostly from Jammu should be set up to work out a system of provincial autonomy. The committee should submit its recommendations, and based on this report, provincial autonomy should be adopted in the new Constitution. After the framing of the Constitution, fresh elections should be held, but before that, the Assembly should pass a resolution confirming the accession of the State to India. To heal the wounds of the recent period, the appointment of an impartial investigation committee would be very useful. This committee would look into all the incidents of firing in Jammu Province. He argued that such an inquiry was required as the Government claimed that only 11 persons were killed in the firing, but the widespread conviction of the people was of many more. An impartial inquiry would put an end to speculation. But he cautioned that those chosen to conduct the inquiry should be people of eminence and integrity and suggested two retired judges, one each from the State and from any other part of India.

He informed Prime Minister Nehru that at that particular time, a demand for an investigation had overshadowed all other demands, which showed how exercised the people were over firings and deaths, and that it needed to be addressed as a priority. He also wrote that the grievances and difficulties that had arisen due to economic reasons should be addressed at the earliest. He pointed out that, as it was, some of the economic grievances had already been referred to the Wazir Committee set up in January 1953, and it had validated the objections of 'Yuvraj Karan Singh' about differing productivity and fertility of land in Jammu and the Valley. It had recommended that the ceiling limit be raised to thirty-eight acres in Jammu and twenty eight acres in Kashmir. Also, it had recommended the abolition of the *Mujawaza*, a kind of food grains tax. All of these interventions were urgent. If timely steps were not taken, Karan Singh warned, the State would 'drift into further violence, bitterness, and disruption'.

By the middle of March, it appeared that his views had

finally begun to prevail. He had, by that time, built a good rapport with Bakshi Ghulam Mohammad, Deputy Prime Minister in Sheikh Abdullah's government, who favoured a close working relationship with the Centre and was free of the Kashmiri chauvinism of hardliners like Mirza Afzal Beg, and of the Sheikh himself. He had good relations with some Dogra leaders of of Jammu as well. Karan Singh's old friend D.P. Dhar, a Deputy Minister in the Sheikh Abdullah government, had also assumed greater importance because of his direct access to Nehru and his ability to effectively communicate with the civil and military administration. Because of them and a few others in the State Government, it began to appear for a while that there could be some movement towards dialogue so that temperatures on all sides could be brought down a little. But it was a false hope.

Karan Singh continued to try. In a letter of 27 March to Nehru he wrote: 'What really disturbs me is the fact that the gulf between Jammu and Kashmir has widened tremendously over the last few months…Neither of the parties seems to quite realize the implications of this, and I fear that we may reap a very bitter harvest in years to come.' He felt only Nehru, given his statesmanly qualities and his sentimental attachment to Kashmir, could find a way out of the challenges that had arisen because of the Jammu agitation and Sheikh Abdullah's attitude. But even Nehru could not do very much without the cooperation of the State Government. Being a Dogra and a representative of the dynasty that commanded universal respect in Jammu, people expected Karan Singh to influence the State Government as the Sadr-e-Riyasat. They did not realize—and their leaders would not tell them—that he was a Head with no real powers. He could do nothing more than issue appeals and try to convince Nehru to move towards the negotiating table, but here again, even if Nehru agreed to talks with all parties, including the Praja Parishad, Sheikh Abdullah would simply stay away. Sometimes it appeared to Karan Singh that the Sheikh had deliberately become intransigent in order to prove to the Dogras how powerless and helpless they had become in the changed circumstances. He seemed determined to humiliate them, and marginalize them completely.

11

A Suspicious Death

In March 1953, a Congress of Commonwealth Universities was to be held in Cambridge in July, and the Syndicate of the Jammu and Kashmir University requested Karan Singh to represent it. Sheikh Abdullah was also keen that he represent the State University. Karan Singh informed Prime Minister Nehru of his desire to also visit France and Switzerland along with his wife, and that he would be away for six weeks. He said he wanted to see Europe's great cities before the next world war destroyed them!

Nehru responded endorsing the idea and asked him to send him his tour programme so that the Indian missions abroad could be informed of any assistance he may need. But primarily, Nehru's mind was occupied with developments in the State, particularly in the context of the Praja Parishad agitation. But more significantly, he wrote in this letter that a group of people in the National Conference government had begun to have reservations about Sheikh Abdullah's authoritarian ways and also his commitment to the State's integration with India. They did not want to be publicly quoted, but they had seen that the Sheikh was making efforts to wriggle out of the understanding that he had with India regarding the Centre-State relations. Karan Singh had gathered something to this effect from his interactions with Bakshi Ghulam Mohammad, D.P. Dhar and Girdhari Lal Dogra—like him, an admirer of Nehru—who was Sheikh Abdullah's Finance Minister. What Nehru was telling him in his letter now confirmed that impression. Nehru said he had been aware of the restlessness among some of Sheikh Abdullah's colleagues and he had made some enquiries, following which, Bakshi and Dogra had called on him and informed him of something they proposed to do. Nehru said that perhaps in deference to the constitutional position that Karan Singh was holding, they had not shared their plan with him. But they had discussed it in detail with Nehru and he had endorsed it. But he had ruled out his and the Indian Government's direct involvement in the matter.

In the rest of the letter, Nehru dealt with some of the issues Karan Singh had raised, like police excesses against the Jammu agitators. He condemned the excesses but said the reports that had been circulated by the Praja Parishad were wildly exaggerated. He believed that the Parishad office in Pathankot was circulating every rumour widely as if that were a verified fact. He also expressed serious concern about efforts by Dr Shyama Prasad Mukherjee and others to convert the State agitation into a national one, and that in this Mukherjee was getting wholehearted support from the cadre of the RSS. Most of these volunteers were drawn from Kanpur, Gorakhpur, etc., he said, and were generally a very poor lot and were being misled and forced into the movement as foot soldiers. Nehru lamented that the agitation had hurt India's interests internationally as well.

In his effort to prevail upon Nehru to hold discussions with Dr. Mukherjee, Karan Singh had in an earlier letter drawn his attention to the softening of the stand by Dr. Mukherjee, as seen in his speeches in the Parliament. But Nehru was not impressed, and said he believed the real reason for Mukherjee's softening was dissension within the ranks of the agitation's national leaders in Delhi, including Dr Mukherjee and N.C. Chatterjee, and that they were looking for a way out so that they could withdraw the agitation. He further said that though he would welcome the withdrawal of the agitation, he did not want the agitation leaders in Jammu and Delhi to pretend that they were the peacemakers. He also said that in this he had the support of the Home Minister Pandit Govind Vallabh Pant, who believed that there should be no dealings with parties like the Jana Sangh and the Praja Parishad, for what they were doing was nothing short of treason. It was obvious that Nehru and Pant were both worried about the fallout of the agitation in the rest of the country—it could drive a wedge between Hindus and Muslims and lead to dangerous sectarian divisions. Both men believed that this was the ultimate plan of the national groups that had joined the Parishad in its agitation.

Apart from the agitation, another factor causing anxiety in Jammu was the future of the State Forces. It was no secret that if Sheikh Abdullah could have had his way, he would have disbanded them long ago. Three Units had already been disbanded, rendering about 3000 people unemployed. But this time, the Yuvraj as Sadr-e-Riyasat was dealing with the subject, and he had a sympathetic ear in Delhi—an advantage that his father never had. The State Forces units had already been put under the administrative control of the Indian Army, and they had given a laudable account of gallantry while standing shoulder-to-shoulder with the Indian Army on the frontline. It was accepted that they would be integrated and absorbed into the Indian Army but the general principle, as applied to the other armies of the princely states, was that all the men, officers as well as other ranks, were to be screened to determine if they were up to the standards set for the Indian Army. Sheikh Abdullah thought the whole issue was pointless. He had a simple solution. He had repeatedly accused the State Forces of unleashing atrocities on the Muslims in Jammu and massacring them during Partition, and now he brought up all that again and the political and economic aspects of the issue, and effectively argued for the complete disbandment of the Forces.

Karan Singh, however, argued with reason and logic and wrote to Nehru on the subject on 1 April 1953: 'Their unique record of service over the last six years in which they have worked shoulder to shoulder in the defence of the nation as an integral part of the Indian Army singles them out for special treatment. Their case does not deserve to be treated on the analogy of other State troops.' He further argued that any further 'pruning and disbandment' would cause unnecessary and undesirable political repercussions as well as economic distress to the disbanded soldiers. It would also be unfair to those who were already anxious and agonizing about their future in the new nation. As it was, thousands of Dogras were still coming to terms with the consequences of the earlier disbandment, and this was tragic for people who had always placed military service on the highest pedestal of national service. He conceded that there could be problems arising out of the absorption and fixing of seniority in the Indian Army, but such minor irritants were far outweighed by their and of their dependents' loyalty to India.

His advocacy for a just cause did not yield immediate results, but Nehru did promise that a fair decision would be taken, and it would be ensured that demobilized soldiers were provided alternate employment. On this assurance, that matter rested for the time being as the attention riveted back to the twin challenges of the agitation and the reluctance of Sheikh Abdullah to implement the Delhi Agreement. Both fed upon each other; the greater the resistance offered by Sheikh Abdullah to the implementation of the Agreement, the greater was the anger and resentment among the Dogras, and consequently, the more intense the agitation.

A new dimension was added to all this when Dr Shyama Prasad Mukherjee decided to defy the 'permit system' required for entry into the State by Indian citizens and was arrested as he tried to cross the State border on 11 May 1953. He was taken to Srinagar and was lodged in a separate accommodation. Karan Singh had met Prime Minister Nehru to discuss the subject of the Jammu agitation on 21 April. Now, after Dr Mukherjee's arrest, he met Nehru again, on 23 May. As before, he spoke at length about the situation, particularly the brutal and criminal behaviour of the Punjab Police in suppressing the agitators. Because of the continued indifference of the Government of India, and callous treatment by the State Government that was creating more ill-will and hatred, Karan Singh confessed that his position had fast become untenable as the people of Jammu questioned him all the time about what he was doing as the Sadr-e-Riyasat and of what use was he to the people of Jammu. As it was, many of them still felt that he had betrayed both the Maharaja—his own father—and the dynasty, and now, if he were to remain a silent and helpless spectator, it would be very difficult for him to continue in office. Pressure on him had mounted considerably after Dr Mukherjee's arrest—a national leader of that stature had come to support the people of Jammu but he had been arrested and put in jail by Sheikh Abdullah, and the Sadr-e-Riyasat was again being accused of doing nothing; of being a traitor to his own province and people.

In the meeting, Karan Singh also emphasized, again, the

Maharaja Hari Singh.

Maharani Tara Devi.

The royal couple with their newborn, Yuvraj Karan Singh, March 1931.

Baby Karan Singh being taken to the Jammu palace in a car with his English nurse, Doris Trunchell.

Mother and son in Jammu, 1932.

Yuvraj Karan Singh—Tiger—with his childhood companions Digby and Bilti.

The three young boys learning to play polo.

The Yuvraj in royal attire, 1940/41.

In 1942, the year he went to Doon School.

One of the many demanding horse-riding sessions that the Yuvraj was required to submit to.

Yuvraj Karan Singh at age 16.

Young Karan Singh in New York, 1948, walking with the help of a cane, following his recovery after a year in hospital. With him are his two companions and support team, Brigadier N.S. Rawat, an officer of the Jammu and Kashmir State Armed Forces (centre) and Captain Ranjit Singh, an aide of Maharaja Hari Singh (right).

In Hyde Park, New York, with Eleanor Roosevelt, former First Lady of the United States (fifth from right) and her son Elliott Roosevelt (far right), January 1949.

Karan Singh shortly after his return to India, with his father (standing to his left). Also in the picture are the two officers who were with him through the difficult year in New York—Brigadier Rawat (sitting, second from right) and Captain Ranjit Singh (sitting, third from left).

Regent of Jammu and Kashmir, at age 18.

With Jawaharlal Nehru in the late 1940s (in the background is the legendary photo journalist Homai Vyarawalla).

With Dr Rajendra Prasad in the mid-1960s, during his second term as President of India.

With Sheikh Abdullah (second from left in the photo above) and Nehru, in October 1949, at the first formal convocation of the Jammu and Kashmir University, Srinagar—where, being Head of State, Karan Singh became Chancellor.

Karan Singh and his father, Maharaja Hari Singh, with C. Rajagopalachari, probably in 1949 or '50

Yasho Rajya Lakshmi of Nepal marries Karan Singh, 1950.

The young couple after the marriage ceremony.

The newlyweds *(centre)* with Maharaja Hari Singh and Maharani Tara Devi.

As the first (and only) Sadr-e-Riyasat, walking into the Jammu and Kashmir Constituent Assembly with the Prime Minister, Sheikh Abdullah, 1952.

Saluting the Indian flag as Sadr-e-Riyasat on Independence Day, 1953.

The Sadr-e-Riyasat with the people of Jammu.

In Leh, wearing the traditional Ladakhi dress.

Karan Singh and Yasho Rajya Lakshmi in the early 1950s with Nehru, at Teen Murti House, New Delhi.

Karan Singh and Yasho Rajya Lakshmi—Asha—in the early 1950s.

The First Lady of Jammu and Kashmir, Yasho Rajya Lakshmi, welcoming the Soviet Premier, Nikita Khrushchev, to Kashmir in 1955.

Khrushchev and his delegation in a procession through the streets of Srinagar, accompanied by Sadr-e-Riyasat Karan Singh and Prime Minister Bakshi Ghulam Mohammad.

Karan Singh and Nehru with His Holiness the Dalai Lama in Delhi, on his first visit to India, 1956.

Karan Singh, in his capacity as Chancellor of Banaras Hindu University, presenting an Honorary Doctorate Degree to Prime Minister Lal Bahadur Shastri, 1964.

Karan Singh with Indira Gandhi and G.M. Sadiq at Dachigam, Srinagar in the 1960s.

Karan Singh (second from right) in Mirtola Ashram with his gurus Sri Krishnaprem and Sri Madhav Ashish (third and fourth from the right, respectively).

With President Zakir Husain, 1968.

Karan Singh and Yasho Rajya Lakshmi in Srinagar with Maharani Tara Devi and their three children, Jyotsna, Vikramaditya and the youngest, Ajatshatru, in the late 1960s.

Karan Singh and Yasho Rajya Lakshmi with King Baudouin and Queen Fabiola of Belgium during their visit to the Raja of Benares (standing next to Karan Singh), 1970.

The couple in Moscow, on an official visit to the Soviet Union in the 1960s.

Karan Singh being sworn in by President Dr. Radhakrishnan as the youngest Cabinet Minister in Indira Gandhi's cabinet, 1967. His first portfolio was Tourism & Civil Aviation

Karan Singh, as India's Tourism and Civil Aviation Minister,
and his wife during their visit to Greece in 1969.

Travelling around India as Minister of Tourism.

With his wife and the then Chief Minister of Andhra Pradesh, P.V. Narasimha Rao, after inaugurating the construction of Tirupati Airport in 1970.

At the United Nations Conference on the Human Environment in Stockholm, 1972.

Being interviewed by the BBC, sometime in the early 1970s.

Being cheered and greeted by people at the Jammu Tawi Railway Station, probably during its inauguration in 1975.

Karan Singh and Asha, enthusiastic world travellers, in Egypt *(above)* and China *(below)*.

Karan Singh and Asha with their children Jyotsna, Vikramaditya (standing, right) and Ajatshatru in the early 1970s.

With Prime Minister Indira Gandhi as she inaugurates the Amar Mahal Museum and Library in Jammu on 13 April 1975.

need for speedy absorption of the State Forces in the Indian Army without screening. That was not only fair, it would also assure a segment of Jammu that justice was being done to them. Nehru agreed with all that Karan Singh said, including his accusations against the police, about which he had already written to the State's Home Minister and Deputy PM Bakshi Ghulam Mohammad. But about dealing with the agitation and the arrest of Dr Mukherjee, he could do little. He could not interfere in the working of the State's government. He could only advise them.

This, Karan Singh knew, Nehru had tried to do many times. Only recently, on his visit to Srinagar that had coincided with the session of the National Conference between 16 and 21 May, Nehru had invited all the leaders of the party to talk about the situation and warn them of the dangers that lay ahead if the present turbulence and division in the State were not handled with maturity by both the State and Central governments. While the others listened, Nehru found that Sheikh Abdullah was silent and seemed hostile. He remained recalcitrant throughout the Indin Prime Minister's stay in Srinagar. Not surprisingly, Nehru had returned to Delhi a disillusioned man. But he was still not willing to give up on the man he had trusted and considered a friend, and had sent Maulana Azad to talk to Abdullah, but he too returned after being ignored and insulted during the Eid prayer.

And yet, Nehru continued to hope. The problem, as Karan Singh saw it, was that for Nehru, the Kashmir issue still hinged on his relationship with Sheikh Abdullah, and as most observers could see, the Sheikh had been using the question of a plebiscite to good effect as a means of blackmail. Nehru had created this monstrous problem for himself in his idealism. By sticking to Mountbatten's conditional acceptance of Hari Singh's accession and allowing the matter to go the UN, he had given his unreliable friend a potent weapon. Now that friendship was showing signs of strain and Nehru was getting disenchanted, but he had put all the eggs in the Sheikh's basket. At the end of a recent conversation with Karan Singh, Nehru had conceded, 'I quite agree that if our agreements are thrown overboard or something like that, your position becomes absolutely impossible.' Nehru appeared hurt and bewildered by the actions of his friend and protégé.

There was another portent in the air that was a fair indication of the direction the wind was blowing. The question about the non-implementation of the Delhi Agreement, which sought to make the terms of the Accession more balanced, was being asked of Nehru in and outside Parliament, and he had no answer. He had therefore written a letter to Sheikh Abdullah about it, as he wanted the matter resolved before he left for a foreign tour and also attend the coronation of Queen Elizabeth II. To his bewilderment, Sheikh Abdullah did not even acknowledge his letter, let alone reply.

In the meantime, Sheikh Abdullah's dictatorial style of functioning and his efforts to rescind the commitments he had made to India had begun to cause unease among his longtime colleagues in the State, too. Bakshi Ghulam Mohammad knew better than Sheikh Abdullah what had happened to the Valley when the invaders had arrived. Sheikh Abdullah had then been enjoying the hospitality of Nehru in Delhi, while the innocent people of Muzaffarabad, Uri and Baramulla had borne the brunt of the atrocities and barbarism of the invaders. During those dark hours, it was Bakshi Ghulam Mohammad who had rallied the people in support of the Indian Army, which had made a timely intervention to save Srinagar and the rest of the Valley. Therefore, he realized very early that the well-being and survival of Kashmir were within the safety net of India. The differences between the two stalwarts of the National Conference, which Nehru had learned about a couple of months ago, had come out in the open by now. Bakshi had a fair hold on the party, and the pro-India faction had begun to gain a majority not only in the Working Committee of the National Conference but also in the State Assembly.

Even as the internal struggle within the National Conference was intensifying, Karan Singh had a private meeting with Sheikh Abdullah, which gave him the clear impression, too, that the Sheikh had decided to go back on the solemn agreement with India. These views had also been expressed by Abullah in public meetings in Jammu as well as in Srinagar. He claimed that communal violence in Jammu and the inability of the central government to quell the 'communal activities' in Jammu had forced him to reassess the situation and relationship with India. He also pointed out that the State had acceded only on the three subjects of Foreign Affairs, Defence and Communications when Maharaja Hari Singh signed the Instrument of Accession, and therefore, he claimed, the State enjoyed complete autonomy in all other matters.

To achieve his reframed goal, Sheikh Abdullah resorted to the same technique that he had used to marginalize the Maharaja. When he wanted to wriggle out of an agreed position, he would come back to Srinagar and encourage a debate within the party regarding the agreement he had entered into in Delhi in such a manner that he would have an excuse to go back to Delhi to inform the Central Government that his party was not prepared to accept the terms of the agreements they had made. In the past, he had succeeded as the Maharaja could be sacrificed, but the Delhi Agreement signed in 1952 was a different matter and going back on it would make India's position embarrassing, and also potentially damage the communal atmosphere in the country. These developments had also begun to cause unease among the Kashmiri Pandits of the Valley, many of whom had been hitherto closely associated with the National Conference. But in the wake of Sheikh Abdullah's attempts to renege on his commitments to India, this minority community had begun to panic.

On June 1, Karan Singh sent a report to Nehru, who was in London to attend the coronation ceremony of Queen Elizabeth II, warning him about the turn things were taking in the State. Some days later, he noted in his diary that after his last meeting with Sheikh Abdullah, it had become clear that was openly 'refuting all agreements with India'. The Sheikh had also said 'that 'Panditji and Mukherjee wanted the same thing—integration, only their methods were different...and that the only way was to completely get out of the Indian Constitution and revise the relationship with India.' Karan Singh also noted that there were sharp divisions within the National Conference, and that a showdown was imminent.

By the 7th of June, Karan Singh was mentally prepared for any such showdown and to act decisively if it happened before the return of Prime Minister Nehru from Europe in a few days. That afternoon, Vijayalaxmi Pandit, Nehru's sister who was President of the UN General Assembly at the time, visited Karan Singh with her two daughters and Padmaja Naidu, and during their conversations she told him that their movements were being watched and that Sheikh Abdullah was trying to force them out of Srinagar as soon as possible. Mrs Pandit also said that she had come to know that Sheikh Abdullah was preparing to deliver a speech on the occasion of Eid with statements which she had gathered would be most undesirable from India's perspective. According to her, Sheikh Abdullah had compared himself to Jinnah during a recent meeting of the National Conference Working Committee, perhaps hinting that he would get Kashmiris a separate homeland, just as Jinnah had got Pakistan for the Subcontinent's Muslims. Both Mrs Pandit and Padmaja Naidu agreed that 'if anything happened to Kashmir, it would kill Panditji, literally and not just politically and figuratively.'

For dinner the same evening, Karan Singh had Major General Jai Singh of the Indian Army over, and both went over the possible crisis that could arise due to any action by Sheikh Abdullah, and the steps that would then have to be taken. He found the General a reliable man who would deliver in case any emergency arose. Talking to the General, Karan Singh felt that Sheikh Abdullah had started down a path from which he would not turn back, no matter how much Nehru or anyone else tried to persuade him. So, the earlier the showdown took place, the better it would be for all concerned. Karan Singh wrote in his diary that night: 'I have decided that when Panditji comes back, if nothing has happened till then, I will give him an ultimatum and try and force a showdown. I have become convinced that unless we tighten and consolidate India's position here very soon, the matter will be out of our hands. It is now or never. Either you wash your hands of Kashmir...or, act and present a fait accompli to the world.' With each passing day after that, the tension and excitement grew. Karan Singh's dreams of those days reflect his state of mind—one night, he dreamt of a boy standing over him with a knife, ready to stab him, and when Karan Singh asked him who had sent him, the boy said, 'Sheikh sahib'.

By 19 June 1953, events picked up pace. Bakshi Ghulam Mohammad had taken a firm decision. When he met Karan Singh, he informed the Sadr-e-Riyasat that he was about to arrest Karra and Hamdani, two pro-Pakistan leaders, for inciting violence and acting against the State, but Sheikh Abdullah had stopped him. He also said the Sheikh was trying to change the portfolios of those ministers who disagreed with him, but he, Bakshi, and his other colleagues of similar thinking were determined that they would neither allow him to change their portfolios nor would they resign if he asked them to do so. The only course left for him then, Bakshi told Karan Singh categorically, would be to resign, and if he did that he would move to displace the Sheikh and form a new government, because he and his supporters were confident of a majority in the Working Committee of the National Conference as well as in the State Assembly. Bakshi also disclosed that he had arranged for the President of the Praja Parishad, Pandit Prem Nath Dogra, to be brought to Srinagar and a meeting had been arranged between Dogra and Shyama Prasad Mukherjee. He said Hukum Singh, a Member of Parliament from the Akali Party, had also met Dr Mukherjee. Karan Singh was both surprised and delighted by the speed with which things were moving. He knew, of course, that Bakshi would have told him all this only after first informing Nehru and getting his consent to take the Sadr-e-Riyasat into confidence.

Later, Hukum Singh also called upon Karan Singh and gave his assessment about the situation in the State. He said he was afraid that Sheikh Abdullah was not at all interested in solving the problem that had arisen due to the Jammu agitation and was exploiting it to achieve his own goals. He had also understood that the Bakshi group was strong in the National Conference but was afraid that Sheikh Abdullah, with the support of the communal Islamic elements in the Valley, would try and weaken Bakshi.

Since the Akali Party too had pitched in the agitation, Karan Singh suggested to Hukum Singh that, in the interests of the country, the agitation should be suspended as a gesture of goodwill and magnanimity, and that this would greatly strengthen Bakshi's hand and also his own. He was also confident that if the agitation was suspended, it would be easier to persuade Nehru to take a reasonable stand, and the real communal forces of the Hindu right-wing that were exploiting the situation would stand exposed. Importantly, it would give respite to the leaders of the Praja Parishad who also appeared to have painted themselves into a corner.

On 22 June 1953, the situation took a sudden turn when Karra and Hamadani addressed a congregation in Srinagar, and slogans of 'Pakistan zindabad' and '*Hind fauj jao jao* (Indian Army go away)' were raised, giving Bakshi the excuse to arrest Karra and Hamdani against the wishes of Sheikh Abdullah. The latter's resistance to the arrests lent credence to the widely held belief that the congregation and the raising of anti-India slogans were masterminded by him. Meanwhile, Col. I.S. Hassanwalia, Assistant Director of the country's Intelligence Bureau, also called upon the Sadr-e-Riyasat and informed him that a daily situation report was being sent to Nehru, who was furious at the perfidy of Sheikh Abdullah but thought that before action was taken, he ought to be thoroughly discredited. Nehru also wanted that, before anything was done, Bakshi should ensure mass support. Karan Singh wrote to Nehru that the time for 'waiting for a favourable public opinion before acting is gone. Now we must act first, and then everything else could be arranged. If we do not act immediately, the whole game will be lost'. The bold talk apart, the final decision had of course to be taken by Nehru. Privately, impatient for a swift resolution, Karan Singh was critical of his hero and mentor, observing in his diary that Nehru's 'Kashmir policy of appeasement has been a total, thorough, absolute and dramatic failure. He must choose between giving up Kashmir (which I feel will not only be his political fall but also his physical end, as the shock will kill him) or acting firmly and swiftly'.

The 23rd of June 1953 began lazily. Karan Singh was late waking up and it was 10 a.m. by the time he had finished his morning puja. Just as he was finishing the puja, Yuvrani Asha came, trying to say something, but he waved her away. No sooner had he finished, the Yuvrani came again to inform him that Vijayalaxmi Pandit was ringing up to enquire if the lunch party they had planned was still on. Baffled by the query, he asked why the lunch would be off, and she, equally surprised, asked him if he did not know that Dr Mukherjee had died. At first he thought that Mukherjee, the Governor of Bengal, had passed away. But when he realized who had died, he was stunned. His first reaction was that Dr Shyama Prasad Mukherjee had been poisoned on the orders of Sheikh Abdullah. So overwrought was he after months of tension when he had felt besieged, rejected by his own father and his community, pushed and challenged by Sheikh Abdullah and, despite Nehru's constant support, utterly alone, that his mind was inflamed and he turned instinctively to the image of Goddess Kali in his puja room in a rage. He records in his diary, '[I] asked her if there was any justice or goodness left in this world…[and] prayed that if they have been treacherous enough to do such a deed, they should be very soon wiped off the face of the earth.' In his interview for this biography, he says, 'It was an extreme reaction. I had not realized how great a toll the events of the past year had taken on me psychologically. Some kind of explosion was waiting to happen and it did that morning. But I still believe the tragedy could have been prevented. He was a remarkable man, whether you agreed with him or not. He did not deserve to go like that.'

When he left the puja room, he was in a state of turmoil. After a while, when he was in a calmer state, he reflected on the whole affair and concluded that it could not have been a murder. Instead of gaining any advantage, Sheikh Abdullah's people would have landed themselves in a difficult situation by attempting anything so insane. Moreover, Sardar Hukum Singh had also told him that when he met Dr Mukherjee, he had lauded the State Government for the manner in which he had been provided and cared for in detention. But the bottom line was that the world would only know that a detenue without trial had died while in custody.

Karan Singh's mind went back to the two meetings that he had had with Dr Mukherjee. The first meeting had been a year ago, when Mukherjee had come to Srinagar to meet Sheikh Abdullah, and then, only a few months ago, in Delhi. That second meeting had been on Dr Mukherjee's invitation. It had been a cloak-and-dagger affair as Karan Singh had left Imperial Hotel secretly, giving the slip to his security, and met the Mahasabha leader in his home and engaged in a long conversation regarding the affairs affecting the State. He had found Dr Mukherjee to be not only youthful, with his sparkling eyes, but had also been so impressed by his demeanour and knowledge, that he had believed Mukherjee might even succeed Nehru as Prime Minister of India. Now, deeply affected by the leader's death, Karan Singh sent a telegram of condolence to his only daughter. It was only later that he was informed that Dr Mukherjee was also survived by an aged mother. He was very upset that Sheikh Abdullah and many others had gone to the airport as the body was flown out, but no one had thought it necessary to inform him, the Sadr-e-Riyasat.

In the evening, Sheikh Abdullah came to see him and could do nothing more than offer lame excuses regarding his inability to inform the Head of the State so that he could have accompanied the body to the airport. Karan Singh was further upset when the Sheikh remarked that if Dr Mukherjee had to die, why could he not have died somewhere else and not in their State. It seemed an insensitive remark, although, considered objectively, an understandable one, for the tragic event would certainly not make Sheikh Abdullah's and his government's life easier. Karan Singh used the occasion to discuss the current political situation with the Sheikh. At one point he asked plainly if he was comfortable with the proposals of the Delhi Agreement, and Sheikh Abdullah answered with an emphatic 'No!' He argued that the Kashmiri Muslim was not at all prepared to go beyond the Instrument of Accession in any manner, which Karan Singh thought was a spurious argument since the common man had not been told of the economic advantages that would follow full integration with India. He was further shocked to find that Abdullah had started to equate India and Pakistan, and when reminded of what had happened when the tribal raiders had unleashed havoc in the Valley, he had shrugged that away by saying, 'If we want a settlement, we must forget past history'.

12

'Chit of a Boy' Strikes

ON 26 JUNE 1953, Karan Singh wrote a letter to Prime Minister Nehru, warning him that since his last letter of 10 June, the situation in the State had further deteriorated, and unless firm and speedy action was taken, it would become 'irretrievable'.

Karan Singh was to learn later, from B.N. Mullik, Director of the Intelligence Bureau, that when Maulana Azad returned from Srinagar in mid-May, after failing to even meet Sheikh Abdullah, the Maulana had heard and seen enough to understand how serious things were and had advised Nehru to dismiss Sheikh Abdullah before he got up to more serious mischief. Among the many indications of this had been a recent visit by the American politician Adlai Stevenson, head of the Democratic Party. He had long meetings with Sheikh Abdullah and it was generally believed that the Sheikh was seeking American support for an independent Kashmir.

Soon after that, Nehru had gone abroad to attend the coronation of Queen Elizabeth and visit other countries. While he was away, Sheikh Abdullah grew more strident in his speeches, almost as if he were daring Delhi to react. After Nehru returned, he addressed the issue in a long letter to the Sheikh. He warned him of the serious consequences of his actions, but also appealed for mutual understanding. He repeated his invitation for discussions and suggested that Abdullah bring along his confidant Mirza Afzal Beg—who had a strong hold on the masses in the Valley and was now Revenue Minister—and Bakshi Ghulam Mohammad as observers. He added that 'recent developments have, however, led me to think that you have either changed your mind completely or are not clear about your thinking…You told me that there were only two courses open for Kashmir: either full integration or full autonomy, whatever that might mean. I did not agree with you on this, nor do I agree with you even now, but there are many other middle courses. To me, it has been a major surprise that a settlement arrived between us should be bypassed or repudiated, regardless of the merits. That strikes at the root of all confidence, personal or international. No treaty would be worth the paper it is written on if it is to be repudiated soon after. So far as I am concerned, no power in the world would make me go back on the pledge that I gave in that Agreement. If my Parliament or my people in India repudiate that, they repudiate me…It is always painful to part company after long years of comradeship, but if our conscience so tells us, or in our view an overriding national interest requires, then there can be no help for it…'

Nehru had also written in that letter, of which Karan Singh learned later, that Sheikh Abdullah's government was no longer harmonious and pulled in different directions. He also noted that his organisation, the National Conference, was disintegrating, and warned that if that happened, then Kashmir would relapse into sectarianism and political backwardness. Sheikh Abdullah, as expected, refuted the allegations and asserted that he had 'been in intimate touch with Kashmir and its people for the last 22 years' and he knew what they wanted; there was no confusion in his mind. It was obvious he knew exactly what he was doing. It was only Nehru who was vainly clinging to a friendship that had dried under the scorching heat of power and ambition.

Even as Karan Singh, Bakshi and others, like Vijayalaxmi Pandit, Maulana Azad and Rafi Ahmed Kidwai—a veteran Congressman who was Nehru's trusted political confidant—were trying to convince Nehru that his friend of yesteryears had drifted away from him, Nehru continued to hope that wisdom would dawn upon Sheikh Abdullah. At the same time, Abdullah had found a very influential ally in Delhi. Mridula Sarabhai, an old and committed Gandhian, whose opinion carried considerable weight because of her moral authority, became a very vocal supporter of Sheikh Abdullah. Sarabhai tried to convince both the Congress stalwarts and confidants of Nehru that if Nehru and Abdullah would sit down for a heart-to-heart talk, an amicable decision could be taken. But by the middle of July, even she was shocked when Sheikh Abdullah refused to come to Delhi on Nehru's invitation by saying that 'no useful purpose can be achieved by carrying on [about] oft-talked subjects'.

The Sheikh had made up his mind, and he made three speeches that left nothing to the imagination. The first was in Mujahid Manzil, the headquarters of the National Conference, the second in Khanyar and the third in Ganderbal. In all three speeches, he told his audience that the future of Muslims could not be safe in India, where communal forces were dominant. Because of this, he believed that Kashmir needed to re-address its relationship with India. To Karan Singh and other observes it was now obvious that he had used Nehru and India to achieve his ambition of an independent or autonomous Kashmir. To begin with, he had manipulated Nehru in a way that he had made himself a party to the endorsement of Accession, even though legally only the Ruler had that authority. Later, he had said in the

Constituent Assembly that he and the National Conference had endorsed the State's accession to India because of the shared ideals of secularism and economic policies. But now it was apparent that the endorsement was a ploy to prepare the Kashmiri Muslims for his plan to keep Pakistan out of any option for them. Having achieved that goal, he had now unfolded a plan to get out of any relationship with India, and have an independent Kashmir.

Caught in a Hamlet-like dilemma, on 28 June 1953 Nehru wrote Sheikh Abdullah a long letter in which he could not hide his turmoil. He wrote, among other things: 'Thus far I have proceeded on a basis of friendship and confidence in you and have been vain enough to expect the same approach from you. Whether that is justified now or not is for you to say. Individual relations should not count in national affairs, and yet they do count and make a difference.' Nehru had written a long letter, and the reply too was equally long, and both appeared moved by emotions, but neither Nehru nor Abdullah lost sight of where they were heading. Sheikh Abdullah reciprocated the view of Nehru and wrote, 'I agree that personal relationship between individuals should not be a consideration where larger national interests are involved.' Thus, both knew that they had burnt their bridges and that it was time for them to part, and yet they delayed the final thrust.

Meanwhile, the rift within the National Conference had come into the open completely. Blinded by ambition and the arrogance of power, Sheikh Abdullah had not quite realized that he had lost the support of his colleagues of many years. He had the strong support of hardliners led by Mirza Afzal Beg. But they were a small minority. Most of the other senior leaders and cabinet ministers, including Girdhari Lal Dogra, Shamlal Saraf, Ghulam Mohammad Sadiq and D.P. Dhar, had aligned with the Deputy Prime Minister, Bakshi Ghulam Mohammad. Bakshi was in regular touch with Karan Singh, meeting him at his home. D.P. Dhar, who had an excellent relationship with Nehru, was a frequent visitor, too. While they kept Karan Singh and Delhi informed about the conflict within the National Conference, Karan Singh waited in anticipation of a green signal from Delhi.

Bakshi and Mirza Afzal Beg went to Delhi to meet Nehru. Beg represented Sheikh Abdullah, who had excused himself by saying that the present atmosphere was not conducive for talks. Before going, Bakshi told Karan Singh that he was going to serve notice on Nehru regarding the urgency to act. G.M. Sadiq, who was in Srinagar, was equally determined that it was time for action. That day, Karan Singh noted in his diary: 'I am fully convinced that unless Panditji decides to act immediately, we may have to take the initiative ourselves. Otherwise, Kashmir, India and the sub-continent may very easily be set ablaze…I shall either act or quit, and then, in all fairness, tell the people of India clearly how their interests are being completely ruined.' In the whole affair, Karan Singh's position was extremely delicate and difficult. His relations with his father had been strained; the people of Jammu, whose representative he was supposed to be, had been alienated from him after his acceptance of the Sadr-e-Riyasat post and they could not be won back unless he did something spectacular. On the other hand, Sheikh Abdullah was aware that Karan Singh would do all that was possible for him to do in order to thwart his plans, and therefore, the Sheikh would use every chance he got to further embarrass Karan Singh in Jammu. The only support that Karan Singh had was from Nehru and his government in Delhi, and if he failed in his effort to convince them to take action against the Sheikh, he would be left to fend for himself.

C.S. Venkatachar, Secretary in the Central Ministry of States, who was in Kashmir then, also agreed about the need for immediate action and lamented that his Minister, K.N. Katju, was completely ineffective with Nehru. Then there appeared a ray of hope when D.P. Dhar returned from Delhi and reported on his meetings with everyone who could be interested in the Kashmir affair, including leaders of the Communist parties, the Jana Sangh, and of course Panditji. Dhar also appeared optimistic since Rafi Ahmed Kidwai, who had the reputation of a 'doer', had entered the scene. On 12 July 1953 came the depressing news that Nehru had turned down Bakshi's request to act against Sheikh Abdullah immediately. Bakshi had returned dejected and depressed. Karan Singh too was disturbed by the failure, as he was convinced that the Sheikh had made up his mind to demand that the Indian Army be withdrawn from the State. If that happened, there would be so much international focus on Kashmir and Sheikh Abdullah that taking any action against him would become impossible.

Frustrated by Nehru's unwillingness to act, he chose to switch his mind from the political challenges and focus on a visit he had planned to the Amarnath Cave, the famous shrine dedicated to Lord Shiva high up on the Amarnath Mountain, surrounded by glaciers. The strong desire to look inward in times of difficulty had become almost second nature to him after the year in hospital when the image of the Devi had been his greatest comfort. As he was to write years later, 'I have found repeatedly that an outer crisis is an excellent time to deepen one's inner aspiration, that the thicker the battle presses the more significant becomes the voice of the inner charioteer.' Surrounded by the breathtaking beauty of the high Himalayas, he felt uplifted by the majesty of Nature. It was to be one of his earliest 'spiritual', rather than religious, experiences that took him out of himself and connected him with something ineffably vast and liberating: 'The torrent of time slackens, the problems and strife of life pale into insignificance and I am lost in deep contemplation. I cherish a desire in the recesses of my heart to one day build myself a small Ashrama in such surroundings where, with the body and mind made pure and free from the tentacles of desire and fear, ego and attachment...'

By the time he returned from the pilgrimage, there was a quiet and resolute belief that events would, in the end, take the desired course. All that he or any other individual in a similar position could do was to act with courage and conviction.

On 13 July 1953, Sheikh Abdullah made another speech which was yet more proof that he was trying to rally the Kashmiri Muslims behind him in his effort to get out of the constitutional relationship with India. Simultaneously, he was also provoking India to trigger a crisis so that the whole question of accession would be reopened. On 15 July, Khwaja Umar Butt, a local leader, called upon Karan Singh and in a veiled manner castigated his ineffective role as Sadr-e-Riyasat. He pointed out that the situation of the people, economic or otherwise, was much worse than it had been in the past. He said the people expected the Sadr-e-Riyasat to intervene wherever and whenever an injustice took place. He was also of the opinion that India was doing a disservice to the State by not taking a keen interest in the internal functioning of the State Government, so it was, in effect, propping up an inefficient and corrupt regime. On the same day, Bakshi came to see Karan Singh. He apprised him of the political developments and the growing dissension and bitterness within the State cabinet, and said that Sheikh Abdullah could be constitutionally removed from his position through a no-confidence motion in the Assembly. Karan Singh was not entirely convinced this could be achieved so easily. And in any case, he needed clear directions from Delhi.

By then, Rafi Ahmed Kidwai had also concluded that if a crisis of greater magnitude was to be averted—the Kashmir issue was being revived in the UN and other international forums—Sheikh Abdullah needed to be removed from office immediately. Finally, there was an indication that Nehru had made up his mind. Although distraught that his friendship of many years was about to end, and worried that Sheikh Abdullah's dismissal could throw Kashmir into turmoil and that India's position in the UN might be undermined, he had decided that the matter could not be allowed to drift any further. Things began to move fast after this.

Together with advisers from Delhi and in Srinagar, Karan Singh went over all the possibilities. D.P. Dhar was the finest of all the minds involved in the meticulous planning. Major General B.M. Kaul of the Indian Army, who had played a decisive role in the 1948 war with Pakistan over Kashmir, had been drafted to tie up all loose ends about meeting an emergency. Major General Jai Singh and Wazir Lakshman Das were to control the law and order, while P.K. Bamzai was entrusted with the task of managing the flow of information. Delhi's eye on the whole affair was Rafi Ahmed Kidwai, who had sent his Secretary, Jain, for that purpose. All the while, Karan Singh was acutely aware of the high risk in what was being planned. By then, so many people were involved in planning a correct course of action that there was always a possibility of Sheikh Abdullah coming to know of it. In that eventuality, it would not have been past the Sheikh, as the State's Prime Minister, to get the Sadr-e-Riyasat Karan Singh, Deputy Prime Minister Bakshi Ghulam Mohammad and D.P. Dhar arrested on the charge of plotting a coup against an elected government. Karan Singh knew that there was nothing to stop the Sheikh from doing this—the Government of India could not intervene in the internal affairs of the State. In that case, the worst fears of his father would have come true and he would be forced out of the State for good. He knew he had to act before Sheikh Abdullah came to know of what was to happen to him.

The showdown happened soon enough, precipitated by Sheikh Abdullah himself, who, as always, was impatient and overestimated his strength. Having finally realized that some of his party colleagues had a different view of the State's relationship with Delhi and were in touch with the Indian government, he decided to get rid of them. On 7 August 1953, he peremptorily ordered Sham Lal Saraf to resign from the ministry. Saraf was the senior-most member of the National Conference and ranked second only to Sheikh Abdullah in the Party. Saraf, instead of resigning, wrote to Sheikh Abdullah that 'the manner in which you have created a dangerous situation in the country by making highly inflammatory speeches before the public, combined with your authoritarian attitude in the Cabinet, have convinced me that instead of helping the difficult situation my resignation will encourage you to pursue your policies unbridled. Such a course would be suicidal for the country.'

By demanding Saraf's resignation, Sheikh Abdullah had not only precipitated a crisis but had also walked into a position for which Sadr-e-Riyasat Karan Singh, Bakshi, Dhar and others were well prepared. Technically, the Sadr-e-Riyasat appointed and removed ministers on the advice of the Prime Minister, but to have his advice implemented, the Prime Minister had to approach the Sadr-e-Riyasat, who would then act according to the advice given. But Sheikh Abdullah had by then become a prisoner of his image of an all-powerful leader and believed that he could snap his fingers and everyone, including the Sadr-e-Riyasat, would carry out his command. He could not imagine that his colleagues opposing him in the cabinet and the party had prepared themselves for such an eventuality. They drafted a memorandum and sent it to Sheikh Abdullah. A copy, signed by Deputy Prime Minister Bakshi, Finance Minister Girdhari Lal Dogra and Health Minister Sham Lal Saraf, was also sent to the

Sadr-e-Riyasat. It accused Sheikh Abdullah and Mirza Afzal Beg of wilfully flouting the agreed policies of the cabinet. They pointed out that the implementation of the Delhi Agreement, negotiated by Sheikh Abdullah and ratified by the National Conference and the Indian Parliament, as well as the State Cabinet, was being deliberately delayed, to the detriment of the State and its people. In addition, through his public speeches, Sheikh Abdullah had launched a campaign to denounce the Agreement and encouraged sectarian and communal politics.

The memorandum also accused Abdullah of publicly lending support to Mirza Afzal Beg's efforts to arbitrarily rupture the relationship with India and the unity of Jammu and Kashmir. Because of the failure of the majority within the national Conference to persuade Sheikh Abdullah to revert to the path chosen by the party as a whole, the memorandum concluded that 'the Cabinet, constituted as it is at present and lacking as it does the unity of purpose and action, has lost the confidence of the people in its ability to give them [the people] a clean, efficient and healthy administration'.

This was a piquant situation. A cabinet minister had defied the State's Prime Minister and refused to comply with his demand to resign. The constitutional course was that just as the Prime Minister would have approached the Sadr-e-Riyasat if he had wanted to appoint a new Minister, and the latter would have been obliged to swear him in, similarly, if he had wanted any Minister to be removed, he should have approached the Sadr-e-Riyasat to do so. But strangely, Sheikh Abdullah was not prepared to do so. The only explanation could be that megalomania had so consumed him that he considered it beneath his dignity to approach the Sadr-e-Riyasat with a request. On the other hand, the Sadr-e-Riyasat too had to make a constitutionally correct decision in the absence of any guideline as might have been framed by the

Constituent Assembly. But the Assembly had framed neither the powers nor the duties of either the Prime Minister or the Sadr-e-Riyasat. In such a situation, just as the Prime Minister drew his powers from the State Constitution of 1939, the Sadr-e-Riyasat too drew his powers and functions from the same Constitution. The Constitution of Jammu and Kashmir of 1939 enjoined upon the Head of the State that he must act on the advice of the ministers and he must not act contrary to the Constitution. In this situation, the Prime Minister of the State had not advised the Sadr-e-Riyasat even when it was obvious that the cohesiveness in the government lay in tatters and governance had greatly suffered.

Technically, the Sadr-e-Riyasat, who was the appointing authority of the Prime Minister as well as other Ministers, could have dismissed the Prime Minister straight away, yet the Sadr-e-Riyasat thought it was only appropriate that he call the Prime Minister over for a discussion. PM Sheikh Abdullah was to leave for Gulmarg that afternoon on a holiday, but he came over to the Sadr-e-Riyasat's office before his departure and narrated three long but petty incidents related to Saraf that were the reason for Abdullah asking him to resign. Sadr-e-Riyasat Karan Singh expressed his deep concern at the developments and rued the lack of unity in the Cabinet, and invited the Prime Minister to come over to his residence with his colleagues the same evening to find an amicable solution. But Sheikh Abdullah, instead, launched into a tirade against the Indian press that, in his opinion, had vastly exaggerated the differences in the State Cabinet. But when the Sadr-e-Riyasat continued to press him for the need to do something to defuse and rectify the situation, the Prime Minister bluntly told him that no internal solution was possible until there was some external solution which was acceptable to India as well as Pakistan. With this, he left no doubt at all about his true intention—he was working towards an independent Kashmir. This was the reason why he had been holding up the implementation of the Delhi Agreement which would have further cemented the relationship between the State of Jammu and Kashmir and the Union of India.

There was now not an iota of doubt that any further delay in dismissing Sheikh Abdullah would mean inviting disaster. The Sadr-e-Riyasat had prepared himself for this moment during the preceding months, but he knew that the Sheikh's dismissal was no small matter as he was the most popular figure in the Valley, and if, after dismissal, he decided to take the issue to the streets, he could easily arouse 'acute communal and chauvinistic sentiments among the Kashmiri masses, which would result in serious and violent disturbances'. In addition, it was known that anti-national elements and agents were active in the Valley and, given the chance, would not hesitate to plunge the State into turmoil.

On the political front, Bakshi Ghulam Mohammad had been prepared to take over as the Prime Minister of the State, but when the hour of reckoning arrived, he lost his nerve. He refused to go along with the plan unless Sheikh Abdullah and Mirza Afzal Beg were arrested. If they remained free, he feared not only for his own safety but also for the peace and stability of Kashmir. Karan Singh was not in favour of arresting Sheikh Abdullah, but he also knew that Bakshi's fears were not unfounded. With all the other people involved in the operation agreeing that there was no option but to do what Bakshi wanted, Karan Singh then proceeded to tie the remaining loose ends and drafted the orders to dismiss Prime Minister Sheikh Abdullah and dissolve the ministry, and sent it to him with a covering letter that recalled the sequence of events leading to his dismissal. He reminded the Prime Minister that he, as Sadr-e-Riyasat, had made him the offer of a last-minute effort to defuse the crisis, but the offer had been spurned. Therefore:

> 'Under these conditions, I, as Head of the State, have been forced to the conclusion that the present Cabinet cannot continue in office any longer, and hence I regret to inform you that I have dissolved the Council of Ministers headed by you. A copy of my order in this connection is attached herewith.
>
> 'I need hardly add how deeply distressed I am at having to take this action, but the vital interests of the people of the State, which it is my duty to safeguard, leave me no alternative. I trust that this will in no way affect the mutual regard and cordial feelings we have for each other.'

The order passed by the Sadr-e-Riyasat read:

> '...And whereas, finally, functioning of the present Cabinet on the basis of joint responsibility has become impossible and the resultant conflicts have gravely jeopardized the unity, prosperity and stability of the State...I, Karan Singh, Sadr-e-Riyasat, functioning in the interests of the people of the State who have reposed the responsibility and authority of the Headship of the State in me, do hereby dismiss Sheikh Mohammad Abdullah, from the Prime Ministership of the State of Jammu and Kashmir, and consequently the Council of Ministers headed by him is dissolved herewith.'

This order, however, had to be served and executed, and done in utmost secrecy, as any leakage of the decision would have brought the people onto the streets.

By the time the order and covering letter were ready and approved, it was late evening. The weather had turned stormy, with sheets of rain pouring down from a thunderous sky slashed by lightning. Karan Singh's ADC, Major B.S. Bajwa, was entrusted the job of personally delivering the letter to Sheikh Abdullah in Gulmarg. A police party accompanied him. Torrential rain and bad roads delayed their progress, and Karan Singh and his advisors waited in Karan Mahal, tension growing with every passing hour because the chances of Sheikh Abdullah finding out about the operation through some leak were very real. And if he did find out, he would react in absolute fury and there was no telling what crisis might be unleashed.

As it turned out, fortune stayed firmly on the side of the Sadr-e-Riyasat and the Government of India. The Sheikh was completely unaware of what awaited him. He and Begum Abdullah were fast asleep when Bajwa reached their Gulmarg residence very late at night. He had to knock long and hard on the door before it was opened. It was the Sheikh himself at the door. When he was handed the letter and he read it, he exploded, 'Who is the Sadar-i-Riyasat to dismiss me? I made that chit of a boy Sadar-e-Riyasat!'

Bajwa also had a warrant of arrest with him. The police had already surrounded the house.

The Sheikh was allowed two hours to say his namaz and pack. It was later discovered that during this time he burned some files and papers. The police suspected this but did not interfere, as they had strict orders to be courteous and patient. They would not, in any case, have dared to be anything but—the Sheikh was still the tallest leader of Kashmir, despite all his faults. It was just before daybreak that Sheikh and Begum Abdullah were finally escorted to a car and driven out of the Valley to the Tara Niwas guest house in Udhampur—once the residence of Maharani Tara Devi—where they were kept in detention. Mirza Beg and other loyalists of Sheikh Abdullah were also arrested in different parts of the Valley.

The operation was over, but not quite. There could be no constitutional gap in the administration of the State. Once news of Abdullah's arrest was confirmed, the Sadr-e-Riyasat wrote a formal letter inviting Bakshi Ghulam Mohammad to meet him, ending the letter by saying, 'the continuance in office of the new Cabinet will depend upon its securing a vote of confidence from the Legislative Assembly during its coming session'. Bakshi was already on the scene. It had already been decided that no time should be lost in swearing in the new government. The Chief Secretary, M.K. Kidwai, was summoned. He was completely unaware of what was happening, and Karan Singh recalls that when he learnt that Sheikh Abdullah had been dismissed and arrested, 'he sank down on the steps holding his head in his hands, and was revived only after he had been plied with a couple of stiff whiskies'.

Dawn was breaking when the Sadr-e-Riyasat administered the oath of office to Bakshi Ghulam Mohammad and Girdhari Lal Dogra, so that they could effectively deal with the complications and turmoil that would certainly develop when news of the dismissal and arrests became public.

It was early morning of the 9th by the time the entire operation was over. Karan Singh telephoned Nehru and gave him an update over a hissing and crackling line. 'I had not slept a wink that night and found myself in a curiously detached and light-headed mood,' Karan Singh writes in his autobiography. 'I knew that what I had done was for the national good, and that all the danger and risks were worth taking...Asha had also sat up anxiously in her room all night. Slowly I climbed up the steps and walked into her room. "It is over," I said, and we both smiled; she sixteen going on seventeen, I twenty-two going on twenty-three. I was asleep almost before I hit the bed.'

13

Stability and Early Spring

As feared, protests followed Sheikh Abdullah's dismissal and arrest, leading to the death of 46 and injuries to 148, proving that Bakshi Ghulam Mohammad was right in refusing to take oath as Prime Minister if Sheikh Abdullah was not arrested. Had he been only dismissed and not arrested, the situation in the Valley would have been beyond control, and Pakistan and the Western powers would have found a very good opportunity to force a solution of their choice. Now, with Sheikh Abdullah out of the way, Bakshi got the freedom to demonstrate his administrative and leadership skills, and within a short period, the streets became quiet and normal. As a result, Independence Day could be celebrated peacefully. The day began with the swearing-in ceremony of Sham Lal Saraf and Syed Mir Qasim, also as cabinet ministers, and pro-India celebratory processions were taken out. The Friday prayers that followed were also peaceful.

A few days later, D.P. Dhar and Ghulam Rasool Renzu were added to the cabinet as Deputy Ministers. Apart from establishing law and order, Bakshi was quick to win over the confidence of the National Conference cadre and leaders, and they all stood behind him as they realized the futility of pursuing the dream of complete autonomy or independence. Elements hostile to India had tried to rally the Muslim officials of the State and make them resign in order to paralyse the administration, but the move fell apart in the absence of support. Apart from a few odd resignations, there had been no marks of protest.

The news of Sheikh Abdullah's dismissal and arrest evoked hysterical reactions in Pakistan but was welcomed across India and congratulatory telegrams to Karan Singh came pouring in. The reaction in Jammu was, as expected, euphoric. Another unintended, but pleasant consequence, was that the episode marked the thawing of Karan Singh's relations with his father. On getting the news about the dismissal of Sheikh Abdullah and his arrest, the Maharaja immediately wrote a letter to the Yuvraj: 'All one can say and wish is that what has taken and is taking place may turn out to be for the good of the people and the State. That is also my prayer. You must be having a lot of strain in these exciting and busy days. Please take very good care of yourself.' He also expressed his apprehension about the Yuvraj's safety and asked him to tighten the security arrangements, and when Karan Singh and the Yuvrani went to Bombay, the Maharaja greeted him, saying, 'Well done! You and the Sheikh!!' The resentment that he had nursed for the past four years appeared to have vanished, and that was, perhaps, the only time he had spoken words of unrestrained praise to his son face to face.

In Jammu, the common refrain was that the son had avenged the humiliation of the father. Not even the most rational in Jammu could resist this feeling, with the consequence that, buoyed by the development, the old courtiers of the Maharaja began dreaming of reversing the clock and became actively involved in planning the next move to bring back their beloved Maharaja. For Karan Singh, dealing with these people was a constant challenge, and he could never be certain about their loyalty to him because of the unequal and unfair comparison with his father. They were two individuals living in different times and facing different challenges, whereas the former courtiers and the leaders of the civil society, fiercely loyal to the Maharaja and recipients of bounties that had been showered upon them during their long association with him, continued to live in the past. They were always very courteous and showed due deference to Karan Singh, but were hard to placate. With the dismissal and arrest of Sheikh Abdullah, he had established himself as a person who could handle the politics of the day, but the coming days proved that the loyalists began to nurse unrealistic expectations.

As the changes sank in and the rule of Bakshi settled down, one perceptible change that could be seen was that for the first time, Yuvraj Karan Singh, the Sadr-e-Riyasat, was able to function like the head of the State. This was something that Sheikh Abdullah had denied him, but now that he had played an active role in bringing about the changes, he had the moral authority to assert his constitutional authority. He began to periodically meet the administrative Secretaries and Heads of the Departments in small batches over a cup of tea to acquaint himself with administrative matters. The people of Jammu had not failed to see this change, and they thought that the old days were about to return.

In such circumstances, at the end of October 1953, Captain Dewan Singh, aide de camp of Maharaja Hari Singh, arrived from Bombay and claimed to bring a message from the Maharaja. He said that the Maharaja wanted to return to the State, even if as a private citizen, to vindicate his honour. He also said that there was a very strong rumour in the State and also in Delhi, that if a plebiscite became inevitable, then the Maharaja would be asked to return to the State to help win it, and the Maharaja would willingly return for such a cause. He added that in case the Maharaja was asked to return to help, then he was willing to stay in the State for as long as he was required, otherwise, he would be happy with a short stay of a few days, and in no case exceeding a month. But, in the meantime, Karan Singh should exercise his influence on Prime Minister Bakshi Ghulam Mohammad to make a public statement that there was no ban on the Maharaja's entry into the State. This would go a long way in assuaging the hurt feelings of the Maharaja. Captain Dewan Singh urged Karan Singh to take up the matter in all earnestness and suggested that in the meantime, he should not make any statement in Jammu that might suggest that he was not keen on the Maharaja's return to the State. To add emphasis to what he had said, Dewan Singh said that it was the express desire of the Maharaja—and as his son, it was the Yuvraj's duty—to go out of the way if he had to, and get the Maharaja's desire fulfilled. He also wanted Karan Singh to take up the issue of arrears of Rupees 38 lakhs, which the Maharaja claimed were due to him.

During this period, Brigadier Ghansara Singh, the last Governor of Gilgit, also called upon Karan Singh and informed him that efforts were on to get the Maharaja back in the State. Other sources from Jammu also brought a similar message, though no one knew the origin of the speculation. It defied logic, as there was no proposal before the Government of India, and it was not likely that Nehru would even remotely entertain the thought. The old loyalists of the Maharaja had been working overtime to cook up such quixotic plans. They had refused to acknowledge the changes that had taken place, and the fact that Karan Singh had signed the order to dismiss Sheikh Abdullah and put him behind bars did not mean that he had been vested with the absolute powers of a monarch. The decision regarding the Maharaja was not in his hands. He could only let the matter be and wait for the deluded courtiers to come to terms with reality.

This episode was embarrassing, as the loyalists of the Maharaja began to propagate that the son had deliberately not tried to work for his father's return, however brief it might have been. Karan Singh knew that he would have to put up with such moments, and all that he could do was to work to the best of his abilities and leave the rest to the will of God. Unknown to the people of Jammu, he had always tried to help Jammu as he felt that a bad hand had been dealt to them by the combination of Sheikh Abdullah and Nehru. While he was never in a position to persuade the former, he had tried his utmost to convince the latter to engage in a dialogue with Jammu to find an amicable solution to the Jammu agitation. He had not been successful in his efforts but he had succeeded in convincing Nehru that Sheikh Abdullah was perhaps deliberately aggravating the situation by refusing to negotiate and was thus prolonging the agitation so that it could be dubbed as communal, and then he could argue that Muslims would be insecure in a country that was 'slipping' into Hindu communalism, thus building a case for a separate and autonomous, if not independent, Kashmir. This was how Karan Singh saw the Sheikh's plan, and in this argument, he had received no mean support from the likes of Maulana Azad and Rafi Ahmed Kidwai. This, however, was not the case as far as the Maharaja was concerned, as Nehru and his confidants were convinced that the Maharaja was not willing to accept the changes that had taken place and also that turning to him would be a retrograde step.

Karan Singh had, therefore, remained focused on the immediate challenge of meeting the aspirations of the people. The emotional hurt that had been caused to the people of Jammu had been assuaged, but real and substantial change had to be brought to their lives to make the changes meaningful for them. And change had to be brought to the State as a whole and not to one region at the cost of the others. There could be no let-up in Kashmir as any misstep would mean that the pro-Pakistan elements would be in a position to exploit the failings. Kashmir needed to feel that Bakshi was a better alternative to Sheikh Abdullah, and for this, Karan Singh would be required to use his influence in Delhi to get more and more aid for the State.

In the days following the dismissal of Sheikh Abdullah, a tirade of acerbic comments had been directed against India in general and Nehru in particular. *The Daily Telegraph* said that the dismissal of Sheikh Abdullah had undone the commendable work done by the Karachi Agreement of 1953. The reference was to Nehru's visit to Karachi, where he was accorded a tumultuous welcome by the people of Pakistan and the two Prime Ministers, Nehru and Mohammad Ali Bogra, had set a timetable for naming the Administrator of the Plebiscite. But when Sheikh Abdullah was dismissed, a chorus of condemnation rose from the Western world and the Kashmir issue was brought to the centre stage. *The New York Times* observed that no equitable solution to the Kashmir problem was possible without a free plebiscite. *The Daily Mirror* had gone as far as describing Nehru's attitude as 'that of an imperialistic conqueror not subject to the UN'.

Even in certain quarters in India, and of course in Kashmir, Nehru had come under serious attack, making things challenging for the Sadr-e-Riyasat and Prime Minister Bakshi, but they decided the only way to handle the situation was to focus on development. As a first step, the Bakshi government made education free from primary school to the degree level. The old practice of *Mujawaza*—procuring food grains from the farmers at a fixed price, which in practice meant that the produce of the farmers was procured at a cheap rate, thereby depriving them of their legitimate profit—was abolished. This single step went a long way in establishing his authority and making him acceptable among the masses. Emboldened by the positive response of the people, Bakshi was soon in a position to convene a Convention of the National Conference. Except for the hardliners, who were in a minority, almost the entire leadership and active workers attended it. This success helped to convince the majority of the population that the policy of positive cooperation with the Government of India was better than the confrontational politics of Sheikh Abdullah.

When Prime Minister Bakshi decided to visit Jammu, he was firmly saddled in Kashmir. The Jammu people, already buoyed by the dismissal and arrest of Sheikh Abdullah, greeted him with a grand ovation on his arrival. Karan Singh, too, was in high spirits because of this happy turn of events and used the opportunity to bring the issue of Ladakh to the forefront. He wrote to Nehru: 'I feel at this stage a goodwill gesture to the people of Ladakh, who are bitter and resentful as a result of the treatment they received from the previous regime, will be of considerable value. I have discussed with Bakshi the idea of taking a Ladakhi as Deputy Minister for Ladakh Affairs, a gesture which will not only be much appreciated by the Ladakhis but will also make the task of administration via-a-vis Ladakh much easier and smoother.' He, finally, prevailed upon Bakshi Ghulam Mohammad to induct Kushak Bakula, the head Lama from Ladakh, as a Deputy Minister in his Cabinet. It was a small but significant step.

With Sheikh Abdullah, Karan Singh had failed to develop any satisfactory working relationship, but with Bakshi, he was not only comfortable but also offered suggestions whenever he thought they were for the advantage of the State. Among these was his suggestion to fly of the National Flag on the Jammu Secretariat when the Capital moved there, which was accepted and mollified the people of Jammu to some extent. This did not mean that Bakshi was a pliable Prime Minister, as he jealously guarded the rights of the State within the parameters of Article 370 of the Indian Constitution which gave special rights to the State. He was aware that he could not be seen to have surrendered all the rights that the State had secured through long negotiations to which he also was a party. But he remained focused on solving the problems that the people faced.

Before long, however, corruption became a problem, and Karan Singh brought this to the notice of Prime Minister Nehru. He wrote, '...there are officers who are known for their corruption. I feel it is a pity that there has yet been no full enquiry into charges of corruption...Conventions and other political activities have their own undoubted value, but recent experience has shown that the integrity or otherwise of the administration is in the final analysis a decisive factor.' Such corrupt elements of the bureaucracy had also begun to draw support from the political and communal sections of the polity. Because of these facts, he wrote, utmost vigil was needed, as any laxity would allow the political and communal nexus to develop into a dangerous tool capable of destroying everything that has been achieved.

With his newfound freedom to function as the Head of the State, Karan Singh had begun to participate in governance. Sheikh Abdullah had barred him from travelling within the State to meet people and attend public functions after the Kheer Bhawani incident because of his insecurities. Bakshi suffered from no such complex, and Karan Singh made full use of the opportunity, visiting different parts of the State, including Jammu, where he travelled extensively.

The approach of the Bakshi government towards the Constituent Assembly, too, was very different from that of the previous government. Whereas Sheikh Abdullah had balked at implementing the Delhi Agreement, Bakshi declared soon after becoming the Prime Minister that the Agreement would be implemented in toto. In another significant step, the customs duty on goods entering the State was abolished. It led to the lowering of prices of several goods and went a long way in removing the psychological barrier between the people of the State and the rest of the country.

The otherwise positive year of 1955 was, however, marred by an unexpected and unpleasant exchange between him and those who had arrogated to themselves the responsibility of safeguarding the 'honour' of the Maharaja and the royal family. Maharani Tara Devi, who was living in Alhilal, Kangra, in one of the royal family's newly acquired properties, had fallen ill, suffering frequent fainting spells due to depression and acute low blood pressure. She was usually attended to by doctors from the nearby Yol Camp Military Hospital, but her condition worried everyone on this occasion. When he was informed, Karan Singh immediately had a doctor of his confidence visit her from Jammu, but it was obvious that although she was in the company of many of her relatives, she pined to be in the proximity of her son. He, too, felt that as a son he was duty-bound to look after her. Much had changed in the State, and with Sheikh Abdullah no longer in power, Bakshi would not have any objection to her return. At least, Karan Singh thought, she could come to Srinagar or Jammu for a month or two for her treatment, and began to make efforts accordingly.

On 8 August 1955, he wrote to his father that he and Asha had been to Alhilal and 'were shocked to see how very run-down Mummy was looking after her recent severe illness'. Giving details, he wrote:

> As you know, she has not been keeping at all well for the last two years, and each successive illness has been weakening her still further and reducing her stamina and power of resistance. For some time, the doctor has been advising and I have been trying to persuade her to come up to Srinagar for a couple of months, but she had adamantly refused on the ground that she would only go back when you went and not before...Her stay [in Srinagar] will cheer her up and be of inestimable value, as one of her complaints is mental depression with a tendency towards hysteria...I do not think it is necessary for anyone to accompany her from here except a couple of maids and servants, because my staff will be at her disposal here.
>
> I am sure you will have no objection to this course of action because I remember that even in 1949, you were of the view that at least Mummy should accompany me to the State. If I remember correctly, you mentioned the matter in one of your letters to the late Sardar Patel, in which you wrote there was no possible reason, political or otherwise, why a mother should be separated from her only child. In view of all these factors and the doctor's strong advice, I have persuaded her to come up for a month or two. Before she does that, it is my duty to bring the matter to your notice as head of the family.

His father responded from Poona on 21 August: 'As regards what you say in your letter of 8th August about your Mummy, I am afraid there is nothing for me to say in this matter. It is for the person concerned to think over the matter and decide. The question of what I thought about this matter in 1949 and your anxiety to bring it to the notice of the Head of the family are now beside the point...[It] is for the person concerned to see what is and what is not correct in the matter.'

Karan Singh's parents had been living separately since June 1949, except for a brief period during Karan Singh's marriage in Bombay. In his letters, the Maharaja mostly referred to her in the third person. Yet, Karan Singh felt that this response which suggested that he did not care what the Maharani did or did not do, and a complete disregard for her condition, was unusual. He realized that his father had been affected by the many communications he had been receiving for his 'well-wishers'. In the days before his father replied to his letter, there had been a flurry of telegrams from Jammu from many old loyalists of the Maharaja to the Maharani in Alhilal and to Karan Singh, with copies to the Maharaja in Bombay. All these telegrams had the same theme: the need to stop the Maharani from coming to the State without her husband. The Maharani's health and the fact that the royal couple's marriage might have irretrievably broken down was of no consequence to them.

On 19 August 1955, Rao Bahadur Kartar Singh, Wazir Ganga Ram, Thakur Haqiqat Singh, Thakur Dhanantar Singh, Rao Sahib Ratan Singh, and Thakur Nanak Singh addressed a telegram to Karan Singh: 'Her Highness's visit to the State without His Highness is most improper. Kindly persuade her not to come', and sent a copy to the Maharaja. Simultaneously, the same set of loyalists sent another telegram to the Maharani in Alhilal, warning her, 'Your Highness's visit to the State without His Highness most detrimental to the interests of Royal family and will not be appreciated.' Again, a copy was sent to the Maharaja in Bombay. Chain Singh, Munshi Ram, Dhani Ram Wazir, and Thakur Kandhara Singh also sent similar telegrams, and each one of them sent a copy to the Maharaja. Surprisingly, the Praja Parishad too jumped into the fray with its top leaders Pandit Prem Nath Dogra and Chatru Ram Dogra sending a telegram to Karan Singh instructing him to 'Kindly persuade Her Highness not to come without His Highness', with a copy to the Maharaja, and another telegram to the Maharani, saying, 'Your visit to Kashmir without His Highness most inadvisable,' also with a copy to the

Maharaja. Not to be left behind were the sundry citizens of Jammu who sent a letter signed by 71 of them to Karan Singh, sermonizing that '...in the love of her husband lies the worldly or the otherworldly happiness of a wife'.

Understandably, Karan Singh, not anticipating such an insensitive reaction, was hurt by the response that was orchestrated, and on 20th August, responded in a letter addressed to Wazir Ganga Ram who was the first name in the telegram, with a request that all others, including Pandit Prem Nath Dogra and Chatru Ram Dogra, be also intimated of the contents of his letter. He appreciated their loyalty to his father and also their concern for the well-being of the dynasty and added,

> Our doctor has strongly advised that in the interests of her health, she must be moved as soon as possible to Srinagar, for a variety of reasons—not the least important of which is that I will be near her. I can assure you that her visit is not a pleasure trip but is the result of strong medical advice, which, as her son, I can under no circumstances ignore and which overrides any other consideration.
>
> As for her visit being improper, I fail to see the impropriety of a mother who is seriously ill coming to live at a world-famous health resort in her own home with her only child...I am confident that in the light of these facts you will shed [any] misgivings that you may have, so that a delicate personal matter may be spared controversy.

But the gentlemen were adamant and Wazir Ganga Ram sent a response on behalf of others: 'The return of Maharani Sahiba to the State when His Highness the Maharaja Bahadur does not find the situation to be congenial for his return can never be appreciated by the people who will take it as an attempt on the part of interested persons to keep Shri Maharaja Bahadur out of the State forever. According to the religion and traditions of the people here, the proper place for a woman is at the feet of her husband and nowhere else. It is also apprehended that the visit without the consent of Shri Maharajadhiraj may adversely affect the social and political relations of the Royal Family.' This, Karan Singh chose to ignore and by the end of September, when he was able to convince his mother to come up to Srinagar, he informed his father that she had arrived by road on 29th September and wistfully added, 'How nice it would be if you also were here so that we could all live together again like in the old days. It is a strange Fate that for the greater part of my life has kept me apart from both my parents.'

The year 1955 also turned out to be momentous for the country at a time when it was beginning to appear that the USA had turned hostile towards India because of Nehru's refusal to join the Western Boc in the Cold War and remain non-aligned. India stood completely isolated in the Western world. Pakistan, however, had, over the previous six or seven years, aligned with the USA completely, even offering its air fields for use by the American military forces. By 1954, it had become part of the USA-sponsored South East Asia Treaty Organization (SEATO) against communist China, and in 1955, it also became a member of the Baghdad Pact against the USSR. This happened at a time when churning in the foreign policy of the USSR had begun with the dismantling of Stalin-era politics. After its initial disinterest in the Kashmir affairs and abstaining from voting in Kashmir-related debates during the 1947-48 period, it spoke about it only in 1952, when referring to the Western plans, a Soviet representative said, 'instead of speaking for a real settlement, efforts were aimed at prolonging the dispute and at converting Kashmir into a trust territory of the US and the UK under the pretext of giving it assistance through the United Nations'. By the time the Baghdad Pact came into existence, USA became openly hostile to India as it had emerged as a leader of the non-aligned countries, all of them developing and underdeveloped countries. The USSR was by then forced to take India as a serious player in international affairs, and Prime Minister Nehru was invited to visit the USSR in 1955. In November of that year, the Soviet leaders, Nikita Khrushchev, First Secretary of the Communist Party of the Soviet Union and Chairman of the Council of Ministers, and Nikolai Bulganin, Premier of the Soviet Union, came calling to India as a part of the tour of Afghanistan and Burma (now Myanmar).

The Sadr-e-Riyasat Karan Singh and his wife happened to be in Delhi at that time and after finishing their schedule were about to return to Jammu when his Aide de Camp, Captain Goverdhan Singh, suggested that since two great leaders of a world power were visiting the national capital and there was considerable buzz about it, the Sadr-e-Riyasat might consider delaying his departure and see what happens in Delhi. Karan Singh found the suggestion attractive and postponed his return to his State. When Nehru came to know of the young couple's presence in the capital, their names were added to the list of invitees for the dinner in honour of the Soviet leaders. During conversations over that dinner, Karan Singh invited the two Soviet leaders to his State, telling them that it was the most beautiful place on earth. The conversation had rested there, but no sooner had the young couple returned to Jammu than Nehru informed Karan Singh that his invitation had been taken seriously by the Soviet leaders and they wanted to visit the State. It was an important development, as for the first time leaders of a superpower was to visit the State, thereby acknowledging it as an integral part of India. The Western world still continued to treat it as a disputed territory. Given the importance of the visit, Nehru was worried that Bakshi Ghulam Mohammad would feed the guests the famed *gushtaba*—the meat-ball dish of Kashmir—and other spicy dishes and upset their digestion, and told the Yuvraj to immediately reach Srinagar and ensure that everything went smoothly!

Winter is not the usual time to visit Kashmir, but a casual conversation had now brought two world leaders to the State and they would soon change the international response to the Kashmir problem. When Yuvraj Karan Singh hosted them for lunch at Karan Mahal, the two presented him with two lovely ceramic figures of the 'King of the Sea' and the 'Queen of the Sea', and the host cheekily remarked that he thought that the communists did not believe in kings and queens. Khrushchev laughed uproariously and said they were all right as long as they were ceramics! The high point came in the evening when a civic reception was hosted at the Rajgarh Palace on the Jhelum under chinar trees in the crisp winter air. It was then that Khrushchev made that landmark speech when, for the first time, the Soviet Union came out openly in support of Jammu and Kashmir being an integral part of India. During the speech, referring to Kashmir's geographical proximity to the Soviet Union, he said: 'If you are ever in difficulty, all you have to do is to climb on top of these mountains and shout, and we will come to your aid.' These sentiments had not been expressed on the spur of the moment, as Khrushchev repeated them on 11 December 1955 while delivering a farewell speech before his departure. For India, battling against the combined opinion of the West as far as Kashmir was concerned, spring had arrived in winter.

14

A Happy Phase

SHEIKH ABDULLAH HAD BEEN in detention since that dramatic night in 1953. At the start of 1956, Nehru expressed his unease at the prolonged detention without trial. Karan Singh felt that since the Constituent Assembly was still in session and the final ratification of the accession and finalization of the Constitution was yet to take place, there was the danger that a released Sheikh Abdullah might wean away the members of the Assembly from Bakshi and topple his government. Nehru pointed out that ever since the visit of Khrushchev and Bulganin to the State, there had been a positive effect, internally and externally, in India's favour. Moreover, the situation in Pakistan and in Occupied Kashmir was bad, making people believe that India was the right choice for the State. All this, Nehru believed, would make it difficult for anyone to mobilize public opinion against India. But he said it would be best to let Bakshi take a final call on when and how to face the fallout of Sheikh Abdullah's release.

The year also saw the publication of the States' Reorganization Committee's Report, which had recommended the creation of new states by merging and reorganizing the old ones. For obvious reasons, Jammu and Kashmir had been excluded from it, but Karan Singh used the occasion to point out three issues to Nehru—first, the State could at least have been included in the North Zone under the zonal set-up recommended by the Committee for discussing common problems and challenges of the zonal states. Second, the Committee's recommendations regarding linguistic minorities should have applied to the State, as the Dogras and Ladakhis deserved similar safeguards as were provided to other linguistic minorities in the country. Finally, he wrote that instead of the State Assembly electing the Head of State, just as the President of India nominated Governors for other states, the President should be empowered to nominate the Head of State for Jammu and Kashmir as well. It would take nine years for this last suggestion to become a reality.

That year, Karan Singh was finally able to travel abroad again. His father was pleased to hear of this and took a keen interest in planning his first trip as the Head of State, drawing up a list of items that Karan Singh and his wife needed to take with them. For his son, he even suggested the number of visiting cards that he should carry. He also told the couple that he would have a passport case ready for them to carry their passports, tickets, health certificates, letters from various Embassies, etc., and suggested places to stay and eat, and the cabs to hire—they were told *not* to hire the big Daimler as it looked like a hearse! He appeared as excited about the trip as me might have been about his own first trip as Crown Prince. On the couple's arrival in Bombay, he ensured that their luggage was properly packed and personally oversaw the weighing so that they did not have to pay for the extra baggage. He had also arranged for Victor Rosenthal to make all the purchases that he had wanted and asked his old friend Beryl Stileman, living in Sussex, England, to reach Paris to give company to his son and daughter-in-law, and also make all the necessary arrangements for Wimbledon, Oxford, the House of Commons and the theatres before they reached London.

The high points of that trip to Europe—the Yuvrani's first—were visits to the various churches of Italy, and meeting with Earl Attlee, who, as Prime Minister of Britain, had decided to dismantle the British colonial rule in India. Maharaja Hari Singh, too, had met him in London on one of his earlier trips to Europe and had, in his letter to his son, remarked, 'We must recognize him as a very far-sighted statesman, especially because of what he did in connection with our country.' In London, during a visit to the House of Commons, Edward Heath, a future Prime Minister and then a Parliamentary Secretary, hosted the young couple for lunch. Throughout the tour, which also included West Germany and Switzerland, the couple kept in touch with the Maharaja, who was very amused to learn that his daughter-in-law had lost only one umbrella so far! It was, in all, a happy tour before they returned on 21 July 1956. Foreign travel would become a favourite annual activity for the couple. It was their best time together; and their time alone—they made it a point to travel when the children were in boarding school and could not insist on accompanying them!

On 15 February 1954, the Constituent Assembly of the State unanimously ratified the accession to India, thereby freeing India from the obligation of referring the matter to the people. Whatever arrangement that existed from that point onwards was between India and Jammu and Kashmir—J&K—as a state of the Union, and no outside power had any role to play. Another subject of great importance to the State was resolved that year when finally, the State Forces, the officers, and the other ranks, were absorbed into the Indian Army without any screening. Even more heartening for Karan Singh was the fact that the Regiment had retained its identity, though in order of precedence, it was just above the Gorkha Regiment. No other army of the Princely States had been given this honour and a multitude of reasons could be attributed to this achievement, not the least being Karan Singh's diligent pleading of the case with not only Prime Minister Nehru but also all those in the Indian Army, particularly General Thimayya, who dealt with the subject.

When the exercise of assimilation of State Forces had been completed, knowing that the subject was very dear to the heart of his father, Karan Singh informed him on 22 March 1958: 'You will be glad to know that our State Forces officers and men have, as a result of our constant efforts over the last few years, received a wonderful deal—far better than the terms which were given to other State Forces. All our officers, except for one, who is under-matric, and a few others who are not in medical category 'A', have been given permanent regular commissions in the Indian Army, and will get their seniority under the rules. What is more, Jammu and Kashmir Forces will remain a separate group for the time being, and the Training Centre will also remain. As for the other ranks, not a single person is being disbanded unless they want to retire…our whole existing force is virtually integrated en bloc in the Indian Army.' The Maharaja had fought for the honour and security of service for the State Forces with limited success; Karan Singh had continued the fight. The final resolution—which exceeded even their own expectations—was a matter of great pride and satisfaction for both.

The Maharaja was also particularly pleased that Karan Singh had begun to take a keen interest in the affairs of the Dharmarth Trust. With the Maharaja away and Sheikh Abdullah's campaign to control its funds, many of the temples that the Trust managed across the State had fallen into neglect. In his letters, the Maharaja wrote to his son that he appreciated his efforts in getting the Trust funds released and hoped he would also sort out the matter of the interest amount on the Imperial Bank deposits that Sheikh Abdullah had frozen, causing monetary loss to the Trust.

Karan Singh kept up a regular correspondence with his father. Since racing and foreign travel were the only passions left for the Maharaja, Karan Singh also keenly followed the races of Bombay, Poona, and Bangalore through the newspapers. For a person who had hardly any serious enthusiasm for horse riding, he had a remarkable knowledge of race horses and their trainers and was bold enough to comment on the abilities of his father's jockeys and trainers. Whenever any of his horses won a race, the Maharaja would telegraphically inform his son, who would dutifully send a telegram of congratulations. To the Maharaja's delight, Karan Singh also took an interest in the stud farm he had set up in Nagbani and kept his father posted about it—the foals, fillies and horses, and the plantation that he had started there. Some of the happiest moments for the Maharaja in Bombay during those years were when his son was visiting and would accompany him to the races—and his happiness would multiply manifold if, on those days, his horses won.

The Maharaja also looked forward to his son's visits because he had grown extremely fond of his daughter-in-law. No member of the family had ever dared to take liberties with the Maharaja, but Asha managed to breach the stern Maharaja's defence. She could joke with him, make him laugh, and there grew between them a very special bond, each caring for the other. In an interview she gave Aasha Khosa, a correspondent of *Kashmir Times*, in 1984, the Yuvrani said that it was her father-in-law who taught and groomed her—advising her on her wardrobe, teaching her how to conduct herself in public and hold conversations, how to cook dishes that were relished by her guests. A letter the Maharaja wrote his son on 27 October 1954 describes an interesting tussle between father-in-law and daughter-in-law. Asha had sent a radiogram with instructions that it be installed in a particular room that was close to the Maharaja's room. The Maharaja believed that she had done this on purpose, so that on her next visit to Bombay, she might play it loudly and take delight in annoying him. But he would not let her succeed in her mischief, he wrote to his son—he had decided to give Asha a room that was farthest from his room on her next visit!

Asha loved to spring surprises and, therefore, kept her preparation for the Bhushan examination a secret from the Maharaja. It was a Hindi exam equivalent to Intermediate. She had forbidden her husband also from informing her father-in-law, as she wanted to inform him after passing it. When she finally did so, the Maharaja's broad smile and the sparkle in his eyes left many amazed, for they had thought it impossible that anything apart from a win at the races or a successful hunting expedition could put him in a happy mood. But a similar decision by the son to hold back information from his father in the hope of giving him a happy surprise drew a mild chastisement. On 4 October 1956 the Yuvraj wrote the Maharaja a letter, telling him he would become a grandfather sometime in February 1957. On 7 October, the Yuvrani received a telegram from her father-in-law: 'Much guarded secret which I have known now confirmed. Blessings heartiest congratulations. Best wishes love. Daddy'. Another telegram followed. This one addressed to his son: 'Letter received. Overjoyed heartiest congratulations. Best wishes. Daddy.'

This was not the end of the matter. After making arrangements for the birth of his grandchild and getting in touch with Beryl Stileman to get her over to India, the Maharaja turned his attention once again to his son and daughter-in-law. To her, he wrote in a tone of complaint, 'After receiving your letter No. 4 wherein you dropped a hint that you were going to give me some interesting news, I was expecting something definite in your last letter…But I may warn you that I have not lived for 61 years in vain, and nothing now surprises me, and perhaps your closely guarded secret will not do so.'

To his son, he wrote: 'Your letter of 4 October brought the very welcome news for which I have been waiting for nearly six years. Actually, it was a confirmation of what I had heard weeks before. That it was so should not surprise you, as Kashmir is a place where you cannot keep a secret. All I can tell you is that neither Beryl nor Shangloo wrote to me about it. You must realize that these things cannot be kept a secret for long, and sometimes attempts to do so leave a bad taste in the mouth. You admit that you have known it for some time, and it does not carry conviction to be told that some kind of confirmation was needed before the news could be broken to the one person who has been pining to hear it.' Then he came to the more substantive subject and conceded that where his daughter-in-law should be during the confinement was for her to decide, but he was ready to have her in Bombay if she so desired. He also informed the Yuvraj about the arrangements that he had already made and suggested that Asha should travel only after Beryl arrived in Srinagar, as she would escort her to Bombay. The old Maharaja was back in action. He had taken control of everything, from choosing the nursing home to who was going to stay where. The soon-to-be grandmother was left out of the picture completely.

The Maharaja kept himself and others busy with his instructions in anticipation of the big occasion. He instructed his son to ask Wazir Amin Chand, who kept all the family records regarding the birth ceremonies of the sons of Dogra kings, to look up the records connected to the birth of the Yuvraj so that he could bring a copy of that to Bombay. It was evident that the Maharaja was confident that the child would be male. Karan Singh, his wife, and Beryl arrived in Bombay in the middle of December 1956, and after a stay of about ten days, Karan Singh returned to Jammu, where Vice President Radhakrishnan was to arrive for the inauguration of the marvel of a tunnel connecting the Ramban side of the Banihal with the Valley. It was an important moment as it provided an all-weather road connecting the two provinces. After the inauguration, when the cars reached the other side of the Banihal tunnel, Karan Singh was pleasantly surprised to see the Valley covered with snow. It was ironic, and probably a commentary on the dynasty's relationship with the Valley, that the scion of the family that had ruled the Valley for a century had not seen snow in the State before that moment. The Dogra royals would move to Jammu to escape the winters of Kashmir, which can be harsh.

All the anticipation and excitement at the possibility of having a male grandchild—heir to a throne, the loss of which the Maharaja appeared not to have reconciled himself to—ended in a sort of anti-climax for the Maharaja, as a girl was born on 24 February 1957. There is clear evidence to suggest that the Maharaja was hoping for a male grandchild so that he could transfer his personal properties to him and be rid of a worry. But he soon overcame the disappointment, and continued to call the shots—when the time came to name the child, he gave her the formal name of Jyotsna but otherwise called her Jyoti. He took good care of the mother and the baby and did not allow them to travel till the time Beryl had selected a suitable child nurse.

Without any indication from the Maharaja that she was needed, or would even be welcome, the Maharani had stayed away. Praying, as she did, for a safe delivery and a male child. She took a longer time to recover from the news of the birth of a girl. Finally, Karan Singh brought his wife and newborn to Jammu only on 11 April 1957 as it was considered to be an auspicious date.

This was a very eventful period in other ways too for Karan Singh. On the last day of May, the result of his MA examination was announced, and he topped the University. It was a load off his shoulders, as now he was free to read some of the books that he really wanted to read. He also began to think about becoming a research scholar for his Ph.D. in Political Science. His father also appeared to be in a happy space, as he began to make arrangements regarding the transfer and gifting of the properties in the State through a power of attorney. A stickler for procedure and protocol, he also allowed his son to dispose of the Dharmarth property at Varanasi, whose maintenance had become expensive, provided the sale was discussed and ratified by the Dharmarth Council and was not against the constitution of the Trust.

The year 1957 had seen two political developments of considerable note. After the completion of the first term of the State Assembly, new elections had been held, but unfortunately, the precedent of arbitrary rejection of nomination papers and intimidation of the opposition candidates set by Sheikh Abdullah was also followed by the Bakshi Ghulam Mohammad administration, only the scale was smaller. Wisely, this time the Praja Parishad had not boycotted elections and, amidst allegations of rigging, had secured a few seats to give voice to Jammu in the Assembly. This had been followed by elections to the Legislative Council and then, with the expiry of the Sadr-e-Riyasat's term in November, Yuvraj Karan Singh had been re-elected for a second term.

That year also saw the completion of the construction of the Raja Amar Singh Rajput School Hostel, for which his father had donated Rs. 30,000, and was now ready to admit its first students. The Rajput Commerce College had also grown, and had become much sought after as students from the rural areas found it useful in preparing for and finding new job opportunities. Until now, students from the rural Rajput community, in particular, had known little about careers outside of the army. Karan Singh took a keen interest in the progress of both institutions. Meanwhile, work was also completed on a new house for the Yuvraj and Yuvrani and their daughter in the National Capital, on land that the Indian government had offered some former princely states for purchase near Central Delhi. It was close to the area allotted to some foreign embassies and was almost a jungle, where Karan Singh remembers seeing foxes and Neelgai and hearing wolves after dark.

While the birth of a girl-child in the dynasty might have become a temporary disappointment for the grandparents, it was to have a major impact on the social life and responses of Jammu. It turned out to be a boon for many unborn female children. Up until then, female infanticide was not uncommon among the Rajputs, but Karan Singh, the Yuvraj, taking great pride in becoming the father of a girl-child, and celebrating the birth as none of his predecessors had ever done, became a turning point in the Dogra society and soon this obnoxious practice, which had been, on paper, banned since the time of Maharaja Hari Singh, was completely eradicated. The little princess also became a harbinger of a social change that was to transform Dogra society—the gradual end to everyday discrimination against girls, who were often denied the benefit of education. This change ought to be seen in the context of her mother's desire and efforts to educate herself, not only academically but also intellectually. Barring a few exceptions, no females among the royalty had groomed themselves intellectually as the Yuvrani did, and before long, she could hold her own in the company of some of the finest minds of the times, like the Nobel laureate couple of Alva and Gunnar Myrdal, Rosemary and Clovis Maksoud, Raj and

Romesh Thapar, Professor Ralph Purcell and Professor John Galbraith. Karan Singh was an avid learner, and Asha followed his example. She influenced Jammu society by appearing in examinations with other students and encouraged many other young women to educate themselves, too. After the conclusion of each examination, she would host a tea-party for all the examinees.

In March of 1958, in a major development, Karan Singh informed his father that he had secured a grant of Rs. 35,000 from the Government of India to construct an auditorium which would be used by both the Commerce College as well as the Rajput School in Jammu, and would be named after the Maharaja. During this time, considerable improvement had also been effected in the functioning of the Dharmarth Trust Board, and it had taken up the construction of an imposing main gate of the Raghunath Temple and a pavilion at the Shankaracharya Temple. In addition, Karan Singh had succeeded in getting sanctioned a sum of Rs. 30,000 for the new campus of Sanskrit Mahavidyalaya. This Mahavidyalaya had under its care rare Sanskrit manuscripts written on birch bark and many scholars in the country had expressed the fear that they would be lost to posterity due to neglect. Sanskrit scholars like Dr. Sampurnanand, who was also the Chief Minister of Uttar Pradesh, had approached Karan Singh so that those manuscripts could be handed over to institutions in his state for better preservation. Karan Singh politely refused the offers and embarked upon a mission to seek expert advice and help for their preservation. Ever since, no one has questioned their safety, and scholars continue to come from all over the world to study them.

Thus, he remained busy in the work that he loved most, and so did his father, whose time was consumed by the races in Bombay, Poona and Bangalore. As the monsoon was about to approach in 1958 to put an end to the racing season in Bombay, his father sent him a record of the complete statistics of the racing season of 1957-58. He had won four Indian Classics and was second in the Derby but lamented that 'it was not possible to beat Gwalior as he had almost four times my number of horses'.

In the summer of 1959, Karan Singh and the Yuvrani planned another foreign tour. This time they chose to visit the Soviet Union and the Scandinavian countries, and to return via London and Paris. Once again, the Maharaja took charge of their preparations and drew a functional list of items that they needed to carry with them and also sent them by Railway Parcel three crates containing one attaché case and two suitcases for his son, two for Asha and two for Jyoti and one tea case as common family property. In a letter, he wrote, 'I hope these will be useful, particularly when going abroad. The cases are light and strong. Their size prevents taking anything unnecessary, thus automatically saving Extra Freight Charges.' He ended the letter with, 'I hope you will now get rid of your ghastly suitcases!'

Before their departure, a nurse, Helen, had to be employed to look after little Jyoti, and the Maharaja asked his son to instruct her that a fortnightly report about Jyoti should be sent to him so that he was up to date about the child's health and general well-being. After reaching Moscow, Karan Singh gave his father a detailed account of Russian life and how they lived. The response of the Maharaja reflected how little people in India knew about Russia and perhaps how deep-seated were the prejudices nursed by the privileged classes about Communist societies. He wrote: 'It is interesting to know about your impressions of Russians. I was surprised to read that the Russians have attained a good general standard of living and that they are steadily improving…I am glad you have gone with a receptive mind. This will enable you to take full educational advantage of your tour.' And the tour did indeed have an impact on Karan Singh. Always sympathetic to the socialist world view, he had always been deeply distressed by the unconscionable gap between the rich and the poor in feudal and capitalist societies. And here was a country where life was not rosy for everyone, but everyone had a house to live in, a job, and access to good healthcare and education.

On his return, he submitted a detailed report to the Central Government about the visit, also mentioning his impressions about the development model used by them. It was ironic that someone born to royalty was drawn to the communist model of development.

Two events darkened that otherwise good year. Before the last quarter of 1959 had begun, Asha suffered a miscarriage. The couple accepted the misfortune with relative equanimity but the Maharaja, they knew, would be upset. He had indicated his desire for a grandson in several small ways, once in a light-hearted manner he had said to his son about his granddaughter, not yet three, 'Tiger, you need to have a second child soon, this one is too headstrong!' But he wasn't upset for long after Karan Singh informed him of the miscarriage, and explained the necessary medical steps that had been taken. Not one to ignore any instance of carelessness, real or perceived, the Maharaja wrote a letter reprimanding the Yuvraj and instructing him to take good care of the Yuvarani the next time.

This, however, was a personal misfortune that had no bearing on public life. However, sometime before, the State had been rocked by a controversy. Kashmir is prone to floods, but that year they were exceptionally severe, and a large segment of the population had been affected. That year, Assam too had experienced unprecedented floods, and the whole country was alive to the devastation they had caused. In the State, there existed the Prime Minister's Relief Fund to which donations were made during such natural disasters. But in other States, apart from the Chief Minister's Relief Fund, many had the Governor's Relief Fund, too. Prime Minister Nehru advised Sadr-e-Riyasat Karan Singh to open such a Fund in his State too, which he did after duly consulting the State Prime Minister, who also contributed to finalizing the names of the committee members of the Fund. The response to the Sadr-e-Riyasat's well-publicized appeal brought liberal donations from all over the country. But mischievous elements in the State, led by a senior bureaucrat who had been dismissed from service on charges of corruption and misbehaviour during Maharaja Hari Singh's time, but had been brought back into service by Sheikh Abdullah, tried to create a rift between the Sadr-e-Riyasat and Prime Minister Bakshi. The two Funds were sought to be presented as if they competed with each other, instead of being complementary. When the Yuvraj and Yuvrani, with a few members of the Relief Fund, went to a village in Baramulla, the local National Conference leaders and prominent workers were conspicuous by their absence. This resulted in negative coverage in a couple of local papers about the Sadr-e-Riyasat working at cross purposes with the government. Both newspapers carried an identical report about the visit, which wasn't surprising since neither had sent a reporter to cover it. It transpired that the 'news' they carried had been fed to them by the office of the senior bureaucrat.

It was apparent that mischievous elements were on the lookout for opportunities to drive a wedge between the Head of the State and the Prime Minister, and they had found one in this case. The intention was to put the idea in Prime Minister Bakshi's mind that the Government of India had used the Sadr-e-Riyasat to show that without the Centre's support, the State

Government was not in a position to provide relief to the flood victims. In exasperation, Karan Singh told Bakshi that if there were any apprehensions, he was willing to turn his Fund over to the Prime Minister as he had no desire to drag his office into any controversy. Ultimately, the whole affair was put to rest, but not before it had been demonstrated that while on the surface everything appeared calm and normal, below the surface troublemakers were always at work. Even more worryingly, the episode again pointed to latent Kashmir-Jammu tension that could be easily exploited by conspirators.

15
The End of an Era

POLITICALLY, KARAN SINGH AND the country had entered a new phase, and he felt restless. The more he saw of the country and the world, the more he began to fret in the narrow confines of the State, and that too within the boundaries of a complicated constitutional role. He yearned to be on the bigger stage, even if he would have a smaller role there. However, the national leadership thought he was needed more in the state than at the Centre, as there was a continued need to strike a balance between Kashmir and Jammu. By this time, Karan Singh's interest in spirituality had led him to two remarkable mystics, Gopalda and Ashishda who had an ashram in the Himalayas, in Mirtola. They had become his spiritual Gurus, to whom he often turned for advice. They also did not think it was time for him to move to a bigger arena. Thus, he continued as Sadr-e-Riyasat, though with some reluctance. To manage his restlessness, he decided to focus on earning a Ph.D. degree, for which he enrolled with the Delhi University under the guidance of Professor C.J. Chacko.

In 1957, the Indian Philosophical Congress was held in Srinagar, and Karan Singh, as Head of the State, was asked to inaugurate it. It was a great occasion for him to dwell on the unique, almost uninterrupted, philosophical and multi-religious tradition of Kashmir, which had successively nurtured the Vedic, Buddhist, Shaiva, and Sufi traditions. The fact was that while he was looking for a bigger and more challenging role in the secular world, he was also gradually being drawn towards exploring the self and spiritualism. The journey, still incipient, could be said to have started during his childhood under the influence of his mother. But while hers was a simple religious faith, for him the religious ritual was opening doors to something deeper and bigger and he now wanted to engage with and understand that. The first conscious effort in this direction was made with the help of Pandit Paramanand, the retired Auditor-General of the State, a Kashmiri Pandit, who offered to teach him Sanskrit. It had all begun with the simple recitation of *shlokas* from the Bhagavad Gita, and it was amazing to discover the ease with which the *shruti*—the learning-by-listening tradition of the Vedic era—came naturally to him. Perhaps his training in classical singing came in handy as the Sanskrit shlokas have a rhythmic and melodious quality, and he found it easy to follow them. The depth and the sweep of the poetry fascinated him, and he wanted to have more of this new world. Therefore, he soon accepted Pandit Paramanand as his Guru and was introduced to the *Shakta* philosophy. He also visited the Bagla Mukhi Temple in Kangra, one of the most important Shakti-peeths of the country, and continues to be its devotee.

All this while, he had not rejected the Vaishnava tradition, so dominant in Kangra, inherited from his mother, whose *Ishtdeva* was Lord Krishna, and he was able to harmonize the two traditions. In 1953, he had gone on a journey to the Holy Amarnath Cave and had written an account that was published in *The Hindustan Times*. He had received many letters from people who had read and liked the account, and among them was a reader called Ram Peare, who suggested that it appeared that he was ready for spiritual guidance and that one Raushan Nath could be of help to him. A few months later, Raushan Nath, popularly known as Nathji, appeared at Karan Singh's Srinagar home and taught him the technique of the evocative chanting of 'Aum', a word and sound that finds mention in the Upanishads and the Bhagavad Gita. It turned out to be a powerful instrument for psychic development, and Nathji remained a part of Karan Singh's life for quite a while, thereby arousing his desire to develop his *Kundalini*—a serpent power believed by Yogis to reside coiled at the base of the spine.

At about this time, he came across a book, *Among the Great*, written by Dilip Kumar Roy, and read an essay about one of the 'greats', Sri Aurobindo, the celebrated philosopher and a major influence on the freedom movement of the country. The essay contained a reference to Ronald Nixon, an Englishman who had settled in India in search of enlightenment, taking a new name, Krishnaprem. Fascinated by the discovery, the Yuvraj wrote to Dilip Kumar Roy to know more about him, who sent him another book, *Sri Aurobindo Came to Me*, which contained a complete chapter about Sri Krishnaprem, which so riveted the Yuvraj's attention that he resolved to meet him in person. The problem was to locate where he resided in the hills of Almora, and he sought the help of Dr. K.M. Munshi, an erudite man with a deep knowledge of Hinduism, who was then the Governor of Uttar Pradesh. Having secured Sri Krishnaprem's address, he began a correspondence with him, and regular replies came not from him but from Sri Madhav Ashish, his disciple, who, too, like his Guru, was an Englishman. Ronald Nixon, or Sri Krishanprem, had been a fighter pilot in the Royal Air Force during the First World War and was brought by his destiny to India, where, after a while, he built with his Guru, Sri Sri Yashoda Ma, an ashram with a temple dedicated to Lord Krishna in Mirtola, Almora. He had written many books, notably on the Gita and the Upanishads. He also drew upon the Western philosophy of Plotinus, Hermes Trismegistus, Meister Eckhart, Helena Blavatsky and others, to show that the spiritual quest was a universal yearning and was not necessarily connected to a particular religion.

Thus, Sri Krishnaprem—whom his followers and students called Gopalda—became Karan Singh's second Guru, but importantly, he struck a relationship that had a lasting influence on him. The nature of their relationship is best seen in the light of the following advice that Sri Krishnaprem gave when they met: 'I am not prepared to advise you on what to do or what not to do, but I will say one thing—do not lose the light that is within you. You have it, and it is more precious than your intelligence, fame, and wealth. It is the only thing that will last; do not lose it. Follow what seems to you the highest. You will never regret it.' Along with Madhav Ashish—Ashishda—they they would sit long into the night discussing everything, politics, relationships, dreams, and books, linking every subject with outer activity and inner aspirations. Both Gopalda and Ashishda, with their intellectual perception and deep emotional empathy, analyzed life situations for Karan Singh in a manner no one else had ever done before. They had both attained an inner peace that also rubbed off on others.

Politically, this period was one of churning at the borders of J&K that would manifest itself in a conflict that would redefine the entire region and affect the lives of millions in the coming years. In late December 1956, the enigmatic Chinese Premier Chou En Lai and his delegation visited India to a rousing reception. One of the members of the delegation was the young Dalai Lama, with whom Karan Singh interacted briefly, enchanted by his beatific smile. No one could have imagined that not far into the future, the young Dalai Lama would be returning to India along with thousands of his followers to seek asylum after the communist boots of China's Revolutionary Army had decided to follow the footsteps of Imperial China to invade and annex Tibet. The year 1959 was the year of the tragic denouement of Nehru's Tibet policy. It was a combination of many factors that led to it; perhaps, an otherwise brilliant reader of history, India's ambassador to China, K.M. Panikkar, had drawn faulty conclusions from the developments that were taking place in Lhasa and had inaccurately reported about them or, the idealism of Nehru had fallen flat in the face of the hard realities of national interests, but either way the consequence was disastrous. Tibet had lost its political and cultural identity, a loss that could possibly have been averted if Nehru had recognized Tibet as an independent country soon after India attained freedom and thus helped it gain membership of the United Ntions. But that opportunity had been lost, and when the Chinese Army struck in Lhasa, the State of Jammu and Kashmir was directly affected by it. At that time, about 500 Ladakhi monks were under training in Tibet, and there were serious concerns about their safety. Moreover, there were many religious and family bonds between Ladakh and Tibet. Therefore, the brunt of the refugee influx would be borne by this region of the State.

But this was still in the future. There were other concerns. Prime Minister Nehru used to regularly write letters to the Chief Ministers of the different states. The Prime Minister of J&K also received these letters, a copy of which was sent to Karan Singh. These letters were not directives but were rather, as Nehru called them, 'loud-thinking'. One such letter was written on 13 July 1958, which dealt with the problems facing the country and the world, and then went on to point out the economic problems of the country that had been exploited to such an extent by the colonial power that it had been reduced to abject poverty. Significantly, he also wrote, among other things: 'In considering these economic aspects of our problems, we have always to remember the basic approach of peaceful means; and perhaps we might also keep in view the old Vedantic ideal of the life force which is the inner base of everything that exists.' Inspired by the views, Karan Singh wrote a lengthy response that very day and pointed out the challenges that needed to be urgently tackled as a priority. One of the issues was corruption in public life. He wrote, 'Corruption has established itself at almost all levels of public life, and it is this above all that corrodes the idealism of youth.' It is obvious that he was deeply disappointed by the accusations of rampant corruption under the Bakshi dispensation, which, in his opinion, had completely negated the good political work that he had done. Among other acts of corruption, he was referring to the widespread use of official and muscle power to intimidate the prospective candidates during the second Assembly elections, thereby devaluing the democratic process. In his letter to Nehru, Karan Singh went on to add, 'Whether or not a spiritual motive permeates us, there is no doubt that we will be judged, and our democracy itself will be judged, by the extent to which we can solve our economic problems and ensure to the people of India a reasonable minimum standard of material goods and services,' and then went on to point out an aspect related to development that had not been paid attention to. He wrote, 'We are spending hundreds of crores upon numerous development projects, but are we spending enough upon family planning and birth-control on a mass scale…unless we do the same all our plans and schemes will be greatly jeopardized and we will never succeed in lifting the mass of our people out of the morass of poverty to which they have been sunk for so many centuries.' After a few days,

Nehru wrote back: 'I read your note with great interest and, I think, profit. What appealed to me especially was a young man of your generation looking at the world as it is. I wish I could enter a little more into the minds of your generation.'

On the political front, hectic activity had been taking place in J&K. The Permit system needed to enter that State had been abolished, a Bill had been passed bringing the Judges of the High Court on par with those of the rest of the country, and the authority of the Indian Election Commissioner had been extended to the State. But the widespread corruption that was reported from every sphere was taking the sheen off these changes. Prime Minister Bakshi had gotten his brother, Bakshi Abdul Rashid, elected as the President of the National Conference, and he had his fingers in all the profitable pies. In Kashmir, humour has always been an armour against the blows of life and fate, helping people cope with the trouble and hardship, and the Bakshi brothers came to be known as BBC—the Bakshi Brothers Corporation, which monopolized corruption in the State. But there were leaders like G.M. Sadiq, Mir Qasim and D.P. Dhar who found it hard to stomach corruption. Thus, along with the Speaker of the Assembly, G.R. Renzu, they drifted away from Bakshi to form the Democratic National Conference. Karan Singh found himself in sympathy with this breakaway group, as on an intellectual plane, he felt an affinity with them. On the face of it, the Bakshi government was strong and he had firm control over the administration and the Party, but Karan Singh, having seen the end of his father's rule and that of Sheikh Abdullah, had learned that in politics no government is ever as strong as it looks. It does not take long for the strongest to disintegrate in no time.

At such a juncture, Bakshi became so confident that he took the risk of releasing Sheikh Abdullah from detention. When this happened, Bakshi's popularity was still rising and he soon proved that his confidence was not misplaced as, in a short period, he worsted Abdullah twice in confrontations: once when the Sheikh had organized his followers with the declared threat of marching to Mujahid Manzil, the headquarters of the National Conference, to capture it, and then on the occasion of the celebration of the Republic Day of India. It was generally believed in Kashmir that whoever controlled Mujahid Manzil controlled the Valley; therefore, upon his release, Sheikh Abdullah had given a call to his followers to gather at the Pathar Masjid from where they would have marched to Mujahid Manzil to reclaim it. But Bakshi was ready with his followers, and in an anti-climax to the feverish war of words, the whole build-up petered out tamely as Sheikh Abdullah could not muster enough courage to lead his followers to their declared destination. The first round having been won resoundingly, Bakshi was prepared for the second round when Sheikh Abdullah gave a call to his followers to boycott Republic Day celebrations and fly black flags from their homes. However, Bakshi's workers outnumbered Abdullah's followers, and not only were the black flags taken down, processions celebrating Republic Day were also taken out in downtown Srinagar, apart from the official celebrations where all the government employees participated. Probably, it was for pro-India actions such as these that the Central Government ignored many of Bakshi's indiscretions and alleged acts of corruption.

Realizing the mistake he had made by releasing Sheikh Abdullah, ignoring Sadar-i-Riyasat Karan Singh's advice, Bakshi had him arrested again. But by that time the Sheikh had used his brief period of freedom to set a template that was to assume gigantic proportions in the decades to come, and in the process destroyed the *Kashmiriyat* that had kept the Hindus and Muslims of Kashmir together. In its place, he developed a religion-based politics that undermined the traditional bonds in Kashmiri society.

In addition, he remained focused on Kashmir to the exclusion of Jammu and Ladakh. In fact, from the beginning of his political career, he had used the Hazratbal Shrine for his political speeches after the Friday prayer. Otherwise, too, his speeches always began with some quotes from the Holy Quran. Thus, he had mastered the art of whipping up religious emotions and then using them to build political mass hysteria. He also used the Plebiscite Front established by Mirza Afzal Beg, for this purpose. Soon, almost all the mosques in the Valley became platforms for the Sheikh to whip up emotions against India, which he described as a 'Communal', 'Hindu' nation.

The instability this would create was still in the future. Meanwhile, in 1960, the Srinagar-Leh Road was opened, marking a historic day for the backward regions of Kargil and Leh. This was soon followed by another new road, linking Udhampur to Dhar in Himachal Pradesh. These were both initiatives that Karan Singh had championed along with others.

Intellectually, this was a very productive period for Karan Singh, as he came in contact with some of the finest brains that came to India. One of them was to drag him into a controversy that was entirely based on speculation. He had invited the American Ambassador in Delhi, Professor Kenneth Galbraith, to Jammu. Galbraith had a reputation for being an excellent teacher of economics and had been handpicked by President Kennedy for the ambassadorial role in India. In Jammu, Karan Singh arranged for Galbraith to meet some professors and intellectuals so that they could profit from the learned visitor and he, in turn, could know more about how the region thought. This innocent intellectual exercise was blown out of proportion and presented in a left-leaning paper as if America were trying to make inroads into the State. It was embarrassing, but Karan Singh told himself in a vibrant democracy this kind of thing was just one of many occupational hazards. But he was disappointed that in its desire for eyeball-grabbing headlines, the media had chosen to ignore his well-known and often remarked-upon friendship with left-leaning thinkers like Romesh Thapar and political activists like Aruna Asaf Ali. This was another experience that made his desire to leave J&K for a bigger stage, stronger.

In 1961, Karan Singh and the Yuvrani decided to go to England as some exchange was lying in the foreign account there. Once again, they decided to fly from Bombay, after spending some time with the Maharaja. When they reached 19 Nepean Road, they were shocked to see him, for he had grown so frail that he found it difficult to walk. Karan Singh knew that his father was diabetic, but he had not been informed by any of his father's staff members who regularly visited Jammu that the problem had worsened. He was also aware that his father had such a needle phobia that he refused to take insulin injections. As a result, he had developed a serious carbuncle on his neck. Karan Singh and Asha were deeply disturbed to see him in a wheel chair. Yet, he received them cheerfully and gave them detailed instructions on purchasing him a pair of Manchester terriers. He had recently read about them, and they were bred in Scotland. He also told his son to get him a pair of 8x30B binoculars for the races. When the couple were ready to depart for the airport, the Maharaja was lying on his bed and when the Yuvraj bent down to touch his feet, he realized that not since he had suffered the atrophy of his hip muscle and the complication of subsequent operations, had he been able to touch his father's feet. In his semi-jocular farewell, the Maharaja said, 'Be good, and look after Asha.'

Karan Singh and Asha spent ten days in London, shopping at Harrods and succeeding in procuring the pair of dogs that the

Maharaja wanted. Karan Singh left the pair with his Secretary, Dewan Iqbal Nath, with instructions to bring them back to India and proceeded to Rome on 26 April, intending to visit Naples after staying in Rome for two days. In Rome, while the couple were planning to take a bus tour in the belief that they were incognito, the Indian Ambassador in Italy, S.N. Haksar, rang up to say that he was coming over immediately to see them. Even as the Yuvrani was unpacking, Karan Singh walked down to the foyer to meet Haksar, only to be informed that his father had passed away.

It was a stunning blow. All his life, the presence of his father had been so dominating that it was impossible to imagine that he was no longer alive. The Yuvrani who had for the last twelve years been the family member closest to the Maharaja, broke down on hearing the news. Meanwhile, Ambassador Haksar had very thoughtfully booked two seats on the Air India flight to Delhi late that evening. On the flight back, the Yuvraj could not sleep as memories of his father came back to him again and again. He saw his father, resplendent in his uniform and medals, riding a white horse ahead of his troops as he inspected the Dussehra parade at Batmaloo grounds. There were other images: his father sitting in the Thricker fishing lodge, sipping his whiskey and laughing at the jokes his staff officers cracked; on the lovely lawns of Gulab Bhavan in Srinagar, cooking delicious recipes along with his mother and a huge entourage. He also recalled that when he was to return home from Doon School on vacation, his father would drive down to Anantnag to receive him. He was not the one to express his affection in words, but this gesture of his coming down to Anantnag was worth a million words. He recalled, too, that such was the Maharaja's intimidating presence that once, when he sat beside his father during a shoot, keeping tab on a counter of the number of ducks his father shot, so awed had he been by his father's reflexes that he had blurted out, 'Well done', but was immediately horrified by his audacity and had timidly added, 'ji' to make his appreciation more respectful!

When Karan Singh and Asha reached Bombay, the cremation had already been carried out as per the will of the Maharaja according to Arya Samaj rites. This was news to all those who knew the Maharaja, as he was more of an agnostic and had not, to the knowledge of anyone who knew him, renounced his Sanatani past. He may not have been very particular about observing the daily religious rituals, but never had he denounced or demonstrated his disinclination to observe them when the occasion arose. When and how he had decided to accept Arya Samaj as his creed, no one in the family knew. The only person who followed Arya Samaj's rites and was close to him was Mehr Chand Mahajan, his former Prime Minister, who had remained his advisor even after he settled in Bombay. But Arya Samaj rituals were what he had chosen according to his will, and, accordingly, the remains of his bones were, instead of being immersed in the Ganga at Haridwar, immersed in the Arabian Sea. In his will, he had instructed: 'My *asthis* [bones] should be thrown into the sea, but my ashes should be placed in a silver urn and taken up in a specially chartered plane and scattered over Jammu city, the place of my birth. The silver urn should then be deposited in the Agricultural College hereinafter mentioned in a suitable place with a suitable inscription.'

Following the will, on 28 April, the Yuvraj and his wife carried the urn on its final journey to Jammu in a chartered DC-3 plane. Before landing, the plane circled the city thrice, and the Yuvraj scattered the ashes out of the window over the soil below. In the city there was a sea of humanity to pay their last tearful homage to their beloved king who had, effectively, been exiled from his kingdom for the final twelve years of his life. The open car carrying the Yuvraj with his hands clutching the silver urn passed through a familiar route which, on happier occasions during the reign of the last Maharaja of the Dogras, would be lined with cheering crowds; now there were the sounds of wailing and mourning. Upon reaching Amar Mahal, the Yuvraj found his mother dressed in white, the traditional colour of mourning worn by Hindu widows. The reality of death finally sank in.

According to the will of the Maharaja, his son was not obliged to carry out any of the ceremonies that follow a Hindu death. But the Yuvraj considered it his duty to go through the traditional thirteen-day period of prayers and rituals for the departed soul. But after the thirteen days, the practical affairs needed to be attended to and the first step the Yuvraj took was to write to Prime Minister Nehru, reminding him of the issue of notification by the Home Ministry consequent to the passing away of his father. He also sent a copy of that letter to Lal Bahadur Shastri, the Home Minister. This notification was to be issued by the Government of India to recognize a successor when any former ruler of a princely state died. It was a legal and constitutional requirement flowing from the accession of the princely States to the Indian Union. The other issue was the Maharaja's will. From 1952 onwards, the Maharaja had transferred all the family estates in the State to his son, and in 1959, had legally made him the sole trustee of the Dharmarth Trust. But to everyone's surprise, he had left all his property and assets in Bombay, Poona, Bangalore, and abroad, to an Arya Samaj charity, and two residential houses in Jammu and everything in them to those who had served him. This raised the question whether he had the right to give away this property, all purchased with money that came to him on account of him being the Maharaja. He had no private income. The fabulous jewellery that he possessed—what he had inherited from his ancestors and what he had bought as Maharaja—had simply disappeared. No one could say with any certainty what happened to it as it was never seen again. What was of great shock was that he had left nothing to his wife, even depriving her of her *stree-dhan*—gifts received at her marriage—which had been taken away from her in 1949 when she decided not to accompany the Maharaja to Bombay. He had justified himself by writing in his will that he had given enough to his wife, son, daughter-in-law and granddaughter in his lifetime.

Many people, including K.M. Munshi and the Maharaja's friend Beryl, thought that the will ought to be contested because of the inherent injustice and, possibly, contravention of civil laws, in its provisions. In hindsight, Beryl remembered that on one occasion, the Maharaja had told her that he would make sure that his wife was unable to lay her hands on his wealth through their son. Now, to the great disappointment of his son, he had executed his intent. It was difficult to accept that an otherwise fair man like him would go to such lengths to spite his estranged wife. The idea of challenging the will was a practical one, but on reflection, Karan Singh decided against the advice as their reputations would have been smeared forever, and he would have had to live with the guilt of having challenged his father, however just his cause might have been. So, he let the matter rest there and moved on to deal with the challenge that had been mounted on the Dogra dynasty all over again by the Kashmiri lobby and small-minded men who had their axes to grind. The issue of succession, a subject that was governed by a covenant between the ruler who signed the Instrument of Accession and the Government of India, was sought to be converted into a weapon to launch a fresh attack on the Dogra Dynasty.

16

Succession and After

The thirteen-day period of mourning after the demise of Maharaja Hari Singh had barely passed when leaders and their proxies in Kashmir tried to cloud the issue of succession to his titles, privy purse, and privileges. Dina Nath Mahajan, Mir Qasim, and M.A. Shahmiri, members of the State Ministry and senior National Conference leaders, questioned if Yuvraj Karan Singh should inherit the privy purse and also the title of Maharaja, which his father held.

In a letter dated 27 May 1961, after raising these twin questions, they conceded that if the privy purse was admissible to the Yuvraj, then the State Government should not have any objection, but the inheriting of the title needed to be given serious thought. They wrote, 'The consideration of this question requires careful examination of the terms of the covenant or the agreement which the late Maharaja entered into with the Dominion of India before the commencement of the Constitution.' Then the three gentlemen went on to concede that since the Privy Purse was to be disbursed from the Consolidated Fund of India, that may not be a problem for the State, but the inheritance of the title could pose certain problems. They added, '[after inheriting the title] he will continue to be what he is today, namely, the constitutional head of the State. But with all that, the Sadr-e-Riyasat of Jammu and Kashmir being recognized as Maharaja or Ruler by the Central Government will in all probability be an exploitable issue and may stir the interested elements in the State to rouse passions. The emotional aspect of this question cannot be overemphasized, and it must receive proper consideration by the State and the Central Governments.'

They argued that with effect from 21st August 1952, the hereditary monarchy had been abolished by the State Legislature and that accordingly an amendment had been carried out to Article 370 of the Indian Constitution whereby, 'in the explanation appended to sub-clause (b) of clause (1) of the aforesaid Article, the words "the person for the time being recognized by the President as Maharaja of Jammu and Kashmir" were replaced by the words "the person for the time being recognized by the President on the recommendation of the Legislative Assembly as the Sadr-e-Riyasat of Jammu and Kashmir." Thus, if the Sadr-e-Riyasat of the State also carried the title of Maharaja, it may give an easy handle to interested elements of the State to raise the slogan that the decision of the Constituent Assembly to abolish the Rulership and to have a wholly democratic form of Government in the State was being flouted.'

Taking a cue from this letter, many more voices joined in, and it appeared that they had the tacit support of the State Government. In Delhi also, there was some hesitation, though the terms that had been set between the Government of India and the Maharaja of the State at the time of accession and then when the Maharaja agreed to the appointment of the Yuvraj as his Regent while he stayed out of the State, were very clear. These read: 'The Government of India also agrees to guarantee the succession to the titles, dignities, privileges, and privy purse according to law and custom of Your Highness's family.' Prime Minister Nehru was aware of the obligation to which the Government of India was bound, but his inherent inability to accept Rulers in a democratic set-up made him wish that the Rulers would, of their own volition, give up the titles in a Republic. The State Government had made its views known through the letter written by the three senior members of the Government, but the fact was that Yuvraj Karan Singh's recognition as successor to his father, along with the privy purse and the titles, was a constitutional necessity for the Government of India. Ultimately, a way was found by Jawaharlal Nehru, who asked the Home Minister, Lal Bahadur Shastri, to convey to Yuvraj Karan Singh that as long as he was the Sadr-e-Riyasat, it would be inappropriate of him to use the royal title as the State had constitutionally abolished the monarchy. The Yuvraj agreed to the suggestion and on 7 July 1961, wrote to the Home Minister: 'Although I have succeeded to the title of my late father His Highness Maharaja Hari Singh, I do not wish to use these titles so long as I hold the office of the Sadr-e-Riyasat of Jammu and Kashmir, and during this period I should like to be addressed as Shri Karan Singh.'

Consequently, on July 10, the Home Ministry issued an order to be published in the Gazette that the President was pleased to recognize Yuvraj Karan Singh as the successor to late His Highness Maharaja Sir Hari Singh Indar Mahindra Bahadur with effect from 26 April 1961. After this, the Home Ministry issued a press note announcing that as successor to the late Maharaja, Yuvraj Karan Singh was entitled to the use of the titles His Highness and Maharaja but he had informed the Government that as long as he held the office of the Sadr-e-Riyasat he did not wish to use the titles and that he wished to be addressed as Shri Karan Singh. In addition, he also surrendered his salary of

Rs. 5,500 per month as Sadr-e-Riyasat since he was to get a Privy Purse from the Government of India. The Government of India was to give Rs. Ten lakhs annually as Privy Purse to Karan Singh, and out of this, Rs one lakh was to be paid to the Maharani during her lifetime, after which Karan Singh was to get the full amount. All discussion on the subject should have ended there, but those who were bent upon creating a controversy and lived on it found plenty of reasons to create disaffection among the people. The first occasion was found when, after his official recognition as the successor to his late father, Karan Singh arrived in Srinagar, and there was a beeline of friends and well-wishers who called upon him to congratulate him. In response, he extended the common courtesy of hosting a dinner party for them. But in a lapse of judgement, instead of sending the invitations in his name, they were sent on behalf of his Staff Officer. This allowed the anti-Dogra forces to say that Karan Singh was officially celebrating his coronation and foisting the titles of the monarchy on a people who had abolished it.

The dinner was to be held on 4 August 1961, but Prime Minister Bakshi met Karan Singh three days before the dinner and pointed out that the invitations should not have been issued on behalf of the Staff Officer but on Karan Singh's behalf. Correcting the mistake, Karan Singh immediately wrote letters to Bakshi and his cabinet colleagues, requesting them to attend the dinner. But the State Government, dominated by Kashmiri leaders, was not going to let this opportunity go. A day before the dinner, *Kashmir Post* commented on the whole affair under the heading 'Succession as Maharaja'. It made the suggestion that the dinner 'smacks of a planned campaign for revivalism in this State, well set on the path of democracy'. Writing to his Prime Minister on the same day, Karan Singh pointed out that the general perception of the people was that *Kashmir Post* wrote what was endorsed by the State Government and pointed out that the public allegation against the Head of the State had 'dangerous and schismatic implications'. He demanded of Bakshi that the editor of *Kashmir Post* should publicly apologize for making such a sinister accusation. Bakshi replied on 10 August and claimed that he disapproved of the content published in the said newspaper and that he had asked the Director of Information to sort the matter out who, after holding a meeting with Ved Bhasin, the Editor of *Kashmir Post*, reported to the Prime Minister that Bhasin had claimed that he did not mean to be discourteous to the Head of the State and had been trying to 'focus public attention on what had become a raging controversy both here [Srinagar] and in Jammu'. He said he had received reports of various elements trying to 'exploit the conferment of the Maharaja's title on the Sadr-e-Riyasat for a revivalist programme'. It was very obvious that the whole controversy had the backing of the State Government and was meant to embarrass Karan Singh and also widen the differences between Kashmir and Jammu.

This innocuous dinner was to reverberate for a little while longer as interested people informed Prime Minister Nehru that it did appear as if the dinner was indeed a kind of coronation ceremony. Karan Singh had come to know that this had caused Nehru some disquiet, so he was constrained to explain the whole affair through a letter on 30 August. He wrote that since a large number of citizens from all walks of life and faith spontaneously called upon him to offer congratulations upon his succession to his late father's royal position, he had, to fulfil his social obligations, decided to host a dinner party for about four hundred guests. He had carefully drawn up the list of guests so that no section of the citizens of Srinagar was left unrepresented. He further explained that since the party was on the occasion of his succession, he had thought it indelicate to extend the invitation himself; therefore, after some consideration, it was issued by his Staff Officer. It was only in hindsight that he realized that it would have been better if he had issued the invitations himself. But he protested that turning a social function into a weapon to impute motives to him was grossly unfair. He pointed out that certain interested political sections who opposed his continuing in the office of Sadr-e-Riyasat had been waiting for an opportunity to attack him but in the present instance, the way they came after him was an outcome of a conspiracy since long before the Presidential Order announcing his succession to his father, the mischievous campaign against him had been launched in press and public. Finally, he pointed out that the dinner had been hosted in good faith by incurring considerable personal expense.

This controversy, however, continued to dog Karan Singh for a few more months as every social and religious act in connection with the death of the Maharaja and the subsequent recognition of his son as the head of the family was sought to be dragged into controversy. The family had planned that the ceremony where the son is recognized as the successor to his father should be held sometime in October 1961. No sooner had this news broken than the critics were back. Rumours were afloat about the 'coronation' and the 'hectic activities' that were taking place in that connection in Jammu, the citadel of Karan Singh's family. It was also rumoured that there were serious differences on the issue between the Sadr-e-Riyasat and Prime Minister Bakshi and that the ruling National Conference would never allow it to happen. What was true was that the 'coronation' had been planned for October, that is, six months after the demise of his father, but it had been postponed on the insistence of his mother, who wanted all such ceremonies to take place only after the completion of one year of mourning.

In an interview with V.I.K. Sarin on behalf of the newspaper *Current,* Karan Singh said that the controversy had been created by those interested people who thrived on disorder and conspiracy theories and insisted that 'being the Head of the State does not debar me from fulfilling my social, religious and family obligations, and I don't think anybody should have any objection to it'. He then went on to affirm that the ceremony would take place in April 1962. This unnecessary controversy, he said, was the handiwork of those who were bent upon destroying the identity of the Dogras. They had not been satisfied with the reality of the Parliamentary form of government, where, in this case, the power structure in the State had tilted towards Kashmir on the strength of numbers. Kashmiri leaders, therefore, had no reason to create mischief. But Karan Singh also observed that Jammu too needed to be realistic, for democracy had favoured Kashmir; therefore, every statement or act taking place in the Valley did not need to be responded to or resented. There was still so much more to do and aspire for, and Karan Singh had no intention of getting bogged down by inane controversies.

Putting all the controversies behind him, Karan Singh focused on completing his doctoral thesis from Delhi University and also plunged himself into the activities of the State. He had turned thirty and was full of energy as well as curiosity and, therefore, chafed at the narrow confines of his role as Head of the State. He would have loved to play some active role in party politics, but, for obvious reasons, that had to be ruled out. So, he took an active part in other activities that were offered by his role as the Chancellor of the Jammu and Kashmir University. As Chancellor, he presided over the meetings of the Syndicate and played an active role in planning the buildings there. He also presided over the meetings of the Red Cross and the Board that looked after the interests of the ex-servicemen. While finding ways to make himself useful, he also kept a vigilant eye on the political activities in the State.

His wife, Asha, too, had matured and trained herself in more ways than one. She had cleared the Prabhakar examination, which was equivalent to graduation, after passing an additional paper in English. Apart from this, she had groomed herself to hold her own in the company of guests from the rest of the country and abroad. As the wife of the Head of the State, she was the Chairperson of the State Social Welfare Board, in which capacity she was involved in several projects in Srinagar, Jammu, and Leh. This remained her passion throughout her life. In this work, she was assisted by the indefatigable Bageshwari Dhar, a Kashmiri Pandit widow who had assisted Mridula Sarabhai in recovering and rehabilitating abducted women in the aftermath of Partition.

During this period, Kashmir also became a favoured destination for important seminars and conferences, which provided Karan Singh more opportunities to widen his horizon as he had to make inaugural speeches. This involved wide reading and research, which was an intellectually rewarding experience. Apart from his ever-increasing desire to walk on a bigger stage, it was a satisfying phase of his life, but for the fact that with the new year came the third general election for the State legislature, and to Karan Singh's disappointment, it was no different from the earlier elections.

The Congress Party had no presence in the State, so it supported the National Conference and even Nehru came to the State to campaign for it. The 1962 election was marred by the allegation that ballot boxes had been tampered with. This was serious, as it put a question mark over the sanctity of the whole process, and Karan Singh wrote to the then Election Commissioner, K.V.K. Sundaram, who flew down to Jammu and held consultations with Prime Minister Bakshi and the opposition before adopting measures to make the ballot boxes more secure. But this incident had caused enough damage to the integrity of the process, and when the results were declared, which were hardly any different from the earlier two elections, the suspicions about rigging seemed confirmed. In the Jammu region, where the Praja Parishad was expected to do well, the National Conference had won 26 of the 29 seats, and it was obvious that the margins of victory did not truly reflect the mood of the people. In the Valley, 34 seats were won by the National Conference after the nomination papers of all the opposition candidates were rejected on flimsy grounds. In the end, Bakshi's National Conference had won 70 of the 75 Assembly seats. The template for elections set by Sheikh Abdullah in 1952 had been scrupulously followed by Bakshi in 1957 and now in 1962.

The year 1962 also witnessed the liberation of Goa from Portugal and the general election for the Parliament, which resulted in a resounding victory for the Nehru-led Congress for a third term, after which he was once again elected leader of the Congress Legislature Party and Prime Minister. The year also brought an end to the Presidency of Dr. Rajendra Prasad and with it, the world witnessed a rarity with three great intellectuals occupying the highest political posts in the world's largest and most vibrant democracy. Dr. Rajendra Prasad was replaced by the widely respected and erudite Dr. Radhakrishnan, and his place as Vice-President was taken by the equally cultured and scholarly Dr. Zakir Hussain. With Nehru as the Prime Minister, this triumvirate presented to the world the best of intellectual minds, with all of whom Karan Singh had a special relationship. The same year, Karan Singh also had the good fortune of meeting and listening to two Nobel Laureates in Delhi. He attended a fascinating lecture delivered by Dr. C.V. Raman on 'The Gateways of Human Knowledge' and another delivered by Pearl S. Buck, the famed author of *The Good Earth*, who addressed an overflowing audience at the India International Centre. He met her after the lecture and she graciously accepted his invitation to dine at his Delhi residence, Mansarovar. According to Karan Singh, after the great Helen Keller, she was the most remarkable woman he had met. Keller, who had lost her sight and hearing when she was just an infant, had triumphed over the misfortune and become a remarkable writer and disability rights activist. Her story had been a strong inspiration for Karan Singh when he was recovering in the New York hospital. Several years later, he had met her at the Jammu airport when she transited through it, and one of his abiding memories was of Keller feeling his face with her soft hands and then declaring that he was handsome!

Later, in the summer of the same year when a visibly tired and unwell Nehru came to Srinagar to enjoy his holidays, Karan Singh visited him and after discussing the political situation of the State, gave him the manuscript of his doctoral thesis on Sri Aurobindo, titled *Prophet of Indian Nationalism*, and requested him to write its foreword. Nehru obliged and wrote: 'In commending the study of Sri Aurobindo's political thought, I would like to point out that the young man who has written it, is a scion of a princely state in India. At present, he is the political Head or Governor of the State of Jammu and Kashmir. It is significant to note that he should have devoted himself to his studies and, more particularly, to this analysis of the political thought of Sri Aurobindo during a crucial period of our history, instead of occupying himself with the normal activities of Indian princes, that is, shikar, polo and high society.' The acknowledgment of these facts was very satisfying, as Karan Singh had consciously deviated from the conventional life of the princes and had even defied his formidable father. Soon, thereafter, the thesis was published by Allen and Unwin in London. It was, in fact, his third book. The earlier books were *Varied Rhythms*, a collection of poems and essays in 1960, and *Shadow and Sunlight*, a collection of Dogri-Pahari folk songs with musical annotations and English translations in 1961. A few months after he had renounced the titles of His Highness and Maharaja, he was awarded his doctorate, and he earned the title 'Doctor' of which he has remained very proud all his life. Soon after, as if to give him a special reward for having given up his inherited titles, President Dr. Radhakrishnan informed him by a telegram that he had been appointed to the honorary rank of Major General!

Much before the year had closed, India had been brought down with a thud from the high perch of idealism it was sitting on. Warning signals had been emanating for quite some time, and even Karan Singh had pointed out that the Chinese had been setting up posts in the areas that were legally part of the former State of Jammu and Kashmir and, therefore, India. In his fortnightly report to the President dated 1 November 1961, he had written that the Chinese had set up another post at 'Chipchap' within India's borders. He had added: 'It seems fairly clear that the Chinese have no intention whatsoever of vacating the territory they have occupied, and are, in fact, busy stabilizing and consolidating their positions there.' His warning was prophetic as Indian diplomacy fell between two proverbial stools as New Delhi could not deal with the historical ambiguity that was part of the northern borders, both in Ladakh as well as the North-East. Signs of the impending trouble were unmistakable when, in July 1962, there was a skirmish with the Chinese soldiers in Galwan, though a major clash was averted. The fighting qualities of the Indian Army were second to none, but unfortunately, changes had been made in the traditions of the Army with the appointment of Krishna Menon as the Defence Minister. An otherwise brilliant mind, Menon's strong will, arrogance, and suspicious nature led him to push his favourites to important positions. Among them was Major General B.M. Kaul, who was appointed as Chief of the General Staff. With a weak General P.N. Thapar as the Army Chief, 'an overly trusting Prime Minister, arrogant and power-oriented Defence Minister, and over-ambitious Chief of the General Staff', India was led into a debacle when the Chinese attacked in October 1962. The war ended in November, but by then, much of what Nehru had achieved lay in shambles. Nehru was never the same again, even though he was still the undisputed leader, but with all his peers from the days of the struggle for Independence gone, he sat on a lonely perch where there was none to offer him frank and honest advice. The 'Hindi-Chini Bhai-Bhai' slogan had gone up in smoke, and with it the dream of an Asian resurgence.

On 29 October 1962, even as the short war was on, Karan Singh was elected Sadr-e-Riyasat by the State Assembly for the third time, but there was no time for celebration as people and their support had to be mobilized for the war and defence effort. The war turned out to be a blessing in disguise for the Dogra youth as they earned Emergency Commissions in large numbers. The Dogra youth that had, since 1947, felt orphaned and had led an aimless life, discovered that they were wanted and that too in a profession close to their heart. More than any government campaign for national integration, the drafting of the youth, who were otherwise unable to crack the written examinations for securing Army Commission, helped them to meet and integrate with people from other states, and when living with their families at different military stations of the country, they imbibed the idea of a 'diverse but one' India. Politically, Nehru became weaker, and he was aware of it. Internationally, his idealism and the much-publicized Panchsheel as the guiding principles for international relations took a beating. The Anglo-US lobby tried their best to pressure Nehru into settling the Kashmir issue, but to his credit, weak though he had become, he stood firm. Various proposals were suggested, and the most ridiculous one would have left only Kathua district in India, which meant only 300 square miles out of the 85,000 square miles of the State of Jammu and Kashmir. Nehru, though, had to agree to reopen negotiations with Pakistan, which were led by two brilliant leaders in their chosen methods. Pakistan was led by the mercurial Zulfiqar Ali Bhutto, much given to histrionics, and India by Sardar Swarn Singh, a master in the art of diplomatic stonewalling.

In the summer of 1963, an aged, tired and visibly diminished Nehru, accompanied by his daughter Indira Gandhi, came to Kashmir to rest and recover. He stayed at the Chashmashahi Guest House and was left largely undisturbed, and only when Indira Gandhi sent Karan Singh a note that Nehru wanted him to come over for tea, did he visit his mentor and was saddened to see him so diminished. It was during this stay that Indira Gandhi was seen getting involved in politics. She enjoyed the company of Karan Singh, Sadiq, Mir Qasim and D.P. Dhar. All of them were liberal in thought and shared a dislike for the corrupt way Bakshi ran his government. It was obvious to all of them that Bakshi had such a vice-like grip on the government and the National Conference that it was hard to imagine the State without him. But in his short career, Karan Singh had also learned that in politics, even the most formidable are undone by a slight twist of fate. And that was what happened with Bakshi.

It began in 1962 when the acting Mirwaiz of Kashmir, the highest religious functionary in the Valley, died. The official Mirwaiz was Maulvi Yusuf Shah, who had fled to Pakistan-occupied Kashmir in 1947, and in his absence, the government had proclaimed Maulvi Atiqullah as the Mirwaiz. On his death, Bakshi had Maulvi Yusuf Shah's nephew, Maulvi Mohammad Farooq, appointed as Mirwaiz. This turned out to be a serious error of judgment on Bakshi's part, as the new appointee soon became the rallying point for the anti-India and pro-Pakistan forces in the Valley.

In another unrelated development, more challenges emerged for Nehru when, in the wake of the Chinese debacle, three bye-elections were held for the Parliament in Amroha, Farrukhabad and Rajkot constituencies. Those opposing the Congress were Acharya Kriplani, Dr. Ram Manohar Lohia, and M.R. Masani, who were articulate and vocal critics of Nehru. With the aura of Nehru fading, the three opposition stalwarts stunned the Congress with their massive victories. The defeats so stupefied the party that there was talk of its disintegration. To check the slide, a plan was devised, and Kumaraswami Kamraj, then Chief Minister of Madras State (now Tamil Nadu), resigned from his post to rekindle the spirit of sacrifice and go to the people to work and strengthen the party. Six Union Ministers, including Lal Bahadur Shastri, Jagjiwan Ram, Morarji Desai, and S.K. Patil, and six Chief Ministers followed suit. The meeting where the decision to resign was taken was also attended by Bakshi, who should not have been affected by it since he was not a member of the Congress party, but inexplicably he also chose to follow suit and resigned. There were rumours that his services would be utilized at the national level, either in the government or the Congress party. None of that happened, though that would have been remarkable, as it had the potential of bringing Kashmir close to the rest of the country. He was thus deprived of the honour of being the first Kashmiri leader to play a role at the national level. On being asked about his sudden resignation by Karan Singh, Bakshi said that since he had played a significant role in the discussion about the Kamraj Plan, he thought that his resignation would strengthen the hands of Prime Minister Nehru. This explanation was hard to digest, but many people were happy to be rid of him as he had outlived his utility and was fast becoming a cause of disillusionment for the youth.

For many days, uncertainty prevailed as Bakshi Abdul Rashid, Bakshi's cousin and also the General Secretary of the National Conference, launched a campaign of processions, demonstrations and resolutions protesting against his cousin's resignation and demanded that Nehru and Bakshi himself reconsider the resignation. Sadr-e-Riyasat Karan Singh was inundated with deputations urging him to intervene as Bakshi's departure would be politically disastrous. The Pro-Pakistan Political Conference, however, urged the Sadr-e-Riyasat to accept Bakshi's resignation—ironically, while taking out processions, it raised pro-India slogans. Many of its leaders averred before Karan Singh that they had become pro-India!

The turmoil caused by the resignation continued for some time as Bakshi Abdul Rashid, who knew that his brash and uncouth style would never be acceptable to the Government of India, wanted the next best thing, that is, a replacement who was pliable. He had managed to win his brother to his cause, and therefore, Bakshi informed Delhi that he was not in a position to get Sadiq, the most suitable candidate, elected as his successor. Finally, Khwaja Shamsuddin, the revenue minister in the outgoing cabinet, was elected as the leader of the Legislature and sworn in as the third Prime Minister of the State. With it ended the decade-long rule of Bakshi Ghulam Mohammad, who had taken command at a very critical period of history and had consolidated the pro-India forces in J&K. He had also addressed, to some extent, the challenges and problems of Jammu and Ladakh. As a final gesture of his commitment to India, a few days before relinquishing his office, he wrote to the Sadr-e-Riyasat on 3 October 1963: 'As this was to be the last session of the Legislative Council to be attended by me as Prime Minister of the State I made an announcement of the following policy directives for implementation by the successor Government:

a) That the designation of the Head of the State (Sadr-e-Riyasat) and that of the Head of the Government (Prime Minister) should be changed to 'Governor' and the 'Chief Minister' respectively, as in other States of the country; and

b) That there should be direct elections to the Parliament instead of the present system of nominations...'

His successor, Shamsuddin, found himself suddenly catapulted into a position for which he was politically and psychologically unprepared. In administration, he had some outlandish ideas like morality training for the corrupt, and when, after a few months, a crisis of gigantic magnitude hit Kashmir, he was found woefully wanting.

17

The Crisis and Change of Guard

WITH THE APPOINTMENT OF Shamsuddin as the Prime Minister of the State, there was a spurt in political activity that was unrelated to him. The Praja Parishad, the Jammu-based party, decided to merge its identity with the Bharatiya Jana Sangh, the political wing of the RSS. Pandit Prem Nath Dogra, who had piloted the Praja Parishad ever since its inception, became the first President of Bharatiya Jana Sangh's Jammu and Kashmir unit. With this, a national political party had entered the State for the first time. This change was soon followed by the announcement that another national party, the Praja Socialist Party, had decided to extend its activities to the State with Balraj Puri, a political activist, social worker and author, as the President of the State unit. Not to be left behind, Kashmir-based Mohammad Shafi Qureshi announced the establishment of a new outfit, called Jammu and Kashmir National Congress. As the name of this new party suggested, it reflected the urge, however weak it might have appeared at that time, to reach out to the national mainstream.

But even before the new changes could make some difference to the political activity in the State, a crisis of unprecedented magnitude overwhelmed it. On the early morning of 27 December 1963, Rahim Banday, the Senior Nishan Dez (the seniormost keeper of the Holy Relic of Prophet Mohammad) at the Hazratbal Dargah, found that the side door of the passage leading to the room where Moe-e-Muqaddas (the hair of the Prophet) was kept in safe custody, had been broken open, the wooden box containing the Moe-e-Muqaddas had been taken out, and the small bag containing the crystal tube that encased the Holy Relic had been removed and taken away. The shocking news spread like wildfire, and by the afternoon, the streets of Srinagar were full of protesters demanding the immediate restoration of the Relic to its designated place. No one knew for certain what had happened and as people continued to arrive in the vicinity of Hazratbal, another red flag was waved at the already restive people when Bakshi Abdul Rashid, the General Secretary of the National Conference who had made an abortive bid to succeed Bakshi Ghulam Mohammad and was also a component of the much-derided BBC—Bakshi Brothers Corporation—a synonym for rampant corruption, arrived there in an open jeep and brusquely asked the crowd to disperse. Tactlessly, he said that the Holy Relic had disappeared on earlier occasions too but had returned to its place, as no power on earth could remove the Relic from its permanent place of rest.

His arrogant style angered the already emotionally charged people, and they responded violently. It was after considerable effort that he was rescued by the police, but by then the crowds were uncontrollable. A hotel and a cinema hall owned by one of Bakshi's brothers were set on fire. Led by faceless leaders, the emotional crowd moved towards Kothibagh Police Station and set it ablaze too. In response, the police opened fire, killing three. By then, the protest marches against the sacrilege had crystallised into a general protest against the government and the rampant corruption that it was accused of, resulting in complete paralysis of life in the Valley for many days. The longer it took for the Holy Relic to reappear, the more agitated the people became. Pouring oil on the fire were the various rumours that had begun to circulate in the Valley. With each passing day, masses of people arrived from villages far and near. The Valley went into mourning, and people wore black. Women came out onto the streets wearing black gowns, crying and wailing, and only those cars were allowed to move that flew black flags. Fortunately, there was no communal Hindu-Muslim tension. But it was obvious that a time bomb was ticking and Pakistani agents were working overtime to divert the pain and anger of the people towards the government, both State and Central.

It being winter, the State Government was in Jammu, and Prime Minister Shamsuddin, who too was in Jammu, moved to Srinagar to meet the crisis, but he was like a deer caught in the headlights of a speeding car. Paralyzed by the magnitude of what had happened, he could not move out of his residence as he dared not face the people and answer their questions or even console them. He spent much of the time praying in the confines of his home. On the day of the theft, Bakshi Ghulam Mohammad was in Delhi, but he left immediately for Srinagar. Representing the government, only Sadiq and Mir Qasim were present in Srinagar to make some meaningful efforts to control the situation.

Sadr-e-Riyasat Karan Singh was given the news when he was in Varanasi to preside over the convocation of the Banaras Hindu University, since he was its Chancellor. He immediately boarded the first available train for Pathankot, the railhead for J&K. On reaching Jammu, as a first step, he recorded a radio message for the people, expressing his deep anguish and the hope that the Holy Relic would soon be recovered. Arriving in Srinagar, he discovered that multiple forces were trying to influence the course of events to serve their own nefarious goals. He, therefore, decided to fly to Delhi on 2nd January 1964, by an Indian Air Force plane, to apprise the Centre of the developments and the possible consequences that might follow. Meanwhile, forces in Pakistan were gloating over the theft and accusing the Government of India of engineering the theft to humiliate the Muslims of the Valley. They were also suggesting that this was part of a larger conspiracy to suppress the people of Kashmir.

The Centre deputed B.M. Mullik of the Intelligence Bureau to take charge of the investigation, for which he was ably assisted by the Inspector General of the State Police, Thakur Lakshman Das Wazir. On the other side were the protesters who had formed an Action Committee under the chairmanship of Maulvi Mohammad Syed Masoodi, and including two important names who were to play significant roles in the future. One was Maulvi Mohammad Farooq, the same person who had been appointed as the Mirwaiz of Kashmir by Bakshi Ghulam Mohammad and who had become the rallying force for all anti-India and pro-Pakistan forces in Kashmir; and the other was Sheikh Abdullah's eldest son, Farooq Abdullah, then known as Sheikh Farooq. By this time, the city had been completely taken over by the volunteers of the Action Committee, who organized free kitchens at various places. People kept coming from the countryside, often bringing their beddings, food and firewood, and camped on the frozen streets in the falling snow, listening to the speeches of the Action Committee members. As for the ministers of the government, they dared not step out of their homes that were protected by the police. The real power had shifted to the Action Committee.

While the Sadr e Riyasat was in Delhi, Thakur Lakshman Das Wazir, who knew the local ethos very well, had convinced Mullik that there was more to the theft than met the eye and worked on identifying the people and the motive for the audacious attempt.

He was certain that it was an inside job. Meanwhile, the Sadr-e-Riyasat reached Srinagar and decided to follow his instinctive desire to reach out to the people who were emotionally stunned by the outrage. His impulse dictated that rather than reaching out to the people over the radio or through press releases, he should reach out to them physically, face to face. But as the Head of the State, he knew that he would never be allowed to go into the troubled crowd unescorted. Going with the official armed escort or as the representative of the Government would have been fraught with risk, too. Therefore, instead of heading to the Karan Mahal from the airport, he decided to stay with his cousin Nasib Chand,who managed his orchards and lived in a snug house called Cherry Grove facing the Dal Lake. On the 4th of January, he decided to visit Hazratbal without informing or consulting Shamsuddin, as he knew that on security and political grounds, he would not be allowed to go. So, he went with Nasib Chand, taking the steering of the car, accompanied by a Staff Officer and without a flag. He also did not allow the pilot car or the security to accompany him, as any demonstration of power would have been most inappropriate. Trusting in God's will, he went towards Hazratbal, and no sooner had the people who had been camping there ever since the Relic had disappeared seen him, they mobbed him by the thousands. Pressing against him, they kissed his hands and embraced him, declaring emotionally, '*Hamara Badshah aa Gaya* (Our king has come)'. It was a deeply moving moment and gave the lie to the decades of propaganda carried out by Sheikh Abdullah and his party. Even in their hour of anguish, they retained deep regard and affection for the Dogra heir, the demagoguery of the politicians notwithstanding.

At the shrine, Karan Singh offered prayers for the speedy return of the Relic and directed that special prayers be offered on his behalf at all the Muslim, Hindu, and Sikh shrines in the

Valley. After his return, he addressed the administrative challenges with the political leaders and civil and military officials. Sadiq, Mir Qasim and Dhar called upon him and urged him to dismiss the Shamsuddin Government and place the State under Sadr-e-Riyasat's rule. Delegations from Jammu, notably the Praja Parishad, Praja Socialist Party, and Akali Dal, also made similar calls as the government and the ruling Party, the National Conference, had abdicated all responsibility and vanished from the scene when the city was taken over by the Action Committee. Even Sheikh Farooq, alias Farooq Abdullah, supported the call for Sadr-e-Riyasat's rule in the State. Karan Singh, too, was not inclined to give any further rope to the government and the investigating agencies. So, he decided to give twenty-four hours to the team for the recovery of the Relic before he recommended to the Prime Minister to impose Sadr-e-Riyasat's rule. Thakur Lakshman Das Wazir and Mullik were accordingly informed.

Meanwhile, the Pakistan-sponsored-and-controlled 'Radio Azad Kashmir', and a few Islamic countries raised the level of propaganda against India. Mysteriously, posters also appeared all over Srinagar carrying a letter supposed to have been written by the jailed Sheikh Abdullah to Nehru, which referred to a letter written earlier in the wake of the Chinese aggression, demanding that a triple alliance between India, Pakistan and Kashmir be forged to bring peace to the subcontinent. He also accused the Prime Minister of trying to rule through what he called, 'stooges'. Effectively, the alleged letter warned that unless power was handed back to Sheikh Abdullah, there could be no peace in the State. Such demands were orchestrated all over the State through posters and speeches in public meetings, and soon they assumed dangerous proportions with the demand that the recovery of the Holy Relic should be made under the supervision of Sheikh Abdullah; otherwise, even if the recovery was made, it would remain suspect. Faith and politics had joined hands to pose a serious challenge to the Government of India. Various theories were afloat, and investigators were certain that there was a Pakistani conspiracy through Pir Maqbool Gilani, who had allegedly used his influence and contacts for the removal of the Relic. There were also rumours that an elderly lady from the Bakshi family had expressed the desire to see the Relic as her dying wish, and to have it fulfilled, the family had got it temporarily removed, but then had been prematurely caught by the uproar. Thus, investigators were certain that the Relic was in Kashmir, as, considering its history, it was unimaginable that anyone from the shrine or anyone else would connive to have it removed from Hazratbal. The delay in its recovery was creating a tricky situation, and with the Sadr-e-Riyasat present among them, the people expected the dismissal of the Shamsuddin government. Mullik and Thakur were convinced that the removal of the Relic was an inside job, but feared the culprits might, out of fear, throw the Relic into the Dal Lake. To pre-empt this possibility, they decided to give them a chance of surreptitiously returning it. Accordingly, it was publicly announced that all guards around Hazratbal would be taken off for the next 24 hours so that whoever had taken the Holy Relic could return it without arousing suspicion. The next day, at 5 p.m., the Moe-e-Muqaddas had reappeared! The story behind this turn of events was never revealed by either Thakur or Mullik, which gave credence to the belief that it was an inside job and the perpetrators had no intention of permanently removing the Relic from Hazratbal.

Thus thwarted, the Pakistani agents raised the bogey of the authenticity of the Relic as none of the objectives of the Action Committee had been achieved. Sheikh Abdullah was still in detention, Bakshi was not arrested, and no violence, except that of the first day, had taken place, and India remained in control.

But with the next *deedar*—or glimpse—of the Holy Relic due on 6th February 1964, the controversy over its authenticity needed to be put to rest. The Pakistani propaganda had become desperate and it was suggested that *kafir*—or 'infidel'—officers of Hindu India had replaced the Relic with a fake one. As the day of the *deedar* neared, the demonstrations became more aggressive, piling more pressure on the authorities. On 25th January, the situation took an ugly turn when people, incited by the speeches after Friday prayers, turned violent and attacked Punjab Police pickets at many places, and the police in turn opened fire, killing six persons. In its wake, the Action Committee mounted pressure and demanded a special *deedar* be held to establish the authenticity of the Holy relic. The government refused at first but after the Republic Day had somehow passed without serious disruption, Prime Minister Nehru decided to concede to the demand as it was thought prudent to dispel all doubts before 6th February as on that day thousands of people were expected to be present from all over the Valley and any trouble on that occasion had the potential of a catastrophe. To oversee everything, Nehru deputed his trusted lieutenant, Lal Bahadur Shastri, though Gulzari Lal Nanda was the Home Minister.

On 3rd February, everyone, including Shastri, Shamsuddin, Thakur, Mullik, and the members of the Action Committee, along with holy men, gathered in the hall of the Hazratbal. Maulvi Mohammad Syed Masoodi, the chairman of the Action Committee, and no friend of India, took charge of the proceedings and exhorted the holy men to be careful in judging the authenticity of the Relic and handed over copies of the Quran to each member to hold in their hands while pronouncing their judgment. One by one, the members averred that the Relic was real till finally, it was the turn of Faqir Mirak Shah, the holiest of holy men in Kashmir. After carefully examining the Relic, he finally muttered the words '*Haq*', that is, 'true'. A huge wave of relief swept the hall even as the members of the Action Committee were crestfallen. Shamsuddin wept in relief, and Shastri offered a silent prayer of thanks.

With the crisis resolved, it was time for a political overhaul. It was the most opportune time to move beyond Bakshi. He had played his role well and had led the State at a time when it was being pushed by Sheikh Abdullah towards an uncertain future. But he had, during the long years in office, become a tool for his relatives and friends to exercise arbitrary and unrestrained power for their personal gain. Opposition to him was widespread, and Sadiq wrote a long letter to Prime Minister Nehru in which he debunked the supposedly widespread belief that Pakistan had considerable influence on the Muslims of Kashmir. Sadiq went on to pay tribute to the people from all religions of the State who had played a central role in strengthening communal harmony during the crisis and singled out Pandit Prem Nath Dogra for not letting rumours about communal riots in Kashmir affect life in the Jammu region. Sadiq also added: 'Why is it that Dr. Karan Singh, a scion of the Dogra Dynasty, was mentioned with deepest affection and respect in public meetings attended by lakhs of people? Why is it that Sheikh Sahib's son and many other speakers from public platform[s] demanded and continue to demand the rule of Sadr-e-Riyasat in preference to the rule of "Muslim" Bakshi?' Sadiq, in effect, was pleading with the Government of India to destroy the shibboleths of the past and usher in an era based on integrity.

The crisis had exposed the incompetence and irrelevance of Shamsuddin as the Prime Minister, and he made way for Ghulam Mohammad Sadiq, a long-time critic of the Bakshi regime over its corruption. It was clear that Kashmir had been very close to the brink during the Moe-e-Muqaddas incident, and most observers hoped that under Sadiq's stewardship, a new era would be ushered in, and the process of bringing the State closer to the Union by the use of the Presidential orders would also be accelerated. Meanwhile, Prime Minister Nehru, who had never been comfortable with the idea of Sheikh Abdullah being put in detention, had begun to have second thoughts about his Kashmir policy. With Bakshi out of the equation and a confident Sadiq in the saddle, steps to resolve the issue had to be taken. Sadiq's liberalism was an asset, and he did not have any objections to the Sheikh's release. After extensively consulting the Centre, a decision was taken to unconditionally release Sheikh Abdullah, Afzal Beg and others, and an application for the withdrawal of the Kashmir Conspiracy Case was filed in the court on 8 April 1964. Since Sheikh Abdullah did not bear the same grudge against Sadiq that he held against Bakshi, upon his release, he termed him 'an old comrade' in his first press conference. He also conceded that he did not have any solution for the Kashmir problem but expressed his unequivocal opposition to the division of the State.

The very next day, Sheikh Abdullah, along with Mirza Afzal Beg, was to call upon the Sadr-e-Riyasat at Hari Niwas in Jammu. They were to meet for the first time after their confrontation on 8 August 1953—the day Abdullah was dismissed and arrested. Thus, after a little over a decade, the man who was the undisputed leader of Kashmir and who thought his decision or word could not be challenged was to come face to face with the person who had ordered his dismissal from office and arrest. It was natural for Karan Singh to be apprehensive about the meeting. Would the Sheikh be resentful of his captor? Would his bitterness get the better of him, and would there be a bout of recriminations and justifications? Anything was possible, and Karan Singh braced himself and waited, playing out the various possible scripts in his mind. Finally, the door opened, and as the tall and imposing figure of Sheikh Abdullah was ushered in, he warmly greeted Karan Singh with the words, '*Kaise ho Tiger?* (How are you, Tiger?)' With those three warm words, the ice of apprehension melted, and they embraced affectionately and cordially and chatted for half an hour without making any reference to politics. The Sheikh had called upon Karan Singh as a gesture of goodwill and reconciliation, but certain questions needed to be answered before the full political implications of his release as a goodwill gesture could be assessed. He had to be categorical in stating whether he accepted the 'limited accession', or had he altogether rejected 'accession'. More importantly, would he accept not only the accession of Kashmir to India but also that it was on par with the other states of the country?

Pakistan was jubilant at the Sheikh's release, and its mercurial Foreign Minister Zulfiqar Ali Bhutto invited him to Pakistan for a meeting with President Ayub Khan. The Sheikh then proceeded on a tour of the Muslim-majority Doda district of Jammu Province before going to Kashmir, which he entered on 17 April 1964 and received a tumultuous welcome from Anantnag to Srinagar, wherever he went. Ten years out of the limelight had in no way diminished his charisma, and when he urged the people to maintain communal harmony and safeguard the property of the non-Muslims, the message went far and wide. However, his political statements were ambiguous, and soon he began to question the finality of the accession of the State to India and openly supported the Plebiscite Front, established by Mirza Afzal Beg. He also began equating India and Pakistan. It was obvious that for him, all the changes and developments that had happened during his absence were of little consequence, as no change could be legitimized unless it had been initiated and approved by him. His statements caused unease in Jammu, though Sadiq firmly reiterated the finality of accession and rejected Sheikh Abdullah's stance. With the shadow of uncertainty cast over the State, Karan Singh thought that Sadiq and his group had to take full control of the National Conference, or they needed to launch a new political party that carried their message and agenda. At that moment, the masses were with Sheikh Abdullah, the party machine with Bakshi, and in such a situation, the government of Sadiq was not tenable.

In these circumstances, even as Sheikh Abdullah was to visit Delhi and hold talks with Nehru, Karan Singh warned in his fortnightly letter to the President: 'There would appear to be little doubt that if the Sheikh continues on his present path he is bound sooner or later to come into conflict with the legally established Government...But if the Delhi talks do not produce the desired modification in the Sheikh's attitude, a showdown is inevitable with all the grave consequences that will be implied therein.' It was a serious situation with multiple possibilities; therefore, Karan Singh decided to go to Delhi during the last week of April to be on hand to brief the Delhi leaders and meet Prime Minister Nehru, Gulzari Lal Nanda, who was Home Minister, and Lal Bahadur Shastri, Minister without Portfolio. Earlier, in January, Nehru had suffered a stroke from which he had never really recovered, but was still working and trying to make one final effort to resolve and bury the Kashmir Question. From 1949, when Karan Singh became Regent, he had corresponded with Nehru regularly, and the last correspondence was in the form of a note giving him an appointment on 10 May. When he entered Nehru's room with his wife Asha, Nehru rose to greet them, but was visibly seriously ill and in discomfort. Karan Singh requested him not to make the effort, but he brushed him aside, saying that ill he might be, but he had not forgotten his manners! Karan Singh did not think it appropriate to engage him in any lengthy political conversation regarding Kashmir and sidestepped it by informing him that he had discussed the issue in detail with Lal Bahadur Shastri.

At the end of April, Sheikh Abdullah also went to Delhi and had an emotional reunion with Nehru and also stayed with him. He also met other Cabinet ministers and political leaders, including Jayaprakash Narayan. During Karan Singh's stay in Delhi, both Jayaprakash Narayan and Sheikh Abdullah separately called upon him. This was also the time when Pakistan, in illegal occupation of Shaksgam Valley in Aksai Chin, had handed it over to China in 1963, after the Indo-China War of 1962. Even the Anglo-US authorities were concerned about it, but as a solution were pressurizing India to enter into a settlement with Pakistan. An ailing Nehru was persuaded by Sheikh Abdullah to try and build a bridge between the two neighbours and relieve India of the constant pressure over Kashmir. With this backdrop, Abdullah announced his decision to visit Pakistan. Speaking to the All-India Congress Committee, Nehru said: '[Abdullah] hopes that it should be possible for India, holding on to her principles, to live in peace and friendship with Pakistan and thus incidentally to put an end to the question of Kashmir…I hope Pakistan will get rid of its hatred and fear of India. She has nothing to fear from India unless she attacks India. I hope that it may be possible for the two countries to develop closer and more intimate relations to the advantage of both. If Sheikh Abdullah can help in bringing this about, he will have done a great service to both countries. We are prepared to help him in this attempt, but in doing so, we must adhere to our principles as well as our basic attitude in regard to Kashmir.'

On 11 May 1964, Karan Singh returned to Srinagar, and after more consultations and meetings, Sheikh Abdullah arrived in Srinagar on 13 May. There was a marked change in his speeches, as they had become balanced, circumspect and moderate, cautioning the people of the importance of safeguarding the interests of the minorities in India and Pakistan when the negotiations were in progress. The most remarkable change was that instead of talking about 'self-determination', he laid all the emphasis on Indo-Pak relations. Accordingly, he left for Delhi on 21 May and, after further discussions, travelled to Pakistan on 25 May, where he was given a grand welcome that rivalled his welcome in the Valley. On that day and the next, he held discussions with President Ayub Khan and Bhutto and reached Muzaffarabad, the capital of what Pakistan called 'Azad Kashmir' and India, 'Pakistan-occupied Kashmir', on 27 May. It was here that his old comrades from the Kashmir Muslim Conference days, Maulvi Yusuf Shah and Chaudhary Abdul Rashid, had migrated in 1947. However, this visit, which had the potential of redefining the Kashmir issue, had to be aborted when the terrible news of Nehru's demise was announced to the world, and Sheikh Abdullah cut short his tour to return.

On that morning, wrote Karan Singh, India lost a great 'patriot and politician, historian and litterateur, administrator and world statesman'. Karan Singh lost his mentor and political Guru—a wise and affectionate elder who had helped an eighteen-year-old to hold his own against a stalwart who was also an enemy of his dynasty. Nehru had helped the young Yuvraj navigate the treacherous waters of politics, but importantly, had helped him make a smooth transition from the feudal world of his father to the real world of the people—a people who had known nothing but subservience for centuries. Nehru's constant guidance through his correspondence and numerous meetings was to become Karan Singh's political compass that never failed him. Political poise and dignity even in the face of adversity was another lesson the young man learned from the extraordinary elder statesman—as did numerous others who had the good fortune of watching Nehru at close quarters.

An Air Force plane had been requisitioned to fly Karan Singh, Sadiq and Dhar to Delhi, but bad weather did not allow that to happen, and they reached the next day, but well before the funeral procession was to start. Mourning crowds thronged the whole route from Teen Murti to Rajghat, near which Nehru was cremated. Leaders from all over the world had arrived for the occasion, including Zulfiqar Ali Bhutto from Pakistan. In a curious similarity—yet revealing dissimilarity—with the wish of Maharaja Hari Singh that his ashes be scattered over Jammu, according to Pandit Nehru's testament, his ashes were to be scattered throughout the length and breadth of the country. Karan Singh took a portion of Nehru's ashes in an urn by train to Pathankot, the then railhead, on 4th June, where thousands had gathered to pay homage. In Jammu too, there was a large turnout of people, and after allowing them to pay homage, on 8th June, the ashes were immersed in the Tawi River.

Prime Minister Sadiq too carried an urn to Srinagar on 6th June where Karan Singh joined him two days later and both drove in an open car from Rajgarh to Shadipur from where they boarded a white boat, the same which had carried Nehru on many occasions for the river processions during which the people of Srinagar had cheered him from both the banks. Finally, the ashes were immersed at the confluence of the Jhelum and its tributary, the Sind. Kushak Bakula had taken another urn to Ladakh, where the ashes were immersed in the River Indus.

After the immersion of the ashes at different sites across the country, the Congress Party prepared itself to choose a new Prime Minister. For almost a decade, the whole world had been speculating on 'who after Nehru'. It was time for the country to respond and demonstrate that, after independence, the Indian leaders had built sturdy institutions and a vibrant democracy that was capable of marching forward on its own. The question marks over India had been raised because of India's dependence on Nehru and his banyan-like presence. The free world also feared that after Nehru, India could go the Pakistan way since the neighbour's democracy had derailed no sooner had Jinnah died. Their apprehensions were misplaced. The transition was swift and smooth, despite a brief power struggle among senior leaders of the Congress. Immediately after Nehru's death, Gulzari Lal Nanda had been appointed as interim Prime Minister. In less than a fortnight, Lal Bahadur Shastri, the diminutive, unassuming but diligent Congressman, succeeded Nehru as India's Prime Minister and he demonstrated his will while selecting his Cabinet when he refused to buckle under pressure from the senior leader Morarji Desai to rank him number two in the Cabinet. Shastri's appearance and gentle nature were deceptive as he was capable of making hard decisions. Importantly, he had the popular support not only of the Congress Parliamentarians but also of the grassroots workers of the party. When his Cabinet was announced, in a move with far-reaching consequences, he also inducted Nehru's daughter, Indira Gandhi as a Minister.

18

Finally, the Change

NEHRU'S DEATH HAD LEFT Congressmen a little lost, but they seemed determined to carry forward the work that he had begun. Meanwhile, Sheikh Abdullah was left high and dry. It was now his word against the speculation of others as to what understanding had been reached between Nehru and him. On June 11, he addressed a public meeting organized by the Plebiscite Front, where he broke down several times while referring to Nehru. He claimed that his talks in Pakistan with President Ayub Khan had been positive and that he was certain that, had Nehru lived, the two would have reached an agreement. However, he did not elaborate on what would have been the basis of the understanding, though it was widely rumoured that Sheikh Abdullah had advocated a 'confederation' between India and Pakistan where Kashmir would enjoy a special intermediate position.

Karan Singh, meanwhile, pressed forward for the presence of Inia's national political parties in the State and, in his first letter to the President after the death of Nehru, he suggested that the National Conference should be transformed into the

Indian National Congress, the State ministry be expanded and administration be toned up in a manner that it became efficient and corruption free. In a parallel development, Maulvi Farooq, after being ousted as the President of the Action Committee, had formed a new party called the Awami Action Committee. His traditional rival, Sheikh Abdullah, went a step further and extensively toured the whole state, exhorting all those who were pledged to self-determination to come under the banner of the Plebiscite Front. He also became more strident than ever before in his demands. His partisans argued that he had been forced into that kind of competitive politics because of the rising graph of the followers of Maulvi Farooq. His critics, however, were convinced that with Nehru gone, and Shastri, though efficient, lacking Nehru's stature and sheer force of personality, it was time for Sheikh Abdullah to pile pressure on him to get the long-cherished concessions.

The month of July turned out to be hectic as the Commonwealth Prime Ministers' Conference was due in London and was to be attended by Shastri and Ayub Khan. Sheikh Abdullah announced that he too would go to London, suggesting that he would be at hand to help resolve the Kashmir problem when the two leaders met or when the British intervened in the matter. However, his announcement brought about such fierce criticism in the press that he hastily dropped the plan. On the other hand, Karan Singh's constant urgings to transform the National Conference had begun to bear fruit as Prime Minister Sadiq and senior National Conference leader Mir Qasim also agreed that greater integration with mainland India would go a long way in breaking the barriers between Kashmir and the rest of the country. Finally, Sadiq and his friends took the initiative, even in the face of opposition from Bakshi and his group within the party, and Sheikh Abdullah and his followers outside the party, to hold a series of meetings of the National Conference Working Committee and Parliamentary Party in July, and authorize Sadiq to explore the extent and scope of the presence of the Indian National Congress in the State. Consequently, Mir Qasim resigned from the government to become the General Secretary of the National Conference to steer it forward.

Despite losing his mentor, a happy period had begun for Karan Singh. His father had desperately wanted to have a grandson in his lifetime but that had not happened. Karan Singh and Asha understood the Maharaja's wish but it was not a priority for them. They were happy with their life at home with their daughter. Jyoti—Jyotsna—was six years old, a little pampered because she had grown up all alone. Every night, she would wait for her father to come and sit by her bed and sing her songs from the hit list of the year 1948 when he had been in America, listening to the radio most hours of the day in his hospital room. In 1964, Asha was pregnant again. The delivery was due in August, and even though the Maharaja had passed away, they decided to go to Bombay, where Dr. Shirodkar was still active, with his reputation having spread all over the world. To the joy of the young family, their second child was born on the morning of 5 August 1964, and they named him Vikramaditya.

The paternal grandmother of the newborn, Maharani Tara Devi, was informed telephonically from the nursing home itself, and the world came to know when the newspapers broke the news the next morning. The couple brought their son to Jammu and were felicitated by ever-growing crowds from Pathankot onwards. Jammu appeared to be happy once again. The grateful grandmother, of course, showered her friends, staff and servants with expensive gifts. According to his commitment, Karan Singh offered eleven thousand rupees each to their family temple, Sri Raghunath Mandir at Jammu, Harmandir Sahib at Amritsar, and Hazratbal shrine at Srinagar.

On their way back to Jammu, the family had broken journey for a few days in Delhi, where Karan Singh had to attend a meeting of the Nehru Memorial Committee, later converted into the Jawaharlal Nehru Memorial Fund. Since Sheikh Abdullah also was a member of that Committee, he too was there and he called upon Karan Singh at his Delhi residence, Mansarovar, where both had a lengthy conversation during which the Sheikh asserted that he was not committed to any particular solution to the Kashmir issue but was anxious to find some way out. Nevertheless, Karan Singh got the unmistakable impression that he favoured some kind of semi-independent status for the Valley, which had been guaranteed by both India and Pakistan. He also made a personal appeal to Karan Singh to take the initiative and play a proactive role in solving the problem of the State. In sharp contrast, when Karan Singh returned to Srinagar after a short stay in Jammu, he found that the Plebiscite Front had stepped up its activities and had observed 9th August, the day when Sheikh Abdullah was dismissed, as 'Black Day'. A call for a general strike too had been given and a huge procession taken out, in which Abdullah had participated and which he also addressed. The speech was decidedly anti-India, and he not only lashed out at the Government of India and Bakshi but also, for the first time, at Sadiq, Qasim and Dhar. He was frustrated and restive as nothing was working in his favour, and he was again on a warpath with India. The strong and overpowering Kashmiri sub-nationalism, coupled with his massive ego, did not allow him to accept the reality of the State being part of India. He was obsessed with the idea of Pakistan playing a role in letting him have a semi-independent Kashmir.

Unaffected by what Sheikh Abdullah wanted, the National Conference was gradually moving towards merging with the Congress. Conventions to that effect had been held in Jammu and Srinagar, where thousands of workers had endorsed the idea. But while attention was focused on what was happening outside, Bakshi had made all preparations to pull the rug from under Sadiq's feet. Sadiq was completely oblivious to the threat. He and his intellectual friends had gradually taken action against the Bakshi supporters within the party and the Assembly, and Bakshi himself had been threatened with an inquiry into the alleged acts of corruption and pushed to the wall. In a retaliatory move, Bakshi had prepared to overthrow the Sadiq government on the floor of the House and had rallied his supporters for the proposed no-confidence motion. He met Karan Singh and told him that he was determined to see through the no-confidence motion as the Sadiq government had consistently launched a campaign of victimization and vilification against him, and he was no longer prepared to tolerate that.

Karan Singh was horrified at the prospect of the government getting toppled on the floor of the House at a time when Abdullah was on a warpath and the Kashmiris still simmering with anger against Bakshi and his supporters over the Holy Relic crisis. The no-confidence motion would have forced Karan Singh to place the State under Sadr-e-Riyasat's rule, which, under the circumstances, would have been fully exploited by Abdullah, the Plebiscite Front, and Pakistan. After prolonged discussions, it was decided that to tide over the crisis, Bakshi and some of his supporters would be arrested and the Assembly prorogued. It was decidedly an undemocratic step, but under the circumstances was the lesser evil. Bakshi and some of his supporters were accordingly arrested under Defence of India Rules and sent to Tara Niwas, the same State Guest House in Udhampur where Sheikh Abdullah had been sent just over a decade ago.

The State eventually succeeded in tiding over the crisis, but it dawned upon Karan Singh that he had been increasingly drawn into the rough and tumble of politics. He was no longer a detached and aloof constitutional head as he rapidly became a major character in the State's dramatic politics. And he realized that he had also begun to enjoy it. This made him restless, and he strained at the constitutional leash that hindered his urge to play a more active political role. The Sadiq Government had survived the crisis, but it had rekindled Karan Singh's desire to break free of the confines of the State and move on to the bigger national stage. In 1958, he had felt the same urge and had consulted the Swamis of Mirtola, Gopalda, and Ashishda, who had then advised against the move, saying he was not yet ready. In 1964, the urge was stronger, and he decided to visit Mirtola. This time, Asha and Beryl Stileman, who had come out of England, also accompanied him. The three had a very happy time there, and Karan Singh came back in a positive frame of mind as his Gurus had given him a green signal. They advised that if the inner urge was so strong, it should not be suppressed. During this trip, Karan Singh also had a mind-opening encounter with the sun when, one early morning, he decided to go out for a walk to greet the rising sun from the top of a nearby hill. As the sun came up behind a large tree, its shooting rays were diffused in all directions, giving him a sensory feeling of encountering the Brahman, the Life Force, the Infinite One. After this almost out-of-body experience, the sun became an integral part of his philosophy, and when he designed his crest, the sun was a part of it. He returned to Delhi with a clarity of mind and eagerness to find an appropriate occasion and opening to make his much-desired move beyond the State.

He knew he could discuss such affairs with Shastri. He had, of course, been closer to Nehru, but there was a respectful distance despite the great affection, and he could never bring himself to talk to his mentor on equal terms. With the new Prime Minister, he had no such inhibition, and he looked for an appropriate occasion to bring up the subject. By the first quarter of 1965, it had become clear to him that he had outgrown life in the State as Sadr-e-Riyasat. He also yearned for the invigorating and varied intellectual life of Delhi. Whenever he was there, he would call upon President Radhakrishnan as both enjoyed each other's company, and he always came out the wiser after such encounters. But of all the places, it was the home of Clovis Maksoud, the Arab League representative in India, that he loved the most, for it was the venue of the most stimulating conversations. Maksoud, an American-born Lebanese, had studied in Beirut and gone on to George Washington University and Oxford and had built quite a reputation as a debater at the Speaker's Corner in London's Hyde Park. When he came to India as the Arab League's Ambassador, he was already a celebrated thinker and orator and quickly became one of the most influential foreign diplomats in Delhi. Indian and foreign leaders and intellectuals gathered at his home to exchange views and often new ideas and insights emerged over leisurely and lively lunches and dinners. Among the regulars there were Romesh and Raj Thapar, both left-leaning intellectuals whom Karan Singh already knew. They introduced him to their multifaceted and talented friends who were journalists or otherwise engaged in creative and scholarly activities. His yearning for this kind of life grew stronger by the day till he could no longer contain himself from writing to Lal Bahadur Shastri on 1 March 1965: 'In a few days I will be thirty-four and for some time I have been feeling that it would be desirable for me to widen my field of experience. However, the national interest being necessarily uppermost in my mind, I realized that until now, my quitting the present post might have created avoidable complications. With the forthcoming amendment of the State Constitution, the Office of the Sadr-e-Riyasat elected by the State Assembly will be replaced by a Governor appointed directly by the President, and because of this development, I do not think my presence here remains as important as it was previously...With the advent of the office of Governor, a wide choice of talent is now available... [About] myself, I am seriously considering contesting the general elections, especially as the people of this State will for the first time be electing their representatives to the Lok Sabha directly.' He pointed out that the next general elections were due in two years; therefore, he was wondering if he could be appointed as the High Commissioner to the UK, a post that was soon falling vacant. He added, 'It is embarrassing for me to write this, but I do feel that perhaps I could fill that appointment successfully...I have been there several times, and such acquaintance as I have with English life, language, and politics should be a valuable asset. It would also provide me with a new dimension of experience before I enter the mainstream of national politics.'

The Prime Minister replied immediately, saying that when they met next, they would discuss this. When they met in April, Shastri emphasized the uncertain situation in J&K and, therefore, Karan Singh's indispensability in the State. There the matter rested till the next year, when Principal Secretary L.K. Jha called on him, offering the same appointment. But by then, Karan Singh had lost interest in diplomacy and, therefore, declined.

In early 1965, a major step towards bringing J&K under the Indian Constitution was taken with the extension of Articles of the Indian Constitution related to provisions in the event of failure of the constitutional machinery. This drew an immediate outcry from Sheikh Abdullah in his speech in Hazratbal after the Friday prayers. The speech was an inflammatory diatribe against India, as he also clubbed the issue of extending Articles of the Indian Constitution dealing with Centre-state relations with the move to merge the National Conference with the Indian National Congress. He claimed that these moves would mean the end of Muslims in the State and called upon his audience to be prepared to make any sacrifice to safeguard their interests. He also gave a call to the people to subject all National Conference MLAs who joined the Congress to a social boycott. He also dragged in Prime Minister Shastri and described him as a weak man from whom nothing could be expected. Meanwhile, in Delhi, there was a debate about whether Sheikh Abdullah should be allowed to fulfil his long-desired intention to go on Hajj. A section of opinion wanted to deny him permission as he had also declared his intention to contact world leaders to rally public opinion against India and muster support for his demand for self-determination in Kashmir. But in a shrewd move, Shastri allowed Abdullah to go as he was certain that he would only expose himself by misusing his freedom, and if he did not misuse his freedom, then India would occupy a higher moral ground for not curbing his right to travel and freedom of worship.

Through the persistent efforts of Karan Singh, the Indian National Congress was finally launched in J&K on 26 January 1965. He had been pressing for it for a long time because he believed that while constitutional, legal, financial and administrative steps were important, in a democratic system, unless the political parties—and through them, the people—were seen to be participating in the big issues of the life of a state or country, the system could not function. The Congress, being the premier political party with a rich legacy, had to play a role in the integration of the State.

Another important development was the opening of the Social Sciences Block of the Jammu and Kashmir University in Jammu. For quite some time, Karan Singh had been working to get the University bifurcated. This was a welcome first step for

Jammu, as earlier the students had to go to Srinagar for their higher studies. But of even greater consequence was his active promotion of the Dogri language and its literature. Thanks to the influence of his mother, his English upbringing notwithstanding, he had always loved to talk in Dogri when among the Dogras. The folk songs and prayers in Dogri came naturally to him, and whenever he was to deliver a speech in Jammu, he made it a point that it was in Dogri. Earlier, the educated Dogras were prone to deliver speeches in Urdu as they thought Urdu to be the mark of an educated and cultured person. Because of Karan Singh's encouragement, a young generation of Dogras became active in enriching the Dogri literature, and the Dogri Sanstha and its long-devoted Pandit Ram Nath Shastri worked with missionary zeal from a small, single-room office to bring it on par with the literature of other Indian languages. The Sanstha received a boost when Karan Singh provided it with a permanent address in the prestigious locality of Karan Nagar in Jammu.

In February, Abdullah and Beg left for the Hajj. In the State, the government made large-scale arrests of Plebiscite Front leaders and workers. Simultaneously, a Constitution Amendment Bill was introduced in the Assembly providing for a Governor to be appointed by the President of India in place of an elected Sadr-e-Riyasat, and also for the change in the nomenclature of the head of the government from Prime Minister to Chief Minister. These were symbolic but significant changes. With the passage of the Bill and assent of the Sadr-e-Riyasat, when the President appointed Karan Singh as the Governor, he was sworn in by the Chief Justice of the State on 10 April. Thus, he held the unique distinction of becoming the only Sadr-e-Riyasat and also the first Governor of the State. This welcome development was followed by a sad episode in the family. Maharani Tara Devi suffered a cerebral stroke that left her partially paralysed.

Meanwhile, Sheikh Abdullah had done what had been anticipated. He crossed the red line when he met the Chinese Premier, Chou En Lai, who invited him to China, and he accepted the invitation. Understandably, there was such an outcry in the press and the Parliament that the External Affairs Minister was forced to announce that all endorsements on the passports of Abdullah and his party had been cancelled except those that were needed for Hajj. There was some speculation about his next step and some wondered if he would seek asylum in some foreign country and launch his campaign against India but, knowing him rather too well, Karan Singh was sure that he would return as he was a man of determination who had not become a leader of his people by running away from tough situations. He duly returned and was promptly arrested, this time by the Government of India, and flown to Kodaikanal, a hill town in Tamil Nadu, to be confined within its municipal limits.

This coincided with increased activity on the Ceasefire Line between India and Pakistan. It was only in retrospect that it was understood that clashes with the Indian Army by Pakistan in the Rann of Kutch were a prelude to the bigger game that was in the offing. Karan Singh had sensed this as he did not believe that Pakistan was prepared to give up its obsession with Kashmir. On 4 June 1965, he wrote to the President: 'It is clear that we are now closer to war with that country than [we have] ever been since 1947.' Simultaneously, the Action Committee launched a civil disobedience movement, and in the competitive politics of Kashmir, Maulvi Farooq's Awami Action Committee adopted a constitution pledging to secure the right to self-determination for the people of the State.

These developments were, however, overshadowed by the news of devastating fires breaking out in different parts of the Valley. These were obviously not natural events. In a monumental failure of the intelligence agencies, the State, and the Centre, everyone remained unaware of a diabolical operation that Pakistan had launched in the State. How big this failure was can be judged by the fact that days earlier, on 5 August, when Sadr-e-Riyasat Karan Singh had given a large reception at the Oberoi Palace Hotel (now Lalit Palace), Srinagar to celebrate his son Vikramaditya's first birthday, some people were talking about rumours that Pakistani infiltrators had reached the outskirts of Srinagar. Even then, the seriousness of the situation had not been fully grasped.

The next day, Karan Singh left for Delhi, from where he went to Mirtola, as Gopalda had not been keeping too well. Though he welcomed Karan Singh in his usual manner, it was very apparent that he was no longer the robust and vigorous man that he had been. The next day, as Karan Singh bent to touch his feet and take his leave, Gopalda embraced him and held him for several moments. In those moments, as they looked into each other's eyes, they knew that they were not going to meet again.

By the time he arrived in Delhi, news about a Pakistani invasion had broken. He immediately rushed back to Srinagar, where Sadiq and his colleagues appeared shaken, and the unflappable Dhar seemed to have lost his poise, as the State Home Department was under him, and without any doubt, the intelligence agencies under him had failed in a big way. Pakistan had been planning this for a long time, even as the Indian side had slumbered. The operation in the Valley had been codenamed 'Operation Gibraltar' and a large number of Pakistani covert operators had infiltrated the Valley in the hope that when they came overground at a given time, the masses would rise in an uprising against India. The invasion was accompanied by virulent and orchestrated propaganda as huge posters declaring 'Proclamation of War of Liberation' and issued in the name of the 'Revolutionary Council of Kashmir' appeared all over the

State. It was obvious that Pakistan, more specifically, President Ayub Khan and the Army, had banked on a massive uprising of Kashmiri Muslims against India, but no such uprising happened. The arrival of Pakistani guerrillas was followed by the escalation of exchanges across the Ceasefire Line leading to Kargil. The Tithwal and Uri sectors too got involved in a major offensive. Pakistan also launched a conventional military operation in the Akhnur sector of Jammu, codenamed 'Operation Grand Slam'. The objective was to make a move towards Jammu and eventually cut off the Jammu-Srinagar highway. However, it succeeded in only grabbing a large tract of Chhamb, which too was a threat to Jammu. Finally, losing patience with Pakistan, India opened up the Lahore and Sialkot fronts on the international border to ease pressure on the J&K border and succeeded in knocking on the gates of the two biggest cities of Pakistani Punjab. More tellingly, the people of Kashmir had spoken their minds by not only *not* cooperating with the Pakistani infiltrators but also lending a helping hand to the Indian Army in whichever way possible.

Meanwhile, the Pakistani attack on the Chhamb-Jaurian region soon got bogged down, though it made some minor inroads in the Ferozepur sector in Punjab and Rajasthan on the Sindh border, and there the troops remained when, on the intervention of the two superpowers and the United Nations, a ceasefire was announced by both sides. But before the ceasefire, India had made two very significant gains in J&K. It had captured the strategically important Haji Pir Pass separating Uri and Poonch and two mountain peaks that overlooked Kargil and the highway to Leh. But the deadlock between the two countries in the United Nations could not be broken, so the Soviet Union stepped forward to host both countries in Tashkent. The meeting went on for several days, and it appeared that it would remain as inconclusive as it had been in the UN, but a sudden last-minute intervention by the USSR led to an agreement between Shastri and Ayub Khan. It was decided that both armies would pull back to the positions held before the hostilities had started. Which meant that India would have to give up the bulge of Haji Pir and the Kargil peaks. Even as this agreement was being finalized, there came the shocking news that the Indian Prime Minister had suffered a fatal heart attack in Tashkent. Ironically, his death turned out to be a sacrifice for peace as it made the Indian public accept the agreement, which, going by the first reports, was being vehemently denounced by the opposition and large sections of the population across the country.

Once again, Karan Singh and Sadiq rushed to Delhi for the arrival of the body from Moscow. By this time confabulations were on to choose a successor to Shastri. At this time the Congress party was in some turmoil as differences had arisen between the old guard and the younger members. The younger generation was impatient for change, feeling that the party was being held back by traditionalists and status quoists. Indira Gandhi, a member of Shastri's cabinet, had also been feeling uneasy in the government, and it was rumored that she was waiting for the Tashkent talks to end before she tendered her resignation. Many believed that she had been included in the Shastri Cabinet only because she was the daughter of Nehru, but the truth was that she was an active Congresswoman in her own right, having been a past President of the party. But now, with the untimely death of Shastri, the leadership question had been opened all over again, and the Congress Parliamentary Party elected her as its leader, although by a narrow margin. This was a shot in the arm for the younger generation as it signalled a major change. Since Karan Singh too belonged to the younger group of post-Independence Indians, he was excited at her election, and when he called upon her in the Prime Minister's office, she said with a smile, 'I wish you were in Parliament now.'

Buoyed by the comment, Karan Singh was more determined than ever to make the transition from the State to the national level. He had been the head of the state for seventeen long years. The national elections were due the next year, 1967, and he felt that he should resign his office well in advance to prepare for the contest. With this in mind, on 17 August 1966 he wrote to Prime Minister Indira Gandhi: 'You will recall that over the last few months, I have mentioned several times my desire to relinquish the office of the Governor and seek more active participation in national politics. I have been Head of the State for almost half my life since I became Regent in 1949, and I do feel that it will now be desirable for me to change my field of public activity, even though it will be a wrench for me to dissociate myself from close contact with the affairs of the State to which I belong. In view of the fact that the general elections are approaching, I write to seek your approval to my requesting the President to accept my resignation from the post of Governor of Jammu and Kashmir sometime next month.'

Indira Gandhi responded the very next day, and her text suggested that while the two had indeed been discussing the subject for quite a while, the shift could not be rushed. She wrote, '...However, as I have explained to you, we are passing through very critical times in economics and other fields. As the General Elections approach, our problems will increase. The threat to our border also continues. In these circumstances and this delicate situation, I am worried at the thought of a new person taking up your important position. That is why I should like you to agree to stay in your present office for the time being. I hope you will find this possible.'

Karan Singh agreed to wait, because it was clear from Indira Gandhi's reply that his move to the Centre was now only a matter of time. In the State, preparations were in full swing to conduct elections for the Lok Sabha. Since they were to be held for the first time in the State, it meant that constituencies had to be carved out—though the number of seats had been allotted, they were yet to be delimited. When this question arose, Karan Singh and his long-time friend D.P. Dhar, collided over it. Dhar had suggested that Ladakh, having almost two-thirds of the total geographical area of the State and with a distinct cultural and linguistic identity, be made part of the Baramulla constituency. He also advocated that Doda, a part of Jammu province, be made part of the Anantnag constituency. Karan Singh opposed both suggestions since they would have blurred the regional identities of Ladakh and Jammu and would have ensured perpetual Kashmiri domination. The Delimitation Commission under Justice J.L. Kapur agreed with Karan Singh's suggestion, and one seat was allotted to Ladakh; three seats were given to Kashmir—Srinagar, Baramulla and Anantnag; and two to Jammu, where Poonch and Rajouri were clubbed with Jammu, and Kathua and Doda with Udhampur.

Another issue on which the two disagreed was the route of the proposed rail link to the State. The war of 1965 had exposed the vulnerability of the Pathankot-Jammu highway, underlining the need for alternative routes. Then there was the issue of economic activity, which had remained sluggish because of the absence of a rail link ever since the Sialkot-Jammu link had been disrupted in 1947. Dhar suggested that the proposed rail line, after crossing the Ravi from Pathankot, the first major town after Kathua, should be Udhampur, and Jammu should be bypassed. He raised security concerns as the reason for bypassing Jammu, the winter capital of the State. This was vehemently opposed by Karan Singh as it would not only have diminished the importance of Jammu but would also have adversely affected its economic growth by foreclosing options for new economic avenues.

The Jammu and Ladakh regions had been facing neglect, and successive governments had failed to acknowledge that the State consisted of the three distinct regions of Jammu, Kashmir and Ladakh, and all three had their aspirations that needed to be accommodated. This, however, did not happen as the template set by Sheikh Abdullah made it easier for the leaders from Kashmir to promote themselves. The result was that Jammu and Ladakh felt aggrieved and simmered with anger. These differences were symptoms of the underlying desire of Kashmir leaders to not only dominate all possible spaces but to put Jammu in subordinate positions—a malaise with a foreboding of the future. Karan Singh offered a solution to this in a letter to the President on 21 November 1966. He suggested setting up a high-powered Commission under the retired Chief Justice of India, B.P. Sinha, with two other members, to look into the problem and devise ways and means for the more rapid economic progress of all three regions. It was a little later that this suggestion was accepted, and a Commission was appointed under the retired Chief Justice of India, P.B. Gajendragadkar. This, however, did not happen till Jammu had begun to simmer and the situation deteriorated to such a degree that police opened fire on students, killing three and injuring dozens. The situation exposed the weakness of the Kashmiri orientation of the political and administrative authorities, and Chief Minister Sadiq was shaken as he had to face the hostility of Jammu for the first time. It was only with Karan Singh's intervention that the situation was diffused by setting up an Enquiry Commission under Justice Mukherjee.

Finally, when the general elections were announced, Karan Singh secured the Congress nomination for Brigadier Ghansara Singh, a battle-hardened loyalist from his father's times, from the Udhampur-Kathua-Doda constituency. Karan Singh was certain that sooner, rather than later, he would get a call from the Prime

Minister, and in that case, Brigadier Ghansara Singh would resign to pave the way for him to contest the bye-election. The election results for five of the six seats were on expected lines, and the Congress emerged victorious, but the Srinagar seat sprang a surprise with Bakshi winning despite all the efforts of the Congress and the administration. Thus, he proved once again that he still commanded the loyalty of the people of the capital city. At the national level, the Congress under Indira Gandhi secured a clear majority, though the margin was thinner than it had been in the outgoing Parliament. Her leadership in the Congress Parliamentary Party was challenged by Morarji Desai, but she emerged a clear winner, though to maintain party unity, she made him the Deputy Prime Minister and also adjusted many from his camp in the Cabinet.

It was a time when Indira Gandhi needed all the support that she could get, and Karan Singh was sure that it was the most appropriate time for him to jump into the political fray. So, after putting Jyoti in the Lawrence School at Sanawar, he and his wife reached Delhi. However, too embarrassed to broach the subject with the Prime Minister himself, he conveyed his message to her Joint Secretary, Sushital Banerji, who had become his close friend, that he was ready. On 12 March 1967, he and Asha were woken up early in the morning by a call from the Joint Secretary saying that the Prime Minister would like him to join her Cabinet as Minister for Tourism and Civil Aviation. The next day, he submitted his resignation letter to President Radhakrishnan, and on 13 March, he was administered the oath of office and secrecy, along with the rest of the Cabinet.

19

Indira Gandhi's Era

After yearning for a change, when Karan Singh finally got it, he realized that, however long he might have been the Head of State in J&K, Parliamentary life in Delhi was something he had not been prepared for. When he was administered the oath of office, the Parliament was in session, where all Ministers were called upon to answer questions related to their ministries. This was something alien to him. No sooner had he turned 18 than he had become the Head of the State, and he had remained in that position for the next 18 years and had never been called upon to answer any question or be answerable to anyone for any act of his government. However, as a minister, he was accountable not only to the prime minister but also to the Parliament; for that, he had to be well prepared.

He had been sworn in as Union Minister for Tourism and Civil Aviation on 13 March 1967 and had barely settled in his office when the Prime Minister wrote to him about her thoughts on Tourism. She emphasized the need to have programmes that enabled rapid expansion of tourism in India and, apart from the few historical destinations, attract tourists to many other attractions of historical and artistic value. She added that while taking care of the domestic tourists, the immediate attention should be on augmenting foreign exchange earnings, for which a review of the 'existing conditions and facilities such as accommodation, transport, entertainment, and so on' had to be made. She also noted that while the tourists were busy during the daytime, they found the evenings long and dull. Therefore, any plan to promote tourism needed to ensure that, without disturbing local customs, India's social or other values and inhibitions were not imposed upon the tourists. She also emphasized the need for better upkeep of historical places and monuments, and the co-opting of private enterprise in promoting tourism. She ended the letter with the words: 'I should be grateful if you would keep me informed of the steps taken or proposed or the trends of achievement'. Karan Singh presumed that similar letters must have been sent to all other ministers upon their taking charge of their portfolios. The letter made it very clear that the Prime Minister would be keenly watching the performance of each minister to ensure that all ministries moved in the desired direction.

After the initial surprise at discovering the gulf between the State and the Centre, Karan Singh gradually settled down and began to enjoy the challenge of facing the stalwarts of Parliamentary life. They belonged to various parties, came from varied backgrounds, and represented their constituencies with pride and commitment, which made them use every opportunity to corner the government. Oftentimes, he noticed a Minister being relentlessly targeted with probing questions that were unsettling, particularly when the Minister was not well-prepared. It was a fascinating battle that could be enjoyed only if the Minister was well equipped with facts and also possessed wit and the gift of the gab. Compared to them, Karan Singh was a greenhorn, having never faced a situation where he was called upon to explain and justify a decision. But there he was, as if in a Coliseum, ready to face whatever questions were thrown at him.

The presence of Parliamentarians like Hirendranath Mukherjee, popularly known as Hiren Da, of the Communist Party of India, serving his fourth term in Parliament, was daunting for any newcomer in the Parliament. Hiren Da had become a member of the Communist Party in 1936 when Karan Singh was just five years old. An excellent orator, he spoke English in an Oxonian accent and was respected not only for his eloquence but also for the depth of his knowledge of the subject he spoke on. Coming face to face with him in the Parliament was a learning experience for someone who had spent half his life as the Head of State. Luckily, at thirty-six years of age, he was young in politics and capable of acquiring wisdom and knowledge from others. Unfettered by the circumstances of his birth and the past, Karan Singh approached his Parliamentary duties with an open and receptive mind.

Another equally formidable Member of the Lok Sabha was Nath Pai, a freedom fighter who spoke English, French, and German with ease, besides his native Marathi. A committed socialist who represented the Praja Socialist Party in the Lok Sabha, he was a master in the art of putting the ruling party in the box with his consummate oratory that masterfully mixed legal arguments with bursts of emotion. His speeches were liberally interspersed with stories and anecdotes in English, Marathi, and Sanskrit, thereby mixing his erudition with earthy wisdom. His most durable contribution during his Lok Sabha years was the persistent championing of the need for Konkan Railways which transformed the fate of the western coastal regions. Then there were the likes of Madhu Limaye, who, along with Pai, was always armed with not only the legal arguments about the constitutionality of any bill, but also its moral validity. Of the two, Madhu Limaye was ever watchful of any government action that might in any way be impinging upon the freedoms enshrined in the Constitution or any attempt that might lead the country toward authoritarianism.

Another major presence in the Lok Sabha in 1967 was Jyotirmoy Basu, a formidable personality elected from Diamond Harbour, Calcutta, and the undisputed leader of the dock workers there. A member of the Communist Party of India (Marxist), he took a liking for the 'Prince' Minister and, as a mark of his affection, would bring *mishthi-doi*—sweet-curd—for him. To Karan Singh's surprise, he found that even though he came from a princely background, most of the Parliamentarians who took an immediate liking for him were from among the communist and the leftist parties, and that many Congressmen who professed socialist values were either indifferent to or resentful of his presence. Probably they thought that his birth and the circumstances of his State had undeservedly catapulted him to the Centre, whereas they had slogged it out during the freedom struggle or some other struggles for the people. Of all the Congressmen, the most resentful were those who had come to be known as the 'Young Turks'—prominent among them were Chandrashekhar, Mohan Dharia and Krishan Kant, members of the Rajya Sabha. The hostility of Chandrashekhar, in particular, bordered on nastiness. The reason these 'Young Turks' occupied a space larger than they deserved was because of the peculiar circumstances that had emerged in the Congress after the 1967 election results, and their utility as a weapon to put the rightist group in the party in uncomfortable positions. But in Karan Singh's case, they probably disapproved of a person from the feudal order who came to occupy important positions in a free India and made no bones about it. Surprisingly, this group had no problem with Dinesh Singh, a talukdar from Kalakankar, Uttar Pradesh, who remained a minister for much of his career from 1962, when he first entered Parliament as a Member of Lok Sabha, till 1995, when he passed away.

Karan Singh had also cultivated quite a few like-minded friends, and their group came to be known as the Wednesday Club, as they met every week on that appointed day in his office. The other members of this club were Lalit Sen of Suket, Brij Raj Singh of Kota, Yarragadda, a landlord from Andhra Pradesh, Erasmo Sequeira from Goa, Captain Ranjit Singh, a landlord from Uttar Pradesh and a former student of Doon School, and Dinesh Goswami from Assam. All of them were accomplished persons who were, apart from being public figures, excellent company. Lalit Sen came from the hill state of Himachal Pradesh and was a very well-read person who had received his education from St. Stephen's College, Delhi, and Sequeira, though not of the Congress party, was always a much sought-after politician when India had to deal with the Spanish- or Portuguese-speaking countries. Thus, he was always a member of any delegation that had to go to Latin America, himself being a champion of close ties with that continent. The members of the Wednesday Club had their own brand of humour, and while referring to Dinesh Singh, the Raja of Kalakankar, called him 'Lord Blackstone' by literally translating the name of his state. The Maharaja of Dhrangdhar, who spoke in the accent of the English aristocrats, was wickedly named 'Lord Haw-Haw'.

Prime Minister Indira Gandhi had chosen the right time to ask Dr. Karan Singh to join her cabinet, as the election results of 1967 had proved to be a warning for the Congress. A generation had passed since independence, and the people had grown impatient and yearned for speedier economic changes. In 1967, she knew that not only her party but she too was in a precarious situation and that fresh and new ideas and drastic steps were urgently required to recover lost ground. But the Prime Minister had found herself being thwarted by her party, which was controlled by the veterans from the days of the struggle for freedom. These veterans were conservative in their thinking and averse to any radical change, and were probably misogynists, hating to see a woman in a position of authority. However, the popular support of the party cadre and people was with Indira Gandhi. She had read the situation carefully and was gearing up for the challenges that lay ahead, and had, therefore, started building her team, Dr. Karan Singh being one of that new team.

Helped by her Principal Secretary, P. N. Haksar, a Kashmiri Pandit, Indira Gandhi responded to the rightist approach of the party stalwarts with a 10-point socialist programme as an instrument to energize the Congress after the 1967 reverses. She had carefully chosen steps to mark the beginning of a new era that was to also announce the death of British-era politics and norms in India. She had chosen to strike at the princes so that the departure from the established order could be announced loudly and clearly. The second step was the nationalization of banks, as they were important tools in the shaping of the Indian economy and winning the support of the masses. These banks held 85 percent of the bank deposits in the country. Thus, the 14 private banks were nationalized on 19 July 1969, and within two weeks, the Parliament had also ratified the Bill. This, however, was challenged in the Supreme Court, which struck down the government's move, after which it became a lengthy process to pass and implement it all over again. However, the process itself galvanized massive public support for Indira Gandhi.

The move to nationalize the banks had been welcomed by the jubilant masses, as in a short period, thousands of new branches were opened all over the country. These banks gave liberal loans to small industries and enterprises, unleashing a new middle class that energetically supported Indira Gandhi. However, she had another score to settle before she could embark upon the task of transforming the country. During the twenty years of independence, the country had witnessed the steady return of the princes of the erstwhile states into mainstream politics by winning elections with handsome margins. The 1967 elections had returned 75 princes to the Parliament, and among them, fewer than half were aligned with the Congress. During the first two general elections, the princes had either sided with the Congress Party or had remained neutral after having received their privy purses and privileges. But with the establishment of the pro-market, anti-socialist Swatantra Party in 1959, most of the former princes from Orissa and Gujarat had veered towards the new party. Meanwhile, in Madhya Pradesh, marking an early sign of that state moving towards a Hindu-supremacist ideology, the former princes had aligned themselves with the Bharatiya Jana Sangh. To the consternation of the Congress, these former royals were popular and wielded considerable influence, as a result of which the Congress had lost in 10 State Assemblies during the 1967 elections. This did not sit well with Indira Gandhi's radicalism, and she marshalled her supporters who, during the meeting of the Congress Working Committee, proposed to abolish the privy purses and privileges of the princes. By the middle of July 1969, this had gathered pace as it helped in contrasting the plight of the common man with the idle opulence of the princes. With this, all eyes were set on those princes who were elected on the Congress ticket and were the Ministers in the cabinet.

On 11 May 1969, newspapers reported that 'all 14 former princely rulers in the Congress Parliamentary Party, including Minister Members, had reportedly signed the 40-member representation seeking the Prime Minister's permission to vote against the resolution to abolish privy purses and privileges.' The news also claimed that the Civil Aviation Minister shared these views and had met the Prime Minister in that connection. The same day, Karan Singh condemned the speculative reporting, saying, 'I hardly need unauthorized and anonymous spokesmen to express my views, and I would like to state categorically that as a member of the Congress Party and Government, I stand firmly by the policy decision on this matter.' Dinesh Singh of Kalakankar pointed out to the Prime Minister that the move to abrogate solemn covenants signed with the princes could cause concern among the rulers of Sikkim and Bhutan, as they too had treaties with India. However, he did not push the matter any further.

By the middle of February 1970, Home Minister Y. B. Chavan, who had spearheaded the move to abolish privy purses and privileges, had drafted a note on the proposal, a copy of which was forwarded to Karan Singh by Indira Gandhi. He responded on 15 February 1970 and urged that the matter be dealt with in a spirit of fairness, equity and dignity, and that though the abolition was in keeping with the spirit of the times, it would have been better if it could be done by mutual agreement. He suggested that while abolishing the privy purses and privileges, the princes be paid transitional payments, which should be worked out based on ten times for privy purses of Rs. 10 lakhs and above, twelve times for purses between 1 lakh and 10 lakhs, and fifteen times for purses below 1 lakh. Of the amount thus calculated, 50 percent should be paid immediately in cash, and the balance 50 percent should be paid immediately in the form of special interest-bearing bonds. He also suggested that some minor privileges be continued for a certain length of time. He also cautioned that care be exercised while framing the law in light of the reverses suffered by the government in the Supreme Court over the nationalization of banks.

Unfortunately, the former rulers not only took a rigid stand but also approached Lord Mountbatten through the Maharaja of Jaipur, since Mountbatten had played a leading role in negotiating the treaties with the princely states at the time of Independence. However, the Commonwealth Relations Office in London discouraged him from intervening and taking the risk of spoiling relations with India. In a show of unity, the princes had also constituted a Concord of Princes, and with the former ruler of Dhrangdhara, in Gujarat, as their spokesman, they adopted a maximalist position, ruling out any compromise formula. The government then went ahead with the 26th Amendment to the Constitution, but once again failed in getting the nod from the Supreme Court. Indira Gandhi, however, persisted and was able to achieve her goal after the next general elections. In the meantime, she made her political point in no uncertain terms.

While the process of nationalizing the banks and abolishing the privy purses and privileges was long, the third step, which led to Indira Gandhi's total victory and dominance over her opponents in the Congress Party, was the most decisive. The first two years of the new term of the Parliament were of mild jostling and pushing for more political space and allocation of funds for the welfare activities that were championed by the Prime Minister and her faction, and the tight-fisted control over funds by Morarji Desai, her Deputy Prime Minister and Finance Minister, who was an advocate of the US-style free-market economy. The first two years passed with Indira Gandhi marshalling her resources and chalking out a plan for winning public support as well as initiating steps to accelerate the socialist economy. On the other hand, the faction led by Desai and Congress President Nijalingappa was determined to assert the superiority of the party, which was under their control, and its Working Committee. They claimed that the policies of the government were to be formulated by the party, and the government had only to implement them. They also wanted the government to be accountable to the party, which was unacceptable to Indira Gandhi. Thus, she was thwarted in her efforts to make the government reconnect with the people who were feeling disillusioned, as unemployment was widespread and the cost of living had skyrocketed. She was convinced that the old guard, better known as the Syndicate, was out of touch with the masses, the realities of their lives and their aspirations.

The showdown between the two happened in July 1969, when the Congress Parliamentary Board met to choose a candidate for electing a new President after the untimely demise of President Zakir Hussain. The old guard suggested the name of Neelam Sanjiva Reddy, who was aligned with them, as the party's Presidential candidate, but Indira Gandhi put forward the name of the veteran Dalit leader Jagjivan Ram. When pressed for a vote in the Parliamentary Board, Indira Gandhi lost by four votes to two. She accepted the decision and also filed the nomination papers of Sanjiva Reddy, but she was determined to hit back and wrest control of the party when she saw a chance with Vice President V.V. Giri, a trade union leader, deciding to contest the election as an independent. At the last moment, Indira Gandhi gave a call to her followers to exercise conscience-vote in the presidential election, thereby taking away the majority of the Congress votes from the official Congress nominee. The candidature of Giri was also supported by the communists and other left-leaning parties, which led to his narrow victory. Peeved at the defeat, the party bosses expelled Indira Gandhi from the party, but they had overplayed their hand, and a majority of the members of the All-India Congress Working Committee walked out of the party to side with her. This faction came to be called Congress (R), as they had requisitioned a meeting of their own, and the other faction became Congress (O). Karan Singh was among those who had decided to be with Indira Gandhi.

Away from politics, he had remained involved in the affairs of his State in general and Jammu in particular. He had kept his interest alive in the promotion of Dogri and its literature, and within two years of his arrival in Delhi, he succeeded in having Dogri literature recognized by the Sahitya Akademi. By the time he had arrived in Delhi, he had already earned the respect of the literary and intellectual circles of Delhi, and when the idea came up to institute an annual award to any work of literature that was written in any of the languages included in the Eighth Schedule, he was made a part of the select few who deliberated the details of the award. In 1966, when the first award was given to Sankara Kurrup, a prominent author of Malayalam, Karan Singh was a member of the jury. By 1970, Dogri literature had come to be widely accepted and the language was recognized as one of those that were eligible for Sahitya Akademi awards, and Narendra Khajuria became the first recipient. It marked an important step towards Dogri being incorporated in the Eighth Schedule. For this, Karan Singh had worked ceaselessly, composing devotional songs in Dogri, usually singing and recording them too, in order to popularize the language. Equally significant was his single-handed effort to popularize Dogri poetry in the rest of the country with his translation of Padma Sachdev's poems into English. However, he had to wait for three more decades to see Dogri being included in the VIII Schedule of the Indian Constitution through the 92nd Amendment Act of 2003. Karan Singh was a member of the Rajya Sabha then, and the announcement was made by Lal Krishna Advani, the then Home Minister and Deputy Prime Minister.

Politically, as dramatic events with far-reaching consequences unfolded during the years 1967-69, the Minister of Civil Aviation also faced the challenge of not only improving the functioning of Air India to make it globally competitive but also to make it the face of the new and confident India that was eager to make its global presence felt. In addition to the Civil Aviation, Karan Singh also held the Tourism portfolio and was responsible for attracting foreign tourists to earn foreign exchange. His major challenge as Tourism Minister was to wean foreign tourists away from the traditional tourist destinations to the less frequented destinations at affordable rates. This was a challenging task and needed the imagination and cooperation of the tour operators and the local entrepreneurs. Karan Singh devoted himself to meeting the challenge by creating infrastructure for flying, in order to make the experience of exploring different parts of the country more enjoyable. In reality, he became the pioneer of the discovery of 'Incredible India' for foreign tourists during that period.

In aviation, J.R.D. Tata, the pioneer of flying in India, had been the long-standing but part-time Chairman of the Board of Directors. Few objected to his being at the helm as he was an acceptable name, and everyone acknowledged that, as a founder of Air India, he had proven credentials in creating a presence for India even among the developed countries. Though a part-time chairman, he devoted considerable time and energy to the job, as even after the nationalization of Air India, he still considered it his baby. However, when Karan Singh decided to revamp the Board and bring in Mohan Kumarmangalam as a member, Tata protested vehemently as he was convinced that the presence of a communist in the decision-making process would ruin the otherwise well-managed airlines. The Civil Aviation Minister, however, reasoned with him to be patient and at least give Kumarmangalam a reasonable chance to prove himself. He assured Tata that in case he still believed that Kumarmangalam was a disruptive force on the Board, he would immediately remove him. It was true that even though Kumarmangalam came from a family of landlords of Tamil Nadu and was educated at

Cambridge, he had embraced communism from his student days and was also a cardholding member of the Communist Party of India. However, by 1966, like many others all over the world, he had begun to drift away from the ideology of communism and had begun to identify himself with the left-of-centre Indian National Congress. He had been subsequently appointed Advocate General of the then Madras State (now Tamil Nadu). Ideologically, Prime Minister Indira Gandhi, too, was closer to the less rigid members of the communist party and had succeeded in inducting many former communists into the Congress. But a capitalist like J.R.D. Tata was less inclined to accept communists with the same benevolent spirit, and he resisted as hard as he could against the appointment of Kumarmanaglam on the Board. However, as the year progressed, Tata discovered to his surprise that far from being inefficient and disruptive, Kumarmanaglam had had a positive influence. To Karan Singh's delight, Air India was rated one of the five best international airlines when the 'communist' Mohan Kumarmangalam was on its Board, and Tata had to admit to the Minister that he had given the Board its best member ever!

This was a period when the Congress was also riven with factionalism. After the election results of the 1967 general elections, there had been a leadership tussle between Indira Gandhi, representing the left orientation of the Congress, and Morarji Desai, the chosen leader of the right-wing faction of the party, and in an attempt to maintain unity in the party, it had been decided to make Morarji Desai the Deputy Prime Minister. As a result of this compromise, the party had remained divided, and no occasion was allowed to pass without one faction trying to put the other faction down. In this, Indira Gandhi had found the socialists and left-leaning members useful, thereby giving greater clout to the so-called Young Turks. They were very effective in putting the right-leaning Ministers to extreme discomfort with constant criticism and embarrassing questions. Since they usually hogged the headlines, they became a potent weapon for the Prime Minister. Karan Singh was known to be a close follower of Indira Gandhi, but he also enjoyed a very cordial relationship with Morarji Desai and had genuine respect for him because of his learning. But being an unapologetic rightist, Mararji shared Tata's distrust and dislike of communists and when Karan Singh appointed Romesh Thapar, one of his earliest friends in Delhi, who was also a man of taste and ideas, as the chairman of the Indian Tourism Development Corporation (ITDC), Desai expressed his unhappiness in no uncertain words. Even as Chairman of ITDC, Thapar continued with his other activities, which included editing and publishing the journal *Seminar*. As Thapar was a member of the Communist Party of India (Marxist), his journal also published well-reasoned socialist views, which, by their nature, were anti-establishment and usually highly critical of the government policies. On days when his views in an article appeared critical of the government, Morarji Desai never failed to tersely ask Karan Singh, 'Have you read your chairman's views?' And Karan Singh would innocently reply that he had not, but now that his attention had been drawn to them, he would go and read! The senior leader's remonstrations were always brief, but they left no doubt about what he thought.

Karan Singh's friendship with communists and their sympathizers baffled many, particularly in Jammu, where many people wondered how he could encourage and patronize a poetess like Padma Sachdev whose entire work in those days was full of anti-royal rhetoric. In 1971, she became the second writer of Dogri to be conferred the Sahitya Akademi honour.

During this period, Air India caused another point of disagreement between the Minister and the Chairman of the Board over the modernization of the fleet when tenders had been floated, and the choice was between Airbus and the latest and first supersonic jet, Concorde. There was a lot of hype about the Concorde, and many international airlines had begun to opt for it. Tata was also inclined towards this state-of-the-art aircraft, but after more consultations, Karan Singh ruled in favour of Airbus. However, with time, Airbus proved to be a money-spinner for Air India and Tata graciously agreed that once again the Minister's judgement was correct. As a minister, Karan Singh was having a good time as Air India had done exceedingly well. Since he also held the Tourism portfolio, he traveled abroad to promote tourism in India. On such occasions, he was always accompanied by his wife Asha, whose airfare was always paid by him from his account.

Meanwhile, determined to pursue her economic agenda, Indira Gandhi redoubled her efforts to nationalize 14 leading private banks, though the party had only wanted social control of the banks. These were measures that were needed if the economic disparities had to be reduced, though they were denounced by the opponents as populist measures. This measure brought about a sea change in the politics of India, as Indira Gandhi had put the focus on the common man, who genuinely came to believe that revolutionary changes were about to happen in life.

Buoyed by popular support, in March 1971 Indira Gandhi called for early Parliamentary elections and won them with a thumping majority. It marked a wider generational change, and Karan Singh was happy to be part of it. His track record in public life had demonstrated again and again that he had rooted for those socio-economic changes that made a difference to the lives of the people and, therefore, he had had no hesitation in supporting the bank nationalization or the amendment to the Constitution that abolished privy purses, even though he was going to be affected personally by the amendment. Had his father been alive, he would have been bitterly critical of it, as it would have been another instance of a new India where solemn promises had no sanctity. The Bill for the abolition of the Privy Purses was introduced in the Lok Sabha on 5 September 1970, where Karan Singh spoke in favour of the abolition, drawing bitter criticism from the rest of the princes who dubbed him a traitor. Before the introduction of the Bill, a serious effort had been made to find an amicable solution to it, but the maximalist position taken by the former rulers, led by the Maharaja of Dhrangadhra, had made any compromise impossible. Finally, the Lok Sabha passed the Bill, but it failed by one vote to muster the two-thirds strength required in the Rajya Sabha. The same day, President Giri signed an ordinance giving effect to the Amendment, but when it was struck down by the Supreme Court, Indira Gandhi called for the general election, which gave her 352 of the 516 seats. This allowed her to pass the necessary law to complete the process. After that, Indira Gandhi was to remain unchallenged till 1977. The former rulers understandably felt betrayed, and Bhanu Prakash Singh of Narsinghgarh, a Deputy Minister, resigned in protest.

As far as Karan Singh was concerned, the election of 1971 tested him vigorously as his Bharatiya Jana Sangh opponent, Thakur Baldev Singh, received considerable financial support from the princes who wanted to teach the 'traitor' a lesson. In the end, he coasted home comfortably. His wife once again proved to be a great asset as women flocked around her wherever she went.

But the resounding victory of the Congress in 1971 also underlined the magnitude of the challenges that awaited the new government.

20
Aviation and the Finest Hour

IN DELHI, KARAN SINGH learned early that while formulating policies and making decisions, Indira Gandhi always kept the bigger picture of India's interests in mind. Soon after he had taken charge of his Ministry, Mauritius was to hold its first general elections before its independence, and the island nation of the Indian Ocean, with a population of predominantly Indian origin, looked towards India for support in more ways than one. The Prime Minister had promised Dr. Ramgoolam, Premier of Mauritius, that by April of 1967, an air link would be established from India to Port Louis, the capital of Mauritius. The earlier Civil Aviation Minister had failed to address the airlines' objections regarding its projected losses on the route, and the deadline had come and gone. An exasperated Indira Gandhi impressed upon Karan Singh, the new Minister, the need for India to come good on the promise. She was worried that India's failure to establish an air link with Mauritius would adversely affect the elections in that country, and the failure would also allow Pakistan and other countries to exploit the situation. Karan Singh prevailed upon the reluctant Air India and, in the process, learned that every job had multiple dimensions, beyond the financial implications, and that an eye had to be kept on the larger national interests. He overcame the technical and financial problems for the flight and suggested the inaugural flight to take place on 15th August, Independence Day, as that would also then become a political message for both countries.

By the last week of May, he had also made a detailed study of Tourism, the subject on which the Prime Minister had shared her views, soon after he had been sworn in, and he sent her his views in a detailed note. He recognized the potential and scope of tourism in the economic development of the country and in augmenting foreign exchange earnings, but also recognized that the challenge was to convert the potential into reality. For this, he identified the need to bring in more commercial flights, which in turn would require better and upgraded terminal facilities. He earmarked new and bigger planes and better terminal facilities as a necessity if India was to benefit from the advent of the 'Jumbo' and 'Supersonic' jets. But once the tourists had arrived, they needed decent hotels and hospitality, which at that moment were non-existent. Surface transportation also needed to keep pace with the rising footfall, as well as the means of entertainment during the evenings, as the tourists needed to be engaged beyond the daytime tour of sites. He also proposed to develop new areas of tourist interest and also carry out tasteful publicity abroad. His proposals also kept an eye on the domestic sector and suggested the establishment of Workers' Homes, youth hostels, and adequate facilities for India's middle class. He hoped that the measures he proposed would also help promote national integration. He pointed out that domestic tourism had always been a part of the Indian lifestyle—not only since Adi Shankaracharya established the four Peeths in the different corners of the country, but also in the Buddhist era before that, when scholars, students and pilgrims within the Subcontinent and from China and other lands travelled to different sites, from the north to the south. Thus, he had a very clear roadmap for the development of tourism and assured the Prime Minister that the targets would be met.

However, very soon the young Minister realized the kind of bureaucratic hurdles that kept popping up during a routine day's work. Ten weeks after he had taken charge of his Ministry, he was still without a Secretary to his Ministry, and when a name was finalized, he found that the person suggested was on the verge of retirement whereas he needed someone youthful and energetic. The term of the Chairman of the Indian Airlines too was coming to an end, and the Minister was again keen on having someone dynamic and capable of meeting the goals set by him and the Prime Minister. Again, it turned out to be a longer process than he would have liked, as the appointment had to be ultimately decided by the Appointments Committee of the Cabinet, even though he had warned that any delay would adversely affect the Corporation.

The Ministry of Tourism and Civil Aviation had been carved out of the Ministry of Transport and Shipping when, in 1967, the importance of tourism had been realized. To further strengthen the new Ministry, Karan Singh proposed that the Department of Archaeology be transferred to it. He argued that a vast number of foreign tourists visited India to see the historical sites and monuments; therefore, their upkeep and beautification should be put under the control of the tourism department, just as the research and study of their significance was under the education department. He also advocated the establishment of catering schools, national parks, wildlife sanctuaries, and a Construction Wing, as the construction of airports and tourism-related infrastructure required specialized skills. But to his disappointment, his plans and enthusiasm were not shared by the Planning Commission, which, instead of enhancing his Ministry's allocation during the Fourth Five-Year Plan, almost halved what was expected. This meant that many of the targets that had been set suddenly became unrealistic and overly ambitious.

As Minister, Karan Singh discovered that the confrontational politics that had manifested itself in public life when the progressives and the conservatives within the Congress came face to face in 1969, affected not only the politics of the country but was to also affect the relationship between the management and workers of almost all sectors. In aviation, there was no doubt that India needed to grow at a faster rate and also needed to ensure that the development was equitable and spread across the board. For this, every sector needed to be modernized and made more efficient. Karan Singh had discovered that civil aviation was afflicted by all the ailments that had begun to plague life in general. He understood that it was unrealistic to expect that it would be free of the influences of society simply because it was a better-paid job than the others. In addition, he discovered that aviation required massive investment for modernizing, not only the fleet but also the general infrastructure of the airports, manpower, equipment and technology. Since he also held the Tourism Ministry, he knew that if foreign tourists had to be attracted to India, then an attractive face of the country had to be presented as soon as they landed at any of the international airports. In addition, they needed comfortable and affordable hotels to stay. The truth was that the fleet of Air India and Indian Airlines had been aging for quite some time, the airports offered only basic facilities, and the hotels at the tourist destinations were either too expensive or lacking in decent facilities. The concept of budget tourism had not yet arrived.

As soon as he set his heart to the task of modernizing

the aging aircraft fleet, he discovered that many lobbies were jostling to promote the various aircraft manufacturers that they represented. The proposal of purchasing new planes for the Indian Airlines had been put before the Cabinet on 8 November 1968, a little over a year after he had taken charge of the ministry. A Cabinet committee had gone into it and had reported back to the Cabinet on 12 December 1968. In the meantime, a team had been sent to USSR, UK and USA to study the viability and technical efficiency of the three shortlisted planes and it had concluded that the choice was between Boeing-737, BAC 111-500, and the DC-9, as the Soviet TU 154 was not only technically inferior but also did not measure up to the operational economics. However, two Cabinet colleagues, Fakhruddin Ali Ahmed and Dinesh Singh, advocated the purchase of the Soviet plane as a quid pro quo for the Soviet purchase of various goods from India. Aware of the bigger picture and close and friendly relations with the USSR, Karan Singh argued that had the Soviet plane been only marginally inferior, then the decision could have been made in favour of the Soviets, but in the case under question, that would harm Indian interests. To balance things, he offered to purchase Soviet hydrofoil boats for tourist purposes and also secure from them the details of TU 144, the Soviet supersonic passenger plane, so that it could be considered along with the Concorde and the Airbus for Air India.

The committee constituted for the purchase of the planes was headed by Bharat Ram and also had Kumarmangalam as a member, whose ideological proximity to the left was no secret. The Americans, too, had noticed this, and US Ambassador Kenneth Keating called upon Karan Singh to express his apprehension about a fair deal as the American plane belonging to the Douglas company had been dropped from consideration, with its representative being accused of offering bribes to a senior officer of the Indian Airlines. Keating suspected that with 'communist' Kumarmangalam as one of the members of the committee, the decision-making had veered in favour of the Soviets. Karan Singh assured him of a fair process and explained the reason for excluding one of the American planes. When the CBI established a prima facie case against the representative of American Airlines and an Indian officer, the DC-9 was eliminated from the process. After making a careful assessment with the help of facilities available at the Computer Centre in New Delhi, a recommendation for the purchase of Boeing-737 was made, and the Cabinet approved it on 9 January 1970. The plane chosen in the face of intense lobbying by the various interest groups had a proven track record, as even at the time of issuing the letter of intent to Boeing's manufacturer, it was in use by 25 airlines in 14 countries. For Indian Airlines, it turned out to be a money spinner.

It was not just the Americans who were wary of the left-leaning people. J.R.D. Tata's antagonism towards them was understandable as he was a capitalist, but a large section of the politicians too was fiercely opposed to anyone whom they suspected of being a communist. This was also on display when the Air Corporations (Amendment) Bill, 1970 was tabled in the Parliament. Even though the subject was regarding the Air Corporation that was supposed to expand its field of operations, like setting up and running hotels and the hospitality industry, it soon veered towards the subject of the suitability of Mohan Kumarmangalam as the Chairman of the Indian Tourism Development Corporation and the inability of the Minister to recruit an adequate number of air hostesses in the Airlines. Rajya Sabha member Krishan Kant had gone to the extent of remarking that a handsome, young Minister could not find beautiful air hostesses! Ironically, while most of the members conceded that

Air India was doing well, they failed to see that the kind of support that was needed to make an airline successful had not been forthcoming.

Lok Nath Misra, a member from Orissa, also launched a personal attack on Kumarmangalam even though he was not a member of the House, and it fell upon Karan Singh to defend him, which he did vigorously. He pointed out that it was factually incorrect to say that Kumarmangalam was a communist as he had resigned from that party in 1966, but in any case, a communist had not been barred by the Constitution of India from holding any government position. He also pointed out that there was an elected chief minister who was a member of the communist party, and that Kumarmangalam should have been acceptable to the critics, particularly when he was devoting a lot of his time without availing rent-free accommodation and never availing free passage when not travelling for any work unrelated to airlines. This stout defence forced Misra to acknowledge that he would not have been so critical of Kumarmangalam if the airlines had not been working so 'shabbily'. Karan Singh accepted that there were many ailments afflicting the Corporation, but these could be eradicated only after the new planes arrived and finances were made available for overhauling the infrastructure. On the question of the suitability of Kumarmangalam as Chairman of ITDC, he asserted that in his opinion, the job required a person who was 'intelligent, who can understand the trends in the industry and who can look ahead and plan'. He insisted that the Chairman had fair managerial and executive ability that had been demonstrated during his years as a labour leader. There were many other minor objections, all of which were suitably addressed by Karan Singh, whose approach made it clear that he favoured lateral entry into the government of people who had ideas, dynamism and the will to contribute to the task of nation-building.

His first three years as Minister of Tourism and Civil Aviation had been satisfying on many counts, not the least on account of its markedly improved performance. In 1968-69, Indian Airlines made a profit of Rs. 1.66 crores and Air India of Rs. 1.84 crores. Further, whereas Indian Airlines would be raising Rs. 50 crores from its resources for new investments, Air India had planned an investment of Rs. 75 crores during the Fourth Five-Year Plan, out of which it would invest Rs. 60 crores from its own funds. The Minister was hopeful that it was possible that the entire amount could come from Air India's funds. But when he presented the Air Corporations (Amendment) Bill, 1970 in Parliament, the debate turned out to be, in more ways than one, a continuation of the power struggle that had erupted during the 1967-69 period when the first round had decisively gone to Indira Gandhi.

Karan Singh was once again subjected to intense pressure when the airworthiness of the Avro came into question. The plane was being manufactured by Hindustan Aeronautics Limited (HAL), and foreign manufacturers were trying to run down the home production. Karan Singh called for all the technical details and sought the opinion of the most neutral of experts, but at the end of the day, everything boiled down to accepting or rejecting expert opinion, and he decided to accept the expert advice from HAL that it was safe to fly the Avro. But no sooner had he made that forceful defence of the aircraft in question, the crash of a trainer plane was reported on 15 March 1973, putting him in an awkward position. It was deeply embarrassing for him as he felt that his forceful defence appeared to have been an exercise in misleading the Parliament. He also felt as if he had let down his Prime Minister by making inaccurate claims about the safety of the Avro. So, in the highest tradition of Parliamentary democracy, where accountability was paramount, he decided to take responsibility and sent his resignation to the Prime Minister. Not very long ago, the late Lal Bahadur Shastri too had resigned over a railway accident, therefore, he was only upholding that tradition by putting in his papers. Indira Gandhi sent a note to Karan Singh expressing concern over the accident and drew his attention to reports that the senior pilot and the other two on the flight were reputed to be heavy drinkers and that the senior pilot had not been entirely sober before the flight. It appears that she had obtained that information from her son Rajiv Gandhi, who too was a pilot with Indian Airlines. She also emphasized the need to make breathalyzer tests a part of routine procedures for pilots. However, on the same day, she wrote another letter to Karan Singh, saying that he had 'done good work in [the] ministry and brought a fresh outlook to bear on many problems. Hence, I am not accepting your resignation and would like you to continue as Minister.' That turned out to be the only occasion when Indira Gandhi turned down an offer to resign by a minister.

Interestingly, the high point of that period for Karan Singh was, on the face of it, unrelated to either Civil Aviation or Tourism. True to her panoramic approach to the growth story of India, Indira Gandhi was also concerned by the depleting number of wild animals, particularly tigers. She was also among the early world leaders to recognize the importance of wildlife and forests and, hence, conservation. During a meeting, when this issue came up, she asked Karan Singh if he would like to head the National Board for Wildlife. It was the apex body for wildlife conservation, but it had been without a leader as no one seemed interested in it. Not one to shy away from a challenge or shirk any duty, Karan Singh accepted, and put his heart and soul into the job and soon realized something obvious that had been missed till then. The lion had been named the National

Animal of India, but Karan Singh pointed out that the natural habitat of the lion in India was confined to the Gir forest in Gujarat whereas the tiger existed in all the states and regions of the country except regions of extreme climatic conditions, like the Thar desert of Rajasthan and the snowbound and cold desert of Ladakh. His suggestion was to replace the lion with the tiger as India's National Animal. Happily for him, the Prime Minister agreed. From then onwards, the Jim Corbett National Park, in present-day Uttarakhand, began to be viewed as an important national project to preserve wildlife and nature, and became a template for many other national parks in the country.

While Karan Singh had been focused on transforming the aviation and tourism industry, the country had begun to grapple with a crisis that was to finally culminate in changing the geographical boundaries of the subcontinent. In December 1970, Pakistan held general elections in which the Awami League, with support only from the Bengali-speaking East Pakistan, won an overall majority but was denied the opportunity to form a national government by the Pakistan Army and political parties from West Pakistan. This denial led to massive protests and an uprising of the people in East Pakistan, which was suppressed by the use of brutal military force. On 23 March 1971, the Pakistani military massacred students and intellectuals and unleashed a reign of terror in East Pakistan, forcing people to flee to the safety of India. Thus, India, which was struggling to feed its people in the wake of consecutive monsoon failures, found itself saddled with millions of Bengali refugees from East Pakistan. It was also creating a crisis in West Bengal, as most of the refugees came to that State and stretched its limited resources. India pleaded with the world powers to make Pakistan see the folly of waging a war against its own people, but the Western world remained impassive as Pakistan and its President General Yahya Khan had facilitated the breaking of the ice between the USA and China. Unwilling to let anything spoil the newfound bonhomie and restrain Pakistan, the USA felt irritated by the persistent efforts of India to rouse the world's conscience. It was obvious to everyone except the Americans that the refugee crisis was testing Indira Gandhi's and the country's patience, and unless the carnage in the east was stopped, India and Pakistan would drift towards another war.

In June 1970, a few chosen Ministers were sent to various countries to canvass support for India's position with the world leaders. While Indira Gandhi went to the USA and USSR, she deputed Karan Singh to visit the German Democratic Republic (East Germany), Romania, Yugoslavia, Spain and Iran. Of the five countries, three were part of the Soviet bloc, while the last two were autocracies aligned with the West. During his visit to Yugoslavia, he discovered the deep interest that the intellectuals there had in India, and, on return, he suggested to the Prime Minister to explore the possibility of establishing an institute of Indological Studies there. He also built a lifelong personal bond with President Marshal Josip Tito and his wife, who had taken a personal liking for him and his wife during their meetings. Later, as the Soviet Union collapsed, Yugoslavia, an unlikely federation of various ethnicities and nationalities, fell apart after Tito's death. But Tito was well aware of this possibility and had nonchalantly accepted this during a conversation with Karan Singh. On another occasion, he had invited Karan Singh and Asha to his Dacha, an exclusive island, for a holiday, and when he returned empty-handed after a hunting trip, he complained to Karan Singh that he must have prayed hard for the animal!

In other countries, too, Karan Singh succeeded in striking

a friendly chord, but the most significant visit was to Iran. The Shah of Iran had visited India, along with his Foreign Minister Zahedi, in 1969. During that visit, Karan Singh was the Minister in Attendance and had struck a cordial relationship during their twelve-day visit. The trip had given him enough time to converse with them informally and find out their views that were not for public consumption. The Shah of Iran refrained from making any overt statements that could give the impression of favouring Pakistan, but his Foreign Minister, who had married the Shah's sister, had not been that circumspect. He had told Karan Singh that Kashmir needed to be made an independent State and that the Islamic world would never accept Kashmir as a part of India because, he said, it was anti-Muslim. The visit in 1970 had changed little except that Karan Singh noticed that though the Shah appeared to be in total control of his country, there were murmurings against the one-man rule at the Tehran University and other intellectual centers. Little did he know that the benign murmurings of 1970 would build into a roar in just about a decade, causing an upheaval that would create divisions in world politics perhaps for all times to come.

Even as diplomatic efforts to arouse the world's conscience continued, Indira Gandhi, aware of the dependence of the USA on Pakistan to further its global interests, decided to counter that by negotiating and signing an Indo-Soviet Friendship Treaty, but without joining the Soviet Bloc. Meanwhile, India also lent all support to the Government-in-exile established by those of the East Pakistan Bengalis who were abroad when the military crackdown had commenced. They had also organized an Army of their own—Mukti-Bahini—that waged a guerrilla war against the Pakistan Army. Finally, on 3 December 1971, Pakistan overreached itself by launching an air offensive against India from its western wing. The Parliament was already in session when a full war broke out on India's western front, though for India, it was more of a defensive measure as its focus was on keeping the war on the Eastern border short, swift and decisive. The whole nation followed the progress of the war, and people remained glued to their transistor radios to get the latest updates. Finally, on 16 December 1971, as Karan Singh sat on his designated seat just behind the Prime Minister's, he saw Indira Gandhi virtually run into the Lok Sabha and say, 'Mr. Speaker, I have an announcement to make,' and as the House became dead silent, she added, 'Dhaka is now the free capital of a free country.' At those words, the House exploded with spontaneous and tumultuous applause. That was the most glorious hour of Independent India and Indira Gandhi.

Her announcement had an electrifying effect on the country and marked the pinnacle of her success. From 1969 onwards, her timing had been perfect, and it appeared that she could do no wrong. But just when a human being appears infallible, signs of fallibility begin to appear. At the time of the cease-fire, India was in a strong position, not just because it was in control of strategic locations and large tracts of Pakistani territory in the west but also because India had approximately 90,000 Pakistani soldiers as prisoners. This had put Pakistan under tremendous pressure from its people, and it was desperate to bring them home. In such an atmosphere, both countries decided to meet in Shimla. While Indira Gandhi led the Indian team, Pakistan was led by its Zulfiqar Ali Bhutto, now the country's President. Both were assisted by their respective advisers, but the Indian team was packed with bureaucrats belonging to the Pandit community from Kashmir. There was not even one member who belonged to any other State or community. The key adviser was P.N. Haksar, on whom Indira Gandhi had been banking since 1969 and who had helped her by giving shape to her socialist policies while confronting her opponents in the Congress party. Also on the team were Karan Singh's old friend D.P. Dhar, who had now moved to the Centre and become a close confidant of Indira Gandhi's; and P.N. Dhar, who was to be later appointed her Principal Secretary.

One of the riddles of India's relationship with Pakistan is that while India utilized the services of Karan Singh to normalize political equations in Jammu and Kashmir before 1970, it neither consulted nor involved him in any of the negotiations with Pakistan. Indira Gandhi often liked to use him as a sounding board for new ideas, and the notes and observations that he used to send to Indira Gandhi regarding the countries he visited were valued by her, but she never consulted him on Indo-Pak relations. In 1972, when the two sides met in Shimla in June-July, Karan Singh was left out of the negotiations. Perhaps, her advisers thought that, being the son of the person who had signed the Instrument of Accession in India's favour, his presence would put off the Pakistanis. But it was strange that the presence of so many Kashmiri Pandits never raised any eyebrows. The Shimla Agreement was signed on 2 July 1972 and, among other things, India agreed to free all the Pakistani prisoners of war. Most experts felt that India had let go of a chance to regain those areas of Jammu and Kashmir that had gone under the control of Pakistan in 1948. It was hard to understand the inability of India to extract a concrete advantage from its position of strength, as it was known that the bulk of the Pakistani PoWs were of Punjabi origin, and President Bhutto was desperate to get them back. But the grapevine had it that Pakistan had come well prepared and knew beforehand that the key person from the Indian side was the all-powerful P.N. Haksar, the Principal Secretary of Indira Gandhi, and Bhutto assiduously built an understanding with him. It was Haksar who convinced the Indian Prime Minister that if the Pakistan President was sent home empty-handed, that country would slip into the hands of religious fanatics and political hardliners, and a chance to build bridges with Pakistan would be lost. Thus, an opportunity to put the Kashmir debate to rest had been missed. But importantly, after becoming the Prime Minister, that was the first time that Indira Gandhi had not secured a complete victory.

In the Civil Aviation Ministry, the moves to revamp Air India and Indian Airlines had continued, as had the process of renovating and improving the existing airports in the country. Karan Singh had developed excellent relations with the Parliament and the media, and when he offered to resign in the wake of the Avro Trainer plane crash, his gesture was appreciated by all. But soon this goodwill evaporated when a Boeing plane crashed over Palam, New Delhi, on 31st May 1973. In the crash, 48 of the 65 passengers lost their lives. Among the killed was Kumarmangalam, who, after serving as an Air India Director, had been Chairman of the Air Corporation before being elected to the Parliament to become Minister of Steel and Mines in 1971. Many people, including outside forces, had attributed the crash to the abysmally poor infrastructure and unacceptably poor environment and functioning of the Air Traffic Control tower, and this had led to the speculation that foreign airlines were about to ban flying to and out of India. This would have dealt a crippling blow to the fledgling tourism industry that had just begun to blossom. Karan Singh, as the Civil Aviation Minister, appointed a Commission of Enquiry under the chairmanship of a retired High Court Judge, and after evaluating every available evidence, it concluded that the crash had been caused by pilot error. Visibility had been so poor due to bad weather, that the crew had been unable to locate the runway. Yet, the pilots had decided to continue with the descent and the plane had crashed into power cables near the airport and burst into flames. An experts' report concluded that the reason for the crash had been 'Wrong approach configuration and poor flight planing on part of the flight crew.'

The debate that followed the horrific crash became an occasion to analyze almost every aspect of flying, and questions were raised over how the periodic assessment of the flying abilities of the pilots was conducted. The report found that all the technical parameters regarding the aircraft, the pilots, the weather, the audio system, etc., were in perfect order and that while landing, the pilot had made the fatal error of inaccurately judging the runway and the height at which the plane was flying at the time of landing. It was also pointed out by the report that the co-pilot had failed to give proper call-outs during that critical period. But the bottom line was that 48 precious lives had been lost, and many Members of Parliament wanted to pin the responsibility on the Minister and the management. The Minister's assurance that there was no proposal by international pilots to boycott Indian Airports had not satisfied them. What, however, could not be denied was that there was a serious deficiency in the working of the pilots. Even during the Avro crash, the subject of alcohol consumption by pilots before their flight had been raised by no less a person than the Prime Minister.

The Indian Commercial Pilots Association (ICPA) had extracted a major say in the selection of Check Pilots, Instructors, and Examiners in 1966. Now, putting his foot down, Karan Simgh directed that in the future, these were to be selected by the Director General of Civil Aviation (DGCA). He also proposed creating posts of three Examiners under the DGCA, who would be tasked with constant monitoring and assessment of the flying proficiency of the pilots. He also decided to get 50 sets of breathalyzers immediately, with 100 more soon. Strict action against those pilots who had imbibed alcohol before the flight were put in place. In addition, as the Air India pilots had begun to resort to partial strikes, the government decided not to tolerate such tactics and, if needed, to invoke the Essential Services Maintenance Act. Karan Singh also highlighted the fact that Indian Airlines had been working without a full-time Chairman, which affected its efficiency, and that the Chairman of the International Airport Authority lacked drive and dynamism and was also a heart patient, which hampered the working of the Airports. He also pointed out that in the recent past, three air crashes had taken place around Palam—the Japan Airlines, Royal Nepal Airlines, and the Indian Airlines Fokker Friendship—and the inquiry reports had found that all three were due to pilot errors. There was a clear case of indiscipline and negligence by the pilots, but Indira Gandhi cautioned him and advised him to deal with the matter gently through negotiations.

It was very clear that a serious problem had evolved with the running of Air India and Indian Airlines, and the country's airports. Either the personnel were inefficient or lacking in motivation to excel, or were just not physically fit for the job. This required hard decisions, but the Prime Minister did not favour any drastic steps to discipline the pilots, although they were earning princely salaries compared to other sectors in the country. It was possible that with her elder son a pilot with Indian Airlines, she was only getting the perspective that was given to her at her dining table. Karan Singh, though, was convinced that unless hard decisions regarding discipline were taken, there was no chance of improving the efficiency and profitability of aviation even with the new and bigger planes.

Karan Singh had been Minister of Tourism and Civil Aviation for more than six years, and he began to feel the monotony of dealing with similar problems and challenges year after year. So he was relieved when the Prime Minister reshuffled some of the portfolios and assigned the Health Ministry to him on 9 November 1973.

21

The Years of Conflict

On 8 August 1958, when Karan Singh had responded to Jawaharlal Nehru's fortnightly letter that had a note titled 'loud thinking' appended to it, he could not have imagined that he would one day be given the responsibility of dealing with a problem that, according to him, had been offsetting all the successes that the country had achieved after independence. He had written to Nehru, 'We have, of course, achieved a good deal since Independence, but the expectations of our people always expand faster than our capacity to meet them, with the result that the gap remains and even grows. I am no economist so I will not venture to say anything with regard to...our economic planning, but there is one matter which I feel bound to mention and that is the question of population...however much we may increase our food output per acre, however much we may extend our irrigation and improve our methods of production, our huge and rapidly increasing population will inexorably swallow up all that we produce and millions will remain in distress...' By appointing him the Health and Family Planning Minister, Prime Minister Indira Gandhi had unwittingly thrown the challenge at him to contribute towards solving a problem that he had underlined fifteen years ago.

Within a couple of days of taking charge, he had identified the problems facing the Ministry and broadly outlined how he wanted to energize the Family Planning programme that was refusing to take off for lack of conviction, commitment and prudish attitudes among the policymakers. The Prime Minister, in her letter to him, had laid stress on the improvement of the conditions of the hospitals in the Capital and ensuring that the health facilities provided to the central government employees were not confined only to the VIPs. When he went to visit the Safdarjung and Willingdon Hospitals, he was appalled by the overcrowding. He, therefore, proposed that the Central Government Health Services (CGHS) beneficiaries be treated at separate hospitals so that they did not add to the burden of the two main Hospitals. For that, he began to explore the possibility of utilizing some buildings in Delhi that could be used to exclusively treat the CGHS beneficiaries. Also, to his surprise, he had found that originally, there had been no provision in the Fifth Five-Year Plan for the improvement of hospital facilities in Delhi.

Within a month of his taking charge of his Ministry, Karan Singh had also made Family Planning a focal point. His suggestion to recalibrate the birth rate targets had been accepted, but he pointed out that even those could be achieved only after a massive and concerted effort of the Ministry and the State Governments. He, therefore, mooted the idea of putting the mass media to good use in spreading messages about hygiene and birth control, and information about the country's Health and Family Planning services. At that time, Hindustan Latex, the producer of contraceptives under the brand name of Nirodh, had only one manufacturing unit in Trivandrum (now Thiruvananthapuram) but since the demand would soon increase manifold, he proposed the expansion of the existing unit along with the establishment of many more factories of that kind. He had also pointed out the inadequacy of the functioning of the Indian Council for Medical Research (ICMR), but was hopeful that with Dr. Coluthur Gopalan taking over as the new Director General, after his recommendations, restructuring and reform of the ICMR would take place to improve matters.

To meet the targets set for the Fifth Five-Year Plan, Karan Singh held detailed discussions with the State Chief Ministers, as well as the State Health Ministers, as, ultimately, they would lead the mission among the people of their states. Significantly, Karan Singh also met the representatives of various unions in the Delhi hospitals in addition to opening up a dialogue with the medical profession through the Delhi Medical Association. From the early feedback that he received, he suspected that if corrective steps were not taken in time, the Government would soon be faced with serious difficulties in Delhi and elsewhere. Barely two months into his tenure as the Health Minister, he was proved right in his judgment as the junior doctors in Delhi went on a strike at midnight on 31st December 1973.

Much before the junior doctors went on strike, the national capital, like many other cities across the country, had begun to simmer with anger, with scarcities and escalating prices triggering lightning strikes with occasional bursts of violence. The criticism of the Government was widespread, and even the friendly media acknowledged that the plight of the 'workers' was pathetic and that only 'black marketeers and hoarders' were prospering. In the medical profession, it was not just the junior doctors who had been at the rough end of life; the nurses and paramedics shared their plight. Karan Singh was sympathetic to the junior doctors, but when he approached Y.B. Chavan, the Finance Minister, with a proposal for their wage hike, the Minister was not prepared to loosen his tight fist even slightly. Chavan responded by reminding his fellow Minister of his princely ancestry, saying that Karan Singh belonged to the illustrious line of Raghuvanshis (belonging to the dynasty of Lord Ram) and therefore his hand was always willing to give doles but he, as the Finance Minister, had to carefully watch the outflow of money and be mindful of many other factors.

The unrest among the junior doctors had been simmering long before Karan Singh was assigned to the Health Ministry. To look into their demands, the Kartar Singh Committee had been set up in October 1973, but before it could submit its recommendations, the storm had broken. Karan Singh had met the doctors before they had gone on strike and had assured them that the government would announce its decision before 31st January 1974 and had invited them for talks, but they had not turned up. They did meet him later, but only on the third day of the strike when positions had hardened. The strike had led to widespread disruption of health services. The Kartar Singh Committee submitted its report on 10 January 1974 and recommended substantial enhancement of emoluments and stipends. It was at that point that Karan Singh had pleaded with the Finance Minister, and he, in response, had made that 'Raghuvanshi' retort.

Karan Singh knew that the salaries of the doctors were unjust and an insult to their profession, but he could do nothing as the financial condition of the country was such that the Finance Ministry was finding it hard to strike a balance. Many sections of society had been taking out protest demonstrations or going on strike. The striking doctors not only struck work but also sat in protest outside Karan Singh's residence in Chanakyapuri, periodically raising slogans that increased in intensity when the Minister entered or went out of his home. After about a week, some of the young doctors became almost like familiars of long association and some mornings or evenings the Minister and they would even exchange greetings! His wife, Asha, was very sympathetic to the doctors and, on one occasion, having come to know that it was the birthday of one of the protestors, she had a birthday cake sent over to them.

Karan Singh pressed for a just and equitable solution. He understood that the junior doctors were young and volatile and leaderless, and were, therefore, susceptible to the influence and infiltration of extremist elements. So he was not certain the Kartar Singh Committee recommendations, if they were accepted by the Finance Ministry and announced, would be accepted by the striking doctors. He recommended to the Prime Minister that rather than give in bit by bit, it would be better to take a principled position and then stand firm by it. But he also warned that the government should be prepared for any eventuality arising out of the rejection of its offer by the strikers. The main problem, in his opinion, was an alarming credibility gap between the current generation of young doctors and the government, which was 'symbolic of the growing alienation of the younger generation throughout the country'. He pointed out to the Prime Minister that he did not view his job as restating the official position, as he was convinced that the junior doctors had been dealt a very raw deal in the past. The note of the Finance Ministry that rejected almost every item of the agreement that he had worked out for the junior doctors came as a rude shock, because in his considered opinion, the financial impact of higher wages could not be termed as huge.

The matter was also raised in Parliament, where members like Jyotirmoy Basu, otherwise favorably inclined towards Karan Singh, always had their knives sharpened for attack. On 19 February 1974 when Karan Singh wanted to make a statement on the junior doctors' strike in the Lok Sabha, Basu led one of the most stinging attacks against him by saying that while the expenditure on a Minister was more than Rs. 50,000 per month, the government was not prepared to concede to the demands that, according to him, were just. In his reply, Karan Singh had pointed out that the strike had also affected the medical education and services in other parts of the country, and to address the protestors' concerns, he had offered a hundred percent hike for some categories of doctors while assuring others of favourable consideration of their demands. He further pointed out that 'the whole system of medical education needs to be restructured and streamlined to make it a more effective instrument for meeting the growing requirements of our people.'

Finally, it was only on 6 April 1974 that Karan Singh was able to resolve the deadlock and inform the Prime Minister that the junior doctors had called off their strike after a closed-door meeting with him in which a fair hike in salaries had been agreed to. After the crisis had ended, he wrote to the Prime Minister, asking her to change the Secretary to the Health Ministry, as he was rigid and authoritarian in his attitude and was never on the same wavelength as his Minister. He pointed out that these were not traits that were needed in the Ministry at a time when it was looking to change outmoded procedures and attitudes. With the massive campaign for achieving Family Planning targets in the pipeline, he did not want a secretary who did not share his outlook and was obstructive by nature. In the end, Karan Singh had cleaned his Ministry of most of the cobwebs and devoted himself to the goals that he and the Prime Minister had set for the Ministry.

In hindsight, what stood out for Karan Singh was the inability of the political class to anticipate problems and tackle them, and the obstructive and status quoist attitude of the bureaucracy, which buffeted the country from one crisis to another. The junior doctors' strike had lingered for over three months because of the insensitivity of the Health Ministry and the obstinate insistence of the Finance Ministry on its inability to concede even the rightful and just demands. But the medical profession had not been alone in their grievances. Almost every segment of society was groaning under the weight of stagnated wages, escalating prices, and long working hours and almost inhuman expectations. Among the worst affected were the employees of the Indian Railways who had continued to work under the same conditions that had been imposed by the British. Even the Third Pay Commission had failed to pay heed to their plight, and this had led to sporadic strikes at the local, regional and national levels. The consequence was that the Railways Unions had gone under the control of socialist leader George Fernandes, who, in the eyes of the management, the government, and the public, was effectively a militant leader. When the Government failed to pay heed to the railway strike of 1973, the unions resorted to an all-India strike in May 1974—a few months after the junior doctors strike.

The government had prepared itself well for the strike by stocking food grains in the deficit states, coal and minerals for the power and steel plants, and when the time came, the railway strike was brutally suppressed through mass arrests, dismissals and eviction of families from the railway quarters. More than 50,000 permanent and 30,000 casual workers were summarily dismissed and their families brought on the roads, thereby breaking the back of the strikers. The largest strike in the world, with 1.7 million workers participating, was withdrawn by the end of May. The railway workers' strike left deep scars on Indian life, with bitterness and deep divisions becoming part of normal political discourse. It also changed the people's perception of Indira Gandhi, as the middle class saw a ruthless and dictatorial leader in her. The opposition, down and out since 1969, felt it had found a chink in her armour.

Meanwhile, life for Karan Singh had irreversibly changed. After coming to Delhi in 1967, he had to adapt himself to the hot weather of Delhi and the rest of the country, where his work often took him. No longer could he escape from the sweltering weather of the summer months and be in the cool and salubrious environs of Kashmir. During the seven years that had passed, he had barely spent a few days in Karan Mahal, Srinagar, which provided a 360-degree view of the city. But, in June 1974 he managed to steal ten days in his favorite place. He had planned visits to some of the medical establishments in Srinagar, Baramulla and Anantnag. This was also the time when Sheikh Abdullah had been released, and the Valley was rife with talk of ongoing negotiations to bring him back to power. The people appeared to be excited at the prospect, though those who had established their 'spurious legitimacy' had been feeling nervous and frustrated. Among his other visits, Karan Singh also added a visit to Soura, where Sheikh Abdullah had planned to carry out an ambitious project of building a medical institute that could match in size and functioning the famous PGI of Chandigarh. Estimated to cost rupees ten crore, it was being constructed under the aegis of the Sher-i-Kashmir National Medical Institute Trust, set up by the Sheikh. During the construction, he had already started running a Polyclinic where local doctors came to work voluntarily by turns. A small function had also been arranged there, and Karan Singh, as Union Minister of Health, announced a grant of one lakh rupees for each year of the plan and promised more help in the future. What took Karan Singh by surprise during this visit was that Sheikh Abdullah was not only cordial but also spoke glowingly about him. He too reciprocated warmly as it was obvious that the Sheikh did not seem to be carrying any grudges from the past. Given the ongoing negotiations between the two sides, Karan Singh also responded positively to his gestures of rapprochement, sending positive signals to Sheikh Abdullah's followers. Later, Abdullah gave a guided tour of Hazratbal Dargah, which Karan Singh had not visited since 1964 when he had come there to offer a hand-knitted carpet as a mark of thanksgiving after Vikramaditya's birth. The Mosque was getting renovated, and Sheikh Abdullah had chosen a design that would match the Grand Mosque of Istanbul.

Meanwhile, the two defining strikes had left a deep impact on the social and political life of the country and had exposed the frailties of the system, which caused the Prime Minister to ponder over the challenges as well as the hurdles facing her and the country. Together, the two strikes had touched the lives of every section of society. But looking to the future, Indira Gandhi agreed with Karan Singh about the necessity of family planning for all Indian families and kept her eyes and ears open to the reasons for resistance to it. She was receptive to the feeblest of signals as her brief note of 14 August 1974 to him made clear. She drew his attention to a TV documentary on Sadar Bazar, Old Delhi, in which the interviewer had raised the issue of family planning, where all the Muslim women, even from the poorest class but with big families, disapproved of small families on the grounds of faith and the will of God. The note did not make it clear if she was citing that example to underline the difficulty in making the programme a success or as a warning to him not to pursue it with too much zeal. But the Minister was confident that he had drawn up an elaborate programme to give a push to family planning and that with the massive and creative use of mass media, he would be able to achieve his targets.

From his interactions with Indira Gandhi, it appeared to Karan Singh that she was aware of the rising discontent in all sections of society. She was aware of the rising prices, the impact of three consecutive failed monsoons, and lack of employment for the young. She wrote to some of her party colleagues, including Karan Singh seeking suggestions to improve the administration. But there was something amiss. Karan Singh sensed for the first time since he had known her, a lack of decisiveness, as if she wasn't entirely in control of things, or was at a loss. And like some other observers, he felt that the harsh manner in which she had dealt with the railway strike and other protests was a sign of some kind of insecurity. While it was true that her immense popularity after the Bangladesh war had made her somewhat autocratic, Karan Singh had not personally witnessed this. What he had witnessed was the rising influence of her son Sanjay Gandhi, whom he had had very little interaction with. What little he had seen of Indira Gandhi's younger son suggested to him an unremarkable young man, but also a bit aloof, impatient and possibly spoilt.

On 12 June 1975, at the Allahabad High Court, Justice Jagmohan Lal Sinha delivered his judgment on the maverick politician Raj Narain's election petition filed in April 1971 against Indira Gandhi, challenging her election from Rae Bareli on various charges. The judge not only set aside her election but also debarred her from elective office for six years. It was an unprecedented situation. The judgment had unseated a sitting Prime Minister who was still the most popular person in the country on a technicality of no great consequence. It caused an upheaval, and her supporters came out in large numbers, though her opponents accused her of stage-managing crowd support. The opposition, still smarting from its humiliating defeat in the 1971 elections, with many among them driven, Karan Singh feels, by misogyny, smelt an opportunity and demanded Mrs Gandhi's immediate resignation. They had found an opportunity that had been denied to them by the people and grew impatient with each passing hour. Even Jayaprakash Narayan, an old colleague of Jawaharlal Nehru, but long retired from active politics, entered the domain of active politics, and gave a call for 'total revolution' to overthrow Indira Gandhi. Armed with the Allahabad High Court order, the opposition took to the streets even as Indira Gandhi's supporters asked her to dig her heels in, with 125 Congress MPs and several members of the council of ministers saying 'the Party and the people' had immense 'faith and confidence' in her leadership, and hence urged her to continue to lead and guide the country as Prime Minister. Karan Singh had been holidaying in Srinagar, and he immediately returned and wrote to her on arrival in Delhi, reiterating his support but also suggesting some steps so that her 'image in the general public is not eroded and the psychological initiative regained'. Like other party colleagues, he also suggested filing an appeal in the Supreme Court, which he was certain would stay the High Court's strange order and ultimately vindicate the Prime Minister's position. To tide over the period till the Supreme Court verdict, he suggested that she offer to the President that she would step down from office pending the top court's verdict. The President would then reject her offer, and then she could address the nation the same night in a special broadcast.

However, this sane advice was not followed as the voices of self-serving loyalists far outnumbered those of reason, even as confusion ruled the country. Also, that was the first time that Indira Gandhi did not respond to his letter. Perhaps, she had already reached a stage where she heeded only those opinions that she wanted to hear. Taking advantage of the turmoil, those in the opposition who had never reconciled to the 1971 electoral verdict gave a call to the people to take to the streets, not cooperate with the elected government, and went to the extent of giving a call to the men in uniform to defy the government's orders. It was in such an atmosphere that Karan Singh was woken up by an early morning call from the Prime Minister's office, informing him of a Cabinet meeting at 7 a.m. He, like the other colleagues, reached for the meeting, still wondering what the agenda was and what the urgency was. It was only during the meeting that the Cabinet was informed that a National Emergency had been imposed in the country at midnight, and that most of the leaders of the opposition parties had also been taken into custody.

It left everyone stunned and speechless, but the decision was endorsed post facto. The meeting had ended, with many still dazed by the development, when Karan Singh and K.C. Pant, the Minister of State for Home Affairs, close friends and former schoolmates from Doon, decided to discuss what had happened. For more than an hour, they drove on the roads of Delhi discussing the pros and cons of the situation. Both agreed that at that moment, Indira Gandhi had begun to depend upon unscrupulous people, because in the current situation, it suited her. Both admitted that what had happened was morally wrong and probably unconstitutional, too, but they also knew that any display of defiance would mean their detention in prison. Moreover, they agreed that if they abandoned Indira Gandhi at a time when the country was facing internal turmoil and the possibility of external threats, she and the country would drift towards dangerous waters, and therefore, they should stick with her. In this way, they hoped to offset, or at least balance, the advice Mrs Gandhi was receiving from those who were devoid of political morality and were dodgy public men. If party men like Karan Singh and K.C. Pant also left, there would be none to express an opinion that was both in the interest of the country and the Prime Minister. Thus, deciding to continue supporting

Indira Gandhi, the two friends parted to go to their respective homes.

By the time Karan Singh reached his home, news of what had happened had been broadcast over All-India Radio. He knew that neither his wife nor his daughter Jyotsna would approve of what had been done. His daughter had, only a day earlier, attended Jayaprakash Narayan's massive rally against Indira Gandhi at Ramlila Maidan which had triggered the imposition of the Emergency that night. One of the closest friends of his wife was Raj Thapar, wife of Romesh Thapar and a left-leaning activist in her own right, and none of the leftists were about to support Indira Gandhi's Emergency. Romesh Thapar too stood in opposition to the extreme and unwarranted step that also brought in censorship of the press. He was the editor-publisher of *Seminar*, and in that role, he had always been critical of the government. But Karan Singh had already decided, along with Pant, that some reasonable element of the Congress should remain in the government, so he set his heart to the task he had on his hands. On 28th June, he sent a note to the Prime Minister, giving suggestions to deal with the economic, political and international challenges that India faced. After that, he focused on the problems facing his Ministry.

The preceding period, however, had not been without achievements, foremost among them was when his Ministry took up the challenge of eradicating smallpox. In the year 1974, the smallpox epidemic had infected 188,000 people in India, leading to 31,000 deaths. This had caused concern, and even the WHO had expressed dismay. The problem, however, was that with more than a million villages spread over vast distances, widespread poverty, and lack of education, making people aware of vaccination was a herculean task. Karan Singh mobilized all his resources and galvanized the health workers, as well as the grassroots community leaders and teachers all over the country, to keep a watch over any outbreak and also lead periodic and sustained vaccination programmes. Even before his tenure as Health Minister had ended, the WHO had recognized that India had eradicated small-pox and a special function to honour India was held in Geneva where Karan Singh led the delegation that also included two stalwarts, Dr. Gopalan, the Director General of ICMR and Dr. Ramalingaswami, the Director of AIIMS, New Delhi, who were so antagonistic that they even refused to speak to each other. Karan Singh invited the Director General of WHO, Dr. H. Mahler, to Delhi, where a memorable function was organized in the Jawaharlal Nehru Auditorium in AIIMS. At the function, Karan Singh presented Mahler with a beautifully sculpted Nataraja that continues to occupy a pride of a place in the WHO Headquarters in Geneva.

Away from such successes, more serious challenges were still ahead, with Indian politics on the verge of writing an ignoble chapter.

22
Emergency and the Dilemma

UNLIKE HIS FATHER, KARAN SINGH had raised his children in an affectionate and liberal environment. As an individual, he had matured with the new India that emerged after Independence, under the guidance of perhaps the most broad-minded democrat among India's prominent leaders—Jawaharlal Nehru; therefore, he had also encouraged free and frank expression of opinions by his children, so that they would grow into independent-minded individuals themselves—it would be for them to choose, as they grew up, what and how much of their family's legacy would be part of their identity; what balance they wanted to strike between tradition and modernity; what their world view and politics would be. He may or may not agree with them, but he would try not to hold them back. This conviction would be tested sometimes, and looking back, Karan Singh feels that on balance he acquitted himself well in those situations. His daughter, Jyotsana, for instance, growing up in the liberal atmosphere of Delhi and then Lawrence School, Sanawar, had grown into a freethinking person who spoke her mind even if her views appeared rebellious for a person coming from her background. During the Emergency, she was openly critical of the Indira Gandhi government in which her father had made a considered decision to continue as a Cabinet Minister, but she was never told to change her position.

When Jyoti was born, Karan Singh's life as the Sadr-e-Riyasat had been fairly leisurely, giving him time to be part of her early years. By the time his sons, Vikramaditya and Ajatshatru, were born, in 1964 and 1966, respectively, he was swamped by his official work and social and political obligations, but still, he made it a point to be with his family for every meal, unless he was travelling. In the evenings, the whole family would be present in the puja room for the prayers, where Ajatshatru would be the most ardent of the three children. As time passed, all three of them grew into distinctive individuals, with Vikramaditya developing into an avid polo player who revived polo in the national capital and also became an adventurous biker, off-roading into the mountains. Though neither of the boys took to books and serious scholarship like their father, Ajatshatru at least can claim to have inherited his trait of learning Sanskrit shlokas by *shruti*. Jyotsana developed a deep interest in academics and later chose teaching as a career.

In some ways, their mother was even more remarkable than their father. She was just thirteen when she was married to Karan Singh, himself only nineteen. While he had had the advantage of modern education at home and school in Srinagar, before being sent to Doon School, where his eyes had opened to the vast world under the guidance of some of the finest teachers India had at the time, Yasho Rajya Lakshmi—Asha had no such advantage. The granddaughter of the last Rana ruler of Nepal, she was born into an extremely traditional society. When she was married, she could just about read and write in her native language, Nepali; she had had no access to formal education, nor any exposure to modern ideas. Surprisingly, her father-in-law, the otherwise unapproachable Maharaja Hari Singh, took to her immediately, and she became for him the daughter he had never had. Patiently, he groomed her, guiding her as she learned to fit into one of the most prominent royal families of India. She was a good learner and soon became proficient in Hindi as well as English, and learned to negotiate her way through elite, even 'high', society. In the initial years of her marriage, she followed the advice of her father-in-law. She observed how senior people conducted themselves and spoke in the company of others, and gradually she came into her own, interacting and holding conversations with the eminent, and the rich and famous. In the company of her ever-learning husband who was often put into worlds that would have challenged people twice his age and experience, she became a constant learner herself. She learned to play a supporting role in his public life without being intrusive.

More importantly, Asha found purpose for herself. As the wife of the Sadr-e-Riyasat, she had become the Chairperson of the State Social Welfare Board and immersed herself in her work for the deprived sections of society. When the couple moved to Delhi, she found a larger platform and working among underprivileged women and children with special needs became her lifelong calling. She also formed close friendships, and two of her closest friends in Delhi were Raj Thapar, the activist who had co-founded *Seminar* magazine with her husband Romesh Thapar, and Manmohini Zutshi, a social reformer who, like Raj, was a strong advocate of democratic rights and freedom of speech. Soon after the Emergency was imposed, Asha would drive out in her car at night, pick up Raj and Manmohini, and together the three of them would paste hastily printed posters on the walls in Central Delhi, denouncing the dictatorial regime, the suspension of fundamental rights and press censorship.

During the Emergency, the Karan Singh household was

deeply divided, with the two ladies being in opposition to the anti-democratic measure, and Karan Singh who, though not in support of the draconian measure, yet found some justification for remaining in government and standing by Indira Gandhi. Eighteen-year-old Jyotsana, like many youngsters of her generation, had been attracted by the agitation of the students in Gujarat and Bihar as they were convinced that the country needed a new set of values and leaders. Jayaprakash Narayan's call for 'Total Revolution'—the culmination of the opposition parties' agitation that had come to be known as the JP Movement—had appeared attractive to Jyotsna; she believed it would transform India for the better. She was not convinced by her father's opinion that JP's call to overthrow an elected government by undemocratic means was dangerously irresponsible and had the potential to push the country into nihilistic chaos. Father and daughter argued about this, but agreed to disagree.

Another person close to Karan Singh who disapproved of the Emergency was Ashishda, the Swami from Mirtola, with whom Karan Singh shared all his thoughts, including dreams. Since Gopalda had passed away in 1957, Karan Singh had taken to addressing his letters directly to Ashishda, and naturally, he shared his fears and apprehensions about the road taken by the Prime Minister. On 21st August 1975, while discussing the Emergency, Ashishda wrote to Karan Singh, 'I cannot contemplate the concept of a nation apart from the characters of the individuals who make up the national group. The nation is strong when its typical unit is a free individual and not an anonymous cipher, or depersonalized mass.' Tellingly, he also directly addressed the impact that the Emergency might have had on Karan Singh. He wrote, 'I am distressed on your account. I fear that your enjoyment of power and privilege may lead you to accept the sophistical apologetics that interpret this move as a great blow for, not *against*, democracy. Every fear is attached to hope, and I hope you will not be permitted to distance your inner growth in the interest of personal status. I would prefer to see you in the yogic backwater you dreamed of.'

The three persons who were among those dearest to Karan Singh stood in opposition to him, and he was torn by the dilemma of remaining loyal to Indira Gandhi who, apart from being the daughter of his political mentor and like an elder sister, had always been kind to him and had also depended on him for reasonable advice and opinion. He also genuinely believed that people like him needed to be around Indira Gandhi so that her own and her sycophantic cabal's extreme views could be tempered. He owed her this for the opportunity she had given him that neither Nehru nor Shastri had.

It would be some time before the general public began to suffer the brunt of the Emergency. In the first few months it even appeared that there was support for the draconian measure among the masses. With most leaders of the opposition parties, along with the second line of leadership, put behind bars, and with censorship imposed, there were no critical voices to be heard in the country. Government employees had been warned that no indiscipline would be tolerated, so they reached their offices on time, and the piles of files on their tables were dealt with and cleared quickly. Trains ran on time. Red tape disappeared, and so did petty bribery. Even the functioning of the police stations improved, bringing down the crime rate. Hoarders lived in fear, so there were fewer shortages of essential commodities. Production in factories went up. All this added up to a strong argument in favour of the Emergency.

There were other arguments too. The period of turmoil that

had hit the country had worried many people, especially the opposition parties' plan to cripple the Indian economy through the railways strike and other protests. JP's call to the police and Army to defy government orders had led not only the government but many objective observers to also fear that a violent movement was in the offing. Karan Singh had this apprehension too. He could not have believed that in the new India that had been built, there could be any threat to life because of one's political affiliation or inclinations. He had, therefore, been shocked to receive, several months before the Emergency when the JP Movement was at its height, an anonymous letter warning him of a threat to his life if he visited Muzaffarnagar, UP as he was scheduled to. He changed his programme, but a sense of disbelief persisted till, soon after, a bomb blast claimed the life of Indira Gandhi's trusted Railways Minister, Lalit Narayan Mishra, on 3rd January 1975. To the surprise of many, it was later found that a socio-religious organization called Anand Marg was involved in it. The organization had the stated aim of transforming society, if need be, by the violent takeover of the government. Such examples convinced many fence-sitters too that there was some kind of conspiracy to destabilize the country and, therefore, the need to take drastic steps.

However, there was a downside to the situation, which most failed to see because of tight control over the flow of news and information. Imposition of the Emergency had been recommended by Siddarth Shankar Ray, the Chief Minister of Bengal, and D.K. Barooah, the President of Congress (I), but before long both found themselves relegated to the margins with the emergence of Vidya Charan Shukla, the Information and Broadcasting Minister, Om Mehta, the Minister of State for Home Affairs, and Law Minister H.R. Gokhale. How the equations had changed among the senior and junior ministers was best reflected by the fact that though Bramhanand Reddy was Cabinet Minister for Home Affairs, the Home Ministry was being effectively run by Om Mehta, his junior minister, simply because he had better access to Sanjay Gandhi, who had become the de facto Prime Minister because of his influence over his mother. With censorship in place, there was no way for the people to know if what was being claimed by the government was true. V.C. Shukla and Om Mehta became the most powerful ministers who controlled the narrative of the Emergency. Most of the newspapers complied with the instructions of the I&B Ministry, and neither any criticism of the government nor any negative reporting saw the light of day. Thus, the doors to introspection had been closed. Not only the people, but the Prime Minister herself and her Cabinet had no access to objective information, or intelligent and constructive opinion about the state of affairs in the country.

Ironically, during this period of severe censorship, on 14 August 1975 *The Indian Express* published on its centre page an article based on some 'Secret Papers' of the American administration, implying that during India's Partition, the then heir apparent of Jammu and Kashmir had instigated the massacre of Muslims and when faced with an imminent rebellion by the troops, had sought India's help by acceding to it. Karan Singh was outraged and refuting the wild allegations, he also wrote to Indira Gandhi, pointing out that at that time not only was he just sixteen years old, he was also on his way to New York for medical treatment. But the question was that at a time when insignificant pieces of news were being censored, how did that patently false and incredible story, damaging to the reputation of a Minister in the government—a government headed by Indira Gandhi, who had imposed the Emergency and censorship—get published? Were the censors negligent or complicit?

There were even more strange examples of the working of the censors, as in the case of the infamous Turkman Gate tragedy in Delhi. To clear the area, a demolition drive was carried out there on 18 April 1976, and horrifying excesses were committed by the police, but since the government had ordered that nothing should be published, this was not reported in the newspapers, though the BBC announced it to the world. However, three days after the incident, on 22nd April 1976, *The Statesman* published a Home Ministry statement about the incident, blaming the people themselves for the police firing that killed dozens. It said that a mob of 'anti-social' elements became violent, leaving the police with 'no alternative except to open fire to prevent serious harm to life and property'. Thus, a news that had been suppressed was now made by the censors themselves!

In New Delhi, if Shukla and Om Mehta became powerful ministers, then in some of the other states, notably Uttar Pradesh, Madhya Pradesh, Bihar, Rajasthan, Haryana, and Punjab, the chief ministers became overzealous in implementing the policies and directives coming from 'Delhi'. Their 'zeal' was underlined by Home Minister Reddy's advice to chief ministers to prevent 'needless violence'. In a very short time, Sanjay Gandhi and his coterie began sending directives to officials directly, bypassing the relevant Ministries. In Delhi, for instance, Jagmohan, who was then the head of DDA (Delhi Development Authority) took upon himself the task of beautifying Old Delhi, where foreign tourists flocked during the winter months to visit the Jama Masjid and the Red Fort. This involved demolishing slums and making hundreds homeless. Similarly, P.S. Bhinder, leading the Delhi Police, took it upon himself to clean the streets of Delhi of 'criminals', which in fact meant harassing and persecuting innocent, poor people.

As the period of Emergency continued for longer than anyone had expected, competition among the chief ministers to outperform one another in over-achieving targets set by Sanjay Gandhi also increased, with disastrous effects. Like many other observers, Karan Singh believes that had the general elections been called on schedule by Indira Gandhi in early 1976, there would have been the possibility of reaping the electoral harvest since the the discipline and efficiency that immediately followed the declaration of Emergency had made a deep impression among the people. Instead, a constitutional amendment had given the Parliament a tenure of six years instead of the usual five years, thereby providing an excuse to delay the scheduled elections. By that time, public opinion had turned strongly against the Emergency due to the excesses committed by overzealous men implementing Sanjay Gandhi's reckless policies.

Meanwhile, Karan Singh, blindsided by the impact of censorship, had been busy preparing the National Population Policy of 1976, the country's first comprehensive policy on the issue. Presented with great fanfare, this National Population Policy was completely different from all previous reports and recommendations. It was hitherto believed that development and education would themselves restrict the rate of population growth, and the government's programme was limited to motivating people to accept family planning and providing clinical facilities and other services. But the 1976 policy boldly stated that waiting for education and economic development to bring about a drop in fertility was not a practical solution. The rapid increase in population made economic development near impossible and unless proactive measures were taken, India would remain mired in poverty. So, besides measures like raising the minimum age of marriage for males to 21 and females to 18, the Policy introduced very clear incentives and disincentives to encourage men, especially, to opt for sterilization. The Policy also gave states the mandate to adopt a policy of compulsory sterilization after

India's Ambassador to the USA, Dr. Karan Singh, and his wife
with the US President George W. Bush (Sr), 1989.

In 1986, the 25th Anniversary of the World Wildlife Fund (WWF) was held in the Basilica di San Francesco in Assisi, Italy. The then President of WWF, Prince Philip, Duke of Edinburgh, proposed the idea of bringing representatives of five great faiths of the world—Hinduism, Buddhism, Judaism, Christianity and Islam—on a common platform to address the issue of humanity's impact on the environment. Karan Singh was invited to present Hinduism's message on Man and Nature.

Karan Singh presenting his book *One Man's World* to Pope John Paul II, during the latter's visit to India in 1986.

With Nelson Mandela sometime in the late 1990s.

With Queen Elizabeth II and Prince Philip at Rashtrapati Bhavan, New Delhi in 1997.

Honouring the great Carnatic vocalist M.S. Subbulakshmi with the Swaralaya Puraskar, 1997.

With the legendary artist M.F. Husain sometime in the 1980s.

Karan Singh and Yasho Rajya Lakshmi in Mongolia in 1992, to inaugurate a school proposed by the Indian Ambassador Kushak Bakula Rinpoche.

With Giani Zail Singh, President of India, mid-1980s.

Karan Singh with His Holiness the Dalai Lama.

Karan Singh at Auroville in the early 1990s, shortly after he was appointed Chairman of the Governing Board for the Auroville Foundation. (Photo courtesy of Ireno Guerci.)

'Should [Karan Singh] be our next President?'—cover story in *The Telegraph Magazine* of February 1996, over a decade before Karan Singh's name was formally proposed for the country's highest office by the Congress Party.

Karan Singh with President Pratibha Patil as she presents the Jawaharlal Nehru Award for International Understanding to Angela Merkel, Chancellor of the Federal Republic of Germany (right), on 31 May 2011.

With King-Father Norodom Sihanouk and Queen Mother Monineath Sihanouk during a visit to Cambodia in 2011 as President of the Indian Council for Cultural Relations (ICCR).

Dr. Karan Singh as the Chancellor, Banaras Hindu University, presenting an Honorary Doctorate Degree to Prime Minister Manmohan Singh at the university's 90th Convocation Ceremony, 2008.

With U.S. Secretary of State Hillary Clinton, President of the Congress Party, Sonia Gandhi, and Congress Committee General Secretary Rahul Gandhi in July 2009.

With Prime Minister Narendra Modi, March 2021.

Presenting his book *Shiva: Lord of the Cosmic Dance* to Member of Parliament and celebrated author, Shashi Tharoor.

At the office of the Inter-Faith Harmony Foundation of India with Khwaja Iftikhar Ahmed, the Founder President of the Foundation.

With the renowned classical flautist Hariprasad Chaurasia.

The CD cover of Karan Singh's popular album of Dogri folk songs.

With the noted filmmaker, poet, designer and artist Muzaffar Ali at the opening of an exhibition of his 'Karbala' series of paintings.

In Kashmir, with his older son Viramaditya, daughter-in-law Chitrangada, granddaughter Mriganka, grandson-in-law Nirvan and great-granddaughters Amaaya and Anahat (in Chitrangada's lap).

At Amar Mahal, Jammu on his 94th birthday, with members of his family (left to right): Ranvijay (grandson), Chitrangada (older daughter-in-law), Martand (grandson), Jyotsna (daughter) with her granddaughter Leela, Pradeep (son-in-law), Ritu (younger daughter-in-law) and Ajatashatru (younger son).

In Kashmir with his first cousin Basant Usha in 2024.

At his office-cum-study in Delhi with his younger sister-in-law Bharati Chadha.

With his old friend King Juan Carlos of Spain at the Zarzuela Palace in Madrid, April 2014.

At the Tawi Festival of Arts and Ideas in Jammu, with his long-time friend Rachna Imhasly Gandhy, the pioneering Jungian analyst and transpersonal psychologist, and granddaughter Viveka in February 2024.

Three generations: Karan Singh with son Vikramaditya and grandson Martand.

Four generations; with son Vikramaditya, granddaughter Mriganka and great granddaughter Amaaya.

Karan Singh with his granddaughters Viveka (left), Mriganka (second from left) and Adishree (right) during Mriganka's wedding festivities in 2017.

At a new year lunch with his family at The Claridges, New Delhi.

At the launch of his book *The Eternal Religion: Glimpses of Hinduism*, at the India Habitat Centre, New Delhi, 2023.

Receiving the Memorial Medal of the Tree of Peace of the Servare et Manere from the Slovak diplomat Patrik Líška in April 2022.

With his trusted attendant Praveen in the Karan Mahal garden, Kashmir.

At his puja in Mansarovar, his home in Delhi, December 2025.
(Photo by Abhishek Sharma.)

(Above and below) Karan Singh's puja room in his Delhi home. (Photos by Abhishek Sharma.)

In his study at Mansarovar, Delhi, where he spends most of his time.
December 2005. (Photo by Abhishek Sharma.)

three children, if they felt the need for it. In the light of what later transpired during the Emergency, and in hindsight, Karan Singh believes he should have been cautious in writing that last clause of the Policy. 'I have to admit I made a serious error there,' he says. 'I did not realize I was leaving the door open for coercive measures.'

Ashishda, living in the Almora hills, away from the power centres, among people who would be affected by the New Population Policy, realized what his spiritual student did not. He wrote to Karan Singh in May 1976: 'I am not impressed by your National Population Policy statement. It seems to have just the right mix of compulsion, coercion, and self-determination for success. What I fear is the application of compulsion at a time when the population has been deprived of its democratic system of safeguards against the abuse of just such powers.

'Where there were previously high-sounding policies without implementation, now, with the swing of the pendulum, there are progressive policies with over-implementation. The credibility gap is as wide as it ever was. The abolition of freedom [Emergency] is being interpreted in the lower echelons of the bureaucracy to mean that he who does not press extremist policies to the limit is suspect in his loyalties. In fact, no sooner were the compulsory powers for sterilization given than one hears of their abuse.'

The truth was that by that time, the family planning programme had been hijacked by Sanjay Gandhi and his cabal. Karan Singh had set realistic targets for all the states and had backed them with mass media and advertising outreach. But Sanjay was in a hurry. He had recently displayed his impatience by announcing his 'Four-point Programme' for the nation—that included promoting literacy, tree plantation, eradication of casteism, and abolition of dowry—as an alternative to the government's 'Twenty-point Programme'. He now added family planning to his programme.

Congress Chief Ministers in the northern states—which was where Sanjay exercised his extra-Constitutional powers with the greatest zeal—displayed extraordinary ardour in implementing his programme, particularly the family planning point. Harideo Joshi, Chief Minister of Rajasthan, during Sanjay Gandhi's visit to that state, assured that 350,000 vasectomy operations would be carried out. Others joined the bandwagon, falling over each other to curry favour with the Prime Minister's powerful son, and soon men across northern and central India, many of them unmarried or too old, were being herded into hospitals, dispensaries and makeshift camps by force to undergo vasectomy operations. In some places there was resistance, leading to police firing and deaths.

The true extent of the outrage became apparent only after censorship was lifted. In all, during 1976-77, more than 5.5 million operations had been carried out. While the Emergency was on there were only rumours and word-of-mouth reports and no one was sure what exactly was happening, or how bad the situation was. Karan Singh tried to speak to Indira Gandhi but she had made herself unavailable. He convened meetings of State Chief Ministers and Health Ministers, urging them to ensure there was no coercion. Unsurprisingly, few ofthem paid any heed. 'Sanjay's influence on several of them was decisive,' says Karan Singh. 'Some of them were actively involved in the terrible coercion by giving their babus and the police carte blanche.' Meanwhile, officials in his Ministry kept assuring him the reports of coercion were exaggerated.

Karan Singh received the most honest and reliable critique from who else but Ashishda. On 10th October 1976, Ashishda wrote, 'Local abuse of the vasectomy program continues. The abuses are logical outcomes of the manner in which the principle of reward and punishment is being applied…A woman MLA is seizing ration cards from unoperated men…The vasectomy programme has now reached the point where men are being arrested and taken away by force by the *patwari*. Several men are reported to have taken to the jungle…The present crude scramble to get an unpleasant task finished barely touches the surface of the problem.'

At one point, Karan Singh considered resigning as Minister. Ashishda replied, 'It might seem to you that your acceptance of my basic position [should] logically lead to your surrendering your official position. Personally, I do not see that it follows. As I suggested to you, I would honour your keeping your position in order to temper the injustices that must stem from…the basic faults of the regime. But I would not approve of your staying in the interests of personal status and power, no matter how good the regime.' He, however, assured his disciple that he would continue to support him, whatever turn the future might hold. 'However much we may discuss rights and wrongs, you must get one thing straight about my place in your life. Whatever line of action you may choose to take, I will stand by you, trying to turn it to your advantage, even though I may not approve of the actions themselves.'

It was a difficult period for the country, as well as for Karan Singh. In the end, he decided to stay in the government and do what little he could. At work, he faced the challenge of delivering on the promises he had made to himself, though all power had been taken away from him. At home, he faced the disapproval of his wife and daughter who continued to oppose the Emergency regime. These were indeed testing times, but he had given his family the freedom to think and act according to their judgment. Now he had to face the consequences and demonstrate that he practiced what he preached. He could have forbidden his wife from going out and putting up anti-Emergency posters at night. It was a terrible thing for the wife of a Cabinet Minister to do what she was doing, but stopping her would have been hypocritical. So, all that he could do when she returned home late at night was to thank God for letting them sleep another day in their own home and not in jail. In the mornings, he would pray for the safety of his family and go out to perform the duty that he had taken upon himself.

23

Fall Out of Emergency

In June of 1974, when Karan Singh had gone to Kashmir for his brief holiday, he discovered that the possibility of Sheikh Abdullah returning to power in the State was widely anticipated in the Valley, and the people were excited at the prospect. In a bid to put Kashmir's relationship with India beyond any debate and on par with that of other states, Prime Minister Indira Gandhi decided to open a dialogue with Sheikh Abdullah. By then, it had also become clear to the Sheikh that after the determined manner in which India had played a role in dismantling Pakistan in 1971, he could no longer use the bogey of Pakistani aggression to extract concessions from India. Indira Gandhi realized this, and felt it was the most opportune time to settle the issue with Sheikh Abdullah. Gopalaswami Parthasarathy, on behalf of the Government of India, and Mirza Afzal Beg, on behalf of Sheikh Abdullah, had held preliminary talks in July 1974. However, the more substantive discussions between the two negotiators took place between January 12 and 15 of 1975, before arriving at certain agreed conclusions.

On 24 February 1975, the Prime Minister made a statement

in the Parliament regarding the agreement's details. Among other details, it said, '...the State of Jammu and Kashmir, which is a constituent unit of the Union of India, shall in its relations with the Union continue to be governed by Article 370 of the Constitution of India.' And that, 'The residuary powers of legislation shall remain with the state; however, Parliament will continue to have the power to make laws relating to the prevention of activities directed towards disclaiming, questioning or disrupting the sovereignty and territorial integrity of India or bringing about secession of a part of territory of India from the Union or causing insult to the Indian Flag, the Indian National Anthem and the Constitution.'

The Prime Minister had also held a meeting during which Karan Singh had made certain points, which he elaborated in a subsequent letter to her. He expressed disappointment that even as a cabinet minister and coming from the state that was the subject of the agreement, he had not been given a copy of the detailed formulations of the agreement. Nevertheless, he raised some of the problems arising out of the Centre-State constitutional arrangement as well as its impact on the internal challenges in J&K. He pointed out that if the initiative was to succeed, then the opinion of the people of Jammu and Ladakh also needed to be considered. No agreement regarding the state could work if the sole purpose was to address the concerns of only one of the three units. He also cautioned against looking at the internal geo-political reality of the state from the prism of communalism. He pointed out that though the Jammu region was predominantly Hindu, nevertheless, it had a substantial Muslim population who also happened to be the most backward in the State. The unpleasant truth, he said, was that the new Agreement had failed to draw any lessons from the recent history of the state, where Sheikh Abdullah had failed to emerge as the leader of the whole state because of his inability to look beyond Kashmir.

He also advocated the cause of Ladakh, which had historically nursed reservations about Sheikh Abdullah. These reservations had only grown since his release, as his insistence on the need to return to the pre-1953 situation created more suspicion than confidence. Sheikh Abdullah had, in fact, also referred to those years in his confidential letter to Indira Gandhi when the negotiations for a settlement had started. On 29 December 1974, he wrote, 'I hope you will agree with me that the only way to repair the vast damage done to the Indo-Kashmir relationship by the Arbitrary action of 9th August 1953 is possible only through complete understanding and mutual trust. If this trust is lacking even in a very small measure, all our efforts to reach an understanding will prove fruitless. Ordinarily, the broad principles of the partition of the subcontinent might well have taken the State to Pakistan in 1947, but for various reasons, things happened another way... [After accession to India] the minorities within the State, no doubt, felt secure once the Leadership of the National Conference decided to throw its lot with India, and their support was, therefore, assured. But what about the Muslim Majority? The Muslims of the State were simultaneously a minority within the Indian population and a majority within their State. Therefore, all fears and apprehensions that they would be dominated by the Indian majority had to be dispelled, and they had to be assured that within the State, their rights as a majority would be guaranteed. Their fear complex could be dispelled only by ensuring complete internal autonomy of the State as envisaged in the Instrument of Accession signed by the Maharaja.' Sheikh Abdullah lamented that over the years, the autonomy of the state had been undermined by what one of the Union Ministers had called an 'egg-shell' emptied of its contents. Ironically, he also questioned the legitimacy of the state elections of 1957, 1962, 1967 and 1972, forgetting that those elections had only followed the template that he himself had set in 1952.

The correspondence made it clear that Sheikh Abdullah was convinced that his dismissal from office in 1953 by Karan Singh had been arbitrary and was at the root of the damage done to Indo-Kashmir relations. That may have been one reason why Indira Gandhi had kept Karan Singh out of the negotiations for the new Agreement she worked out with Sheikh Abdullah, and had chosen not to respond to his subsequent letter.

Among other suggestions in Karan Singh's letter that Indira chose to ignore, was that the pattern laid down in Schedule VI of the Constitution for Administration of Tribal Areas in Assam be incorporated in the Agreement for the welfare of Ladakh. He also advocated setting up of a Regional Council, with elected members from the Leh and Kargil regions, and setting up separate Regional Development Boards for the Jammu and Kashmir regions, for equitable distribution of funds. On the political front, he demanded that when the Chief Minister was from one region, then a deputy chief minister should be appointed from another region. He also used the opportunity to ask the Prime Minister to address the long-pending grievances of the Scheduled Caste population of the state and suggested that Article 335 of the Indian Constitution be extended to the J&K, so that this section of the state's population could enjoy the same benefits that were given to Scheduled Castes in the rest of the country. Similarly, the Gujjars and Bakkarwals also needed to be included among the Scheduled Tribes due to their nomadic existence. For the Dogras, he wanted that when the new government assumed office, an announcement be made that a resolution urging the inclusion of Dogri in Schedule VIII of the Indian Constitution would be passed by the State Assembly.

In addition, Karan Singh urged the Prime Minister to ensure that the Congress would have a substantial representation in the new cabinet, since the new government of Sheikh Abdullah would be in power solely because of its support. Moreover, the Congress high command should decide its nominees and not the new Chief Minister, as otherwise the very concept of a coalition would be rendered meaningless. Finally, he wrote that there was a need to overhaul the Congress party in the State, so that it was energized, as after the creation of a new political party by Sheikh Abdullah, the Congress was bound to face new challenges in the Valley—Abdullah was, after all, still a towering and charismatic figure.

Karan Singh's suggestions in that letter were largely ignored, and his fears were soon proved right. Sheikh Abdullah believed, and he had told the Prime Minister this in no uncertain terms, that the situation in J&K had changed for the worse in the years since 1953, when he had been dismissed. So it wasn't surprising that he did not seem to acknowledge that his interpretation of the provisions of Article 370 was taking him too close to secessionism, and that India could not afford to have such tendencies grow in the country. On this issue, Indira Gandhi stood firm and wrote to Abdullah, 'I am aware of your views on the Centre-State relationship in respect of the State of Jammu and Kashmir. I have already explained to you that the clock cannot be put back, and we have to take note of the realities of the situation. I am appreciative of the spirit in which you have expressed your agreement with the terms of the agreed conclusions. The agreed conclusions have been examined, and I am in a position to inform you that such appropriate executive action as may be necessary to give effect to them will be taken. I have been in close touch with the Chief Minister of the State, who is in agreement with the approach in regard to political co-operation with you and the understanding reached about the relationship of the State with the Union.'

Though Indira Gandhi had been categorical, Sheikh Abdullah continued looking back to the past and hoping to put the clock back. In the process, two things happened. Though Indira Gandhi thought that she was prevailing upon the Sheikh to accept the changes that had taken place during his years of absence, she let him believe that Kashmir was a synonym for Jammu and Kashmir. It was a serious mistake, as it was to cost the state and the country dear, with Kashmir being unapologetically imposed upon Jammu and Ladakh. But an even more serious mistake was that both the leaders in general and Sheikh Abdullah in particular failed to take into account the presence of a secessionist constituency whose midwife had been the ideology that had been so assiduously built and nurtured during the past two decades by the Plebiscite Front. The young in this constituency felt betrayed when the new Agreement between Indira Gandhi and Sheikh Abdullah was announced, since all those years, they had been brought up on the dream of complete autonomy, even independence. Thus, with the announcement of Sheikh Abdullah's return to power with the support of the Congress, but without any of the promises of the past getting fulfilled, a new and probably more militant secessionist lobby was born.

For Karan Singh, the fact that his suggestions post the Agrement had been ignored, and that he had been kept out of the negotiations in the first place, was further proof that although Indira Gandhi sought his opinion and suggestions on all important issues—before the rise of Sanjay Gandhi and the Emergency—Kashmir was one subject on which he would never be consulted. He believes that it is possible that Indira Gandhi, and even successive governments, thought that since the Kashmiri sub-nationalism was born out of opposition to Dogra rule, his opinion and presence could be prejudicial to any agreement. Moreover, she and her advisers at that time also believed that as long as the Kashmiri sentiment was catered to, there was no need to pay attention to either Jammu or Ladakh. Time has proven

Karan Singh right, as the consistent overlooking of the interests of these two regions has pushed the people in these regions away from the Congress party.

After coming to power, Sheikh Abdullah delivered a series of shocks to those who had championed the Agreement signed between him and Indira Gandhi. No sooner had he become the Chief Minister than he announced the revival of the National Conference and suggested that the State unit of the Congress dissolve itself and merge with it. Reacting to this, on 9 January 1975 the working committee of the Jammu and Kashmir Pradesh Congress Committee, while re-affirming its 'full support to the accord which had received overwhelming approval in Parliament and the entire country', declared 'it would not be desirable to merge the Congress with the National Conference...[It] is essential that the Congress Party should continue to function vigorously in the state'.

By August of 1975, the pace of political developments in the state had picked up. Though the Congress did not merge with the National Conference, the Plebiscite Front did, and Mirza Afzal Beg was elected its President. In another development, former Chief Minister Syed Mir Qasim had been elected to the Rajya Sabha, leaving the state Congress unit in a state of confusion and disarray. Karan Singh urged Indira Gandhi that 'steps should be taken urgently to strengthen and refurbish the image of the party, as the present trend, if allowed to continue for much longer, will cause serious and permanent damage'. He suggested that a powerful ad hoc Pradesh Congress Committee be constituted and given the task of reorganizing and revitalizing the party apparatus. But importantly, there was the need to establish an arrangement with Sheikh Abdullah that would ensure participation and consultation with the Congress Party at the highest policy level. Later, the Congress paid a heavy price for ignoring his advice, as very soon, Sheikh Abdullah not only consolidated his hold over the administration but also kicked away the ladder of the Congress that he had used to climb to the high office. Ten Congress MLAs had by then defected to join the National Conference.

When the Emergency was declared in 1975, it had shocked the nation, but the positive response of the general public to the immediate consequences—return of order, increase in discipline and general efficiency and the crackdown on hoarders and black-marketeers—had convinced Indira Gandhi that her old popularity had returned. But as the Emergency lingered, not only did the novelty of it vanish, but the abuse of powers by government officials and the police created an undercurrent of resentment and anger, and it grew stronger by the day. Then, on 18 January 1977, Indira Gandhi surprised the country and the world again—this time by announcing that general elections would be held. No one to this day can say with any certainty what prompted her to do this. Her detractors maintain that she had overestimated her popularity. Others argue that she was essentially a democrat; that she imposed the Emergency because she genuinely believed that the country's stability was in danger and had no intention of putting democracy on hold permanently. The announcement of elections initially drew a tepid response, but within days, the opposition parties were galvanized and decided to come together to contest elections with a common symbol. This newborn alliance got a massive boost when Mrs Gandhi's seniormost cabinet colleague, Babu Jagjiwan Ram, walked out of the government and the Congress to form the Congress for Democracy and then became part of the opposition alliance—the Janata Party. This triggered an exodus from the Congress and gave a huge boost to all those opposing Indira and the Congress.

For Karan Singh, like others, it was time to return to his constituency and ask his voters to reaffirm their faith in him. The Emergency had not been withdrawn, but the press had regained its freedom, making reporting of news easier. With this, the floodgates opened, and news about violation of civil liberties, abuse of power and—most of all—forced sterilization came pouring out. All but a few of the opposition leaders had been released from jail, and together with others who had suffered in opposing the Emergency, they spread out all over the country with a missionary zeal to punish the Congress. It was in this atmosphere that Karan Singh headed to Udhampur to file his nomination papers when he came to know that the opposition alliance had chosen Om Prakash Saraf to contest against him. He was happy and relieved to know that, as he knew that Saraf was a gentleman who would not be carried away by the vicious propaganda that was going on against the Congress. Much later, his leftist friend Romesh Thapar told him that he, along with all those who had vehemently opposed the Emergency, had planned to descend upon the Udhampur constituency to ensure his defeat as he was the head of the Health Ministry, whose family planning programme had led to the horror of forced vasectomies. Fortunately for Karan Singh, they finally decided that though he was the Health Minister, he was not to be blamed for the wrongdoings, as the family planning programme had been hijacked by Sanjay Gandhi. Therefore, they decided to focus their energies on Rae Bareli and Amethi, from where Indira Gandhi and Sanjay Gandhi were contesting.

The contest in Udhampur was between two gentlemen who were above the pettiness into which political contests can degenerate. Saraf was an old Gandhian, and his campaign was civil and his speeches respectful of his opponent. This was fully reciprocated by Karan Singh, who extolled the many virtues of

Saraf as a Gandhian politician and a committed journalist. With the the election fought on principles and without rancour, Karan Singh romped home to an easy victory with a margin of over 24 percent of the votes. The election results from the rest of the country were a massive shock to the Congress, as it was almost wiped out from the north and the Hindi belt. The party could win only 152 seats, all except two coming from the south. Apart from Karan Singh, Nathu Ram Mirdha from Rajasthan was the only Congress person elected from Northern India. To the delight of many, Sanjay Gandhi had been trounced, but to the shock of the country, even Indira Gandhi had been humiliated.

For the first time since Independence, a non-Congress government was formed at the Centre, with Morarji Desai, who had parted with Indira Gandhi in 1969, becoming Prime Minister after a bitter internal battle in the Janata Party. The country was still grappling with the same problems that had posed serious challenges to Indira Gandhi, but unfortunately, the new government focused more on punishing Indira Gandhi. She was arrested and put up in the gazetted officers' mess in Delhi's New Police Lines for the night, but the whole operation had been so clumsy, and the charges so flimsy, that the magistrate she was brought before the next morning dismissed the charges. Mrs Gandhi, with her extraordinary political sense, made excellent use of the opportunity to present herself as the victim of a vengeful combined opposition that had nothing to offer the country except its hatred of her. Her comeback began that day.

By this time, the political atmosphere had already been vitiated when the Morarji Desai Government constituted a widely publicized Commission to look into the allegations of excesses, atrocities and misuse of power during the Emergency. It was headed by Justice Shah, who was later accused by Indira Gandhi of prejudice as he had spoken vehemently against her policy of bank nationalization. Many of the former Congress ministers had refused to testify before the Commission, but Karan Singh had testified because he was asked specifically about the programme of forced sterilizations and his role in it. He told the Commission: 'I must admit that the extent of such coercion was not revealed until after the Emergency was lifted, mainly because of the self-defeating censorship of the press…it will remain a matter of grave sorrow and personal regret that in the name of family planning, Indian citizens, especially those belonging to the weaker sections of the society, should have been humiliated in such a barbaric fashion.' Without naming Sanjay Gandhi, he blamed an 'extra-constitutional centre of power' that was operating in the country. Not surprisingly, after this statement, the relationship between Indira Gandhi and Karan Singh was never quite the same again.

Equations changed in the Congress. Barring two, all the elected leaders of the party belonged to the South, and most of them did not subscribe to the Congress politics that was promoted by Sanjay Gandhi with the tacit support of his mother. All of them blamed him for the debacle the party had suffered, and now that Indira Gandhi appeared to be regaining some of her popularity among the people, he was beginning to dictate terms in the party again. In January 1978, the Congress split for the second time, with a large number of non-elected members opting to remain loyal to Indira Gandhi, and the party came to be called Congress (I). Most of those who had been elected to the Lok Sabha came together under the Karnataka leader Devraj Urs, the President of the United Congress, to form the Congress (U). The memory of Sanjay Gandhi's corruption of his cherished family planning mission still fresh in his mind, Karan Singh too joined the new party. More than that parting with the Congress, what Karan Singh has always regretted is that in the charged atmosphere during that split, he was a little harsh in his criticism of Indira Gandhi. 'She had always been supportive, we had a relationship or mutual regard and affection. A very long time has passed, but the regret has remained.' They had met in 1949, when he was eighteen and she just short of 32. They had taken to each other, and over the years she had become like an elder sister. She would often come to stay with him and Asha when she was on holiday in Kashmir with her sons. It had been a long and fruitful association, strengthened by their shared interest in books, art and culture. She was also an admirer of his wife's grace and striking presence, and on one occasion, in a thank you note, she had written, 'I enjoyed my tea with you and your very beautiful wife. The word beauty is used often and far too casually, but she really has a quality for which there is no other word.' It had been a happy association, despite some disagreements. The political distance that came between them in 1978 was never bridged, although he had 'a personal reconciliation with her some time before her tragic assassination'. In some measure, he was able to make up for the hurt he believed he caused her.

Shortly after that split in the Congress, in July of 1979, the Janata Party government, headed very briefly by Charan Singh after Morarji Desai, fell under the weight of its contradictions. Thus, for the fourth time, Karan Singh headed to his constituency of Udhampur to seek a fresh mandate from the people.

24

End of Electoral Politics

For the first time in his electoral journey, Karan Singh faced a serious challenge. The earlier three elections had been against opponents who had probably approached the elections knowing in their hearts that they had no chance of winning. On all those occasions, he had been the candidate of a party that had deep roots and the support of a well-oiled machinery that was backed by an army of workers who were deeply loyal to him and his dynasty and would come from all over the Jammu region to campaign for him. But in December 1979, he represented a political party, the Congress (U), that had no organizational depth in the state. He and a band of workers who owed him personal loyalty constituted the entire presence of the party in all of Jammu. On the other hand, bent upon settling old scores was Sheikh Abdullah, with his newly revived National Conference. Sheikh Abdullah and the Congress had come to an understanding and had put up Abdullah's cabinet colleague Devi Das Thakur as their joint candidate in Udhampur. Luckily for Karan Singh, the Bharatiya Jana Sangh took a strategic decision of not fielding any candidate in the constituency, to ensure there was no split in votes that might work to the advantage of the NC-Congress alliance.

Karan Singh girded for the campaign. His wife was acutely aware of the stakes and prepared for the battle with determination and enthusiasm. She was the one who was always in touch with the people and had developed a distinctive style of campaigning, in which the empathy that she exuded was her strongest asset. Both of them worked tirelessly and tried to reach out to as many villages and towns as possible, and while Karan Singh addressed public meetings, Asha would go out to meet the women who came in droves just to have a glimpse of the 'Maharani'. It was an unusual campaign that they conducted, as most of their meetings were informal, at roadside tea stalls or anywhere else where people gathered in small groups to catch up and gossip. When Karan Singh and Asha stopped at any such spot, within minutes the news spread like wildfire, and the women, especially, came rushing to see the Maharani, to be near her and talk to her. The couple also travelled to places that could not be accessed by road and when they were tired walking, they were carried in *dandis*. On one such occasion, while going to a remote village in the Kathua district, the dandi carrying Karan Singh broke and he barely escaped rolling down a deep gorge. Every morning, the couple drove out, trying to reach every nook and corner of that vast constituency, covering half of the Jammu region. It was physically exhausting and mentally draining, but exhilarating.

The result justified all the hard work. They won. The odds against Karan Singh had been heavy, with the government machinery having been used against him to the fullest extent. Karan Singh had to admit his and Asha's and his supporters' efforts apart, the victory could not have been possible had the Udhampur Bharatiya Jana Sangh (BJS) leader, Lala Shiv Charan Gupta, not mobilized all the manpower at his command to surround the counting centre in Udhampur as it became clear that the Deputy Commissioner of the district, B.R. Kundal, who was the Returning Officer, was under clear instructions from the State Government to declare the National Conference candidate as the winner. But the BJS leader warned Kundal of dire consequences if the election were rigged, and finally Kundal followed the rules and declared Karan Singh the winner by over 50,000 votes. He had secured more than 56 percent of the polled votes to 36 percent votes for Devi Das Thakur.

In a massive turnaround, the rest of the country, fed up with the shenanigans of the Janata Party, brought Indira Gandhi and her Congress back to power. The excesses of the Emergency had been forgiven, and even Sanjay Gandhi had found redemption among the people of Amethi, who gave him his only electoral victory. Karan Singh, on the other hand, soon found himself sitting among the independent Members of Parliament, but as was his nature, he fully immersed himself in that role too. New Delhi was due to host the Asian Games in 1982. In a letter to the Prime Minister, dated 14 April 1980, he expressed concern that time was running out and unless firm decisions were taken regarding the various venues that would be needed, it would be difficult for the country to hold the Games. The Prime Minister responded in two brief and terse sentences. She wrote: 'Work on the preparation for the Asian Games has begun. It is obvious that all the competitions cannot be held in one place.' On another occasion, when he suggested that a Radhakrishnan Centre of Comparative Philosophy and Religion be set up at the Institute of Advanced Studies, Shimla, she replied in a single sentence that his suggestion would be kept in mind.

Karan Singh, however, would not look wistfully at the past, and immersed himself in his new role as a Member of Parliament. Any subject that he thought was of public importance was brought to the attention of the Prime Minister and the

Parliament. Among them, was the mismanagement of the Aurobindo Ashram, Pondicherry, and the Aurobindo Society in New Delhi. Over time, internecine conflict, personality clashes and dubious financial transactions had bogged down the idea of propagating the philosophy of Sri Aurobindo and Mother. He suggested that the most effective step would be for Parliament to pass an Act to take over the whole project as a national memorial to Sri Aurobindo. The Prime Minister was appreciative of the concern and, though the Auroville Foundation Act had to wait till 1988, yet, in December 1980, the Auroville Emergency Provision Bill was passed to take over the Ashram's management for two years. The measure was not enough, but it elicited considerable support not only in both Houses of the Parliament but also among those who were residing in the Ashram. So, Karan Singh pressed for further measures, like having an Advisory Committee that included people who had some awareness about the ideals for which Sri Aurobindo and Mother stood.

But the subject that agitated him most was his home state, over which his suggestions and warnings had remained unheeded. He had, from the beginning, expressed his apprehension over the Agreement of 1975—the 'Kashmir Accord'—and he now drew the attention of the Prime Minister to the fact that five years after the Accord, with the stated goal of bringing the Kashmiris into the national mainstream, had been signed, Kashmir was seething with secessionist, anti-Centre and anti-India sentiments. He pointed out that this had been aggravated, if not caused entirely, by the intemperate public speeches and private conversations of Sheikh Abdullah. There were reports of Pakistani agents having infiltrated the Valley, especially in the western Sopore and Baramulla districts. Consequently, he wrote, 'the Kashmiri pundit community in the Valley is under intense pressure, virtually amounting to intimidation, and they are suffering from a deep sense of grievance and insecurity.' It appeared that the national sentiment that had been gradually and painstakingly built by Bakshi, Sadiq and Qasim had vanished with the revival of Sheikh Abdullah.

While Indira Gandhi was not prepared to admit that she had erred in not heeding the warnings of Karan Singh, Sheikh Abdullah continued to flirt with communalism, this time with a more audacious and potentially disastrous plan than before. He allowed more and more Muslim people claiming to belong to Pakistan-Occupied Jammu and Kashmir (PoJK) to come to different regions of the predominantly Hindu Jammu to 'reclaim' the land they said they had left behind when fleeing during Partition. This disrupted the lives of those Hindu and Sikh families who had migrated in 1947-48 to these lands and had settled there. Since no counter-migration to PoJK was taking place, this raised the fear of a destabilizing change in Jammu's demography. In addition, there were reports of large-scale gun licences and ammunition issued to a Muslim community in the Jammu region, adding to the volatility of the situation. In Ladakh, too, the State government was sparing no effort to drive a wedge between the Buddhist and Shia populations of Leh and Kargil, respectively. It was not that Indira Gandhi was not aware of what Sheikh Abdullah was up to, as she had during a press conference remarked that 'he has the habit of saying different things at different times', but she still did nothing to halt the wheels of communalism. Perhaps she had committed herself too far during the negotiations of the 'Accord' and did not know how, or was not willing, to retrace her steps.

In February 1981, an event in far-off Meenakshipuram, Tamil Nadu caused an uproar in much of the country, and Karan Singh was troubled by both the event and the reactions to it. About 200 Dalit families consisting of over 1500 persons had collectively converted to Islam, saying they were no longer prepared to bear the injustice perpetrated by caste inequities. Hindu organizations blamed it on foreign funding to local Islamist groups to lure the poor with money. Karan Singh, however, was convinced the reason lay elsewhere. Reform was needed within Hinduism, for he had always believed the practice of untouchability was a blot on Hindu society. He now took it upon himself to rejuvenate the Hindus. He travelled all over the country, meeting religious leaders, including Jayendra Saraswati, the Junior Shankaracharya of Kanchi Kamakoti Peetham, who had a very positive attitude on the issue of eradication of untouchability. He also met the Tamil Nadu Chief Minister M.G. Ramachandran and discussed the challenge that had arisen due to the conversions.

From then on, he devoted himself to setting up and running a Hindu reform organization, called the Virat Hindu Samaj, and after bringing various groups and sub-groups under its umbrella, held a massive rally on 18 October 1981 at the Boat Club in New Delhi. He emphasized that periodic social reforms that had taken place within the Hindu Samaj, where prevalent beliefs and dogmas had been challenged, had made the faith richer, and the process should continue. 'The deprived and the depressed fifth caste of Hinduism represent[s] an economic, moral and spiritual burden upon the Hindu conscience, which, as Gandhiji used to say, demands heavy atonement from the Hindu society,' Karan Singh said, explaining his mission, and added:

> Coming down unbroken from the very dawn of history, like some great river absorbing numerous streams of thought and action through the centuries and giving birth to equally varied spiritual and social movements, Hinduism has always been the religion of the vast majority of Indians. Even during the so-

called Muslim and British periods, the overwhelming majority of Indians remained Hindus, and in the 1981 census, it is estimated that eighty out of every hundred Indians classified themselves as such...Indian history without Hinduism would be as incomprehensible as, for example, Arab history without Islam or Latin American history without Christianity. This is not to denigrate the role played by other religions in India, but to point out that the cultural and historical primacy of Hinduism remains an unalterable fact of the Indian scene. This being so, the problem of social reform within Hinduism also has great significance for the entire nation...

In a way, Hindu social reform is as old as Hinduism itself, in the sense that its great intellectual freedom enabled each seer to propound his interpretation of the eternal truths enshrined in the Vedas and Upanishads based on his own spiritual experience. Lord Mahavira and Lord Buddha were outstanding reformers who developed new attitudes towards rigid social formulations such as caste and animal sacrifice. The history of Hindu social reform from then onward is replete with men and women of vision and spiritual insight...[who] were able to give a fresh impetus to Hindu thought and interpret the truths enshrined in Hinduism in the light of fresh challenges and changing situations...

Indeed, our freedom movement itself in a way flowed from Hindu social reform movements...More than any other single person, Mahatma Gandhi brought to the surface of Hindu consciousness this sore [of caste oppression] has been festering in the Hindu society for many centuries...The abolition of untouchability in our Constitution, the reservation of seats in State Legislatures and Parliament, the reservation of jobs in Central and State services, and the broad spectrum of social legislation passed since Independence were all attempts to move in the direction that Gandhiji and other great social reformers had indicated. It is true that they have not been able to fully achieve the objective, but it is unlikely that any other nation in the world

> has adopted such a comprehensive set of statutory provisions specifically designed to help the weaker sections of society.
>
> There are those who now say that the measures have had no impact and that the plight of the Harijans in Hindu society remains as bad as it was. This is demonstrably untrue. Nonetheless, widespread discrimination still exists, and it is becoming clear that no amount of progressive social legislation or reservation can really solve the problem unless there is a change of attitude among the vast masses of Hindu society. It is in his context that the Virat Hindu Sammelan acquire[s] special significance. That a million people (give or take a couple of thousand) drawn from all sections of society should gather at Delhi entirely at their own expense, listen in pin-drop silence to an array of speakers for over three hours, and disperse in complete discipline was itself a remarkable occurrence…But the most important aspect of the Sammelan was the fact that all speakers, without exception, condemned untouchability as a blot on Hinduism, and urged the vast gathering to pledge to fight and eradicate this evil.
>
> Indeed, the overwhelming response to the Sammelan shows clearly that Hindu society is once again ripe for a new thrust in the field of social reform. It must be realized that the reiteration of the spiritual power and achievements of Hinduism and the solidarity of its adherents is an essential prerequisite for any attempt at a new social reform movement. They are two sides of the same coin, for without solidarity, the confidence and vitality necessary for reform are not forthcoming, and without reform, particularly the eradication of the poison of untouchability, Hindu solidarity loses all meaning.

He explained that the Virat Hindu Samaj was a platform to coordinate and harmonize the activities of various organizations working for social reforms, and concluded that, 'There is today a new sense of self-confidence in Hindu society, of pride in its past achievements, concern at its present shortcomings and confidence in its future destiny.'

The fact that lakhs attended the public meeting held in Delhi, was to Karan Singh a sign that Hindu society was once again prepared to introspect and draw a roadmap for a happier future. The new organization he had set up thus took upon itself the task of coordinating and harmonizing the activities of various other organizations working in the field of Hindu reforms and social service. Karan Singh's efforts to reform the Hindu social order, by reminding it of the great tradition of the past, were often met with scepticism. Indira Gandhi, too, expressed her reservations about the emphasis that he laid only on the Hindus. Replying to one of his letters, she wrote to him in early 1984, 'I am rather worried about your stress on what seems to be a rather narrow view of Hinduism. Such an approach or any action flowing from it might incite one community against the other, as the minorities feel that some of the new organizations are aimed against them.' In response, Karan Singh expressed surprise that Indira Gandhi felt that he was expressing a rather narrow view of Hinduism, since his intention was exactly the opposite, as he was propagating the universal qualities of Hinduism.

Meanwhile, sensing the new awakening among the Hindus and, with people like Karan Singh, with his credentials of liberalism and yet a pride in Hinduism, at the helm, the newly formed Bharatiya Janata Party (BJP) sensed an opening in the political space after the failure of the Janata Party experiment. The handicap that the BJP or its earlier avatar, the Bharatiya Jana Sangh, suffered from was that when it championed the cause of Hindus, it only had the ultra-conservatives and backward-looking and often chauvinistic leaders to present its case. In the past, when the Congress provided a wider umbrella for everyone to achieve the larger goal of India's freedom, many practicing Hindus, well-versed in the scriptures, had found a space in the party. The erudite and urbane Dr. Radhakrishnan, K.M. Munshi, and Sampurnanand were some of the notable names. They adhered to Hindu traditions and philosophy, and yet they were liberals. The BJP had no such face, but in the recent past, they had noticed that among the next generation of leaders, Karan Singh had emerged not only as a champion of Hinduism but also as its modern and liberal face. His speeches on Hinduism and ancient Indian philosophy were well-received at home and abroad. He was what the BJP sorely missed. So, when he immersed himself in the work of the Virat Hindu Samaj and reformation in the Hindu society, the BJP began to look at him closely.

One fine day, Atal Behari Vajpayee and Lal Krishan Advani, the founding members of the BJP and its tallest leaders, called upon Karan Singh at his residence with the invitation to join the BJP. After his election on the symbol of the Congress (U) in 1980, Karan Singh had resigned later that year from the party and had been sitting in the Parliament as an independent member. In the circumstances, the BJP's offer was interesting, but he knew the cost would be discarding all the liberal values that he had learned under the tutelage of Nehru and Dr. Radhakrishnan. Hinduism, as he understood it, had little in common with the kind that was understood by the BJP or any other political party that wanted to represent the political aspirations of the eighty percent population of the country. Therefore, respectfully, he declined the offer so that, unaffected by the politics of the day, he could focus on mobilizing all forces for the reformation that was needed. In this journey, he found that society did not lack in people who were tolerant of other people's faiths and beliefs, and were yet very proud of their Hindu past and its core philosophy, and he continued to work towards the goal that he had set. He was happy with the work and the response that he was getting, not only from various Hindu organizations and individuals but also from leaders of other faiths. This continued for some years, till he realized that the movement that he had set in motion had become too big for an individual to continue and that the BJP, with the support of RSS and its band of workers spread all over the country in lakhs, had hijacked his agenda as it had seen in it a route to political power. There was the danger of his message and work being misrepresented, or being seen as communal. After that, he had no option but to gradually scale down his Virat Hindu Samaj activities and focus on his role as an MP, and also continue his swim into the 'spiritual waters'.

In September 1982, Karan Singh was in Srinagar when the indomitable foe of the Dogras passed away. Disliked and distrusted by the majority of Dogras, Sheikh Abdullah was undoubtedly the undisputed leader of the Kashmiris, particularly Muslims, whom he brought out of the stigma of being '*zulm-parast*'—worshippers of tyranny, for the centuries of subjugation they were believed to have submitted themselves to—and gave them a voice and strength to stand up and fight for their cause. Karan Singh appreciated this, even as he remained critical of the Sheikh's anti-Dogra mindset. Thus, when a condolence meeting was held, being present in Srinagar, Karan Singh decided to attend it, knowing well the enormous risk his visit would be. He had dismissed the Sheikh and ordered his arrest; therefore, the possibility of a violent reaction by the crowd that would be present there could not be ruled out. But his conscience goaded him on, and when he reached the venue, allaying all his apprehensions, he was warmly welcomed by everyone. He spoke glowingly about Sheikh Abdullah's qualities as a leader of the Kashmiri people and said that while he was the 'Tiger', a name by which even Sheikh

Abdullah addressed him, the Sheikh was the lion, the Lion of Kahmir—'Sher-i-Kashmir'. With these remarks for an opening, the crowd heard him approvingly.

Meanwhile, the estrangement between him and Indira Gandhi following the Emergency and his decision not to align with the Congress (I) had lessened with time. It was a very difficult time for her and the country. The country was rocked by insurgencies and communal violence. Ethnic and religious tension in Assam had resulted in the worst pogrom since World War II—approximately 2000 Muslims were massacred in fourteen villages. They had been branded as 'illegal' Muslim entrants from Bangladesh. In Punjab, radical Sikhs demanding a separate Sikh homeland, called Khalistan, had unleashed a reign of terror. There had been targeted killings of Hindus. Several buses were ambushed and all the Hindu men pulled out, lined up and shot. Adding to the dilemma of the Government of India was the fact that the leader of the Sikh militants, Jarnail Singh Bhindrawale, had occupied the Akal Takht, the holy Sikh shrine within the precincts of the Golden Temple in Amritsar. Inexplicably, facing problems of such magnitude, the Prime Minister chose to go on a week-long trip to Libya and the Maghreb. As the news came, Karan Singh wrote to her on 4 April 1984, expressing his deep reservations about the trip, but could not stop her. Perhaps, by then, Indira Gandhi had become a prisoner of her image of an 'iron lady'. Or, perhaps, it was an escapist response during those difficult months. Her return was followed by Operation Blue Star—when the Army stormed the Golden Temple to capture Bhindranwale and his men. It scarred the Sikhs across India and the world. The repercussions were also felt in Kashmir, where Sikh extremists attacked Hindu temples, and burnt shops and properties. It was feared that with the Pakistani agents active, the Sikh and the Kashmiri militants had begun to team up. That was to be another chapter in the history of Kashmir, but on 31 October 1984, Prime Minister Indira

Gandhi was assassinated by her Sikh bodyguards. Riots erupted across much of India, including the national capital and Hindu mobs butchered thousands of Sikhs. It was in the middle of this pogrom that Rajiv Gandhi was sworn in as the Prime Minister, and he called for immediate general elections to the Parliament.

It is very hard to say if it was destiny or hubris that made Karan Singh change his Lok Sabha constituency in these elections, abandoning Udhampur for Jammu. Udhampur had reposed its faith in him for four consecutive terms, and there was no reason to believe that it would not deliver victory to him again. But in a serious error of judgment, he listened to the advice of some responsible citizens of Jammu, like Nilambar Sharma, who had diligently worked to highlight the problems of Jammu region as one of the conveners of the Jammu Front that Karan Singh had formed many years ago. Nilambar Sharma and others convinced Karan Singh that he had represented the hilly and the mountainous Lok Sabha constituency of Udhampur for much too long, and now it was time to return to Jammu, the *karambhoomi* of his ancestors—the land of their karma—and the place where all the ancestral temples were located. Tempted, Karan Singh filed his papers from the Jammu constituency. The consequence was disastrous, as he not only lost but also trailed in the third position. The winner, Janak Raj Gupta of the Indian National Congress, bagged more than 46 percent of the votes, while the National Conference candidate polled about 25 percent and Karan Singh 24 percent. It was a bitter disappointment. It was the second time that Jammu had let him down, the first time being when it had welcomed him with black flags when he came there as the elected Sadr-e-Riyasat. But more than him, it was his wife, so loved by everyone in the entire Jammu region, who was in a state of utter disbelief and shock and was heartbroken.

But the people had spoken, and it was time for him to move on and open a new chapter in his life.

25
The Quest

FREE OF BOTH THE excitement and the burden of political life and nursing the wound of rejection by people he had considered his own, Karan Singh found himself drawn to the aim that he had articulated back in 1952, when he was barely twenty-one: 'to achieve spiritual enlightenment and peace…[and] spread the message throughout the world' and put it 'on the broad and clear sunlit path of peace, happiness, love and universal prosperity'.

At a very young age, he had learned from his mother that there was a need to connect with the Superior Power and that the basic tool for establishing it was the daily ritualistic worship of God. Thus, he had been initiated into worshipping Krishna even though his family deity was Rama, to whom his ancestors had built the grand Raghunath Mandir complex in Jammu. Then, soon after being introduced to Pandit Parmanand, he had also started to worship the Goddess, Shakti. But Karan Singh's curious mind and spirit had always yearned for something more than conventional religion.

In 1953, when he had, by and large, settled on Lord Krishna, he still recorded in his diary: 'I have as yet not settled down to any one path or any one particular deity. Of course, God is omnipresent, but it is helpful if one worships one particular aspect of Him. I am beginning to get greatly attached to the wonderful form of the Divine Lord Sri Krishna, and a deep and emotional love for him is beginning to grow in my being…I am now keenly awaiting some initiation into some form of Yoga whereby I might really and truly set out upon the path of spiritual illumination.' In this phase, when he and his wife had gone to Alhilal, Kangra, between Palampur and Baijnath, where his mother lived in the Taragarh Palace, he had used that occasion to explore the nearby region of Mandi and Suket and reached Riwalsar, a place sacred to both Hindus and Buddhists. For the Buddhists, the place and the lake have a special place as it is associated with Padmasambhava, also known as Guru Rinpoche, who taught *Vajrayana* in Tibet. Later, while visiting Delhi, he and his wife travelled to Mathura, Vrindavan and Gokul and felt the presence of Lord Krishna as the various spots associated with his life appeared to be still resonating with his *Leela*. However, the blatant and competitive commercialization and exploitation of the pilgrim's faith by the brahmins was a jarring note.

After that, they had visited Calcutta and worshipped at the Kali temple at Dakshineshwar, where Sri Ramakrishna, perhaps the most remarkable mystic of the nineteenth century, had lived. With his extraordinary mystical experiences, he had been instrumental in triggering a spiritual revolution in Hinduism at a time when spiritual and intellectual crises were sweeping across the country. That journey to Dakshineshwar, the first of its kind for the pilgrim soul in Karan Singh, as it turned out to be a moving experience. Before the visit, he had already read about the most illustrious of Sri Ramakrishna's disciples, Narendranath Dutta, better known to the world as Swami Vivekananda. He and his wife also drove to Belur Math, where Vivekananda had founded the Ramakrishna Mission. During the visit to Kalighat, they paid obeisance to the Goddess in her manifestation as Kali, who is the slayer of all evildoers and terrifies all except her devotees and the innocent, for whom she remains the divine guardian-mother.

In July of 1953, Karan Singh, accompanied by Asha, had decided to undertake the pilgrimage to the Holy Amarnath shrine, a full month before the actual pilgrimage date. Because of his leg, he could not make the yatra the hard way as most devotees do; therefore, he was carried in a dandi while Asha decided to walk all the way. They halted at the three designated spots of Chandanwari, Sheshnag, and Panchtarni and were struck by the uplifting power of the beauty of nature. He felt 'the presence of a Power greater, stronger and purer than one's petty self'. The pilgrimage had left a deep mark on him, and, as we have seen, the articles on the pilgrimage for the *Hindustan Times* had brought Raushan Nath—Nathji—to his door. Nathji would often sit with Karan Singh during his puja and chant the primeval sound 'Aum', with Karan Singh joining him. Once, as he was chanting, Karan Singh felt a curious sensation of movement in his spine. This experience was probably the closest that he came to awakening the *Kundalini* or the serpent-power at the base of the spine.

During those years, he would often reach out to Dr. Radhakrishnan whenever he was in the national capital, and learned about Indian philosophy and the various living persons who, in Radhakrishnan's opinion, had attained illumination. In his presence, Karan Singh was like an eager pupil looking towards the Master for some clue or lead to understanding enlightenment. It was during one such session that Dr Radhakrishnan had turned to Karan Singh and said, 'Do you know what is enlightenment? It is like a flash of lightning against the dark blue clouds.' He had sat mesmerized by the words, hoping to experience that 'flash' someday. Dr. Radhakrishnan always spoke highly of Ramakrishna Paramahamsa and the Ramakrishna Mission, and of a young Swami, Ranganathanand, and predicted that one day he would head the Mission. Karan Singh, too, was very impressed by Ranganathanand and rated him among those who had considerable spiritual achievement to their credit. He also met Swami Ashokanand in Kashmir, who had established an ashram dedicated to Ramakrishna Mission at Nagdandi, just beyond the enchantingly laid out Mughal Garden at Achabal in south Kashmir. Many years later, even during the dark phase of terrorism in Kashmir, this Ashram continued to function without being disturbed by the sense of insecurity and violence that prevailed around it.

These journeys and meetings had made Karan Singh yearn for more as he realized that, since time immemorial, travel had been an integral part of any spiritual quest. So, the next year, in 1954, he planned a visit to the south from whence had sprung all the Bhakti movements that then travelled through the Deccan and the plains of central India to enlighten the north. It was during this visit that Karan Singh was made aware of the power and beauty of Lord Shiva. It all began with a visit to the Meenakshi Temple in Madurai, dedicated to the fish-eyed goddess, and the Brihadishwara temple in Thanjavur, which boasts probably the most impressive Shivalingam in India. He and his wife also visited the Shiva temple in Tiruvannamalai before reaching the temple at Chidambaram, where Shiva is worshipped as the Divine Dancer—Nataraja. The moment he laid his eyes on the dancing figure of Shiva, Karan Singh was captivated by its artistic beauty, balance and the spiritual cord that it struck. This first introduction grew into an everlasting bond when he was introduced to what he has believed ever since is the world's greatest solo dance, for the manner in which it combines emotion, melody and rhythm—

bhava, raga and *tala*. The dance was Bharatanatyam, and he saw it being performed at the Music Academy in Madras (now Chennai). The dancer was a young woman who, he later discovered, was a rising film star—Vyjayanthimala. He was captivated. He had seen nothing so graceful and elegant before. It was both a sensuous as well as a spiritual experience, and he became an instant devotee of the dance form.

The tour of South India opened Karan Singh's mind to the many-splendored dimensions of Hinduism, but, more importantly, it made him aware of the richness and diversity that abounded in India, which was unified by a great culture that, he believes, has existed like an eternal river. It was during this journey that he first felt that his State was a space that appeared restrictive in the face of the vastness of the cultural and spiritual landscape that existed outside it. Before he returned home, he also realized that he had not found a spiritual Guru. He yearned for a guide and friend blessed with divinity who could hold his hand and lead him on towards superior consciousness.

It was in 1957, the year his daughter Jyoti was born, that he came in contact with such a Guru. He was led, by Dilip Kumar Roy's book *Among the Great*, to Sri Krishnaprem—Gopalda—the former English fighter pilot who had established an ashram in Mirtola, 17 km from Almora in the Kumaon hills. His correspondence with Gopalda began that year, and continued even after his death with his disciple Sri Madhav Ashish, also an Englishman, popularly addressed as Ashishda, till he too passed away in 1997. After a year's correspondence with Gopalda, Karan Singh had visited Mirtola in 1958. The ashram and temple had been built on an idyllic spot among the mountains, where the only sound he could hear on reaching was the chirping of birds and the rustling of leaves. It was the perfect place for meditation, and Karan Singh took an immediate liking to it.

A brilliant mind, Sri Krishanprem had already written several books, of which Karan Singh had read, *The Yoga of the Bhagavadgita* and *The Yoga of the Kathopanishad,* which also drew upon Western mystical traditions, and had surrendered himself to Krishna, whom he called 'Thakur'. Karan Singh spent three nights at the Mirtola Ashram, joining in the ritualistic *arati* and then the conversations that covered topics ranging from the ancient scriptures to everyday situations. The kindness of Sri Krishanprem touched the core of his being, and he opened up not only about the academic questions that troubled him but also about everyday dilemmas that confronted mankind.

A bond was created that remained as long as the two Gurus lived. It was amazing that, born thousands of miles away in alien cultures, the two Englishmen brought the teachings of the Upanishads to their Indian follower with a combination of intellectual perception and emotional empathy. The lessons thus learned gave him a new awareness of his inner being. That first visit gave a sense of purpose to Karan Singh when he returned to Delhi, and the relationship forged during those three nights became his lodestar—as both Gopalda and Ashishda were always there, whatever the problem or crossroad that confronted him. He turned to them whenever he needed advice, but he was never really told to follow a particular path. He was only made aware of the possibilities and the pitfalls, leaving the final decision to his wisdom. Together, Gopalda and Asishda—who were like one being in two bodies—became the Guru that he had been yearning for, but the *diksha* was given to him by Ashishda and not Gopalda, who had stopped giving *diksha* by the time Karan Singh met him.

By then, Karan Singh had also earned the reputation of being an avid reader, and indeed, he spent considerable time with his books. He had picked up the habit of reading those books that could open up his mind. So, after finishing his official work, he would keep himself busy reading, while Asha looked after the members of their extended family, which mostly included his cousins from his maternal side or someone connected to the paternal family of his wife. During one of his reading sprees, he had come across Aldous Huxley's *Doors of Perception* in 1954. The book had generated quite a debate as it was an autobiographical book that described Huxley's psychedelic experience under the influence of the drug mescaline, popularly known as LSD. The book reflected on LSD's psychological and philosophical impact on the mind and speculated about its possible use as a facilitator for mystical experience. The debate fascinated Karan Singh, and he was curious to know how mystical experiences were triggered. He had always wondered if the doors of perception opened because of long periods of meditation or if they opened because of some revelation or the chanting of some mantra, or was it possible only with the help of an external tool—maybe a Guru. But here, Huxley was suggesting another possibility. Huxley had offered himself as an experimental subject for those who were studying the impact of psychedelic drugs like mescaline. He was convinced that there were many paths to enlightenment and that, apart from meditation and prayer, there could be drugs that broke down the barrier of the ego to draw one closer to spiritual enlightenment.

There the matter remained till 1962, when Aldous Huxley published another book, the novel *Island*. When Karan Singh read it, his curiosity about Huxley and his experiments towards mystical experience grew even more. In the novel, the people of a particular island are depicted as consuming some kind of 'medicine' to attain mystical and cosmological insight. Karan

Singh wrote Huxley a letter, commenting on the novel, and asking where in India those drugs were available, though he had a fair idea that they were mostly for scientific experiments. Huxley responded on 22 December 1962, admitting that the plot that he had woven in the novel was, in fact, a dream, albeit a pragmatic one, and strongly believed that the realization of that dream could make the world fit for evolved humans to live in. As for information about the psychedelic drugs was concerned, he wrote that since they were in short supply and were available only for scientific experiments under qualified people, he could find out about the availability in India from the manufacturers, the Sandoz Company. He also gave Karan Singh the address of a friend of his who was a Harvard Professor and conducted research on the subject. He also informed him that the Professor might be interested in an Indian subject as he was, in fact, looking for someone brought up in a culture outside the West.

Nothing came of this for the next two decades, when he was involved in momentous political events. But throughout this period, he had been drawn towards issues that he thought were more important than politics. Gradually, he emerged as a well-known proponent of and activist for pan-global efforts towards promoting inter-religious dialogue, and became the Chairperson of the Temple of Understanding India Foundation. He acquired an international reputation for his espousal of Indian Philosophy as an enabler of universal values that could help in bridging distances between different religions, philosophies and cultures and moving the modern world towards harmony. In 1981, when UNESCO celebrated the centenary of Jesuit priest Pierre Teilhard de Chardin and held a colloquium, Karan Singh, in his capacity as an independent thinker, was invited to deliver a lecture. The famous priest who often found himself in the crosshairs of the Catholic Church was also a scientist, paleontologist, theologian, philosopher and teacher, and had also authored several influential theological and philosophical books. Among his speculative ideas, often criticized as pseudoscientific, was a vitalist conception of the 'Omega Point'—a final point of unification. On 16 September 1981, Karan Singh presented his paper titled 'A Hindu Viewpoint' at the colloquium, and summed up by pointing out that, 'In the Western tradition, perhaps one could say that Karamyoga was the way of Martha, Bhakti Yoga the way of Mary, Jnana Yoga the way of Plato, and Raja Yoga the way of Eckart.' It was obvious that, free from the limitations of politics, his mind had expanded, bringing him a little closer to his dream of becoming an evolved 'world citizen'.

Before this, as he continued his search for higher consciousness, Karan Singh was introduced to Transpersonal Psychology. This branch of psychology which focuses on human experiences which go beyond the individual self, fascinated Karan Singh, and brought him back to the subject that Aldous Huxley had wondered about. He made enquiries and eventually he came in contact with Professor Stanislav Grof, who, along with Abraham Maslow, had initiated the study of transpersonal psychology and had been striving to get it recognized as a separate subject of academic studies. In 1972, they had established an International Transpersonal Psychology Association (ITPA). The Association held periodic conferences in various parts of the world, and also published a journal that contained articles from experts. Karan Singh got into a regular correspondence with Professor Stanislav Grof and was soon invited to attend one of their conferences in Europe. Subsequently, he also invited Professor Grof and his wife, Christina, to be his guests in Delhi, and they stayed with him and his wife for a few days.

His curiosity about LSD, first aroused in 1962 after reading Huxley, was rekindled after this encounter. But the problem was that it was a banned drug in India, and even scientists experimenting on its effect on the human mind were barred from procuring or using it. However, in several states in the USA, it was a legal drug, and many universities conducted experiments with it. Thus, when Karan Singh and Asha visited the USA next, he got in touch with Professor Grof, who, along with Christina, accompanied them to the Esalen Institute in Big Sur in California, along the Pacific Coast. It was a non-profit retreat centre for 'humanistic alternative education'. In this retreat, LSD was legally available, which made Karan Singh decide to experiment with it to see if his state of consciousness was altered. Professor Grof procured the drug, and it was decided that Karan Singh would take it in the presence of Grof, Christina and Asha. Christina and Asha would take notes, recording their observations about the effect of the drug. These notes were to be compared later with Professor Grof's notes, and Karan Singh's memory of the experiences he had had.

The two beds in the room had been joined so that everyone could sit on them comfortably and observe the changes. There were also a couple of chairs by the beds. Allowance had also to be made for the possibility of a 'bad trip', as that altered state of consciousness was called when things went wrong with the subject. Sometimes, the subjects were known to believe that they were flying; hence, in a bad trip, there was the danger of them trying to jump out of the window. Before consuming LSD, Karan Singh performed a puja. A little over an hour after he had taken the drug, he began to feel a change and got up from his chair to lie down on the bed. In the background, Meera bhajans sung by M.S. Subbulakshmi were playing. Christina sat on the floor and Asha sat on the bed next to him. Soon he felt that the music had gotten louder and he asked it to be toned down, just as geometrical patterns of colours began to move, both inside and outside him, like a constantly shifting kaleidoscope. The music appeared to him to have transformed into a living, pulsating and dynamic texture. His whole being appeared to him to have been flooded with ecstasy, and he felt a different dimension of himself and the world around him—a sensation he maintains our languages don't have the words to describe.

What he does say is that he was entirely convinced that he had witnessed the dance of Nataraja, even though there was no form. Soon he was overcome with astonishment and ecstasy and kept exclaiming in Hindi to Asha—'*Ashcharya-ascharya, adhbhut-adhbhut*'—Astonishing-astonishing, amazing-amazing. His physical consciousness had disappeared, and he only had a disembodied mind that was partaking in the cosmic dance; though he was lying on the bed, he was dancing to the rhythm of a cosmic music. He made ineffectual attempts to describe what he was experiencing, but before he could do so, he would get caught in a new wave of music and ecstasy. His hands moved as if he were playing Shiva's hand-drum, the *damaru*, and although he was far away, everywhere and nowhere, he was aware there were observers and he felt they were an extension of himself, or he of them. Several times he tried to begin a sentence, and every time he was carried away by a new wave of music and the Dance. All the while, he was smiling and holding Professor Grof's and Asha's hands. At that point, Professor Grof asked him if he wanted to tell them something, and he countered, 'Do I have to?' Asha also asked him if he wanted to have another dose, but he declined, as at that moment, the music and the Dance were bliss beyond belief. In that instant, even in his altered state, he knew that if one dose could do that to him, then if he took another dose, he would completely disappear. After a while, he felt as if he was at a great height, and when he tried to make a great effort to communicate the feeling, all he could say was, 'If I don't describe what I feel…' But his voice trailed off before he could complete the sentence and he was consumed by the Dance again.

He then asked for the kirtan *'Om namho Nityanandam, Nityanandam Brahmanandam, Brahmaswaroopam Neelavarnam, Trilokinatham Shreegurudevam, Om namho Nityanandam'* to be played, and as the ecstasy reached new heights, he laughed in joy and said, 'The Dance, the Dance, I always knew it was in the Dance…the link between what is there and what is here!' He also exclaimed that he found it amazing 'how tenuous' were the links between the state that he was experiencing and the ordinary life people lived; that the bonds which we feel so strongly are extremely fragile. He was in a state where he tried to express his feelings as his mind was crystal clear, but felt that his body had disappeared, and he only felt his mind as part of that great Dance, and that he would require a great act of will to come back. He understood that to come back was a deliberate imposition of patterns, that it was like imposing the Vaishnava pattern on the Shaiva pattern. He felt that the ultimate reality and truth were in the Dance of the Nataraja, and that Dance was everything and everywhere—it was; and nothing else was. He was in such a state of bliss that when Asha held his hand, he tried to tell her in Hindi how incredibly grateful he was to Stanislav and Christina for having facilitated such an ecstatic experience. Then he got stuck with the question of 'coming back' from the experience, as it was an act of wilful imposition of 'disharmony'. He had to finally come back, but to do so, a strong centre had to be created. For close to four hours, there had been no body or ego; just the voice, the mind, the music, the Dance—and Light, a universe of light. He reached out to hold Professor Grof's hand but barely felt it and wondered aloud, 'Why would anyone want to come back? It is easier to go, more difficult to come back.'

Meera's bhajans continued to fill the room till 2.00 p.m. By

3 p.m., as he began to return, he felt deep sadness at having to come to normal consciousness and wondered if he required some medicine to regain his centre. There was a tremendous void in him, and he knew that even if he had offered prayers at that moment, he would not have known whom to offer them to. By then, even though the music was there, the Dance had vanished, and he sat up in deep depression. When Stanislav Groff asked him if he could describe a matching situation, he said, 'Definitely a transition stage, either pre-death or post-death.' Finding him thus, Stanislav suggested that he ought to vomit if he was feeling nauseous, but what he felt was not at a physical level, he suffered from the great 'psychic burden' of 'recreating the centre' to again belong to this world. He longed for that experience of having disappeared, 'disappeared from' all human relations, loves, hopes and fears and the ego, into nothingness. He wished to be a part of that incredible ecstasy of the cosmic Dance of Nataraja again. He knew that he had, through the instrumentality of Stanislav and Christina, experienced an encounter of such colossal ecstasy that all his life he would crave for his final merger with it. He never again took any such substance; one overwhelming experience was enough for a lifetime.

After that experience of the combination of *the* Dance and music, Karan Singh realized that even if he had not seen Lord Shiva in his physical form, the multiple flashing lights dancing in changing patterns were indeed Lord Shiva. He was convinced that the Lord of this cosmos was Lord Shiva, who had manifested himself in that Dance. From then on, although he continued to worship other gods as well, Shiva became the centre of his life, and he knew that throughout his life, he would yearn for a merger with the Lord of all that existed.

26

A Philosopher-Diplomat

THE YEAR 1984 BROUGHT a decisive change in Karan Singh's life. After losing the Lok Sabha election from Jammu, he would enter a phase that would turn out to be the most exciting, productive and creative of any that he had known. For the first time since their marriage in 1950, he and Asha were free to explore the world without any official care. Among the new relationships that blossomed in this phase, some were those whose seeds had been sown when he was a minister in Indira Gandhi's cabinet. In a remarkable resemblance of circumstances, an interesting bond developed between four dynasties: three from Europe and one from India. 'You could call it an exclusive club of unprincely princes!' Karan Singh laughs, recounting the days.

One of these 'princes' was Juan Carlos, the King of Spain, born in unusual circumstances in 1938, when his family was in exile after the Republicans, led by communists, established the Second Spanish Republic following the overthrow of the monarchy in 1931. The decade in which Juan Carlos was born was marred by the bloody Civil War between the Republican forces and the Nationalists led by General Franco, in which the latter prevailed after considerable bloodshed and destruction in 1939. It was only after this that the family of young Juan Carlos could return to Spain. In a curious turn of events, General Franco, who had assumed the title Caudillo and remained the military dictator and ruler of Spain till his death in 1975, had declared Juan Carlos as the king just before his death. However, the monarchy thus re-established was to be a constitutional monarchy in tune with the times. Juan Carlos was married to Princess Sophia of Greece and Denmark. She, too, came from a dynasty that had seen better days, and was later abolished.

Another prince of the club whose dynasty was targeted by republican forces was King Baudouin of Belgium. Born the eldest child of King Leopold III in 1930, Baudouin was married to Dona Fabiola de Mora y Argon, who was born in a noble family from Spain. Baudouin became the King in very unusual circumstances when his father was forced to abdicate in 1951 after being accused of treason for surrendering Belgium in the wake of the Nazi occupation of the country in 1940 and collaborating with the Nazis. Public opinion after the defeat of the Nazis was so fierce that King Leopold had to abdicate in favour of his son Baudouin, who turned out to be a popular king, dutifully performing his constitutional duties and not trying to test the boundaries of his powers.

The third European royal to fall into the same league was Constantine II, King of Greece, who had been forced to live the years of the Second World War in South Africa. Born in 1940, he succeeded his father upon his death in 1964 and was a very popular king to begin with, since he was already an established sporting hero, having won an Olympic gold medal in sailing. However, this lasted only for a short period as Greece was still suffering from the consequences of a prolonged civil war when the communists made a serious but futile bid to capture power. The King himself squandered the goodwill of the people by becoming a part of machinations to overthrow the elected and popular government. Greater hostility to the monarchy was also due to the intemperate remarks delivered periodically by the Queen-Mother. Finally, a military coup settled the matter in 1967. Constantine was forced into exile, which was followed by a referendum in 1973, and the monarchy was abolished by popular vote. A year later, it was restored, but it was followed by another vote in which 70 percent of the voters favored ending the monarchy. Thus, in 1974, another dynasty in Europe came to an end.

Complementing the three European Kings was Karan Singh, whose dynasty's story was not dissimilar to others, having seen turmoil overtaking his State, leading to his father's virtual exile and then the end of monarchy and his dynasty's rule. Sharing a common thread of destiny, the four often met and formed a very interesting, but exclusive club of princes. Of the four, Belgium and Spain had been rehabilitated as constitutional monarchs, while Karan Singh, though not a king, inherited the title of Maharaja and enjoyed some degree of political power and prestige in his country.

King Baudouin and Queen Fabiola were a popular royal couple in their country, and their easy access to and keen interest in the lives of their people had helped in erasing the bitter anti-monarchy feelings of the Nazi years. The only thing that marred their happy world was the absence of any children, as none of the pregnancies of the Queen had ended happily. Over the years, a personal bond had developed between the two families from Belgium and India, and many years later, Karan Singh's daughter, Jyotsana, was invited by the affectionate Queen Fabiola to stay with them while she was visiting that part of Europe. When Baudouin passed away in 1993, Karan Singh represented India at his funeral.

In contrast, King Juan Carlos was a gifted and complex personality who had very early in his life earned the reputation of a playboy. He had visited India along with Queen Sophia in 1966 on a private visit and had met Karan Singh in Delhi. When Karan Singh visited Spain in June 1973 as Tourism and Civil Aviation Minister to attend the Air India / Tourism Conference, he renewed his contact with Juan Carlos, who had by then been designated as the King after the passing away of General Franco. The arrival of Karan Singh in Spain coincided with a major reshuffle in the government structure. Several prominent Ministers had been dropped, and new ones were inducted in a clear message that General Franco wanted Spain to be eased into a settled political set-up. During a private lunch with Karan Singh and Asha, the Spanish couple expressed their eagerness to visit India the following year, and since they had already travelled in central India, they hoped to see Kashmir and the South during the next visit. Karan Singh was only too willing to host them during their stay in Srinagar. By and large, King Juan Carlos enjoyed a good period in the history of Spain during which, in 1992, its Catalonian city of Barcelona became the sporting capital of the world for a fortnight when it hosted the Summer Olympic Games. However, his failings caused his ultimate failure as he was accused of financial indiscretions that led to his abdication in favour of his son, who had embraced modernity and had married a commoner.

Of the four, only the royal family of Greece could never claim any sort of rehabilitation in public life. Over time, as the four royals would meet periodically, often travelling incognito, reflecting on the coincidence of their somewhat similar destinies, they all agreed that history demands that humans swim with the ebb and flow of its forces and that swimming against the current invariably brings a swift end to even the mightiest.

Even without any elected office, Karan Singh never had a dull moment in his life as he devoted himself to building understanding and harmony among various faiths. By the mid-1980s, religions and political ambitions and interests had begun to clash on the global stage, and there was hardly a nation that was not combating the new threats. Undeterred, he continued to work on interfaith relationships and build a temple of understanding in as many hearts as possible. He used this period not only to travel and understand different cultures and people but also to carry with him the essential message of the Upanishads. He built relationships with religious leaders from all over the world so that the barriers between different faiths could be pulled down. So, he engaged in correspondence and dialogue with leaders and thinkers of various faiths, putting the core of Hindu philosophy across and understanding their philosophy to find common ground. One of the most fruitful dialogues was with Daisaku Ikeda, a Buddhist leader from Japan who was also a philosopher, educator and businessman, who emphasized that though Buddhist and Hindu religions might differ on certain philosophical aspects, certain elements of Buddhism had been integrated into Hinduism. Though many considered him a divisive figure in his lifetime, he had an important role to play in bringing the West and the East closer. For the followers of Daisaku Ikeda, the 'lotus-mantra' contained the secret of harmony in life, while Karan Singh emphasized the all-embracing philosophy of Hinduism that 'there is but one truth, though the wise men called it by different names'—*Ekam satya, viprah bahudha vadanti.*

During these dialogues with Ikeda, Karan Singh discovered many similarities between Buddhism and Hinduism as he found that the Hindus' concept of the next predicted avatar, Kalki, closely resembled the belief of the Buddhists in the rebirth of Maitreya Buddha. But importantly, he concluded that the 'people of Asian nations needed to rebuild among themselves those links of understanding that had languished during the colonial period'. He was convinced by the end of the dialogue that it was in the minds and hearts of mankind that the bulwark of the new consciousness had to be built and expressed the hope that the ideas the two had articulated would create a ripple effect that would help in forging a new globalism to which both of them were committed. This interaction was published in 1988 in *Humanity at the Crossroads: An Intercultural Dialogue.* During this period, Karan Singh pursued every opportunity he could to interact with the wise men of the world, and the more he did, the more he was convinced of the common values and goals that drove mankind.

All this while, Karan Singh remained in regular communication with Ashishda, seeking his guru's opinions and advice, and also sharing his ideas, and also his dreams, of which he had many—in fact, Karan Singh does not remember a time when his sleep was bereft of dreams. Ashishda remained a steadfast guide, though he knew that Karan Singh had a mind of his own and his advice notwithstanding, was more likely than not to follow what he thought was the correct course. This was evident from a letter of November 1982, when Karan Singh had set his mind to reforming and revitalizing Hindu society. The letter suggests that Ashishda had his reservations about Karan Singh's exertions to hold a Hindu Sammelan, as he feared, correctly as it turned out, that it might be appropriated by people with other objectives who would want to increase communal tensions. He was of the firm conviction that though Hinduism had to be safeguarded from domination by aggressive streams of other faiths, he did not want Hindus, Muslims, Christians, Sikhs or people of any other faith to believe that they were the sole possessors of the Truth. He was also of the opinion that any Hindu who followed the Upanishadic traditions would not make a religious issue of the Arab world's political expansionism and that those who treated it as a religious issue and not a political one suffered from a confusion of the mind. He cautioned that any counter-move to Arab expansionism would not succeed in reducing tensions of polarization, because any such move would be a polarizing one itself. Ashishda had also very astutely read that some of Karan Singh's associates and allies in the Virat Hindu Samaj movement may be using him, because of his popularity and liberal appeal, as a tool—an acceptable, distracting front behind whom they were working to establish their personal power base. He was sure that his disciple would be 'successful' in his venture, but suggested that 'your effect on the world [would] be far greater if you were not identified with a particular religion.' Having said that, Ashishda remarked, 'So you see, I am not saying, Don't do it! (You wouldn't listen to me anyway!)' Finally, on a note of warning, he ended that letter by writing, 'One is always weakened by identification with a form because it drives one to defend and justify.'

Karan Singh had not been fully convinced till the day he was approached by the founders of the BJP, Atal Behari Vajpayee and Lal Krishna Advani, with an invitation for him to join their new political party. If he was still not convinced of the seriousness of Ashishda's cautionary notes, then he saw them clearly when new and strident Hindu outfits began springing up with a barely concealed communal agenda for capturing political power. It was at that point that he had stepped back from organizing the Hindus and started to focus on widening his understanding of the individual's relationship with God. He had reverted to his original for 'the religion of Man', as Vivekananda had said. He also tried to open more doors of perception and hoped one day to experience that 'flash of lightning against the dark blue clouds', as Dr. Radhakrishnan had so eloquently described 'enlightenment'.

It was in this search that he came in contact with the International Transpersonal Association (ITA). When at the initiative of Swami Muktananda, the ITA held its Conference in Bombay in 1982, Karan Singh was also invited and he contributed a paper that was later published by the ITA. After that, he participated in the next Conference in 1983 in Davos and then in Kyoto in 1985, which was a great success in terms of participation but which drove the ITA to bankruptcy. However, it was revived in the USA in 1990 when it was held in Eugene, Oregon, and the next year in Atlanta, Georgia. It was there that, with the inspiration of Christina Grof, wife of Stanislav Grof, a new dimension was added to the ITA when people working in the field of de-addiction began to recognize the vital role spirituality could play in treatment and rehabilitation.

Karan Singh might have had some differences with his father, but there is no doubt that during his early youth, he was keen and happy to follow his father's example in several matters. One of them was hunting, but very soon he had given it up, which was an early sign of him being temperamentally attuned to a spiritual and artistic life. What had survived was a fascination with and respect for wildlife. As a minister in the cabinet of Indira Gandhi, he had been offered the responsibility of taking control of the National Board for Wildlife, and he had not only accepted it but had left a lasting impact by giving it new impetus and importance. This made him an early champion in India of the movement to conserve the environment and wildlife. In this, he was not alone, and there were many influential voices from all corners of the world as the degradation of forests and nature was a common concern. In 1986, the 25th Anniversary of the World Wildlife Fund was held in the historical Basilica di San Francesco, Assisi, Italy. The then President, the late Prince Philip, the Duke of Edinburgh, mooted the idea of bringing the five original faiths—Hinduism, Buddhism, Judaism, Christianity, and Islam—on a common platform to address the issue of the increasing impact of Man on Nature. As a leading thinker of Hindu philosophy, Karan Singh was invited to present the 'Hindu Message on Man and Nature' and said: 'Hinduism believes in the all-encompassing sovereignty of the divine, manifesting itself in a graded scale of evolution. The human race, though at the top of the evolutionary pyramid at present, is not something apart from the earth and its multitudinous life forms. The Atharva Veda has a magnificent Hymn to the Earth which is redolent with ecological and environmental values. Two stanzas are enough to convey the Hindu approach to Nature:

> Earth, on which lie the sea, the river, and other waters,
> In which food and cornfields have come to be,
> In which lives all that breathes and that moves,
> May she confer on us the finest of her yield.
> [...]
> Earth, my mother, set me securely with bliss
> In full accord with heaven.
> O wise one
> Uphold me in grace...

Similar sentiments, drawn from their religious texts, were expressed by Venerable Lungrig Namgyal Rinpoche, representing Buddhism, Father Lanfranco Serrini, representing Christianity, Dr Abdullah Omar Nasseef, representing Islam, and Rabbi Arthur Hertzberg, representing Judaism. It is interesting to note that among all the speakers, only Karan Singh was nearest to the ancient Indian concept of Rajrishi—one who is detached from worldly affairs, even while wielding political power and being a family man!

Politically, Karan Singh had largely withdrawn from party politics as the sudden death of Indira Gandhi had stalled his re-entry into the Congress, and he was not inclined to become a member of any other party. His satisfaction, though, was that before Indira Gandhi's assassination, a rapprochement had taken place with her, as the last correspondence between the two suggested. After a very long time, the coldness of the formal letters was gone, and most of the letters of that period were addressed to 'Dear Tiger', suggesting the return of the warmth of the early years of their acquaintance. It was widely believed then in political circles that his return to the Congress fold was imminent, but after her death, Rajiv Gandhi came in with a new set of advisors and a team that had other ideas. Unfazed, Karan Singh continued with the work that he had been doing. However, on 24 February, the birthday of his daughter, he received a call from Prime Minister Rajiv Gandhi's residence inviting him to tea. When he went, Rajiv Gandhi asked if he would be interested in becoming India's Ambassador to the USA. Karan Singh had no hesitation in accepting the offer, but he put two conditions: first, that it should be publicly known and conveyed to the American President that he had the personal confidence of the Prime Minister, and second, that he would have direct access to the Prime Minister. Rajiv Gandhi not only agreed but also informed him that his appointment would be with the personal rank of a Cabinet Minister. It was a singular honour that came at a very challenging time in the country's history. Sometimes, it appeared that India was under siege, and even the USA, the champion of democracy and liberalism, had succumbed to the pressure of non-democratic forces to aggressively exert its influence against India.

After that, in the whole of March, Karan Singh did not hear anything about the subject. In April, he and his wife left for London and the USA on a private visit, as he was scheduled to deliver the Eighth World Conservation Lecture in London under the auspices of the World-Wide Fund for Nature UK. It was in London that he received a call from Ronen Sen, Joint Secretary of External Affairs, informing him that the Prime Minister was ready to approve his appointment and that he would like him to be in Washington by the end of June. The next day, Karan Singh continued his scheduled programme and delivered a lecture at the Bharatiya Vidya Bhawan, London on Jawaharlal Nehru before proceeding to the United States. In New York, he discovered that the then Indian Ambassador to the USA, P.K. Kaul, was also present, so he called upon him and was surprised to see heavy security guarding him. Karan Singh found Kaul a bitter man since he felt that whatever he tried to do to improve Indo-US relations was systematically sabotaged by the Foreign Ministry, and warned Karan Singh of similar treatment because of the Ministry's pathological dislike of non-IFS (Indian Foreign Service) Ambassadors.

A few days after returning to Delhi, Karan Singh received a formal letter from the Foreign Secretary, S.K. Singh. Soon thereafter, news about his appointment began to appear in the newspapers and was met with enthusiasm. During one of his meetings with the Foreign Minister, Narasimha Rao, he came to know that India had not yet found its feet with the administration of the new President, George W. Bush (Sr.), and had few connections in the White House, National Security Council or Capitol Hill. His job, therefore, was to develop access at all those levels, and at the highest level. Ronen Sen assured him that since Rajiv Gandhi was to meet Bush in Paris in July, he would mention to him Karan Singh's appointment. Meanwhile, Ambassador Kaul had some commitments in the USA, so Karan Singh decided to reach Washington at the end of July. Amidst all the excitement around him, he was acutely aware of what

Sri Krishnaprem used to say about change. He would tell Karan Singh that a change in the outer environment invariably reflected inner development. Retreating from the excitement of Delhi, he and his wife went to Srinagar, where they practiced meditation with an American Buddhist monk, Bhikshu George Churinof, and made a conscious effort to be quiet, read and meditate rather than talk and recite. It was hard, but he succeeded. Meanwhile, press reports about his appointment had been doing the rounds in newspapers, and the Sunday supplement of New York's *The Economic Times* carried a favourable report, concluding that he would be 'a natural hit in the USA'. The *New York Times* and the *Washington Post* also gave extremely positive publicity to his appointment.

Karan Singh was also aware that it was not an easy assignment since the whole world was in a churn. Because of *perestroika* and *glasnost* under Mikhail Gorbachev, the USSR was experiencing a revival of nationalist tendencies that had remained dormant during the Soviet Union years, and it was also poised to embrace the liberal values of democracy. The USA was also dealing with the aftermath of the Iranian Revolution, though Ayatollah Khomeini had passed away. The geopolitics of South Asia too had dramatically transformed relationships in the neighbourhood following the Soviet invasion of Afghanistan in 1980, and the USA needed Pakistan far more than it did in normal circumstances. While India supported the Soviet-backed government in Kabul, Pakistan seized the opportunity to offer all logistical support to the anti-communist forces that the USA had marshaled from all over the Islamic world. Thus, in the fight against the Soviets in Afghanistan, Pakistan became an important pivot and also the frontline state. Flush with American funds and arms and its newfound importance in international affairs, it had also diverted those funds towards reviving secessionism in Punjab and Jammu and Kashmir and took full advantage of some of the missteps taken during the last years of Indira Gandhi. The full brunt of those flawed decisions was borne by Rajiv Gandhi's government. With terrorism in Punjab, many Sikh secessionists had sought asylum in the USA and had begun to fund and give direction to the Khalistan movement. Since India had a reputation for sympathy for the Soviets, the Americans had given the leaders of the Khalistan movement a free run under the guise of freedom of speech. Under severe pressure from the anti-Congress forces that had found a cause in the purchase of the Bofors guns from Sweden, Rajiv Gandhi needed fire-fighters on various fronts, with diplomacy in Washington on top of his agenda.

Almost 23 years ago, Karan Singh had wanted to get out of his State and become a diplomat. He had suggested that since the post of High Commissioner to the UK was to fall vacant, he should be considered for the assignment, but the then Prime Minister Lal Bahadur Shastri had declined his request as he thought his services were needed more in J&K than anywhere else. A year later, he had been offered the same position, but by then he had lost interest and moved on, having set his mind upon the hurly-burly of domestic politics. Now, in 1989, when he had resigned himself to other activities, Rajiv Gandhi wanted him to go to Washington as the Ambassador. As the date for Karan Singh's move to the US approached, Rajiv Gandhi asked him to take his collection of bronzes, artifacts, family portraits and valuable curios along with him, as the walls of the Indian Embassy were almost bare and gave a poor impression of India. Since Americans have a fascination for royalty, Karan Singh suggested to the Prime Minister that though he had given up the use of his title of Maharaja, his wife was a Princess from the Rana dynasty of Nepal, therefore, it might be useful if the couple were allowed to be introduced in the US as Dr. Karan

Singh and Princess Yasho Rajya Lakshmi. Rajiv Gandhi too was enthusiastic about the idea and approved the suggestion with a rider that the royal title not be used on National Days. Back in Srinagar, the J&K Government, now headed by Dr Farooq Abdullah, hosted an official reception in the beautiful Emporium Garden, where stood the tall and majestic Chinar trees, and made a graceful speech. Karan Singh responded by quoting the poetry of Mohammad Iqbal and ended with a Sanskrit prayer to Lord Shiva. Before his departure to Washington, he found out that his appointment had not been taken kindly to by the officials of the Foreign Ministry, when, despite his Cabinet rank appointment, Foreign Secretary S.K. Singh gave him a farewell reception along with two other Ambassadors. But Karan Singh chose to ignore this discourtesy as it was not worth making a fuss.

Before leaving, he had a long meeting with Rajiv Gandhi, where Indo-US relations were discussed, and he also gave two important interviews, to Barbara Crossette of the *New York Times* and Steve Coll of the *Washington Post*. Barbara Crossette's interview proved to be an excellent curtain-raiser and was titled 'Philosopher Coming to U.S. as India's Envoy'. It covered half a page and commented appreciatively on his academic and philosophical interests. Rajiv Gandhi also gave him his FAX number so that he could be in direct touch with him, showing that the Prime Minister knew about the non-cooperative attitude of the Foreign Ministry officials.

In Washington, the couple was officially introduced to the President of the USA as Dr. Karan Singh and Princess Yasho Rajya Lakshmi, and while Karan Singh got busy with his work, she set about unpacking and placing portraits, paintings and art objects in their official residence. In the entrance lobby, she put up a full-length portrait of Jawaharlal Nehru, painted by the Karnataka artist N.S. Subbu Krishna, which portrayed the essential Nehru—full of dynamic energy, running down a flight of stairs. Karan Singh and his wife had landed in Washington on the 1st of August, and on the 9th of August, he presented his credentials to President George W. Bush Sr. Before being ushered in the presence of President Bush, they were led to an ante-room where Karan Singh signed the register, in Hindi and English, as was his custom, and added the National motto *Satyamev Jayate*—Truth alone triumphs.

At the Embassy, the portraits of Karan Singh's ancestors in their regalia adorned the walls of the dining room, and when he proudly described each of the portraits, he noticed with delight that the guests were impressed. The walls of the embassy were done over, and just inside the entrance Karan Singh had two masterpieces put up, which would prove to every visitor the centrality of Punjab, particularly the Sikhs, in Indian consciousness. These were paintings by the celebrated Sikh painter Sardar Sobha Singh—one of Guru Nanak, the other of Sohni-Mahiwal, whose eternal love story resonates in every Punjabi heart. To Karan Singh, since the lovers resided on the banks of the Chenab River, they could also be legitimately claimed by the Dogras as their own. The two portraits together sent out a positive message to visitors of Punjabi origin—that in India even non-Sikhs and non-Punjabis shared the ethos of Punjab. The fact that Karan Singh spoke fluent Punjabi also helped a great deal in endearing him to the Punjabis in general and Sikhs in particular.

The Indian Embassy now had a new occupant who brought with him an ambience that it had lacked earlier. In a clear departure from the practice of his predecessor, P.K. Kaul, he immediately stopped the practice of sending sniffer dogs to any place, even private homes, that the Ambassador was due to visit. The interior of the Embassy now announced not only the history of the occupant's royal family, but also gave a glimpse of the rich art and culture of India through the bronzes and artifacts on display. It was a new and energetic beginning that did not go unnoticed in the US press, and it fell in love with the charming 'royal' couple. That Karan Singh was a Rock 'n Roll Fan, and that he had spent a year in America as a patient and remembered his doctors and nurses with gratitude and affection, endeared him even more to the Americans. Almost as soon as he had arrived, he was also being invited as a speaker at various forums, including universities, where he was introduced as a 'philosopher-diplomat', and he took every such opportunity to speak about the richness of Indian culture and philosophy.

He had literally hit the ground running. During the first fifteen days, he had two memorable encounters. The first was his television interview on the Public Broadcasting System (PBS) with the celebrated American journalist and political commentator Morton Kondrache, and the other a private talk with the redoubtable Dr. Henry Kissinger, who visited him at his residence. The PBS interview turned out to be a forty-minute free-for-all where he gave as good as he got, responding to sharp and prejudiced questions about recent events in India and its internal politics and foreign relations. Later, he was told that it had been well circulated among the Indian community. Karan Singh, by his own admission, has always enjoyed the limelight and also public speaking and a good conversation, so he made the most of this encounter. The Kissinger visit turned out to be an eye-opener in some ways as the influential intellectual and former Secretary of State acknowledged India's dominant role in its sphere of influence. He also acknowledged that he admired Indira Gandhi as an able and ruthless protector of India's national interests. But what surprised Karan Singh was that, according to Kissinger, during the East Pakistan crisis of 1971, and months before the creation of Bangladesh, Pakistan's President Yahya

Khan had told the United States that East Bengal would sooner or later emerge as an independent country. According to Kissinger, Yahya Khan had done this so that the US could play a role in the inevitable and manage things in its own favour and its ally Pakistan's, but Indira Gandhi, determined to ward off outside influence in the region, was not prepared to accept the United States as the godfather of the new country. She wanted to play the pivotal role in the birth of a new nation in India's neighbourhood and had therefore not been averse to a full-scale war. Another point of discord between India and the US was that the Nixon Administration had told Indira Gandhi that it could not allow India to attack West Pakistan during that crisis, but she refused to give that assurance. The conversation brought back to Karan Singh the memory of a jubilant Indira Gandhi rushing into the Parliament to announce the surrender of Pakistan to Indian Forces and the birth of a new nation.

Amidst the positive coverage of the new Indian Ambassador was the harsh reality that relations between Washington and Delhi were hardly satisfactory. Because of ideological and economic reasons, relations between the two great democracies of the world had reached rock bottom and just before the arrival of Karan Singh, an Amendment had been introduced in the House of Representatives, aimed at cutting all aid to India on the grounds of human rights violations. Though the Amendment was defeated, yet the narrow margin had come as a rude shock to India. It was obvious to Karan Singh that while Indian influence in Capitol Hill was at its lowest, the Khalistani lobby led by Gurmit Singh Aulakh had succeeded in exerting considerable influence among the Congressmen.

Another matter that needed urgent attention was trade. The USA, driven by its aggressive Trade Representative, Ambassador Carla Hills, known in India as the 'Super 301 lady' for vigorously championing the US Trade law that retaliated against countries the US thought were inimical to its interests, had succeeded in naming India, along with Brazil and Japan, as 'unfair trading partners'. Initially, it was naively thought that India had just been added to make up the numbers, and that Japan was the real target. But it soon emerged that to the USA, the stance of Brazil and India, the largest developing countries of Latin America and Asia, on GATT—the agreement to reduce international barriers on trade—was unacceptable. Karan Singh had detailed discussions with Carla Hills, who questioned the Indian government's role for obstructing rather than encouraging economic growth, while he questioned the absolute value of private enterprise with no social commitment, because that would create the anomalous position of 'a Trump Tower and Harlem side by side'. Privately, however, he believed that since the whole world was coming to terms with the new economic realities, it was time for India also to show some flexibility without sacrificing vital national interests. He also warned Delhi that a continued impasse would damage India's foreign exchange earnings, important sections of industry, as well as bilateral relations with the US.

Around this time, he wrote an article for the *Washington Post,* which was published on the op-ed page with the heading, 'Pay Attention to India'. The same day, the *International Herald Tribune* commissioned an article, which appeared the next morning on its centre page under the heading 'In All, More Than a Billion Democrats'. Karan Singh had decided he would make a clear case for his country forcefully, without being in the least defensive, nor ungracious. He would demand respect respectfully. He wrote:

> Having been at my post as India's Ambassador to the United States for barely a month, I must record some preliminary observations on relations between the world's two largest

democracies so that I can still use the alibi of being a 'newcomer' in case my analysis turns out to be inaccurate. I have phrased them in the manner of four notable truths, not in any spirit of irreverence, but because of my convictions that, on the state of relations between these two countries could well depend the future of democracy itself, especially in the developing world.

The first notable truth is that India is, to put it gently, peripheral to the consciousness of the United States. This is galling to Indians, because we have been brought up in the knowledge that we are one of the two most ancient civilizations in the world; that we have produced some of the greatest philosophers, poets, dramatists, and thinkers in human history; that our monuments are among the most magnificent in the world, and our freedom movement led by Mahatma Gandhi and Jawaharlal Nehru was unique; and that because of the vibrant democracy we have sustained since we became independent in 1947, one-seventh of the human race in the developing world enjoys democratic rights and freedoms. All these statements are true, but even taken together, they are not sufficient to bring India into the soft focus of the American awareness.

The second notable truth is the reason for this curious situation. Put bluntly, it is because India has neither been an ally nor an adversary of the United States, thus fitting neither into the hagiography nor the demonology of a society obsessed until very recently with the Cold Wars and power blocs and dominated by a firmly dichotomous world view. To get America's attention, a country needed to either be an 'enemy' or a 'trusted friend'. Because India has been neither, she doesn't really figure in any major way in the American consciousness except on the far peripheries. Also, with the memory of our unique freedom movement steadily fading despite the great Gandhi film, the younger generation of Americans has not been exposed to major political events in India. Most of the media coverage tends to be rather negative and reinforces well-established, but outdated, stereotypes about India.

The third notable truth is that the reverse of this is not true; America is by no means peripheral as far as India is concerned. Apart from her superpower status, America is the largest foreign investor in India, our largest trading partner, and our largest single source of tourists. We also recall with gratitude Franklin Roosevelt's role in getting the formidable Winston Churchill to take a more reasonable view of India's demand for independence, and, after freedom, the invaluable American food aid during the early drought-ravaged years, and even effective in the long term, the American scientific and technological contributions to our 'green revolution', which now enables India to feed its 800 million people without having to import food grains. The Kennedy years were of particular importance to my generation, and even the sharply divergent political perceptions later have not diminished the importance of America in the Indian mind.

The fourth notable truth is that this lopsided perception between our two countries is no longer acceptable to India. Apart from the factors already mentioned, we are on the threshold of an economic breakthrough and need much closer links with the United States in order finally to overcome the poverty barrier.

We seek not aid but trade, not charity but technology. India today represents one of the great potential markets of the 21st century. Our burgeoning middle class is steadily developing the capacity to absorb American products. We are, under a youthful, technology-oriented prime minister, in the process of liberalizing our foreign investment policies, and we need an adequate response from American entrepreneurs, including the 750,000 American citizens of Indian origin who are making a handsome contribution to their adopted country and can also help in India's economic growth.

> The present situation, in fact, represents an unprecedented opportunity for breaking the indifference factor and bringing India into prominent focus in the United States. With its shared ideals and commitment to democratic values and institutions, India can become a major partner with the United States in the quest for peace, stability, and economic growth on this planet... America has to be more clearly aware of India's tremendous potential as the most populous democracy on earth.

The argument and eloquence of the new Ambassador was persuasive, and even Carla Hills came to appreciate India's compulsions in not wholly embracing the economy driven by markets. India was, for the time being, off the hook of the threat of sanctions.

Amidst all this, Asha had returned to India as their youngest daughter-in-law was expecting. She gave birth to a baby girl on 19th September. It was a happy time, and for Karan Singh personally, a satisfying one as he had begun to enjoy meeting the challenges of his role and was encouraged by the response that he was getting from the American leaders, public, and especially intellectuals. This, however, had not made him lose sight of his heartfelt ambition to build a majestic Shiva Temple of the dancing Nataraj in the US, and he imagined that it would be on a height that commanded a panoramic view. He had shared his heart's desire with one of his American friends, Bill Gilkey, with whom he got acquainted in New Delhi when he was posted in the American Embassy. Bill Gilkey was a remarkable person with an extraordinary ability to read the events to come by the casting of the I Ching, an ancient Chinese divination text. By the year 1988, the idea of a Shiva Temple in the USA had grown, and Bill, who had by then settled in Japan but was in regular touch with Karan Singh, held out the hope of having such a temple on the Eastern Coast, on a commanding site. He wrote, 'The only part of the US the I Ching liked was the Eastern part of the US…I am not even sure that it means the East is where the temple should be located. But what it does indicate is where the search, the first inquiries, should begin. And that is somewhere in the Washington, DC, Virginia, Delaware, and Maryland area.' He went on to explain, 'The readings (of I Ching) described a sort of Chinese tower on a hilltop that commanded a wide view of the countryside and at the same time could be looked up to by everyone in the surrounding area. From this tower emanates a hidden spiritual power, influencing and dominating people without their being able to understand what is happening. I cannot be sure that this tower is Lord Shiva's temple itself, or whether it is such a place where you might find someone whose power could be of use to you.'

On 23rd September, after lunch, Karan Singh decided to drive down to Swami Satchidanand's Ashram in Yogaville, located on a 700-acre farm in Buckingham County, Virginia. He had known the Swami for years and had also read his literature, but had not visited him. Apart from taking classical Yoga to the West, he was a pioneer of interfaith dialogue and had built an extraordinary community of Western Hindus in Yogaville. Karan Singh was impressed by the community, more so by the LOTUS (Light of Truth Universal Shrine) Temple, a marvel of engineering with the structure designed in the form of a huge lotus. The Interfaith temple, Karan Singh felt, represented in tangible terms the great Vedantic insight that the truth is one, although it may be expressed in many ways. As Swamiji took him around the vast estate, they reached the hill opposite where a new pavilion was being constructed, and it suddenly struck Karan Singh that it was an ideal place to have his Shiva Temple. For years, a seven-foot bronze Nataraj had been with him, but he had not been able to find an ideal place for its installation. It struck him that the hilltop was the place he often visualized, and he found Swamiji as enthusiastic about the idea as he was. It had been almost nine months since Bill Gilkey had mentioned Virginia as one of the sites, as well as finding a person whose energy would be useful in getting the Temple built.

Often, when Karan Singh looks back at his brief sojourn as Ambassador, seven months to be precise, he also remembers that when he had come to the US the first time, on 31 December 1947, he had stayed for thirteen months, which seemed like an eternity as he spent much of his time on a hospital bed. In contrast, the ambassadorial term seemed like a fleeting moment in time, although a great deal had been achieved during this period, not least the fruition of his desire to have a Shiva Temple in the West. After having identified and discussed the idea and the location with Swami Satchidananda, the idea firmed up, and even as India went to the polls in late November, Karan Singh decided to visit Yogaville again. This time, he was accompanied by his wife Asha and the architect Jonathan Isleib, and by chance, Juliet Hollister, the dynamic lady who had founded the Temple of Understanding. All of them were of the unanimous view that the location was ideal.

In India, the election results were not good for Rajiv Gandhi and the Congress, and as later events proved, they were equally bad for the country. Being a political appointee, Karan Singh resigned, though in not very graceful circumstances created by the new dispensation. Away from the huffing and puffing of political moves, the plans for the Nataraja Temple proceeded as planned. Swami Satchidananda had chosen the 10th of March 1990, a day of the full moon, as the day of the ground-breaking ceremony. At the auspicious hour, the ceremony began at the chosen site on the hilltop, which had been cleared. For the actual foundation-laying ceremony, Swamiji had collected hundreds of crystals of varying sizes, and beginning with Swamiji, Asha and Karan Singh, every person in the Ashram, including the children who had gathered, put one of them in the foundation. As planned, the Temple was to be built in alignment with the Lotus Temple and the pavilion below. It was decided that it be called the Paschim Kailash, or the Western Kailash, after the famous Mount in the Himalayas, which traditionally is believed to be the permanent abode of Lord Shiva. In the meantime, Karan Singh made arrangements for having the majestic seven-foot Nataraj bronze shipped over from New Delhi. After an enjoyable cultural evening, Swamiji drove them up to the site once again and they saw the Lotus, which looked like a glowing jewel of rare beauty. For Karan Singh, it was an unforgettable day as he saw the beginning of a long-cherished desire begin to get fulfilled.

His time in the USA had come to an end, and in a few days, he was to return home. He could not help but ruminate over the past few months to find some hidden design of destiny that had brought him to the US. The more he thought, the more he was convinced that since his ambassadorial role had been cut short, even before he could bring about tangible changes in the Indo-US relationship, therefore, the only meaningful purpose of his coming to the US was to be an instrument in the building of the Shiva Temple. Paschim Kailash.

27

The Mandate of '89 and After

RAJIV GANDHI HAD BEEN hopeful of returning to power after the 1989 elections, probably with a reduced majority, and he had elaborate plans about how the country was to be steered during his second term. He was a modern, forward-looking leader who was aware that many of the political shibboleths of the past decades had to be jettisoned if India was to be part of the development story of the approaching twenty-first century. The fact of a unipolar world after the demise of the USSR could also not be ignored. Midway through his first term, Rajiv Gandhi had lost his core team of 1984, and with internal betrayals and the scandal of the Bofors gun purchase unfolding, he was certain to lose the massive mandate he had won in 1984. However, he remained hopeful of being voted for a second term, and Karan Singh was part of his plan to improve the relationship with the USA during that period.

However, the reports coming from India were not very optimistic. Karan Singh's elder son Vikram (Vikramaditya) predicted about 200 seats, well short of the simple majority; the more hopeful estimated enough seats to form a government.

Those who came from India to Washington or New York had the same assessment. In no position to contradict the reports, Karan Singh prepared himself for an early return to Delhi.

The four effective months of Karan Singh's tenure had barely made the US sit up and look at India anew. He, too, had understood the magnitude of the challenge posed by the 'Super 301' list and knew that without India getting off it, the development story of India would get a serious setback. It was a 1974 Act, later strengthened by the Omnibus Trade and Competitiveness Act, 1988, that empowers the US Trade Representative (USTR) to investigate and retaliate against foreign countries accused of unfair trade practices that burden US trade and commerce. If the US chose to act against India, then it could be crippling for the fledgling Indian economy. Karan Singh was confident that given some more time, he could make a positive contribution and bring the two countries closer. While the reports he was getting all suggested that the Congress would fail to get a majority in the Lok Sabha, it was difficult to visualize how the coming together of various opposition parties would form a government. Therefore, he hoped that the Congress would form the next government, albeit with a reduced majority.

The election results belied this hope. The results threw up a very complex picture in which the Congress had emerged as the largest single party, but well short of the halfway mark, and the National Front, even with its poll ally, the BJP, would not be able to form a majority government. The day the results were announced, Karan Singh went to the studio of the Discovery Channel of Monitor Television, where in response to a question he said that since the Congress had been defeated in the north where it had been in power but had wrested the South where the oppositions parties had been in power, it appeared that the results were essentially anti-establishment. He was also asked if he thought that Rajiv Gandhi would retire from politics, and he replied in the negative and added that he was a young man with many more active years ahead of him. Later, he was told that the statement was interpreted as partisan to Rajiv Gandhi.

The very next day, India entered a strange phase of politics. Although the Congress had emerged as the largest single political party, Rajiv Gandhi decided not to stake a claim to government formation. But a strange scenario emerged when the Janata Dal was given outside support by the BJP and CPI(M) (Communist Party of India, Marxist)—that constituted two extreme ends of the political ideology spectrum. After the defeat, Rajiv Gandhi had made a very graceful television speech, which Karan Singh heard as his eldest son, Vikram, had called him from India and held the receiver of the phone close to the television. After listening to the speech, Karan Singh wrote a personal letter to Rajiv Gandhi expressing concern over the disturbing development, and concluded by saying: 'As Panditji and Indira both showed, courage in the face of adversity is a rare quality. You have this fine heritage, and are still young with several decades of political activity ahead. Reverses often give us valuable strength and resilience to grow inwardly regardless of outer circumstances. Please continue to look upon me as a family friend, and let me know if there is anything I can do from here.'

Even before these developments had taken place, Karan Singh, in consultation with his wife, had decided that if the Janata Dal gained an absolute majority, he, being a political appointee, would resign. But a peculiar situation had arisen with the Janata Dal securing only 143 seats in a House of 525. Consequently, the President had given a month to V.P. Singh, the leader of the unlikely coalition, to prove his majority on the floor of the House. Given this, Karan Singh decided to wait for a month and to personally hand over his resignation to the Prime Minister if he proved his majority. He felt that the new government had come with three distinct disadvantages. The first, of course, was the inability to secure a clear mandate. The National Front had barely secured 25 percent of the Lok Sabha seats and less than 20 percent of the popular vote. The second was that the manner in which the Leader of the House had been elected did not inspire confidence, since it had been a cloak-and-dagger affair, with V.P. Singh and Devi Lal combining to hoodwink another prime ministerial candidate, Chandrashekhar, who had been double-crossed. The whole farce of the election of the Leader of the House was shown by *Newstrack*, and the whole country saw the anger on the face of Chandrashekhar when he realized the result of the intrigue masterminded by the supporters of V.P. Singh. It reminded Karan Singh of the manner in which the first anti-Congress coalition of 1977 had avoided a democratic way of electing its leader. The third negative was that the minority government was supported by the BJP and CPI(M), which vehemently differed in their approach to the whole political agenda. This meant that the government would be ineffective and unstable. In the circumstances, one would think that such a government would not undertake a major reshuffle among the diplomats. After all, no one knew how long the government would last, and diplomacy could not be disrupted for short durations when the government changed. Karan Singh, though, had sought a meeting with the Prime Minister for two reasons. He wanted to find out what Prime Minister V.P. Singh wanted, and in case he felt that he did not enjoy the confidence of the PM, then hand him his resignation letter. He had been appointed ambassador by a Prime Minister with a personal rank of a cabinet minister, and, therefore, he did not think it right to go through the Foreign Minister, the usual route for career diplomats. Since there was no word from V.P. Singh's office, he had, in the meantime, spoken to Rajiv Gandhi, who had, in the first place, appointed him, for advice. He was ready to resign, but Rajiv Gandhi said that he had been getting very positive and good reports about his work in the US, and that he should continue in his post if the new government asked him to.

Later that December, Dr. Farooq Abdullah, still the Chief Minister of Jammu and Kashmir, checked into the Medical Centre, Houston, for a check-up, and before he was to fly back to India, Karan Singh invited him to the Chancery. He was to learn later that Mufti Mohammad Sayeed, Farooq Abdullah's political rival in J&K, who was Home Minister in the new government at the Centre, had probably not liked this small courtesy extended to a sitting Chief Minister whom the Ambassador had known for decades. Karan Singh was still in the USA when the news of the abduction of Mufti Mohammad Sayeed's daughter, Dr. Rubaiya Sayeed, was broken. Mufti Mohammad Sayeed, from South Kashmir, had been appointed as the Home Minister in what was considered by many observers a radical move by V.P. Singh. It was much appreciated and lauded by many observers as it was intended to instil confidence among the minorities, particularly after the decade of the eighties, which had been troubled by anti-Muslim communal strife in the country. It was also believed that the Mufti being a Kashmiri, the move would counter the influence of secessionist elements in the Valley. But the hope was shattered, as within days the Mufti's daughter had been taken hostage by the extremists of the Jammu and Kashmir Liberation Front (JKLF), who wanted five hardcore terrorists released in exchange for her freedom. It was clear to Karan Singh that a grim chapter was about to be added to the long and complex history of the State.

Farooq Abdullah, who had rushed back to India to face the difficult challenge, was convinced that the abduction of a girl was such an abhorrent deed in Kashmiri society that the societal pressure would force her abductors to release her, and therefore he was opposed to the release of terrorists in exchange for her freedom. However, with Delhi mounting pressure on him, Farooq finally met the demands of the terrorists. But he was not happy. When Karan Singh spoke to Farooq shortly after this surrender to the militants, in the course of the conversation Abdullah told him that he had spoken with Rajiv Gandhi, with the Foreign Minister I.K. Gujral, and Prime Minister V.P. Singh, and they all felt that he should continue as the Ambassador. Yet, far from granting Karan Singh an interview when he visited Delhi, the Prime Minister kept him waiting without a response. The meeting with I.K. Gujral came as a rude shock. Gujral had known him for years, and Karan Singh thought of him as a personal friend, so the lack of warmth and the perfunctory greetings came as unpleasant surprise. The few comments that he made were negative, and the meeting ended with Karan Singh insisting that he would take a final call after meeting the Prime Minister. Then he sought an appointment with the Deputy Prime Minister, Chaudhary Devi Lal, who invited him for dinner at Haryana Bhawan. He was aware that the Deputy PM had been pressing for a change of ambassadors to major countries, but during the conversation, Devi Lal gave no hint of this. Later, *Sunday* magazine ran a column that Karan Singh's meeting with Rajiv Gandhi was the main reason why he was not asked to continue as the Ambassador.

Karan Singh was scheduled to leave for Moscow on 13th of January to take part in the Global Conference on Environment and Development for Survival, and in the absence of a meeting with the Prime Minister, there was no clarity about his future course of action. On the 10th of January, he called upon the Home Minister in his office. It was a sobering experience to see Mufti Mohammad Sayeed, who had capitulated so tamely to an ant-India militant outfit, occupying Sardar Patel's chair. They discussed Kashmir, and Sayeed's view was that the internal administration of the Valley had completely collapsed, and that law and order could only be restored through Governor's rule. Only after that could long-range political thinking take place. Meanwhile, the Government of India was dropping broad hints through news reports that claimed that all political appointees to diplomatic posts had offered to resign. But Karan Singh still waited for a meeting with the Prime Minister. Just before he departed for Moscow, he had a meeting with Gujral again, where Gujral reiterated the view that political appointees should automatically resign when the government changed, and that an ambassador must have a personal rapport with the Prime Minister. Karan Singh replied that it was precisely to find out if he could have a personal rapport with V.P. Singh, that he had been pressing for a meeting. It was then that Gujral told him that perhaps the Prime Minister did not want to see him since he had not given him any time. He added that Karan Singh's meeting with Rajiv Gandhi had been an irritation, to which Karan Singh reacted indignantly since, apart from being the serving Ambassador to the most powerful country in the world, he had a political and social status of his own in India. He had a personal relationship with Rajiv Gandhi and he did not feel he had to seek the government's permission to meet him. Besides, he added, he considered the Prime Minister's behaviour discourteous. Then he told Gujral that he would send his letter of resignation the next day.

At that point, Gujral said that as he was the Foreign Minister, the letter should be addressed to him, adding that, in any case, he would be responding to that letter, no matter where he sent it. Karan Singh politely declined, saying, as long as he was holding office, he would correspond only with the Prime Minister and not the Foreign Minister. The next morning, he sent his resignation letter to the Prime Minister's House. The text was as follows:

'In the few months since I presented my credentials to President Bush on the 14th August 1989, I took a number of steps to strengthen Indo-US ties, including establishing high-level contacts with the Administration, the Senate, and the House of Representatives; meeting with leading intellectuals and academicians; visiting important States, and interacting extensively with various sections of the Indian-American community and leaders of corporate America; speaking at several universities and scholarly institutions; and developing a high profile presence. I am happy that these measures have already begun to have a positive impact on the whole complex spectrum of relations between the two greatest democracies in the world.'

Later, before returning to the USA via Moscow to pack up and hand over charge to the person who would succeed him as Ambassador, Karan Singh and his wife called upon Rajiv Gandhi, who was astonished by the attitude of the new government, and remarked that if Karan Singh wanted to return to Parliament, there was a seat in the Rajya Sabha from Jammu and Kashmir. Karan Singh thanked him, but said that in his assessment, the State Assembly would have been dissolved by the time the election for the Rajya Sabha fell due. Members for the Rajya Sabha were elected by the members of the respective State Legislatures, and he was certain that the Farooq Abdullah government would not run its full term. Rajiv Gandhi also expressed concern over the Punjab situation, and presciently expressed deeper concern for developments with the Liberation of Tamil Tiger Eelam (LTTE) as he feared that it could result in increased LTTE activity in Tamil Nadu.

On 13th January, the day of Lohri, the seasonal festival of North India marking the peak of winter, Karan Singh left for

Moscow, and addressed the Global Forum on Environment and Development for Survival conference. During his Moscow visit he noticed that, notwithstanding the popularity and success of Gorbachev abroad, in his homeland, the picture was grim, and his position was uncertain. The glittering shops were largely empty, and a violent civil war was raging between Muslim Azerbaijan and Christian Armenia, and the Baltic republics of the USSR were threatening to secede. From Gorbachev's point of view, what he was trying to do was to bring about a shift that was as monumental as the October Revolution. One economic and political model was being sought to be replaced with another, with the outcome being extremely uncertain. Gorbachev addressed the conference on the concluding day and mentioned humanist values rather than religion, and he acknowledged that the importance of ecology had been understood and that it was only through international efforts that a tragedy could be averted. After his speech, he was mobbed by the delegates, and to his huge disappointment, Karan Singh could not approach him. This encounter brought back nostalgic memories of Secretary General Khruschev holding an exclusive dinner for him and his wife thirty years ago.

While he was in Moscow, his wife informed him that Jagmohan had been appointed Governor of Jammu and Kashmir, and Dr. Farooq Abdullah had resigned because he had not been consulted. Karan Singh found it amazing that some other Governors had also been removed and new ones appointed. Many new ambassadors, too, had been appointed, and he wondered what would happen if a government that was inherently unstable and standing with the support of two political parties that were ideologically opposed to each other, fell within a year or so? Would all the new appointees be asked to resign all over again by the government that would follow? India had entered an uncharted territory where the exercise of power seemed to be the be all and end all. He was certain that the consequences of Jagmohan's appointment and Farooq Abdullah's resignation would be unfortunate.

A happy outcome of the Moscow visit was a meeting with Swami Sivaya Subramuniya, who had an ashram on the Island of Kauai, in Hawaii, where he had built a beautiful Nataraja Temple, way back in 1985. On that occasion, the Swami had given Karan Singh a metal bracelet inscribed with the Sanskrit mantra AUM NAMAH SHIVAYA, which he has worn ever since. As far as the conference went, Karan Singh found the experience much more rewarding than the earlier conferences, where he usually participated for a day and confined himself to making his speech. He found that full participation gave a much deeper exposure to the varied intellectual and personal chemistry involved in such meetings. He also noticed that there had been a dramatic increase in the level of awareness regarding environmental problems over the last decade, and the Moscow conference was an important symbol of this.

By the time Karan Singh arrived in Washington, the news of his resignation had been widely reported in India and Washington, and he found himself deluged with letters from the Indian-American community and American friends, expressing their shock and disappointment. The news from his home state was becoming increasingly alarming, and he wanted to make a statement, but held himself back as he was still officially the Ambassador. On 25th of January, he addressed the Women's National Democratic Club on Human Destiny in the Nuclear Age. Seated at the main table was Mary McGory, the eminent *Washington Post* columnist who had known every Indian Ambassador of the past three decades. She wrote a column, 'America's China Syndrome', which was carried by the *Post* on 28th January. Two paragraphs went like this:

> Karan Singh is the most glaring example of New Delhi's weakness for human chess. He has been here exactly five months. He has already been yanked, a casualty of democratic practices. Last December, Indian voters threw out Rajiv Gandhi, and the new crowd apparently cannot wait to get its man in place—or, at least, to get Karan Singh out. It's strange because it is hard to see how they could find anyone more representative of the old India and the new: son of a maharajah (of Jammu and Kashmir), and an alumnus of the Indira Gandhi cabinet; and a linguist, scholar, philosopher, author, composer and a fan of hard rock. What could they be looking for? His wife is a Nepalese Princess who heads an organization for the mentally [challenged].
>
> Singh would not disgrace them if they gave him enough time to do his packing and say his farewells. He went to the Women's National Democratic Club on Thursday and gave a speech on global citizenship and dazzled the audience. He quoted Robert Frost and Bhagavat Gita and closed with a prayer in Sanskrit.'

Karan Singh decided that instead of waiting in Washington for Delhi to accept his resignation, he would continue with his engagements, and in the process had a very rewarding time in which he gave speeches on subjects ranging from Hinduism to Indo-US relations in different cities, mainly at universities. When he and Asha were in Boston, visiting two great institutions of learning—MIT and Harvard—they met the reclusive Nobel Laureate Dr. Hargobind Khurana. They also met Harvard University President Derek Bok, who was married to the daughter of Gunnar and Alva Myrdal, the Nobel Laureate couple whom Karan Singh and Asha had known in their New Delhi days. During that meeting, they were joined by Dr. Diana Eck, the celebrated author of *Banaras, City of Light* and *Encountering God.* Since she was Professor of Comparative Religion and Indian

Studies, a lively discussion ensued that made Bok say that if Karan Singh wanted to return to the US, he would be happy to explore possibilities of a suitable position at Harvard University!

Later, Diana Eck hosted a lunch of Sanskritists and Asian scholars where Karan Singh spoke of the richness of Indian cultural traditions, concluding with a Sanskrit prayer. His lecture at Harvard University was on 'Four Decades of Indian Democracy'. Returning to New York, he inaugurated a fabulous exhibition of Pala Art (8th to 12th century) from India, Nepal, Tibet and Indonesia, which was titled 'Leaves from the Bodhi Tree'. The audience was led by Senator Paul Sarbanes in a packed auditorium, and Karan Singh spoke about art, its multi-splendored manifestations, and its deeper significance. Thus, his interaction with some of the brilliant minds of the US continued, but in the process, old friends also came out to revive memories. Among them were Prof. Stanislav Grof and his equally brilliant wife, Christina Grof. Clovis Maksoud and his wife Ava, too, were in the US. Since Maksoud, with his weight, was always a candidate for a cardiac problem, he had recently undergone an operation. Karan Singh and Asha went to see him and found him as lively as ever.

It had been almost a month since Karan Singh had tendered his resignation, but there was still no response from Delhi, and, therefore, he continued to perform the duties of an ambassador. He had taken a ten-day rewarding tour that took him and his wife across America thousands of miles by air, but gave immense satisfaction since he delivered a speech wherever he was. They were in Dallas on the 11th of February when they saw on television the release of Nelson Mandela after 27 years of incarceration. It was a monumental day to remember as it marked the turning of a new page in modern history when De Klerk, the leader of apartheid South Africa and its President, proved to be a bold and imaginative leader. Globally, humanity was passing through a period of monumental changes, as De Klerk was the second person after Gorbachev to be striving to replace one set of ideals with another. Seeing Mandela on television taking his first steps as a free man was a moving experience; it also marked the culmination of the long and arduous fight against apartheid, in which Mahatma Gandhi had also played a significant role.

By this time, the Kashmir situation had blown up, and the migration of the Kashmiri Pandits, which started as a trickle, had grown into a mass exodus for which the State government was not prepared. The Kashmiris residing in the US were becoming restive, and Pakistan had become aggressive in its diplomatic moves. But since Karan Singh had still not heard anything from Delhi and had no mandate to respond to the challenges this posed, he wrote to Gujral, telling him clearly that he would be returning by the middle of March. Rumours were afloat that his resignation was not being accepted, but Karan Singh knew that the delay was because there were plans afoot to hold fresh elections to the J&K State Assembly, and the government did not want him to come back and canvass support for the Congress Party. On the 20th of February, the Chancery of the Indian Embassy held an internal political meeting and discussed Kashmir. Karan Singh expressed the opinion that India could not say that there was nothing to discuss about Kashmir, as under the Shimla Agreement, India was committed to bilateral discussions with Pakistan on all issues, including 'a final settlement of Jammu and Kashmir'. There was, therefore, a contradiction in India's stand if it said that there was nothing to discuss. Karan Singh felt that the new government did not truly understand the complexities of the Kashmir issue, and that there was considerable confusion in the handling of the State. This was subsequently proved, as the troika of Mufti Sayeed, George Fernandes and Jagmohan began pulling in different directions. Karan Singh wanted to engage in aggressive diplomacy as an ambassador, but in the prevailing atmosphere, he could do so only if specifically asked to do so. But Delhi maintained an enigmatic and frustrating silence.

His tenure had been so brief and hectic that he had not been able to get any of his children to Washington, though under the rules it was permissible. Only the younger sister of his wife visited them in the US during that period. It was March, the month of his birth, when all the packing was done, and Asha and he prepared to return. One of the last items he packed was a pistol of non-prohibited bore he bought. At the Delhi airport, all his luggage was cleared, but the pistol was withheld. He was told by the customs officials that after getting routine clearance from the Home Ministry, it would be delivered to his residence. Like V.P. Singh, Mufti Mohammad Sayeed, who was Home Minister, had also been a member of the Congress party for much of his life and had known Karan Singh well, so what followed came as a rude shock to Karan Singh. The Home Ministry declined his request to clear the pistol, and he was forced to return it at a considerable loss. It was beyond reason and imagination that a former Head of State, Cabinet Minister, and outgoing Ambassador to the most important country in the world would be subjected to such treatment.

It was later that an intelligent guess could be made as to why that inexplicable denial had happened. During the Bofors controversy, the non-Congress parties had accused Rajiv Gandhi of having foreign accounts and because of the toxic atmosphere that had been created, the Rajiv Gandhi government found it very hard to refute the allegations, but a plan was hatched, probably under the direction of the then Foreign Minister Narasimha Rao, to counter the accusations. Under the plan, some office bearers of the Indian Overseas Congress, based in New York, made a counter-allegation that V.P. Singh's son, who was then in the USA, had a secret bank account in St. Kitts, the Caribbean tax haven. Following this, a letter was addressed to Karan Singh by one Ramesh Ravela on 30 October 1989, in which certain allegations regarding the St Kitts affair were made against the Consul General in New York. This was forwarded to the Consul General, Ranjit Rai, for his comments, who said that the allegation against him had no substance. The matter had rested there until 30th January 1990, when Ramesh Ravela and a few other people of Indian origin sent Karan Singh a petition, with copies to Prime Minister V.P. Singh and Foreign Minister I.K. Gujral. Their statement to the press contained, among other statements, the following lines: 'Ambassador Dr. Karan Singh, through his intellectual honesty and dedication to the values of freedom and democracy, won the hearts and minds of all Americans and Indians, and we regret the fact that he has resigned from his position. But [we] must also point out that the alleged abuse of the rights of a citizen took place during Dr. Karan Singh's term as Ambassador and that his office has repeatedly ignored our inquiries into the matter.' The reference was to the St. Kitts affair in which allegations had been made against V.P. Singh's son. Karan Singh realized that an undesirable attempt had been made to hit below the belt by using the Chancery, and he had sent all the papers to Delhi. In due course, V.P. Singh, in all probability, was convinced that the St. Kitts allegations could not have happened without the knowledge of the Ambassador. Apart from this, there is no other explanation for why a Prime Minister would not continue with the services of a person who, from all accounts, was serving the country well.

When V.P. Singh became the Prime Minister, an inquiry had been launched about the St. Kitts accounts in which Ranjit Rai, the Consul General, deposed that Narasimha Rao had specifically told him that Ambassador Karan Singh should not come to know who was involved in accusing V.P. Singh's son of wrongdoings. In the end, Karan Singh came out unscathed, but it reflected poorly on V.P. Singh's government that used power to settle personal scores in a petty manner, by denying permission to import a small personal weapon. It is ironic that V.P. Singh's government did not last long and became a victim of the political ambitions of leaders who could not see beyond their interests. To Karan Singh's satisfaction, within a couple of years of his return, the financial mess in which India found itself forced it to rethink its approach to its relationship with the US, including trade and tariff-related matters.

28

New Directions, Old Concerns

When Karan Singh returned from Washington in March of 1990, the Valley was already in flames. The process that had begun with the return of Sheikh Abdullah in 1975 had finally spun out of control. Neither Sheikh Abdullah nor his successor, his son Farooq Abdullah, nor the Government of India had a fair policy as they oscillated between appeasement and a hard line. Sheikh Abdullah's return had been generally welcomed in Kashmir, but it had deprived a section of the Kashmiri youth of a hero who was willing to make sacrifices, much like Omar al-Mukhtar of Libya, to redeem a promise that he had made to his people. When out of power, he had promised to give his people an almost independent Kashmir. Unrealistically, he had promised to roll back all the changes in the constitution and administrative setup and make a fresh start from the time when he was removed from office in 1953. But now he had eaten the proverbial humble pie and accepted the terms set by Indira Gandhi. He had to remain satisfied with becoming one of the several Chief Ministers of the Indian Union. For the youth, this had amounted to betrayal.

Another faultline in the State was Kashmir's, particularly Sheikh Abdullah's, relationship with the Dogras. All his life, he had thrived on anti-Dogra rhetoric and had used it whenever he had felt that he needed to rally his support base in Kashmir. Moreover, he was also under pressure to prove that he had an identity independent of the Government of India, and this led him to periodically raise the political temperature by warning of a massive revolt in the Valley if the matter of full accession of J&K to the Indian Union was even mentioned, leave alone discussed. Before his return to power in 1975, he had twice called upon Karan Singh, and on both occasions, it had been made clear to him that certain subjects had become integral to the consciousness of Indians of every state, and they could neither be diluted nor challenged. Secularism and integration of the State were two such subjects. Probably, the Sheikh believed that as he had manipulated Jawaharlal Nehru, he could replicate that success with Indira Gandhi. But he forgot that the circumstances had changed; India was no longer a country that was reeling in the aftermath of Partition and the attendant violence, and the challenge to feed its people amidst shortages of foodgrains. During Indira Gandhi's time, a bold and confident India had emerged—as the world saw in 1971, when it successfully ignored pressure from the USA and took the Indo-Pak conflict over East Bengal refugees to its logical conclusion, the dismemberment of Pakistan.

Karan Singh had impressed upon Sheikh Abdullah on every possible occasion to appreciate the changed circumstance, the earliest being in 1968. Karan Singh had stressed that even if the status quo regarding the special status of the State was not very satisfactory, 'Kashmir was a part of India', and no action to change this status could be taken without convincing the people of India. He had further pointed out that 'for two decades our official policy has been an increasingly closer integration between Kashmir and the rest of India, and a whole generation of Indians has grown up to accept this premise. Any reversal would, therefore, require the most delicate handling of public opinion in and outside Parliament.' Karan Singh had seen with dismay that even after the Parthasarathy-Beg agreement and the Sheikh continued to play the politics of polarization between Hindus and Muslims, in addition to packing the government with his relatives, and periodically breaking into a tirade against the Centre. As a consequence, when he died, he left behind a legacy of a polarized society and a weak, corrupt and inefficient administration for his son. The most contentious legacy that he left behind was the Jammu and Kashmir Resettlement Act, 1982, which allowed those who had migrated to Pakistan before 1954 to return and reclaim their lands. Since these migrations had mostly taken place in Jammu, the implementation of the Act would have had the most significant impact there.

When the Jammu and Kashmir Resettlement Bill was first introduced in the J&K Legislature by a member of the National Conference, Karan Singh was in the Parliament, and he had made a long statement to point out that the Bill would effectively mean giving Indian citizenship to people who had migrated to Pakistan at the time of Partition. This, he had argued, was the domain of the Parliament, and the Bill was an inroad into the sovereign right of the Parliament to legislate on this matter. Apart from the legality of the attempt, it had grave political and security implications. When the Bill was passed by the legislature, the Governor withheld assent, and Sheikh Abdullah furiously criticised the critics of the Bill in Jammu as 'Hindu communalists', and expressed deep anger at the delay in the Governor's assent. He delivered a speech at Hazratbal after the Friday prayers, on 28th May 1982, during which he declared that his party was committed to undoing all the laws that were extended to the state after 1953, as they lacked popular support. Karan Singh had warned Indira Gandhi that this rhetoric was likely to intensify the sense of insecurity that was being felt by the minority community in the Valley. But the Bill was passed and became an Act. Fortunately, it was immediately challenged in the Supreme Court and pending a decision, was never enforced, till it was repealed in 2019.

Meanwhile, a new wave of politics had emerged after the debacle of the Congress in the 1977 general elections, and the subsequent booting out of the alternative to Congress, the Janata Party, in 1980. This, however, had given rise to the politics of change through the ballot that made the National Conference leaders realize that the Congress was not the only political party that it had to deal with, and that it had to be ready to build an understanding with other parties that were opposed to the Congress. Thus began a dangerous game between the Congress and the National Conference to control the state of J&K by any means. While the National Conference polarized the Muslims, the Congress took recourse to speaking mainly for the interests of the Jammu region and the Hindus, in addition to using the Constitution to destabilize the state government. When Sheikh Abdullah passed away, he left for his son Farooq a state to govern with the tools of a weak and corrupt administration, a divided polity and opportunistic politicians. It was also a period when militancy and secessionist elements in Punjab, too, had become active, and displaying a serious lapse in judgement, Farooq Abdullah thought that the situation provided him with an opportunity to arm-twist the Government of India. But Prime Minister Indira Gandhi, worried over the possibility of the militants of the two states joining hands and getting support from Pakistan, was equally determined not to allow that to happen, and therefore, decided to oust Farooq Abdullah from power. Accordingly, Governor B.K. Nehru was replaced by Jagmohan, who was known for his ability to overzealously carry out the tasks set for him. A new low in politics was touched when, soon after arriving in Srinagar as Governor of the State, Jagmohan triggered a defection in the National Conference to oust Farooq Abdullah from power.

Hard and ruthless politics for wielding political power had replaced a sensible and pragmatic approach to a state that was sensitively placed in geography and had a complex history and equally complex and competing aspirations. The tug of war between the Centre and the state resulted in the gradual erosion of administrative integrity, and the state appeared to be waiting for something critical to happen. Ghulam Mohammad 'Gul' Shah, the leader of the defectors and the son-in-law of Sheikh Abdullah, succeeded Dr Farooq Abdullah only to lead the state on a disastrous path. Curfew became the norm during his two-year rule, earning him the sobriquet 'Curfew Shah'. Finally, the Congress saw the folly of its misadventure of installing an incompetent leader, and withdrew support to pave the way for Governor's rule.

In Jammu, meanwhile, there was a significant development. The management of the Vaishno Devi Shrine was taken over by the government-constituted Shri Mata Vaishno Devi Shrine Board in 1986 through an act of legislation. This was considered a setback for Karan Singh as until then it was run by the Dharmarth Trust, of which he was the sole Trustee. The move was opposed not only by Karan Singh but also by the hereditary priests of the Shrine, called *baridars*, and challenged in court on the ground that the state had selectively targeted Hindu religious institutions in violation of their rights to manage their own religious affairs. Karan Singh was hurt by the move as it was a family Trust established in 1846 by the founding ruler of his dynasty for the purpose of managing Temples in Jammu and Kashmir. However, it was also true that in recent years, the number of pilgrims to the Vaishno Devi Shrine had seen phenomenal growth, which the management was not equipped to manage efficiently. Soon after the takeover, Karan Singh saw for himself the improvement in the facilities for the pilgrims, and he realized that the pilgrimage had become too big for the Trust to manage efficiently. He, therefore, withdrew his suit in the larger interest.

Meanwhile, in the time that Jagmohan was Governor, fundamentalists had begun to gain ground in the state, but unfortunately, no one paid any attention. Taking advantage of the rise of such forces, Pakistan stepped up its support to the separatists in the Valley. Thus, the fundamentalists joined hands with the separatists, and soon the combination assumed threatening proportions. In a serious error of judgment, Rajiv Gandhi and Farooq Abdullah formed a coalition to contest the elections, and they carved the state between them, leaving no space for other political parties. In their misplaced judgment, they had hoped that their alliance would eliminate both the communal forces of Jammu and Kashmir, namely, the BJP in Jammu and the Jamaat-i-Islami, which had formed the Muslim United Front (MUF) with other like-minded political parties, in Kashmir. The election results showed that the National Conference and Congress combined could muster only 53 per cent of the popular votes but had cornered 87 per cent of the seats. But the threat to the social fabric of Kashmir was visible to the discerning eye as the MUF had polled 31 per cent of the votes, though it could win only 4 seats. In the Hindu-dominated Jammu region, the BJP could win only 2 seats. This situation had left the extremists in both the communities dissatisfied, but while the BJP waited for its time, the Muslim youth of Kashmir were restive since they were now even more convinced that there was no hope for them in electoral democracy.

By the middle of 1989, a mood of drift had set in Delhi since the general elections to the Lok Sabha were round the corner, and probably Rajiv Gandhi thought that Kashmir could be tackled after the elections, just as he had done in the case of Punjab and Assam after he became Prime Minister in 1984. But there was something else that Rajiv Gandhi could start doing immediately so that it could be taken to its logical conclusion during his second term—of which he was confident. Indo-US relations had almost hit rock bottom by this time, and with the Presidential election due in the USA, he wanted someone there who could help improve relations between the two great democracies. This was when, as detailed in the previous chapter, he appointed Karan Singh as India's Ambassador to the USA. The Valley had slipped into the grip of militants by then, and Karan Singh knew that he could do little to influence the course Kashmir had taken. He left the country for the US.

But by the end of that year, there were dramatic changes in the political scene. The Congress was voted out of power. The new government headed by V.P. Singh thought that it had better ideas about dealing with the new situation in Kashmir, and appointed Jagmohan once again by replacing General (Retired) K. Venkata Krishna Rao, much against the warnings of the Chief Minister, Dr. Farooq Abdullah. The helpless Chief Minister resigned in desperation, and soon after, left the country. Consequently, things degenerated even more in the politically abandoned state, with the militants moving around with impunity, and governance was effective only in the Jammu and Ladakh regions. Governor Jagmohan dared not step out into the streets of Srinagar that spewed hostility and danger. There was a painful purge of the Kashmiri Pandits, and the Valley lost a vibrant and creative part of its syncretic society. Tragically, their departure was accepted with pliant resignation. Karan Singh was shocked when news of the overnight flight of the Pandits from the Valley began to emerge. Shell-shocked, they arrived in Jammu in a daze. The anger at how they had been treated by a people with whom they shared so much of their civilizational history was to come much later. Kashmir had been taken over by the culture of the gun. Consequently, those Kashmiri Muslims who could leave also left the Valley—the more resourceful went abroad, and the lesser ones came to the safety of Jammu. Others adopted whatever measures were required to stay alive and merge with the surroundings.

For the next few years, there was a constant tug of war between the Central government forces, which wanted to reestablish order so that the political process could be put back on track, and the forces of anarchy and secessionism. Finally, after a seesaw of six years, during which the Valley saw the siege of the Hazratbal Shrine by the security forces, the abduction and killing of foreign tourists by militants to draw international attention, as well as the burning down of the Charar-e-Sharif Shrine by the terrorists, the security forces and the administration managed to create some goodwill among the people, enough to prepare the state for a return to the process of electoral politics. In 1996, the process began to hold elections to the J&K Assembly and install a popular government.

Even as his home state continued its downward spiral into hopelessness, Karan Singh's diplomatic skills were acknowledged by the Narasimha Rao government and he was called upon to lead the Indian delegation to South Africa in 1993 to celebrate the centenary of the incident at Pietermaritzburg Railway Station where Mahatma Gandhi was thrown out of an all-white compartment by the apartheid South African Government. The incident sparked the beginning of a non-violent movement against racial discrimination and oppression led by Gandhi, and it laid out a path for India's freedom struggle, the Civil Rights Movement in the USA, and Nelson Mandela's movement in South Africa to end apartheid rule. By 1990, Nelson Mandela had been freed after years of imprisonment at the infamous Robben Island and was poised to be the next and the first black President of South Africa. An ardent practitioner of Mahatma Gandhi's non-violent movement and a true champion of reconciliation, Mandela presided over the centenary celebrations event in 1993, and was so impressed by Karan Singh's speech on the occasion, with its message drawn from the Hindu philosophy of universal brotherhood, that he tapped Asha's shoulder and remarked, 'You are a very lucky woman to have such a man for your husband.' The remark, says Karan Singh, could be construed as annoying for some feminists, but it was extremely flattering for the husband!

Karan Singh also represented India during the funeral of King Baudouin of Belgium in 1993, which was also a personal loss to him and his wife. However, a great honour was bestowed upon him the same year when he was chosen as a member of the UNESCO Commission on Education for the Twenty-first Century. It was headed by Jacques Delors, who had a track record for his commitment to human solidarity, international cooperation and brotherhood, and for Karan Singh it was a joy working with Deloros as he turned out to be an excellent chairman. During this period, Karan Singh travelled all over the world in connection with the work of the Commission as it periodically met in various countries. As usual, he was always accompanied by his wife, who loved travelling and shopping for gifts for friends and the children of the family. It was as a member of this Commission that Karan Singh mastered the art of saying what he had to say in six minutes, as the rule during the deliberations was that every member got only six minutes for a speech, after which a short bell was sounded to ask the member to wind up, and there was a continuous ringing if the speaker persisted. After five years of extensive work in studying various cultures and systems of education, the Commission produced a report in 1998 that was aptly titled 'Learning: The Treasure Within', which laid stress on freedom, social justice and solidarity.

In Kashmir, meanwhile, the slide to tragedy continued. There were times when it appeared that, finally, Pakistan had succeeded in its design as the young gave up their studies for guns. There were long periods when schools remained closed because of extended curfew or terrorist activity. The militants had morphed into terrorists, and they roamed around, picking their targets at will. People in the countryside were the worst sufferers, caught between the terrorists who forced them to give food and shelter, and the security forces who would come to their door demanding answers from them for aiding enemies of the state.

On 15 October 1993, armed militants occupied the Hazratbal Shrine complex in Srinagar, and Indian security forces surrounded the complex to flush them out. The stand-off would continue for 34 days. Karan Singh and his wife decided to visit Kashmir when the crisis was at its peak. They had decided that not only did they need to go to their home in Srinagar, but also pray for peace, not only at the Shiva Temple on Shankaracharya hill but also at the Hazratbal Shrine. It was a bold move, reminiscent of Karan Singh's visit to Hazratbal in 1963 when the Holy Relic had been stolen and the streets of Srinagar were teeming with distraught and angry protestors. His visit then had evoked an emotional response from the grieving people and had helped in bringing the situation under control. But 1993 was not 1963. This was a dangerous time, when Pakistan-trained terrorists were calling the shots, and killings were common. Anything could have happened, since the terrorists holed up in the Shrine, most probably of Pakistani origin, would not have the same emotional connect with the former Sadr-e-Riyasat. As it turned out, the decades of anti-Dogra rhetoric, and his almost decade-long absence from the state, appeared not to have diminished the respect he had earned in the Valley. Consequently, the visit evoked a remarkable response not only from the people and the press, but also from some of the terrorists who were holed up in the Shrine.

That response made Karan Singh wonder if, perhaps, he still had some karmic debt to pay to that beautiful state founded by his ancestors. He also wondered if he would ever get a chance to help stabilize relations between India and Pakistan and thus bring peace and perhaps also happiness to the more than 1.75 billion people of the Subcontinent. In fact, this has been his abiding regret—that no government ever thought of using his services for a dialogue with Pakistan. He was convinced that India had fallen short of the role that was envisaged for it by Swami Vivekananda and Sri Aurobindo. They had wanted India not just to be a resurgent nation, but to provide intellectual, moral and spiritual leadership to the human community. He remains convinced that as long as India is locked in confrontational situations with its close neighbours, Pakistan and China, it will not be able to play any kind of leadership role in the rapidly emerging global society.

The phase of militancy and terrorism in J&K had many ups and downs in the decade of the 1990s, and re-establishing a political process seemed nearly impossible. But to the credit of Narasimha Rao, who became Prime Minister in June 1991—and who always stuck to the principle of talking with whoever was willing to talk—his minority government was able to manage enough support to hold elections for Parliamentary seats in J&K in 1996. After him, the Deve Gowda-led coalition government also mustered the courage to hold polls for the State Assembly. After six years of mayhem, the electorate brought back a people's government.

For Karan Singh, the return of the political process in his home state was to be a harbinger of another turning point in his life.

29

A Life Well Lived

WHEN THE LOK SABHA elections were held in May 1996, the Farooq Abdullah-led National Conference had stayed away from the polls as it had wanted autonomy-related concessions as a precondition for its return to electoral politics, which was not acceptable to the Government of India. But when the National Conference saw that the Government had gone ahead with the polls, it knew that it would be suicidal for it to boycott the Assembly polls too, as Delhi was determined to hold elections, with or without Farooq Abdullah's party. However, Prime Minister Deve Gowda had promised maximum autonomy to the State, and this gave the National Conference something to take to the people and thus return to the democratic fold. The apprehensions of the National Conference regarding the wisdom of returning to the polls were understandable, as its leaders and workers had borne the brunt of the militants' ire in the Valley, and hundreds among them had been killed, while many more had migrated out of the Valley or had publicly renounced their association with their party. For some time, they had also been ostracized for supporting India and the national symbols, making life miserable for them and their families. The same fate had befallen the workers of the Congress Party. Farooq Abdullah, who had left the country in 1990 when the storm had broken, had returned, and he now prepared himself and his party to face the people. Six years was a long period to ruminate over how and why J&K had reached where it had in January 1990, when he left the country. And he now approached Karan Singh with a proposal.

Years of reflection must have taught Farooq Abdullah that by pitting Jammu against Kashmir, the politicians had led the state to the precipice. He also realized that when people talked about autonomy, it could not be autonomy only for Kashmir, as that further aggravated the imbalance between the three regions of the state, which could easily be exploited by those who were hostile to the idea of normalcy. So, he mooted the idea of making a fresh beginning in regional cooperation with Karan Singh. Confident of winning the state elections, he proposed that the state also needed strong voices of reason like that of Karan Singh to represent it in the National Parliament after the State Assembly had been restored. When Karan Singh pointed out that his days of electoral battles were over, Farooq Abdullah said that the National Conference would like to elect Karan Singh to the Rajya Sabha. In return, he wanted Karan Singh to nominate either of his sons to contest on the National Conference symbol during the Assembly polls. On the face of it, this was a reasonable proposition and a tacit acknowledgement of the role played by Kashmiri leaders in creating divisions in the state and leading it into a minefield of uncertainty, distrust and suspicion. Moreover, as the Valley had been taken over by secessionist and terrorist elements with the support of Pakistan, it was necessary that the distortions of the past be acknowledged in order to make a new beginning. So Karan Singh agreed, and his younger son Ajatshatru Singh joined the National Conference and contested the Assembly election from Nagrota, near Jammu. The two leaders also agreed that after winning the elections, a Regional Autonomy Committee would be set up so that powers, administrative and financial, could be equitably devolved upon the three regions of the state. This was something that Karan Singh had long been pressing for, and was now happy to see wisdom dawning at least on some Kashmiri leaders. Karan Singh had concluded very early in his public life that the bane of the state was not that it was not completely autonomous, as Sheikh Abdullah had wanted, but that after assuming power, the National Conference had come to believe that it had got the right to lord over the Jammu and Ladakh regions and exercised its power to divert funds from these regions to Kashmir.

A born optimist, Karan Singh accepted Farooq Abdullah's proposal. He was confident that if the regional autonomy plan was implemented honestly, then the dark phase that had left the state scarred would soon be a matter of a distant and regrettable past. Thus, after an absence of twelve years, Karan Singh was back in Parliament, though this time in the Rajya Sabha. Even when away, politics had never been too far from him. It was a combination of factors that had taken him away from the role of an elected representative of his people, and it was again a combination of circumstances that had brought him back. It was ironic that a party that had spared no effort under the leadership of Sheikh Abdullah to erase his dynasty from the state had, after so many decades, sought the support of the son and grandson of the last Dogra Maharaja to help navigate the state through difficult times. On his part, Karan Singh was only too happy to help his state come out of a traumatic phase and move forward.

During the Assembly polls, the National Conference notched a decisive victory, and for the first time, because of the newfound bonhomie between the two adversaries, the National Conference succeeded in making inroads in the Jammu region, in which the two prominent Rajput winners for it were Ajatshatru Singh and Surjit Singh Salathia. Of the two, Surjit Singh Salathia was destined to enjoy a fairly long and successful run in the party and the government till he deserted it to join the BJP after Article 370 was de-operationalized in 2019, and a paradigm shift took place in the state's politics and also the loyalties of many people. Ajatshatru Singh lasted a much shorter time in the National Conference, as he realized that it had not really changed, and shifted to the BJP, since he felt that it alone could safeguard the interests of Jammu.

Very soon, Karan Singh's optimism gave way to disillusionment. Not long after he had agreed to head the Regional Autonomy Committee, he realized that Farooq Abdullah could not resist pressure from his party colleagues who wanted the Committee to simply reiterate autonomy as they defined it, which meant a return to the pre-1953 terms and conditions. Not prepared to lend his name to a committee that was pushing the old agenda, Karan Singh resigned from it. Since no effort was made by Farooq Abdullah to convince Karan Singh to remain its head, or to address his concerns, it only proved that the National Conference had just wanted to use his name. However, Karan Singh continued to believe that Farooq was at the bottom of his heart a nationalist, though to keep his own house in order, he had to occasionally bend to the wishes of his followers. So, although Karan Singh's cooperation with the National Conference at the state level came to a premature end, he continued to plead for the cause of the state in the Rajya Sabha.

At the national level, the era of coalition politics, which had started in 1989, continued. The country saw three Prime Ministers come and go in quick succession after 1996. First Atal Behari Vajpayee for 13 days, then Deve Gowda and Inder Kumar Gujral for under a year each. It was in this backdrop that, out of the blue, one fine morning, Ambica Soni, a confidante of Congress President Sonia Gandhi, rang up Karan Singh in 1999 while he was holidaying in Paris. Ambica Soni said that the Party President was finding it hard to put up a credible face against the BJP stalwart and prime ministerial candidate, Atal Behari Vajpayee, for the Lucknow parliamentary seat in another round of general elections, and wondered if he would take up the challenge. It still surprises Karan Singh that he did not hesitate for a moment. He said yes, but also made it clear that he did not have the kind of surplus money needed to contest an election and, therefore, the Party would have to bear all the expenses, and that a defeat at the hustings would not be held against him for any future arrangement. To both these conditions the Party agreed. The fact was that the BJP was in a strong position in 1999—it was riding a wave of popularity with the polarization of Hindu votes coupled with the incompetence of the Congress in the recent past, and there was also the desire among the people for a change and a stable government after some years of unsuccessful coalition governments. In addition, the BJP was in power in several Hindi-speaking states, including Uttar Pradesh. And notably, in UP it was Kalyan Singh who was Chief Minister again—the same man who had presided over the demolition of the Babri Masjid in Ayodhya, which had begun the process of polarizing Hindu votes. The odds were stacked against Karan Singh, a political outsider in Lucknow, the UP capital.

Accompanied by his wife, Karan Singh reached Lucknow and set up his election office. He also resigned his seat in the Rajya Sabha as he had been nominated by the National Conference and was now contesting on a Congress ticket. Vajpayee was a seasoned election campaigner who had contested from constituencies in Madhya Pradesh as well as Uttar Pradesh in the past; on the other hand, Karan Singh had never tested his electoral mettle outside J&K, where he owed much of his popularity to the dynasty that he belonged to. His only connection with UP had been through the Banaras Hindu University, of which he had been a Chancellor, and Mirtola in Almora, which was still a part of Uttar Pradesh at the time. But he did have a reputation as a great scholar of Indian thought, a popular and impressive orator, and someone who was truly representative of the *Ganga-Jamuni Tehzeeb*—the syncretic culture—of the Indian heartland. Finally, he also had his wife, Asha, by his side, who, on her own strength, was an invaluable asset in any public relations exercise. She was, by then, an expert campaigner and knew very well how to win the hearts and confidence of people. She confidently merged with the local women with ease, and one could never imagine that a Maharani was mingling with people whose culture, dialect and approach to life were vastly different from hers.

In the end, the campaigning got so intense that, contrary to the hope of those in charge of his campaign, Vajpayee had to remain tied to his constituency and could not move around the country freely to campaign for other candidates. When the results were announced, Vajpayee got 3,62,709 votes, and Karan Singh an extremely creditable 2,39,085. But everyone admitted that it was a contest to remember for its intensity and gentlemanly approach, though many tried to drag it into name-calling. The defeat notwithstanding, it was a pitched and satisfying contest, and given the high number of votes that he had polled against the designated Prime Minister, Karan Singh was happy that he had not disgraced himself or the Congress Party. It turned out to be his last electoral battle, and Sonia Gandhi, true to her word, not only did not hold the defeat against him but rewarded him by making him the Congress candidate for the Rajya Sabha in 2000 from the State of Delhi, where the Congress was in power.

Life in the Rajya Sabha was not as hectic as it was in the Lok Sabha, and Karan Singh enjoyed three successive terms of six years each, till he finally bowed out in 2018. All he had to do as a Rajya Sabha member was to adopt one village from the State of Delhi, and he chose Rithala in north Delhi. As was his habit, he took that responsibility seriously and got the Delhi administration to bring all-round development to the village, and when it got the Metro rail link, it was even better integrated with the national capital than ever. In the year 2004, when the Congress-led United Progressive Alliance (UPA) was voted to power, and Dr Manmohan Singh became the Prime Minister, there was a distinct possibility of Karan Singh becoming the Foreign Minister, but the opportunity passed him by as Natwar Singh, a suave career diplomat, was chosen ahead of him. There is no doubt that he would have loved to hold that portfolio, as he always excelled in the role of building relationships on the international stage. His many notes to Prime Minister Indira Gandhi after his numerous foreign visits are testimony to his ability to not only forge relations but also accurately read the ever-evolving situation in world affairs and how Indian interests could be better protected and promoted.

The UPA government, however, had no intention of leaving his abundant talents unused and gave him an assignment in which he revelled the most when in 2005 he was appointed as the President of the Indian Council of Cultural Relations (ICCR). He brought to it his usual energy and dynamism as he immersed himself in the role with a missionary zeal to make the world aware of the rich cultural traditions of his ancient land. During his three tenures that lasted from 2005 to 2014, he revived and strengthened mutual understanding with other countries by promoting cultural exchange with them. It was a matter of some satisfaction to Karan Singh that he had been assigned to perform a duty that had many decades ago been the honour of Maulana Abul Kalam Azad. During his three terms, the number of Indian Cultural Centres abroad rose to 40, where cultural troupes performed regularly, and gradually the world came to understand and appreciate even more than before, the kaleidoscopic culture of India that spoke through the language of a wide variety of classical dances and music, and always with the universal message of oneness in diversity. While Yamini Krishnamurthy introduced the world to the religious themes and ideas of Hindu philosophy through expression, melody and rhythm in Bharatanatyam, Radha and Raja Reddy did the same by means of another South Indian dance form, Kuchipudi. These legends were followed by brilliant Odissi dancers like Sonal Mansingh and Sanjukta Panigrahi, who popularized this dance form that had originated in the temples of Orissa.

Karan Singh also took immense pleasure in spreading around the world the spiritual and philosophical significance of Lord Shiva's Tandav. He had been fascinated by this dance right from the day he was first introduced to it during his first visit to South India as a young man. Nataraja's Dance had also been at the very centre of the near-mystical experience he had had in the one experiment with LSD that he had submitted to in his attempt to connect with the highest Consciousness. So, while others performed Shiva's cosmic dance on the stage, he took upon himself the task of lecturing not only on the philosophical aspect of Shiva, but also on the Upanishads. His work as the President of ICCR was not limited to spreading Indian philosophy and classical dances and arts alone, but also to sharing contemporary culture. Thus, the Boy Bands Festival of the South Asian Association for Regional Co-operation (SAARC) countries was also held in

India, in which pop and rock bands from the different SAARC countries, including Pakistan, participated. Another highlight of his tenure with ICCR was when he roped in the celebrated lawyer Soli Sorabjee, a lifelong devotee of Jazz, to organize a Jazz Festival that remains one of its kind in the Subcontinent's history.

In 2009, Karan Singh became a member of the Board of UNESCO, a position that he held for two terms of four years each. The Director General of UNESCO was the Bulgarian Irina Bokova, who became a good friend and also visited his home in Delhi. He also became the moving spirit in establishing the Mahatma Gandhi Institute for Peace and Education in New Delhi and enjoyed his term there. His term ended in October 2017, and during the farewell speech, Bokova acknowledged that she had immensely benefited from his 'wisdom, vision, and advice' and that if any person embodied the spirit of UNESCO, it was Karan Singh. She also recalled his speech in 2013 to the UNESCO delegates, 'The Universal Message of Swami Vivekanand', which was essentially a humanist message of solidarity, human rights and dignity.

This period also coincided with Karan Singh's appointment as President of the Auroville Foundation with the personal rank of a cabinet minister. He remained President of the Foundation for 18 years. During this period, he was without political power, but it proved to be perhaps the most constructive and productive period of his life, in which he also evolved as a thinker and an educator. This turned out to be an asset for him in the years to come—as he says, 'There is never a dull moment in life. I have never been without work. There is always a lecture to deliver, a book to release, columns and forewords to write. There are always people coming to see me and we talk about religion and philosophy. We talk about culture. Even politics sometimes, but that does not interest me so much any longer, although I'm happy to give advice, if anyone will listen to me!'

One time when his services were sought specifically to help manage a political crisis in India's neighbourhood was when he was called up for a special assignment to Nepal which had been racked first by violence carried out by the Nepali communists, and then by the joint movement of political parties for the restoration of democracy. Nepal was the last of the Hindu monarchies, established by the Shah Dynasty in 1768, and a part of its history bore similarity to Karan Singh's family history. From 1846 to 1951, the Rana Dynasty, the hereditary premiers of Nepal, had been effectively ruling Nepal with the Shah as the figurehead till the revolution of 1951 ended the rule of the Ranas. It coincided with the abolition of the monarchy in Jammu and Kashmir. However, unlike India, Nepal could neither bloom into a modern and functioning democracy nor could it lift its people out of abysmal poverty, giving rise to a strong communist movement. The last decade of the twentieth century saw the communists gaining ground, but things changed dramatically and tragically in 2001 after the massacre of nine members of the royal family, including the king, Birendra, by the crown prince, who was later shot. Following this, the younger brother of King Birendra, Gyanendra, became the king. But he was autocratic, and therefore constantly at loggerheads with the parliament, which he ultimately dissolved, and this resulted in the coming together of all the forces, except the communists, opposed to him under the banner of the Seven Party Alliance, which launched a *Jana Andolan*—peoples' movement for the restoration of democracy.

The movement gathered such momentum that India feared that Nepal would descend into chaos and thus fall into the hands of

Maoists, giving impetus to the Maoist movement in the bordering states of India. Anticipating such a development, Prime Minister Manmohan Singh decided to intervene and asked Karan Singh to go to Kathmandu as his Special Envoy in April 2006. After being appropriately briefed by the Government, Karan Singh carried a letter for King Gyanendra Shah. Upon reaching Kathmandu, he met leaders of all denominations to get a fair assessment of the situation and realized that the country was already teetering at the edge of chaos. Even the King knew of the precarious situation and confessed that, as things were, the communists would take full control of Nepal within a year. Before Karan Singh was to meet the King the following morning, Ambassador Shyam Sharan had wanted to accompany him, but Karan Singh told the Ambassador that he would be going alone for the meeting. Knowing what he was going to do, he had no intention of any third person being a witness to the hurt and humiliation he would have to inflict. So, he went alone and told King Gyanendra as gently and reasonably as he could that Delhi wanted him to immediately hand over power to the Seven Party Alliance and the leader of their choice. Then he handed Gyanendra the Indian Prime Minister's letter and returned to Delhi. Soon thereafter, the King resigned and handed over power as Delhi had suggested.

During his long tenure as a member of the Rajya Sabha, between 2000 and 2018, Karan Singh came to know many politicians who had risen during the post-Indira Gandhi era. Among the most senior among them was Vice President Bhairon Singh Shekhawat, who also presided over the Rajya Sabha. Unlike Dr Radhakrishnan and Dr Zakir Hussain, his early predecessors, Shekhawat was not very well educated, but he was a mature and shrewd politician and presided over the Upper House proceedings in a fair but firm manner in his effort to accommodate all the sections of the House. During Shekhawat's period as Chairman of the Rajya Sabha, the era of bipartisanship, mutual accommodation, and respect hadn't yet ended, and the Parliament still worked without personal rancour. On one occasion, when Karan Singh's starred question was scheduled to be answered by the then Prime Minister, Vajpayee, the Vice President invited Karan Singh to his chamber and requested him not to ask his scheduled question as the Prime Minister was not in a frame of mind to answer it. Pressing his question would have been an embarrassment for the Prime Minister; therefore, Karan Singh tactfully sat out the question hour with fellow members and journalists in the Central Hall, pretending to have forgotten that he had a scheduled question to ask.

Shekhawat was followed by Mohammad Hamid Ansari in 2007, amidst a sad drama that the country could have lived without. Najma Heptulla, a long-time member of the Congress Party had been the Vice-Chairperson of the Rajya Sabha and had hoped to be elevated by her party, but when her ambition was thwarted, she became the first high-profile defection from the Congress to the BJP and was backed by the latter party for the post but lost the election to Mohammad Hamid Ansari, who also went on to enjoy a second term, from 2012-2017. He was well-read, non-political, a career diplomat, and a close friend of Karan Singh's whose company he enjoyed a lot.

It was during the tenure of Vice President Venkaiah Naidu that Karan Singh ended his formal political career, in 2018, amidst glowing tributes from fellow members, including exceptional speeches by Ghulam Nabi Azad and the BJP's Ravi Shankar Prasad. In his farewell speech, which remains one of the finest gems from the parliamentary archives, Karan Singh briefly encapsulated the history of the Parliament, and expressed his optimism and faith in the constitutional and civilizational values of India:

Half a century ago, I came to Delhi…it has been fascinating to see the evolution of the Parliament over these years and how our Constitution gives us the flexibility to adapt to changing economic, social, and political compulsions…

So, this has been a great experience for me, and I've noticed one thing: Despite sharp differences of opinion and ideology, often expressed in intemperate language, one thing is common to all these people. They were all in their own way working for what Pandit Jawaharlal Nehru called the exciting adventure of building a new India. In their own way, every Prime Minister has contributed. Ours is a unique and glorious country…

We are not a closed society. We have been at the crossroads of civilizations. We've produced great ideas. We've received great ideas. That is the genius of India. That is what has kept India going.

I came to the Parliament fifty years ago as an idealistic young man of thirty-six. I now bid farewell as an idealistic old man, because I have implicit faith that India will overcome all its challenges as long as we remain faithful to our constitutional and civilizational values.

So, while expressing my deep gratitude for the unfailing courtesy and consideration I've received from my parliamentary colleagues and for the kind words said by my colleagues Ghulam Nabi Azad and Ravi Shankar Prasad, the secretariat, the staff of the Rajya Sabha, I will leave you with two verses from very different sources.

The first is from Shakeel Badayuni:

हर चीज़ नहीं है मरकज़ पर इक ज़र्रा इधर इक ज़र्रा उधर
नफ़रत से न देखो दुश्मन को शायद वो मोहब्बत कर बैठे

Everything is not always perfectly centered
There is always a slight imbalance one way or the other
Do not look upon the enemy with hostility
He may one day just begin loving you.

The second is from the Upanishad:

सह नाववतु। सह नौ भुनक्तु। सह वीर्यं करवावहै।
तेजस्वि नावधीतमस्तु मा विद्विषावहै॥

Let us work together,
Let us be nourished together,
Let us achieve together,
Let there be no hatred between us.

With this came the end of Karan Singh's parliamentary journey, a glorious one, for which he remains grateful. But there was a greater glory that the Parliament denied him. It is not something that troubles him anymore, but if you ask him about it, he does not deny that when it happened, he had felt let down.

Ahead of the 2007 elections for the new President of India when the UPA coalition, headed by the Congress, was in power, the Congress had put up two names as its candidates. Karan Singh had never made any secret of the fact that he considered himself a suitable candidate for President of the Indian Republic, and when he asked Sonia Gandhi, she told him, 'We have sent two names, one of them is yours.' The other name, it soon transpired, was Shivraj Patil, but most coalition partners in the UPA, including the Left, rejected his name. This made Karan Singh the strongest contender, and the Congress backed him strongly. He also had the support of the DMK. That consolidated his position as the frontrunner, until the Left vetoed his name. When Karan Singh met the DMK supremo M Karunanidhi, who was working to build a consensus in the UPA on the issue, he was told that the Left, particularly the CPI General Secretary A.B. Bardhan, had said that they could not have a Maharaja as President of the country. They also doubted his 'secular credentials'. Karan Singh was flabbergasted and while he tried to argue that he had never been a Maharaja—that he had voluntarily given up that title and also his privy purse—and that the organization he had created for reform within Hinduism was the Virat Hindu Samaj which had nothing to do with the Vishwa Hindu Parishad, he realized soon enough that it was a futile exercise. The UPA core committee finally decided to field a woman against the BJP candidate, Bhairon Singh Shekhawat—Pratibha Devisingh Patil, who was then Governor of Bhairon Singh's state, Rajasthan.

Many observers felt that India had lost the opportunity of having, after decades, a genuine statesman as President—a scholarly and urbane person of the temperament and stature of Dr Radhakrishnan. But after the initial disappointment, Karan Singh put the whole experience behind him and moved on. Speaking of similar situations, he has said that it is self-defeating to feel aggrieved for long. A brief regret is understandable, but bitterness can become a lifelong disease.

In 2009, Karan Singh lost his partner of close to 60 years—his wife, who was to him his 'only true companion'. 'She was my anchor and harbour,' he says. 'If I have ever had a home, it was her.' From the age of 19, when he journeyed out into the world, negotiating his way through challenges and opportunities of the kind that few people experience, she was by his side, always his quiet support. 'I don't know if I was always good to her. There are ups and downs in every marriage, but I don't think we could have made very much of life without each other. We grew up together…emotionally, we were twins.'

She had been with him when he accepted the post of Sadr-e-Riyasat, giving up his royal legacy, and entered an uncertain future, aware that he had risked perhaps a permanent estrangement from his father. She had indicated quietly but firmly, as she sat with him through a sleepless night, that she supported his decision and was with him. She was just fifteen at the time. Two years later, when he took the greater risk of arresting Sheikh Abdullah and saving his State and India from a crisis, she sat up with him, quietly supportive, through another sleepless night. Karan Singh recalls that through all the years that followed, she was involved in all his decision-making, and the few times he had acted without her consultation, he had landed himself in trouble. Contesting for the Jammu Lok Sabha seat—to be rejected by the people he had believed were his own and whose interests he had always safeguarded—was one such decision. 'She was a far better judge of people and situations than me,' he says. 'It wasn't only me, everyone in the family turned to her for advice and comfort. And then one day she was gone.'

Yasho Rajya Lakshmi, affectionately called Asha—the name her father-in-law had given her—breathed her last peacefully at their home, Mansarovar, surrounded by a loving family, including her six grandchildren. She had been ill for some time, and when she was admitted to hospital, she had to be put on dialysis. When treatment appeared to be failing, she had asked for release from the hospital, to go home to meet her end without artificial life support. This, she and Karan Singh had decided long back in their living wills—that when the end was near, they should not be put on ventilator machines. A woman who had loved life and all that was good and beautiful in it, came back home to her family, which had always been the centre of her life. There, she waited for her end. She slipped into a coma and passed away on 24 May 2009. She was 74. Her passing away left a huge void in the household as she was the glue that had kept not only the immediate family together but also the extended family and a large number of friends spread across the globe.

She had also brought hope—*asha*—to many other lives. Particularly the underprivileged and those suffering from some disabilities. She touched many lives, and most of those who came in close contact with her fondly remember her for her unreserved generosity. Born and brought up in luxury, she was strangely drawn to the less fortunate, especially children who suffered from mental challenges, and Karan Singh never ceased to be amazed at the way those children responded to her and felt happy in her presence. Among her most trusted servants was a person from an oppressed caste, whom many from the ritual-bound world she was born into and grew up in, would have kept at a distance. She earned his respect and loyalty and he, her confidence, and she trusted him with the household keys. She was traditional in many other ways, but even there she changed her attitude when there were occasions that demanded that she choose between convention and love. One such occasion was the breakup of the first marriage of her only daughter. She was extremely fond of her son-in-law, and the idea of divorce was also hard to accept for a person with a conventional upbringing. Yet, when the marriage fell apart and became irretrievable, and the divorce proceedings got bogged down in the courts, she stood wholeheartedly behind her daughter, giving her all the support that she needed.

Speaking to her grandchildren, one can see how she remains a living presence in the family. Talking about their liberal and friendly grandfather and how he has shaped or touched their lives, each one of them begins at some point to speak of the grandmother. Over a decade and a half since they lost her, memories of her still light up their eyes.

After bidding farewell to Parliament in 2018, Karan Singh has remained busy with the work that is close to his heart—lecturing, being part of seminars and educating those who desire to learn about Hinduism and Indian philosophy, sharing the knowledge and wisdom that has come his way. He has transferred the property he inherited and the assets that he has built among his children, who, together with the grandchildren, also manage the different family trusts, including the Dharmarth Trust, the Hari Tara Charitable Trust and the Maharaja Gulab Singh Memorial Trust; the Amar Mahal Museum and Library, the Dara Shikoh Centre for Arts and Culture, and the Karan Singh Foundation.

Meanwhile, he continues to reinvent himself and live different lives in one life. Fortunately, age has not rendered him technology-deficient, nor diminished his curiosity and enthusiasm for knowledge. On fixed days of the week, friends or acquaintances with whom he can discuss science or philosophy come over—a research paper on cutting-edge research in artificial intelligence is discussed one evening, a new book on Patanjali's *Yogasutra* on another. Most evenings, he is alone, reading, watching news on the television, or listening to a Meera bhajan by M.S. Subbulakshmi or a Dogri bhajan—or, if he's feeling nostalgic, a rock song from the 1950s or '60s—unless there is a visitor, who could be an old friend from America or Japan, or someone requesting him to write a foreword to or release his or her book. His children and daughters-in-law drop in some evenings, and his grandchildren when they are in town. Afterwards, he goes up to his puja room, assisted by one of his staff, most of whom have been with him for years—respectful, affectionate, caring; there is no bowing and scraping. After an hour or so of puja, it is time for a light dinner. He usually eats his meals alone.

Does he feel fulfilled, one asks him. 'Yes, I can say I have had a good life,' he says without hesitation. What of all the challenges he has faced, repeatedly?

'I was lucky. Temperamentally, I have always been an optimistic person. And I would say life began training me very early on—and it never gave up!' he laughs. 'You see, in my life of almost a century, I have had a variety of experiences. I was a student, with English guardians, and then at Doon School, where I had some difficulty adjusting at first, but I came to like it, before I was pulled out and finished my schooling as a private student. Then, at the age of eighteen I was Head of State and catapulted into an extraordinary political situation with many moments of tension. There I continued for eighteen years, before I became a Minister in Mrs Gandhi's Cabinet, till the Emergency put me in a dilemma. I was Ambassador after that, then with UNESCO, and in the Rajya Sabha for several years. After I retired, my wife and I travelled to almost every corner of the world—so you could call me a traveller, too. And now at this stage, I look upon myself—if I may use the term without sounding arrogant—as a sort of elder statesman, meeting people, listening to them and advising them, delivering lectures. Each one of these is a different world, but I go through them all. I don't allow myself to be fragmented. I am all of them, they have all made me what I am...

'And I must not forget, I was also a patient, that is also an identity I've had. I was in bed for eighteen months, unable even to turn by myself. That is not something you can easily forget. Almost a year in a hospital room in New York, undergoing multiple surgeries, frequently in and out of anaesthesia and afraid I would never be able to get on my feet again. That kind of experience can either make you or break you. I was only seventeen. But I kept my spirits up somehow. Now when I look back, I don't know how I survived that period without having some kind of breakdown. So that's why I say I was lucky. That year in America also made me aware of democracy. It freed me from my feudal background, and then I had Pandit Nehru as my mentor. I would not have had the life I have had without all those experiences...I have been lucky. Life has been good to me, it has been a great gift, and as long as I am here, I intend to make the most of it.'

And so, like the River Ganga, Karan Singh flows on, gathering experience and giving something of himself to his surroundings, making his individual journey to the ultimate ocean that awaits us all at the end.

Acknowledgements

I AM DEEPLY GRATEFUL to Dr. Jyotsna Singh, Chairperson of the Karan Singh Foundation, who took me by surprise when she offered me the opportunity of writing a biography of Dr. Karan Singh for the Foundation. My gratitude is also due to all the Trustees of the Foundation, who not only reposed faith in me but also opened their hearts while talking about Dr. Karan Singh and the late Yasho Rajya Lakshmi. I extend my gratitude to Shri Vikramaditya Singh and his wife, Chitrangada, and Shri Ajatshatru Singh and his wife, Dr. Ritu Singh, for sparing their valuable time for me. My special thanks to Vivasvat Singh Chauhan, Viveka Singh, Mriganka Singh, Martand Singh, Ranvijay Singh and Adishree for sharing their insights into their grandparents' lives. I thank the Amar Mahal Museum and Library, Jammu for providing all the required photographs. Most of all, I am deeply grateful to Dr. Karan Singh, who generously gave his valuable time and was patient with my questions, which were often repetitive.

Words will not be enough to thank my family, who have patiently allowed me to remain focused on my work. Finally, my thanks to Ravi Singh of Speaking Tiger and his dedicated team.

Index